CONTENTS

Commentationes Scientiarum Socialium
33 1986

ONDON

Jukka Gronow

ON THE FORMATION
OF MARXISM

**Karl Kautsky's Theory of Capitalism,
the Marxism of the Second International
ıd Karl Marx's Critique of Political Economy**

ISSN 0355-256X
ISBN 951-653-141-5

ACKNOWLEDGEMENTS

This study was written at the Department of Sociology, University of Helsinki. In 1979–83 it was supported by the Academy of Finland, to which I wish to express my gratitude. A short visit to the International Institute of Social History in Amsterdam in 1983 made it possible for me to become acquainted with the Karl Kautsky archive preserved at the Institute.

I would like to express my special gratitude to the following persons, who commented on my manuscript at different stages: Erik Allardt, Pauli Kettunen, Pekka Kosonen, Arto Noro and Matti Viikari. Erik Allardt and Matti Viikari have also acted as the official examiners of my thesis. None of them, naturally, bears any responsibility for the ideas presented in the final monograph.

I am grateful to Susan Sinisalo for correcting my English. Finally, I am also indebted to the Societas Scientiarum Fennica for including my thesis in this series.

Helsinki, April 1986

Jukka Gronow

Note on abbreviations

The following abbreviations are used in the references:

Lenin CW = Lenin, V.I. (1963−1981): *Collected Works*. Moscow: Progress Publishers
Lenin SW = Lenin, V.I. (1967): *Selected Works*. Moscow: Progress Publishers
MEGA II = Marx, Karl − Engels, Friedrich (1976−83): *Gesamtausgabe*. Zweite Abteilung. Berlin: Dietz
MEW   = Marx, Karl − Engels, Friedrich (1964−1974): *Werke*. Berlin: Dietz

Where reference is made to articles published in newspapers in several parts the respective parts are indicated after the year of publication (e.g. Kautsky 1899: 1).

INTRODUCTION

The quarter of a century of the rise and fall of the Second International (1889–1914) could be called the formative years of Marxism, or scientific socialism as it was solemnly named by its proponents. Karl Kautsky (1854–1938) was one of the leading figures who helped make Marxism the official doctrine of the rapidly growing social democratic mass parties – directly in Germany and more indirectly throughout Europe and North America. As a leading theoretician of the German Social Democratic Party he was understood to represent genuine Marxism by the enemies and friends of socialism alike. Kautsky's Marxism was the target of many polemics and disputes concerning the right interpretation of Marxist doctrine, the scientific validity of the Marxist theory of society, and the political and strategic conclusions drawn from it.

For the first time Kautsky's theoretical authority was seriously challenged in 1899 by the full-scale critique put forward by Eduard Bernstein – a former ally and collaborator of Kautsky – of all the main theorems of Marxism. But neither Bernstein nor later critics could shatter the faith in Marxism as the official party ideology and Kautsky's position as its leading theoretical representative and protagonist. It was not until the end of the First World War and the final organisational and political dissolution of the labour movement that Kautsky's Marxism lost its position of authority. Karl Kautsky became rather an obsolete figure, having no niche in the politically divided labour movement.

Kautsky enjoyed a wide reputation as a leading theoretician of Marxism even before he was commissioned in 1890 to draft the official party programme, later to become known as the *Erfurt Programme* adopted by the German Social Democratic Party in 1891. The *Erfurt Programme* was generally recognised as the party's first Marxist programme. Kautsky was for thirty-four years – from its very founding in 1889 – the editor of the theoretical organ *(Die Neue Zeit)* of the most influential party of the Second International. He was also the acknowledged inheritor of the theoretical legacy of Marx and Engels, the 'Old Ones', and a close collaborator with Engels during his last years. He edited and published many of Marx's posthumous works, including the first published version of *Theorien über den Mehrwert* (see Kautsky 1904; 1905; 1910). Kautsky could thus with good reason speak with the authority of the 'Old Ones' and he was a most influential interpreter and propagator of Marx's and Engels' scientific thoughts. Together with Engels' *Anti-Dühring* (MEW 20), Kautsky's *Das Erfurter Programm* (1906a (1892)) and *Karl Marx' Oekonomische Lehren* (1906c), already published in 1887 before the *Erfurt Programme,* were the basic 'textbooks' of Marxism through which many a generation of Marxists studied and learned their basics of scientific socialism (see Donner 1978).

The choice of Karl Kautsky as the main theoretical figure in the present study could, thus, be justified by the influential position he enjoyed among the Marxists of the period of the Second International. The main purpose of the present study is not, however, to analyse the history of Marxist ideas, and to identify the originators of certain important thought forms or the relations of influence among various Marxists and among different Marxist interpretations and conceptions. The major merit of Kautsky's thinking from the perspective of the present study is that Kautsky was practically the only Marxist theoretician of the time to present a systematic interpretation of what he understood to be Marx's and Engels' theory of capitalism and, in so doing, to develop and formulate a theory of capitalism of his own. As the formation of the Marxist theory of capitalism constitutes the main object of this study, Kautsky's contribution to the development of this theory is of immediate interest.

The focus of the present analysis is thus limited to the history of the social theory of capitalism. It does not intend to discuss in detail problems of philosophical materialism or practical political questions of Social Democracy, only to name two extreme alternative approaches. Compared with Plechanow, another main theoretical figure of the Second International Marxism, questions of philosophical and historical materialism were of relatively little interest to Kautsky and he left the defence of materialism to others, among them Plechanow. The questions of historical materialism were actualised in Kautsky's thinking before the First World War mainly in the context of the discussion concerning the role of ethics in historical materialism (see Kautsky 1906b). But the different versions of and disputes over materialism were otherwise of relatively little interest to Kautsky, as evidenced by the standpoint he adopted in the discussion about Mach and Machism (see Kautsky 1909a). For the practical purpose of the analysis of society and of capitalism in particular it was in his opinion enough to acknowledge a materialist position in philosophy.

Consequently, he did not pay much attention to the development and interpretation of historical materialism or the materialist conception of history, even though he did publish a voluminous work on the subject. *Die materialistische Geschichtsauffassung* (1927) had, however, relatively little to do with his earlier studies and analysis of capitalism. In this later work Kautsky presented an explicitly evolutionist conception of history reminiscent more of the interest in Darwinism of his 'premarxist' years (see Kautsky 1927, 17; Korsch 1971a (1929), 27; B. Kautsky 1955, 2−3; see also Kautsky 1960). The corpus of ideas later to be codified as historical materialism in the Soviet Union had its origin mainly in Plechanow's studies (cf. Negt 1974); Kautsky was, after all, the formulator of the social theory of capitalism of Marxism.

In fact the only Marxist seriously to challenge Kautsky's position as the leading interpreter of Marx' theory of capitalism and as an expert on questions of modern capitalism was Rudolf Hilferding, the author of *Das Finanzkapital* (1968 (1910)), the most systematic single treatise on modern capitalism which was hailed by Kautsky as the fourth volume of *Capital* (see Kautsky 1910–11, 883). On the other hand, it can be claimed that many of the conceptions and conclusions formulated by Hilferding were simultaneously or even earlier discussed and analysed by Kautsky and others as well. Thus there seems in fact to have existed a common corpus of ideas shared by many of the leading Marxists of the time which received its most consequential formulation both in Hilferding's *Das Finanzkapital* and in Kautsky's numerous articles and works on the subject of the development of capitalism.

The emphasis laid on Kautsky as the central and leading representative of the social theory of Marxism does not exclude the fact that many of his ideas and conclusions were also vehemently criticised and polemised against by other Marxists. Some of these disputes are discussed in more detail in this study, but even in such cases it is often possible to recognize a common consensus of what really was thought to constitute the theoretical core of Marxism. A critical reconstruction and a systematic analysis of Kautsky's conceptions about capitalism is of special importance, because he was one of those who perhaps more explicitly than others contributed to the understanding of the fundamental social issues of capitalism. By analysing Kautsky's thinking it is thus not only possible to reconstruct his theory of capitalism, imperialism and the conditions of the socialist revolution, but also to re-examine some of the basic presuppositions of other Marxist theories of imperialism and conceptions of socialist revolution as evidenced by the discussion of Hilferding's and Lenin's theories of modern capitalism in this study.

The purpose of this study is thus not to present a complete history of Marxist ideas at the end of the last and in the beginning of the present century, nor to reconstruct all the theoretical positions of the different factions or emerging schools of thought. The object of the first part of this study is rather exclusively the formation of the Marxist theory of society and of capitalism in particular as represented by Karl Kautsky's theoretical contribution – a contribution that was not a result of the efforts of an isolated intellectual but had at least some degree of representativeness, too.

Karl Kautsky's theoretical conceptions and his contribution to the development of Marxism have been the object of amazingly few studies. No doubt Kautsky has figured as an important personality in various political and intellectual histories of the German Social Democratic Party and of the Bismarckian and Wilhelminian Germany (see e.g. Groh 1973; Rosenberg 1962; Steinberg 1973) and in general histories of Marxism (Lichtheim 1964). Certain important aspects of Kautsky's thinking have been analysed in different contexts; Kautsky has often – undoubdtedly with good reasons – had the questionable honour of representing a deterministic conception of the development of society in Marxism (see Lichtheim 1964, 268–269; Arato 1973–74, 7–8, 33–37; Colletti 1971, 16–18; Scharrer 1976, 17–18). The paradoxical combination of revolutionary vigour and practical cautiousness in Kautsky's thinking was first pointed out by Mathias (1957). The same paradox was formulated in more positive terms by Lichtheim: in Lichtheim's interpretation Kautsky completed the fusion of an essentially pacific and gradualist, democratic and reformist movement with a revolutionary doctrine (see Lichtheim 1964, 259−261).

Despite the fact that different aspects of Kautsky's Marxism have been analysed and discussed in different contexts − one could easily add several other studies to the above list − one can agree with Massimo Salvadori on his comment on the reception and critical evaluation of Kautsky's theoretical and political contribution:

> "In sum, there is an enormous disproportion between the volume of references to Kautsky in the course of history itself and the paucity of critical studies devoted to him. I have come to the conclusion that the main reason for this disproportion is that scholars have so far fundamentally confined themselves to the judgements 'for' or 'against' Kautsky that were pronounced in the thick of political struggles between parties, ideologies, and movements of his own time. One might say that the image of Kautsky has remained fixed ever since in the forms it acquired in that period." (Salvadori 1979, 9).

To this one could perhaps add yet another reason: Kautsky's peculiar political position − later to become known as centrism − did not outlive the split in the Social Democratic movement after the First World War and the Russian Revolution. The effort to establish the Independent Social Democratic Party (USDP) after the war remained short-lived (see Salvadori 1979, 203−215, 245−250). In the post-war socialist labour movement Kautsky fell between the lines dividing Communism and Social Democracy. To the Marxist-Leninists Kautsky has remained a renegade of Marxism ever since the verdict was proclaimed by Lenin, and to the Social Democrats Kautsky is merely a historical figure from the 'pre-history' of the party with only little contemporary interest.

However, there has more recently been what one might even venture to call a revival in the critical re-evaluation of Kautsky's political and theoretical role as evidenced by Steenson's (1978), Salvadori's (1979), Hühnlich's (1981) and Braionovič's (1979; 1982) studies. (Kraus' dissertation on Kautsky's theory of imperialism (1975) is more limited in scope but it may still be added to the above list). Even though not remarkably different in its conclusions from Alter's (1930; see also Furtschik 1929) evaluation of Kautsky as an opponent of Leninism and the proletarian revolution, Braionovič's monograph does include a cautious attempt at rehabilitating Kautsky's theoretical role from a Marxist-Leninist standpoint; Braionovič's verdict of Kautsky is not as complete as usual. Steenson's *Karl Kautsky 1854−1938* (1978) is a general intellectual biography of Kautsky. Hühnlich's study (1981) consists of an overall analysis of Kautsky's political theory but includes many penetrating comments on Kautsky's theory of capitalism and his interpretation of Marx's *Capital,* too. In his *Karl Kautsky and the Socialist Revolution 1880−1938* (1979) Salvadori is mainly interested in the questions of democracy, revolution, and socialism in Kautsky's thinking and Kautsky's intellectual role in the political history of German Social Democracy. The possible shifts in Kautsky's theoretical position at different periods of his intellectual life are one of the main concerns of both these monographs, and consequently they explicitly problematise the Marxist-Leninist thesis that Kautsky had given up his former revolutionary Marxist position.

Hühnlich's and Salvadori's studies have served as invaluable guidelines in orienting my own study of Kautsky's voluminous literary output. (Hühnlich's work includes a comprehensive bibliography of Kautsky's publications; cf. also Blumenberg's earlier bibliography (1960).)

The present attempt at a critical reconstruction of Kautsky's theory of capitalism and imperialism does, however, differ in one important respect from Hühnlich's and Salvadori's analyses, since in this study the relation of Kautsky's theoretical conception to Karl Marx's critique of political economy is of major interest. In this respect the present study ties up with the tradition of the reconstruction of the critique of political economy presented in Marx's *Capital* and in the manuscripts preceding the published version of *Capital*. In the discussions following this tradition, postmarxian Marxism, the emerging theory of the organised working class movement has been understood to have resulted from an essential vulgarisation or deformation of Marx's analysis and critique of capitalism. The misunderstanding included in traditional or orthodox Marxism has mainly been understood to result from two serious shortcomings in the interpretation of Marx's critique of political economy, which show that postmarxian Marxism never understood the main theoretical 'novum' of *Capital* and Marx's specific critical intention. Both these misinterpretations are closely connected with each other.

The main mistake committed by postmarxian traditional Marxism was that it never understood the specific conceptual status of the presentation of Marx's *Capital*.[1] *Capital* was essentially understood to be a theoretical presentation of the historical development of capitalism and of the genesis of capitalism, starting from the presentation of the simple commodity production preceding capitalism and followed by the historical laws governing the development of capitalism. The theoretical and conceptual presentation of *Capital* was understood to follow the actual historical development of emergence of capitalism. According to this interpretattion, Marx's *Capital* does not, however, describe the history of any specific capitalist country; the developmental laws where abstracted from various historical contingencies in the development of capitalism and, as such, they were theoretical generalisations. The most serious result of this procedure of interpretation was that Marx was understood to have presented the laws governing the functioning of a specific historical mode of production preceding capitalism, that of simple commodity production, and its historical transformation into capitalism.[2]

The second vulgarisation thesis concerns the conceptual presentation or logic of *Capital*, too. According to this thesis, the theories of monopoly capitalism or imperialism of traditional Marxism followed from a misunderstanding of the theoretical role of

---

[1] For a discussion of the logic of presentation in Marx's *Capital* see Reichelt (1971), Zeleny (1968) and Backhaus (1974; 1975; 1978; 1981). Haug (1974) presents a more orthodox interpretation.

[2] For a critique of Leninism following this kind of argumentation see *Projekt Klassenanalyse (PKA)* 1972; see also Ebbighausen (1974). In Projekt Klassenanalyse's *Kautsky. Marxistische Vergangenheit der SDP* (1976) there is an interesting discussion of Kautsky's historicising interpretation of Marx's *Capital* and its consequences for his political theory of revolution.

competition in Marx's *Capital*. Following Rosdolsky's (1968) original interpretation of Marx's *Grundrisse* (s.a.) it can be claimed that Marx's *Capital* only covers the presentation of 'capital in general' ("das Kapital im allgemeinen"); the relations of individual capitals or the competition between capitals is not included into the analysis of the capital in general — Marx originally intended to analyse competition in a specific volume of *Capital* (see Rosdolsky 1968, 60) — or they are discussed only insofar as they follow from or correspond to the concept of capital. To Marx, competition was a necessary executor of the inner laws of capital, and free competition is furthermore the specific adequate manifestation of these inner or immanent laws; in free competition the only difference between the individual capitals is quantitative. Free competition guarantees that every single capital receives a share of the surplus value corresponding to its quantity; every individual capital is an aliquant part of the total capital.

In unproblematically stating that capitalism had developed into a new stage, a stage of monopoly capitalism or imperialism which in some fundamental sense had transformed the functioning of the laws of capitalism, traditional Marxism actually thought that modern capitalism had developed through three stages, the stages of simple commodity production, capitalism of free competition and imperialism. Marx's theory of capitalism only covered the first two stages of development and had to be supplemented by a fourth volume of *Capital* presenting the theory of the newest or last stage of capitalism. The relation of the conceptual status of the theory of imperialism to Marx's analysis of capitalism was not generally explicitly reflected. Following Rosdolsky's interpretation of *Capital* and *Grundrisse,* monopolistic competition could only be analysed at the same level as market competition determining the market prices of commodities. Consequently, if Marx's analysis of competition in *Capital* is taken seriously, then it would be much more problematic to write a new Marxist theory of modern capitalism. (See Neusüss 1972; Jordan 1974a; 1974b; Schubert 1973; Gronow 1978.)

The interpretation of the role of competition in the logical structure of *Capital* that was inspired by Rosdolsky's thesis has been challenged by Schwarz (1974; 1980). By analysing the development of Marx's plans describing the structure of the contents of *Capital* Schwarz came to the conclusion that in the final versions Marx did not intend to analyse competition at the level of the analysis of the capital in general, even though competition was planned to be included in the general conceptual analysis of capital. Schwarz's argument opens up the possibility — within the logical structure of *Capital* — of considering monopolistic competition as a modified form of the appearance of the inner laws of capital, but still it does not solve the problem of the explicit status of free competition as the adequate form of realisation of the inner laws of capital.

The first of these theses is more relevant from the point of view of interpreting Kautsky's theory of capitalism — and it is a more fundamental thesis in general, too. Kautsky never postulated that imperialism or monopoly capitalism was a specific new stage of capitalism — as Lenin did — but rather he understood it to be a political method of coping with the contradictions inherent in capitalism. Still, much of what can be said about Lenin's theory of imperialism is valid in Kautsky's case, too. The first thesis is, however, more important; Kautsky explicitly interpreted Marx's *Capital* as a presentation of the historical development of capitalism and even wanted to correct Marx's analysis and complement it by providing it with the relevant historical facts on the basis of which Marx's historical generalisations were reached (see Kautsky 1906c, X−XI).

Kautsky's most original contribution to the development of the theory of capitalism was, however, his interpretation of the law of the accumulation of capital formulated by Marx at the end of the first volume of *Capital*. Kautsky interpreted it to be a historical and empirical law explaining and predicting the future development of capitalism. Together with the theory of immiseration it was understood to predict the increasing polarisation of the bourgeois society into two classes and to show the objective and subjective limits of capitalism. It was thus an essential element of Kautsky's theory of a socialist revolution.

The idea of the basic contradiction of capitalism formed the second cornerstone of Kautsky's theory of capitalism. Following Engels' formulation in *Anti-Dühring* (see MEW 20, 248−265) Kautsky understood the basic contradiction of capitalism in terms of an increasing contradiction between the prevailing private mode of appropriation and the increasing socialisation of production. One of the main theses of the present study is that due to these postulates Kautsky's critique of capitalism came close to a radical version of the natural rights theory; in Kautsky's opinion capitalism was violating the original right of the producer to the products of his own labour. The real nature of commodity production came into appearance in simple commodity production realising the principle of equal exchange, whereas in capitalism the products of alien labour are appropriated by property owners. Due to the development of capitalism into imperialism the exploitative nature of capitalism comes furthermore more evident and accentuated. In imperialism cartels and finance capital are exploiting both producers and consumers in a direct way violating the rule of equal exchange.

It can be claimed that Kautsky's understanding of the social relations of capitalism had important consequences for his conceptions of the socialist revolution, the development of the socialist consciousness, and the role of democracy and dictatorship in the strategy of the working class movement. It can furthermore be claimed that despite the wide spectrum of their political positions Kautsky's interpretation of Marx's theory of capitalism was shared by theoreticians of the Second International from Bernstein to Lenin. It was not the validity of the interpretation of *Capital* that was questioned by the critics of Marxism but rather the empirical validity of Marx's predictions.

By contrasting Kautsky's theory of capitalism with Marx's critique of political economy it is possible to gain a better understanding of some basic ideas in Kautsky's thinking − and in traditional Marxism in general. Such a comparison can also be justified by the fact that Kautsky always understood it as his task to popularise, explicate and develop the scientific socialism developed by Marx and Engels. The purpose of the following discussion is not, however, merely to explicate and critically evaluate Kautsky's theory of capitalism in the light of Marx's *Capital* and its preworks. The task of reconstructing the theoretical conceptions in Kautsky's thinking is demanding as such, but there is a question of even greater interest connected with it, viz. a problematisation of Kautsky's central ideas can be used as a path leading to a re-evaluation and re-interpretation of Marx's thinking, too.

It is quite obviously true that Kautsky misunderstood and misinterpreted many of Marx's central ideas, but the fault was not Kautsky's alone. To Marx the general law of accumulation of capital was not an empirical generalisation explaining the development of capitalism. Neither was Marx's conception of immiseration as straightforward as Kautsky's. Marx never formulated the basic contradiction of capitalism in similar terms as Engels and Kautsky did. Kautsky's main mistake was that he totally ignored the fact that Marx's theory stands in a very specific and important relation to classical political economy, and can only be understood and justified as an explicit critique of the theoretical presuppositions inherent in this tradition of thinking.

A main outcome of this neglect is that there is a fundamental difference between Marx's and Kautsky's critique of capitalism. To put it briefly, according to Kautsky capitalism had to be condemned and was to give way to socialism because in capitalism the products of the working class are exploited by a diminishing number of capital owners violating the right of the worker to the products of his own labour. Marx's critique of capitalism is more complicated and one does not find in *Capital* any simplified critique based on the natural rights doctrine. According to Marx's critical conception, the bourgeois society is a society of exploitation despite the fact that the exchange of commodities follows the rule of equal exchange. Bourgeois society did not hold its promise of a reasonable society guaranteeing the freedom and equality of its members and the human existence and well-being of mankind. It was not the natural society postulated by classical political economy.

It could be claimed, however, that even in *Capital* there is a tendency to positivise the critical intention of the theory and to write a historical theory of the origins and development of capitalism. It is equally true that Marx would not have objected – and, in fact, he even contributed (see MEW 20,VII) – to Engels' formulation of the basic contradiction of capitalism in terms of the private mode of appropriation and socialisation of production. Even in Marx's opinion the material means and the richness of society are nothing but the hidden potentialities of labour only temporarily alienated and objectified in capitalism as the potentialities of capital. In principle they were returnable to labour, even though not as the potentialities of an individual worker, but of the collective working class. It can tentatively be claimed that it was the concept of labour and the labour theory of value critically adopted by Marx from classical political economy that formed the common theoretical core of both Marx's thinking and Marxism. But even in this respect there is a crucial shortcoming in Marxism's understanding, i.e. Marxism neglected almost totally the analysis of the value form of a commodity and of labour power, and consequently its theoretical position can be claimed to be closer to classical political economy than to Marx's critique of it.

There are important consequences resulting from Marxism's theory of capitalism concerning the idea of the future socialist society; in Marxism socialism came very close to what might be called organised capitalism. Even though the idea of an organised capitalism, which had already made the socialist revolution obsolete, was first developed by Hilferding (1973a (1926)) in the 1920s, the characterisation of socialism presented by e.g. Kautsky shared many features with Hilferding's conception of an organised capitalism. It was mainly the fact that, due to the centralisation of capital, the anarchic nature of capitalist production had already been − at least partly − overcome, and elements of the planned regulation of production had been established, which by Engels and Kautsky was understood to form the conditions of socialism ripening inside the very capitalism. In Kautsky's opinion the state was the only social institution capable of organising national production in socialism. Thus all that the socialist revolution had to accomplish was to transform the state from an organ of the power of the bourgeoisie into an organ of the working class and put an end to the still prevailing antagonism of distribution. A socialist society was then essentially a society in which the anarchy of production and the antagonism of distribution had been replaced by state planning and regulation.

Even though Kautsky once referred to socialism as a society which would make an end to the power of the products over the producers (Kautsky 1906c, 264), his socialism could hardly be equated with the communism of Marx. In Marx's communism man would put an end to the prehistory of mankind, to the subordination of the activity of man under reified social relations. His idea of a free association of the producers was reached through an implicit critique of the classical experience manifest in the philosophy of Enlightenment and classical political economy according to which the private acts of individuals unintentionally and unconsciously realise a hidden plan in history; human history has a reasonable goal. Only insofar as there is such a claim of reason in history does Marx's thinking maintain its critical potency. Marx's principle of labour included his historico-philosophical postulate, according to which human history is a result of the objectification of human labour, the productive potentialities and capacities of man, temporarily alienated in a bourgeois society. The present study can, then, be read as a problematisation of this thesis.

The following study is divided into two relatively independent but mutually related parts. In the first part, Kautsky's Marxism is analysed; in the second Marx's critique of political economy is discussed insofar as it is relevant for an understanding of the Marxism of the Second International and for a problematisation of Marx's Marxism. There are three major themes in the first part dealing with Kautsky's Marxism: Kautsky's theory of capitalism, his conceptions about imperalism and the question of democracy and revolution. The elements of Kautsky's theory of capitalism are first introduced by analysing his dispute with Bernstein, and his explicit interpretation of Marx's economic theory. The questions of imperialism, democracy and revolution are especially interesting because by analysing Kautsky's conceptions and their relation to those of other Marxists of the time it is possible to test the fruitfulness of the thesis that Kautsky's theory of capitalism in fact formed the common core of Marxism. Furthermore, Kautsky's idea of scientific socialism and the role of science and intellectuals in the labour movements is of special importance for an understanding of the formation of Marxism.

The second part starts with a discussion of Marx's standards of critique and the character of his theory of capitalism as a critical theory. In the following chapters Marx's critique of the concept of labour and the relation between private property and labour in classical political economy is analysed. In the discussion is also included a short excursion into John Locke's theory of property.

The critical re-evaluation of Marx's critique of political economy, thus, consists mainly of the problematisation of his redefinition of the concept of labour and of the logic of the presentation of *Capital* and results in a thesis about the labour theory of value as the core of Marx's Marxism. Finally, the last chapter before the conclusion presents an answer to the question of whether there is a theory of immiseration of the working class in Marx's *Capital*.

PART I

KAUTSKY'S MARXISM

1. ORGANISED CAPITALISM, THE GENERAL CARTEL AND THE PROLETARIAT

Hilferding's famous treatise on modern capitalism, *Das Finanzkapital* (1968 (1910)), was the most systematic and consequential study of the historical development of capitalism of the period of the Second International. It can be claimed that in *Finance Capital* Hilferding formulated some of the main conclusions drawn from Marx's *Capital* common to traditional or orthodox Marxism. In Hilferding's understanding the various forms of the concentration and centralisation of capital form the main feature of the development of modern capitalism. Accordingly, he understood it as his main task to analyse the new phenomena of the concentration of capital, the establishment of cartels, and to evaluate their consequences for the functioning of capitalism, the strategy of the working class and the Social Democratic Party. It was an understanding and analysis of capitalism shared in the main by Kautsky, too − even though many of the conclusions drawn from the analysis are different in Kautsky's works and articles.

Hilferding's main idea was that there are, in principle, no limits to the centralisation of production and the formation of cartels. The establishment of one single general cartel was − in the end − the logical result of this process:

> "Es entsteht aber die Frage, wo die Grenze der Kartellierung eigentlich gegeben ist. Und diese Frage muss dahin beantwortet werden, dass es eine absolute Grenze für die Kartellierung nicht gibt. Vielmehr ist eine Tendenz zu stetiger Ausbreitung der Kartellierung vorhanden. (...) Als Resultat des Prozesses ergäbe sich dann ein Generalkartell." (Hilferding 1968, 321).

Capitalism was due to develop into a society polarised into two opposite forces: the general cartel responsible for the production and distribution of the national product on the one hand, and the working class to be mercilessly exploited by the centralised capital on the other hand:

> "Die ganze kapitalistische Produktion wird bewusst geregelt von einer Instanz, die das Ausmass der Produktion in allen ihren Sphären bestimmt. Dann wird die Preisfestsetzung rein nominell und bedeutet nurmehr die Verteilung des Gesamtprodukts auf die Kartellmagnaten einerseits, auf die Masse aller anderen Gesellschaftsmitglieder anderseits." (Hilferding 1968, 321−322).

The new economic order solves the problem of the organisation of production. The whole national product is consciously distributed among the cartel and the rest of the people. Money and money prices lose their function of importance, and are substituted by a planned and conscious distribution of goods. The general cartel thus overcomes the anarchic nature of production and the contradictions inherent in production. The society remains, however, antagonistic by its nature, but this antagonism is only an antagonism of distribution. The antagonism of distribution between the general cartel and the rest of the people becomes even more accentuated in a society regulated by a general cartel:

> "Mit der Anarchie der Produktion schwindet der sachliche Schein, schwindet die Wert-gegenständlichkeit der Ware, schwindet also das Geld. Das Kartell verteilt das Produkt. Die sachlichen Produktionselemente sind wiederproduziert worden und werden zu neuer Produktion verwendet. Von dem Neuprodukt wird ein Teil auf die Arbeiterklasse und die Intellektuellen verteilt, der andere fällt dem Kartell zu zu beliebiger Verwendung. Es ist die bewusst geregelte Gesellschaft in antagonistischer Form. Aber dieser Antagonismus ist Antagonismus der Verteilung. Die Verteilung selbst ist bewusst geregelt und damit die Notwendigkeit des Geldes vorüber. Das Finanzkapital in seiner Vollendung ist losgelöst von dem Nährboden, auf dem es entstanden." (Hilferding 1968, 322).

The finance capital — a further result of concentration — ensuing from the combination of industrial and bank capital is manifest as a unified power based on the ownership of the means of production. The specific nature of capital disappears in a society governed by finance capital. Finance capital solves the problem of organising the national economy, and at the same time the capital associations concentrate property in their hands, making the relations of property apparent and accentuated:

> "So erlischt im Finanzkapital der besondere Charakter des Kapitals. Das Kapital erscheint als einheitliche Macht, die den Lebensprozess der Gesellschaft souverän beherrscht, als Macht, die unmittelbar entspringt aus dem Eigentum an den Produktionsmitteln, den Naturschätzen und der gesamten akkumuliererten vergangenen Arbeit, und die Verfügung über die lebendige Arbeit als unmittelbar entspringend aus den Eigentumsverhältnissen. Zugleich erscheint das Eigentum, konzentriert und zentralisiert in der Hand einiger grösster Kapitalassoziationen, unmittelbar entgegengesetzt der grossen Masse der Kapitallosen. Die Frage nach den Eigentumsverhältnissen erhält so ihren klarsten, unzweideutigsten, zugespitztesten Ausdruck, während die Frage nach der Organisation der gesellschaftlichen Ökonomie durch die Entwicklung des Finanzkapitals selbst immer besser gelöst wird." (Hilferding 1968, 323).

In Hilferding's opinion the polarisation of society into a general cartel and propertyless masses has, as such, no economic limitations whatever. From the economic point of view, the development of capitalist society would inevitably lead to the formation of a general cartel. Such a development is, however, impossible to imagine when the political forces are taken into account. The general cartel would sharpen the class constrasts to such a degree — and what is even more important, it would make them visible — that the capitalist society would be changed into a socialist one — the power of the general cartel would be changed into the power of the proletariat — long before the final stage of the general cartel was fully established.

The development or the tendency towards a general cartel has, however, made the task of the proletariat much easier; it has not only created a working class conscious of its historical mission but established an economic order readily and easily changeable into a socialist mode of production as well. The tendency towards the formation of a general cartel has put an end to the anarchy of capitalist production and has thus actually solved the economic problems inherent in capitalism.

The above characterisation of Hilferding's conception of the main historical development of capitalism is, in a sense, the consequential extrapolation of the historical tendencies inherent in capitalism as understood by the majority of Marxist theoreticians during the time of the Second International. In his *Finanzkapital*, Hilferding was both the most consequential theoretician on modern capitalism and the formulator of the strategic perspective of a socialist revolution. It is characteristic of his position that after the First World War Hilferding (1973a (1926)) could formulate a reformist version of the same theory (the concept of an "organised capitalism"). Hilferding's later revisionism does not in any sense diminish his role as the most consequential theoretician of the Second International. On the contrary, the concept of 'organised capitalism' as formulated in his famous speech at the party congress in Kiel in 1926[1] only supports the general conclusions of his *Finanzkapital*. The main difference between Hilferding's conceptions of 1910 and 1926 is that he now recognises the general cartel as the very end of capitalism in itself; the dictatorship of the proletariat has become obsolete, since the economy organised by the big cartels has made it possible to overcome not only the anarchic nature of capitalism but also its inner antagonism. All that is necessary for the social democratic party is to take over the management of the organised economy through the state institutions (see also Schimkowsky 1974a).

One could — by way of a preliminary formulation of the problem — argue that among the Second International theoreticians the theory of capitalism was in a fundamental sense based on two complementary propositions. As already pointed out, Marx's main contribution to the understanding of capitalism and the fate of the working class was understood as being the historical law of capitalist accumulation as presented at the end of the first volume of *Capital*. Hence, *Capital* was essentially read to describe the law-like historical development of capitalism. Marx was interpreted as having claimed that the accumulation of capital was not only producing an increasing amount of wage labourers — the working class — but also as leading to the concentration of capital and the establishment of big industrial enterprises and capital associations. According to the second proposition, this would also complete a change in the laws of commodity production; the law of the appropriation based on ownership of the products of one's own labour is reversed into its opposite. In monopolistic capitalism the exploitative nature of

---

[1] According to Gottschalch (1962, 190) Hilferding used the concept of organised capitalism as early as 1915.

capitalism becomes visible. The law of equal exchange characteristic of earlier commodity exchange is violated, and capitalist private property loses its legitimatory basis. The freedom and equality of the commodity producers of so-called simple commodity production is thus violated. In monopolistic capitalism the accumulation of capital is based on the direct exploitation of wage workers and consumers, too. The accumulation and concentration of capital has led to a relation of exploitation which does not any more express itself in the form of reified social relations; the surplus product produced by the wage workers is appropriated by the capitalist in a direct, one could almost say feudal way. The strategic consequences drawn from this thesis are crucial. Since the exploitation has become quite visible and can be experienced by its objects in a direct way, capitalism − as a fully established mode of production − is politically impossible; its very establishment will inevitably lead to its replacement by a mode of production, the elements of which have furthermore already been developed within capitalism.

In Rudolf Hilferding's *Das Finanzkapital* this kind of reasoning is explicitly presented. In his study Hilferding did not, however, formulate all the political and strategic conclusions inherent in his theory. And Hilferding's later political standpoint − that of an organised capitalism − is already that of a social democrat of the Weimar republic − even though in his own self-understanding he still was a Marxist.

From this point of view it is interesting to study the concept of capitalism and the interpretation of Marxism presented by Karl Kautsky. Kautsky never formulated such an explicit theory of modern capitalism as Hilferding, nor for that matter Lenin did. There is no very systematic presentation of monopolies, finance capital, or imperialism in Kautsky's voluminous work. In many of his works and articles he did, however, quite extensively discuss the problem of cartels, finance capital, export of capital, restrictive tariffs (Schutzzölle), joint stock companies, imperialism etc. He formulated already earlier many of the propositions later to be systematised in Hilferding's work, and after the publication of Hilferding's *Das Finanzkapital* hailed it as a great contribution to the understanding of modern capitalism (see Kautsky 1910−1911, 883).

Despite the lack of a coherent theory of monopoly or finance capitalism, Kautsky shared many of Hilferding's conclusions. Capitalism was essentially viewed as constituting the capitalists and the proletariat, the main relation between them being that of increasing exploitation. The accumulation of capital was understood inevitably to lead towards a polarisation of the capitalist society. And to Kautsky above all, the law of accumulation of capital was a scientific law from which the revolutionary socialist perspective and the necessity of overthrowing the capitalist system of exploitation could scientifically be deduced. The strategy of the working class movement was thus based on scientific knowledge of the development of capitalism. Scientific socialism was supposed to prove both the necessity and the possibility of the goal of the socialist movement. Even though the overthrow of capitalism can − in the last instance − only be the outcome of conscious action by the proletariat organised in a socialist party, the dissolution of capitalism is not a problem as such; it is the necessary and law-like result of the historical tendency of the accumulation of capital.

2. THE DISPUTE OVER REVISIONISM

Some of the main ideas and problems in Kautsky's theoretical thinking — his concept of capitalism and of socialist revolution — can best be presented with an analysis of the first dramatic polemic against Kautsky and the Scientific Socialism represented by him, the "Revisionismusstreit" of 1899, which was the first polemic seriously to threaten Kautsky's theoretical authority inside the party. In 1899 Eduard Bernstein published his critique of Marxism and the *Erfurt Programme,* the theoretical basis of the Social Democratic Party of Germany. Bernstein's *Die Voraussetzungen des Sozialismus und die Aufgaben der Sozialdemokratie* (1904 (1899))[1] was a whole-scale attack on all the main propositions on which Kautsky's position of socialism was based. (Kautsky was the recognised author of the theoretical parts of the programme.) It criticised both the "method", the "programme", and the "tactics" of the *Erfurt Programme.* Kautsky hastened to answer Bernstein's critique already during the same year by publishing his *Antikritik* (1899a).

Die Voraussetzungen had as its main target — as explicated by Bernstein in the preface to the first edition of 1899 (1904, V—VI) — the theory of collapse of Marxism (see also Colletti 1971, 15—18). This theory of collapse referred to a conception according to which capitalist development will out of necessity lead to the destruction of capitalism, to a final crisis in capitalist society. Economic development was understood as leading toward a growing polarisation of society, i.e. to a decreasing number of big

---

[1] Bernstein's revision of Marxism was first criticised and vehemently condemned by "orthodox" Marxists — Kautsky among then — after the publication of *Die Voraussetzungen.* Starting in 1896 Bernstein had, however, already presented his main arguments against Marxism in a series of articles published in *Die Neue Zeit* under the title "Probleme der Sozialismus" (Bernstein 1896—97a, b, c, d, e; 1897—98a, b, c). Kautsky expected from the publication of these articles a veritable development of Marxism and an attempt to understand the new phenomena of modern capitalism from a Marxist standpoint (see Hühnlich 1981, 40). (For an analysis of the exchange of letters between Kautsky and Bernstein during the dispute see Steinberg 1978.) The articles published in *Die Neue Zeit* were already criticised by Rosa Luxemburg in *Die Leipziger Volkzeitung* as representing social reformism even before the publication of Bernstein's *Voraussetzungen* (see Luxemburg 1970 (1898—99); see also Plechanow 1897—98).

Bo Gustafsson has pointed out that Bernstein's break with Marxism can be dated back to his postscript and comment published in the German edition of Luis Héritier's history of the French Revolution of 1848 in 1897 and written in 1895 or 1896. At this time no one paid any attention to Bernstein's critique of the Marxist idea of a revolutionary seizure of power by the proletariat. (See Gustafsson 1969, 109 and 120.)

capitalists and increasing masses of proletarian wage workers. The middle classes, artisans, small scale manufacturers and merchants, as well as peasants are dying out. Economic development furthermore leads to the increasing misery of the working class; immiseration is the other side of the accumulation of capital. The inevitable result of the growing polarisation of society is socialist revolution, the overthrow of capitalism.

It was typical of the polemics between Bernstein and Kautsky that Kautsky did not approve of Bernstein's interpretation of Marxism. According to Kautsky there was no question of either collapse or immiseration in Marxism. Neither the programme of the party nor Kautsky's own conceptions were ever based on any such ideas. The very terms were invented by Bernstein and other opponents of Marxism. Bernstein was fighting against the windmills of a dogmatic Marxism constructed by him. (See Kautsky 1899a, 42−43).

Despite the obvious disagreement over the right interpretation of Marxism, it is all the more astonishing that both Bernstein and Kautsky did, however, seem to share a common understanding of what constituted the theoretical core of Marxist theory of capitalism and socialist revolution. In order to prove that this was indeed the case, it is better to start the analysis of the dispute not with a discussion of the method of Marxism − where the disagreement seems to be the greatest (Bernstein explicitly rejected dialectics and the materialist conception of history) − but with a discussion of the disputants' analyses of the economic development in Western Europe and Germany in particular, and the strategic conclusions drawn from them. It was the question of the accumulation and concentration of capital − and the dispersion of ownership of property − that was the main problem for the both theoreticians.

The whole dispute seems to concentrate on the empirical validity of the economic laws of capitalist development and the Marxist prognosis about the increasing centralisation of capital and the growing proletarisation of the great majority of the population in the developed capitalist countries. They both agreed that if Marx's prognosis is valid, the socialist revolution is a historical necessity. If not, then the revolutionary socialist perspective loses its scientific basis and the way is open to social reforms within the bourgeois society and to an increasing participation of the working class and its political organisations in the political institutions of the bourgeois state.

In the chapter "Die wirtschaftliche Entwicklung der modernen Gesellschaft" Bernstein launched a full-scale attack on the Marxist law of concentration and centralisation of capital. The main question could be formulated according to Bernstein as follows:

> "Grössere Zentralisation der Kapitale, grössere Konzentration der Betriebe, erhöhte Ausbeutungsrate. Ist das nun alles rightig?" (Bernstein 1904, 46).

Bernstein was willing to admit that there is some essential truth in the analysis; such a tendency is active in capitalism, but Marxism has neglected to analyse equally important countertendencies:

> "Es ist richtig vor allem in der Tendenz. Die geschilderten Kräfte sind da und wirken in der angegebenen Richtung. Aber auch die Vorgänge sind der Wirklichkeit entnommen:

der Fall der Profitrate ist Thatsache, das Eintreten von Ueberproduktion und Krisen ist Thatsache, periodische Kapitalvernichtung ist Thatsache, die Konzentration und Zentralisation des industriellen Kapitals ist Thatsache, die Steigerung der Mehrwerthsrate ist Thatsache. Soweit lässt sich prinzipiell an der Darstellung nicht rütteln. Wenn das Bild nicht der Wirklichkeit entspricht, ist nicht weil Falsches gesagt wird, sondern weil das Gesagte unvollständig ist. Faktoren, die auf die geschilderten Gegensätze einschränkend einwirken, werden bei Marx entweder gänzlich vernachlässigt oder zwar bei Gelegenheit behandelt, aber später, bei der Zusammenfassung und Gegenüberstellung der festgestellten Thatsachen, fallen gelassen, so dass die soziale Wirkung der Antagonismen viel stärker und unmittelbarer erscheint, als sie in Wirklichkeit ist." (Bernstein 1904, 47).

A good example of the tendencies acting against the increasing concentration and centralisation of capital is the growth of joint stock companies. These were discussed by Marx in *Capital* but their importance as a tendency working against centralisation was not, however, fully recognised by Marx and his followers. Joint stock companies are a good example proving that parallel to the concentration of industrial enterprises there need not necessarily be a tendency towards the concentration of riches or property:

"Die Form der Aktiengesellschaften wirkt der Tendenz: Zentralisation der Vermögen durch Zentralisation der Betriebe, in sehr bedeutendem Umfang entgegen. Sie erlaubt eine weitgehende Spaltung schon konzentrirter Kapitale und macht Aneignung von Kapitalen durch einzelnen Magnaten zum Zwecke der Konzentrirung gewerblicher Unternehmen überflüssig." (Bernstein 1904, 47).

Bernstein's main task in his empirical critique of Marxism was to test the real distribution of property and income in the capitalist countries of his time. The relevant statistics were, of course, rather incomplete and dispersed — a fact readily admitted by Bernstein. Using various sources he was, however, able to compile data to support his arguments. The main result of Bernstein's research was:

"Nicht 'mehr oder minder', sondern schlechtweg *mehr*, d.h. *absolut und relativ* wächst die Zahl der Besitzenden." (Bernstein 1904, 50).

Bernstein admitted that if the total number of property owners were steadily decreasing, capitalist society would necessarily crash. In Bernstein's opinion the socialist perspective is not, however, dependent on the postulate of the ever-decreasing number of property owners in society. The increase in the number of property owners by no means makes the demands of the social democrats about the just distribution of income and property less important:

"Ob das gesellschaftliche Mehrprodukt von 10 000 Personen monopolistisch aufgehäuft oder zwischen einer halben Million Menschen in abgestuften Mengen vertheilt wird, ist für die neun oder zehn Millionen Familiehäupter, die bei diesem Handel zu kurz kommen, prinzipiell gleichgültig. Ihr Bestreben nach gerechterer Vertheilung oder nach einer Organisation, die eine gerechtere Vertheilung einschliesst, brauch darum nicht minder berechtigt und nothwendig zu sein." (Bernstein 1904, 51).

Even though one were to admit that the concentration of capital in enterprises is an inevitable result of the development of a capitalist economy, there does not necessarily

exist a parallel centralisation of property. According to Bernstein recent developments
in the capitalist countries prove quite clearly that there is an increase in the number of
property owners. Joint stock companies are the means by which the middle classes are
enjoying a new revival. The growth of a new middle class is also made possible because
of the simultaneous increase in surplus product due to the increasing productivity of
labour. (See Bernstein 1904, 46—54.)

Having discussed the dispersion and centralisation of property in society, Bernstein
criticised another central supposition or doctrine of Marxist economics. According to
Bernstein, the necessity of the future disappearance of small enterprises or small production units can be deduced from the doctrine of the concentration of capital. Even
though Bernstein was by no means trying to deny the tendency towards centralisation of
capital as such, he vehemently denied the conclusions drawn from it. The small-scale
enterprise typical of an earlier stage of capitalism is by no means dying out. Even
though typical of modern capitalism, big industrial enterprises do not push small ones
out of the market. There continues to be room for the small producer and there are
even certain factors that are beneficial to the increase of small-scale production in
general in modern society. And as in the case of the centralisation of property, the
statistical evidence collected from the end of last century does not support the thesis of
the ever-decreasing number of small enterprises in general (see Bernstein 1904, 55—61).
In industrial production the small production units are able to preserve their position or
lose it only very gradually. In agriculture the situation is even better. The small and
medium-sized enterprises grow faster than the big ones (see Bernstein 1904, 65). If the
collapse of capitalist society were to depend on the disappearance of the middle steps
between the top and the bottom of the social pyramid, it would not be any nearer to us
today than it has ever been during the earlier development of capitalism (see Bernstein
1904, 65).

In Bernstein's opinion it was thus not possible to generalise any tendency towards
increasing centralisation either of ownership or of production in capitalism. There are
tendencies inherent in capitalism pointing in such a direction, but at the same time
there are countertendencies in action. The total result of these tendencies can only be
clarified after careful analysis of the relevant empirical data. The empirical data at
Bernstein's disposal concerning the concentration in the 1880s and 1890s did not support the thesis of any clear concentration tendencies as such.

The next step in Bernstein's critique consisted of the Marxist conception of crisis
development. Consequently, he criticised various explanations of crises, and a recent
discussion of the causes of crises by Rosa Luxemburg in particular (see Bernstein 1904,
70—75). The most important question taken up by Bernstein was, however, the effect
of the various forms of centralisation on the character of crises. In his opinion the
"Unternähmerverbände", associations of capitalists, cartels, syndicates and trusts, were
obviously able to regulate production. Bernstein was not, however, supporting the
thesis that the cartels were able to cure all the evils of capitalism.

But in any case, new associations of capital, cartels, are a product of the capitalist economy, and not only a product of political intervention into the economy via protectionist tariffs. As such, they are a means of adapting production to the market; they are an effective countertendency to overproduction. According to Bernstein cartels are able to modify the appearance of capitalist crises in the market:

> "Dies leugnen, heisst die Vorzüge der Organisation vor anarchischer Konkurrenz leugnen. Das aber thut man, wenn man prinzipiell in Abrede stellt, dass die Kartelle auf die Natur und Häufigkeit der Krisen modifizirend einwirken können. Wie weit sie es können, ist vorläufig eine reine frage der Konjunktur, denn noch liegen nicht genug Erfahrungen vor, um in dieser Hinsicht ein abschliessendes Urtheil zu erlauben". (Bernstein 1904, 79—80).

It is, thus, impossible to prophesy more precisely the effect of cartels on the crisis phenomena. Bernstein, however, warned the workers' organisations not to neglect the problem of the cartels, even though nothing very definitive could be said about their effects. One should take them into account because they might still modify crises. (See Bernstein 1904, 81—82.)

The general line in Bernstein's critique is not difficult to summarise. He criticised any expectations of an imminent collapse of capitalism, whether the expectations were based on the centralisation of capital, property or income, or on crisis development. On the one hand Bernstein denied the increasing centralisation and polarisation of society, while on the other hand the concentration of capital was, in the form of capital associations, modifying the market problems of overproduction. Collapse and general polarisation of society were not to be expected. Any strategy based on such expectations is false and doomed to failure.

The chief question in the dispute between Bernstein and Kautsky was quite evidently the role of capital concentration in capitalism. The problem is once more taken up by Bernstein at the end of his critique. Bernstein referred to Kautsky's answer to the critique presented at the Stuttgart party congress a few years earlier. Kautsky had made the thesis about concentration the crucial question by saying:

> "Wenn die Kapitalisten zunehmen und nicht die Besitzlosen, dann entfernen wir uns immer mehr vom Ziel, je mehr die Entwicklung vor sich geht, dann festigt sich der Kapitalismus, nicht der Sozialismus." (Cited in Bernstein 1904, 178.)

Bernstein's own comment on this thesis was typical. He not only rejected the increasing polarisation but also problematised its possible consequences:

> "Hinge der Sieg des Sozialismus von dem unausgesetzten Zusammenschrumpfen der Zahl der Kapitalmagnaten ab, so müsste die Sozialdemokratie, falls sie folgerichtig handeln wollte, wenn nicht die Anhäufung von kapitalien in immer weniger Händen mit allen Mitteln unterstützen, so doch mindestens Alles unterlassen, was dieses Zusammenschrumpfen aufhalten könnte. Faktisch thut sie oft genug das Gegenteil." (Bernstein 1904, 179).

In other words, while believing in the inevitable decrease of capitalists the social democrats not only neglected the real historical tendencies but also, in fact, condemned the practical political measures of their own party.

The empirical falsification of the tendencies towards the concentration of capital was not actually needed either, after all, to prove Bernstein's point. Having attempted with great effort to prove that the concentration of capital is not a permanent and unavoidable tendency in capitalism, Bernstein denied the importance of the problem as far as the socialist perspective was concerned:

> "Dass die Zahl der Besitzenden zu- und nicht abnimmt, ist nicht eine Erfindung bürgerlicher Harmonia-Oekonomen. (...) Was hat aber diese Thatsache für den Sieg des Sozialismus zu besagen? Warum soll an ihr, beziehungsweise ihrer Widerlegung die Verwirklichung des Sozialismus hängen? (...) Die Aussichten dieses Kampfes hängen nicht von der Stange der Konzentration des Kapitals in den Händen einer zusammenschrumpfenden Zahl von Magnaten ab, noch von dem ganzen dialektischen Gerüst, wozu diese Stange gehört, sondern von dem Wachstum des gesellschaflichen Reichtums, beziehungsweise der gesellschaftlichen Produktivkräfte in Verbindung mit dem allgemeinen sozialen Fortschritt, insbesondere der intellektuellen und moralischen Reife der Arbeiterklasse selbst." (Bernstein 1904, 178–179).

The above quotation clearly proves that Bernstein was not, after all only trying to falsify the predictions of Marx's *Capital* as interpreted by Kautsky. He was trying to prove something else, namely the irrelevance of the whole "dialectical scheme" for the socialist perspective in general. Socialism could not under any circumstances be the automatic consequence of the economic development of capitalism.

What then is the strategy recommended by Bernstein for the social democratic movement based on his re-evaluation of the economic tendencies in modern capitalism? According to Bernstein, socialism essentially is a 'cooperative social order' (genossenschaftliche Gesellschaftsordnung; see Bernstein 1904, 84). Marxists claimed that in the big capitalist enterprises production is already organised in a socialist manner; it has become socialised. The idea of the realisation of socialism in socialist theory was based on two essential conditions, the first being the high development of capitalism (the socialisation of production), and the second the exercise of political power by the worker's party (see Bernstein 1904, 84–87).

Despite the fact that the big enterprises have developed and had a major position in industry, Bernstein emphasised that smaller enterprises still play an important role in production — even more so in other capitalist countries than in Germany or Prussia. Consequently there could be serious doubts as to the stage of development of the socialisation of production and the realisation of socialist economic order in this respect in the nearest future. The second problem was even greater. The exercise of the political power through the working class was traditionally understood among Marxists in terms of the dictatorship of the proletariat (see Bernstein 1904, 87). Bernstein was expressing rather serious doubts about the willingness of the propertyless classes to support such a socialist course. To begin with, workers are differently placed in accordance with their actual economic position and qualifications. Further, the propertyless in commerce and agriculture, for instance, are in a position very different from the propertyless in industry. Hence, it would be a great miscalculation to suppose that all the propertyless are potential supporters of revolutionary social democracy. On the contrary, political development in England — where the capitalist relations emerged eralier and are more highly developed than on the Continent — seems to point towards serious problems in the socialist movement. Even though the wage workers have been increasing in number, the socialist revolution does not seem to be any nearer today than it was at the beginning of the nineteenth century. (See Bernstein 1904, 88—93.)

As a matter of fact, Bernstein was then questioning all the central dotrines of revolutionary socialism on which the expectation of a socialist revolution had been based. The socialisation of production was not sufficiently developed; it would thus be impossible for the state to take over the organisation of production; and last but not least, the majority of wage workers and other propertyless classes by no means automatically supported the revolutionary course presented in the programmes of Social Democracy. There were no signs of a linear increase in the support of socialist ideals despite the increase of wage labourers. In short, in Bernstein's opinion, it was justifiable to question the conditions of socialism in modern society on which the social democratic strategy rested. It is the important task of Social Democrats to overcome the evident discrepancy between the programme of the party and the Marxist theory on the one hand, and the actual goals and aspirations of the working class, on the other.

The only consequential result of this re-evaluation could be the overthrow of all doctrinary beliefs in a revolution in an immediate future and in an establishment of the dictatorship of the proletariat. In fact Bernstein claimed to have been performing exactly such a revision; the party programme should be changed to answer the needs and the conditions of the present situation:

> "Ist aber die Sozialdemokratie heute etwas Anderes als eine Partei, welche die sozialistische Umgestaltung der Gesellschaft durch das Mittel demokratischer und wirtschaftlicher Reform anstrebt?" (Bernstein 1904, 165).

Kautsky took Bernstein's critique obviously very seriously. As already pointed out he answered it during the same year, in 1899, by publishing his *Bernstein und das sozialdemokratische Programm. Eine Antikritik* (1899a; see also Kautsky 1899b, d). In his anticritique Kautsky took up all the central problems and questions posed by Bernstein in his *Voraussetzungen*. Kautsky did not practically accept any of Bernstein's conclusions. They were all based either on serious misunderstandings or on unreliable empirical data. The historical validity of the law of capital accumulation and concentration was discussed in great detail and in a systematic way in the second part of the work, called "the programme".

According to Kautsky, Bernstein's first mistake was that he did not seem to recognise that Marx's theory of concentration of capital did not include any predictions or prophecies as to the exact development and stage of concentration, even less any prophecy of a collapse of capitalism. Marx had only pointed out the general direction of economic development in capitalism (see Kautsky 1899a, 49). However, Kautsky admitted that there was a real problem pointed out by Bernstein: is there a tendency towards increasing concentration active in capitalism? According to Bernstein, there is no parallel tendency towards the concentration of production and enterprises, and the concentration of property. The first tendency is — with certain reservations — a real one; the second does not necessarily take place at the same time. According to Kautsky, the statistical evidence provided by Bernstein could not, however, prove anything of the kind. To begin with, Bernstein was using statistics referring for the most part to a certain year, and thus they could not prove anything about the historical tendency of concentration. Secondly, the Social Democrats had never denied the possible future existence of small-scale enterprises alongside the big ones. (See Kautsky 1899a, 52—53.) There cannot, furthermore, be any question of a general expropriation of the small capitalists all at once (see Kautsky 1899a, 49). In Kautsky's opinion it cannot be denied that there is, however, a general tendency towards the capitalisation of production and the gradual disappearance of individually owned enterprises operative in capitalism.

This tendency is of crucial importance from the point of view of the socialist perspective. Is it due to it that the proletariat comes to recognise the inevitability of overcoming private property:

> "Die Aufhebung des Alleinbetriebs, der ehedem die herrschende Betriebsform bildete, schafft Proletarier, Lohnarbeiter. Je mehr sich auf den Ruinen des Handwerks die kapitalistische Produktion entwickelt, desto geringer für den Lohnarbeiter die Aussicht, auf der Grundlage des Privateigenthums als isolirter Produzent von kapitalistischer Ausbeutung und Knechtung unabhängig zu werden, desto stärker sein Verlangen nach Aufhebung des Privateigenthums. So entstehen naturnothwendig zugleich mit dem Proletariat sozialistische Tendenzen bei den Proletariern selbst wie bei jenen, die sich auf den Standpunkt des Proletariats stellen, seine Erhebung zu Selbständigkeit, also zu Freiheit und Gleichheit bewirken wollen." (Kautsky 1899a, 53).

The concentration of capital is the crucial question because it creates both the subjective and the objective conditions of a socialist revolution:

> "Es ist die Konzentration des Kapitals, welche diese immer mehr verbessert. Je mehr sie fortschreitet, desto mehr vergrössert und schult sie das Proletariat, wie wir gesehen, desto mehr entkräftet, entmuthigt, verringert sie aber auch die Masse derjenigen, die an dem Privateigenthum an den Produktionsmitteln ein Interesse haben, die selbstständigen Unternehmer, desto mehr schwäht sie deren Interesse an der Aufrechterhaltung dieses Eigenthums, desto mehr schafft sie aber auch die Vorbedingungen sozialistischer Produktion." (Kautsky 1899a, 53).

Kautsky was quite explicit in his theoretical thinking about the laws of capitalist development. The concentration of capital both sets the historical task of the proletariat and creates the means to solve it:

> "Das sind die Elemente, aus denen nach marxistischer Auffassung der Sozialismus entspringen soll. Die Konzentration des Kapitals stellt die historische Aufgabe: die Einführung einer sozialistischen Gesellschaftsordnung. Sie produziert die Kräfte zur Lösung der Aufgabe, die Proletarier, und sie schafft die Mittel zur Lösung: die gesellschaftliche Produktion, aber sie bringt nicht selbst ohne Weiteres die *Lösung der Aufgabe*. Diese kann nur aus dem *Bewusstsein*, dem *Willen*, dem *Kampfe* des Proletariats entspringen." (Kautsky 1899a, 54).

The data about German occupational and industrial statistics used by Bernstein were not, however, totally irrelevant for they could still be used to test Marx's prognosis about the direction of social development:

> "... sie lassen uns zwar nicht erkennen, wie weit wir noch vom Sozialismus entfernt sind, wohl aber, ob wir uns in der Richtung bewegen, die in der von Marx prognostizierten Weise zum Sozialismus führt." (Kautsky 1899a, 55).

Kautsky was, after all, taking Bernstein's empirical studies or the questions pointed out by them seriously. He first took up the question of the concentration of enterprises and the development of small-scale industries or enterprises. In his opinion there was no doubt about centralisation in this respect. Even though the number of small enterprises and their share of the total labour force was still quite prominent in some industries, the general trend was obvious; their share had been diminishing during the latter part of the century. The situation was somewhat different in commerce and in the sphere of circulation, where small enterprises still held a dominant role. They did not, however, support the thesis of the viability of the small-scale enterprise in general. Quite on the contrary, the small enterprises in commerce were becoming more and more "proletarised" and dependent on the bigger enterprises. Moreover, their customers were predominantly proletarian, which lent them a proletarian character:

> "Die Zunahme der Kleinbetriebe im Zwischenhandel und dem Gewerbe der Beherbergung und Erquickung ist aber kein Zeichen der Lebensfähigkeit des Kleinbetriebs, sondern ein Produkt seiner Zersetzung. (...) So werden die kleinen Wirthe und Händler immer proletarischer in ihrem Fühlen und Denken. War ehedem die kleinbürgerliche Denkweise bestimmend für das Proletariat, so tritt jetzt immer mehr das umgekehrte Verhältnis ein." (Kautsky 1899a, 64).

Taken as a whole, the statistical material supported the Marxist thesis about the development of concentration and centralisation in industry and the economy in general:

> "Wenn ja eine Theorie eine glänzende Bestätigung fand, so die Marxsche in den Zahlen der deutschen Berufs- und Betriebszählungen." (Kautsky 1899a, 68).

In agriculture the situation was somewhat different, and Kautsky was forced to admit that the concentration of capital was not as clear in farming as in industry. The share of small farms had been increasing in agricultural production. But even here the tendency towards the polarisation of production relations was quite clear. On the one hand, there were big farms working with wage labourers, on the other, there were small family farms providing work for members of the family for only part of the time. The small farmers were not only no longer able to make a living from work on the farm, their work and means of subsistence had become more and more dependent on industrial production and the capitalist market. It was therefore possible to speak of proletarisation even in relation to agricultural production and the agrarian population. (See Kautsky 1899a, 73.)

Once again the latest development in the economy thus supported the Marxist thesis about the polarisation of society even in the agricultural sector, even though there was an important difference compared with developments in industry. In agriculture there were more countertendencies and, consequently, the direction of the development was not easy to predict (see Kautsky 1899a, 78). There could not, however, be any doubts about the general direction of development in the whole capitalist production:

> "Sind aber die Erwartungen nicht völlig in Erfüllung gegangen, die Marx in Bezug auf die Konzentration des Grundbesitzes hegte, so haben sich um so glänzender jene erfüllt, die er in Bezug auf die Gesammtheit des modernen Produktionsprozesses aussprach. Die 'Kapitalmagnaten', welche alle Vortheile des kapitalistischen 'Umwälzungsprozesses usurpiren und monopolisiren', sind zur Wirklichkeit geworden in der kurzen Spanne Zeit, seitdem Marx diesen Satz niedergeschrieben, und werden immer mehr zur Wirklichkeit durch die Vollendung der Kapitalkonzentration in der Form der *Kartelle* und *Trusts*." (Kautsky 1899a, 78–79).

Having discussed the problem of the tendency towards the concentration of capital in modern society, Kautsky took up Bernstein's second and seemingly more central argument. Bernstein did not, in fact, deny the concentration of capital or enterprises but only the concentration of property. According to Kautsky the greatest problem was what Bernstein meant when speaking about property owners ("Besitzenden"). Marx never presented any theory about the decrease in the number of property owners. On the contrary, the number of capitalists was due to an increase at the same time as the number of wage labourers due to the accumulation of capital. Kautsky was obviously at his strongest in arguing against Bernstein about the meaning of the property owners. It is, indeed, very unclear what Bernstein meant when speaking about property owners and their increase. More specifically, Bernstein was speaking about people with a "higher income based on property", i.e. people who have some property income without or besides the income from their wage labour. Kautsky's interpretation was that Bernstein could have meant one of three possible alternatives, namely either the increase in the number of property owners referred to the capitalists, which was not in contradiction with Marx's theory, or it referred to the increase in the middle classes with some independent sources of income of their own. The thesis about the increase in the share of the middle classes is more serious and according to Kautsky it contradicted the ideas presented in the *Communist Manifesto*. If the share of the capitalists and the wage workers was increasing simultaneously, then there could not possibly be any simultaneous increase in the share of the middle classes (see Kautsky 1899a, 84–85). The third alternative was that Bernstein was simply referring to the increasing well-being of the wage workers in modern society. It would, however, be rather strange to speak about property in relation to wage workers and their income.

Once more the statistical evidence is found to be problematic. To begin with, it was restricted to too short a period, and, secondly it is very difficult to interpret the income statistics in terms of sources of income. As a whole Kautsky was not convinced of Bernstein's critique of Marxism and the concentration thesis. He was, however, willing to accept that economic developments in capitalism would not lead to the straightforward destruction of the middle classes but rather to the transformation of the traditional middle classes (merchants, artisans, etc.) into a new kind of middle class. (See Kautsky 1899a, 98.)

The argument about joint stock companies was presented by Bernstein as further evidence of the important role of the middle classes in capitalism. According to Bernstein joint stock companies function as a counterfactor against the centralisation of property despite the centralisation of production. The evidence presented by Bernstein of the effects of joint stock companies on the dispersion of property was found to be quite inadequate by Kautsky. But even his theoretical arguments were – in Kautsky's opinion – misleading and wrong. It is quite true that joint stock companies make the dispersion of ownership of capital possible in principle, but this does not prove anything about the actual dispersion taking place:.

> "Die Zunahme der Zahl der Aktionäre beweist gar nicht die Zunahme der Zahl der Besitzenden; sie beweist nur, dass in der kapitalistischen Gesellschaft die Form der Aktie immer mehr die vorherrschende Form des Besitzes wird." (Kautsky 1899a, 100).

Further:

> "Weit entfernt, die Wirkungen der Konzentration der Kapitalien aufzuheben, ist das Aktienwesen vielmehr das Mittel, sie auf die Spitze zu treiben. Die Form der Aktiengesellschaft erst ermöglicht riesige Unternehmungen, denen das Einzelkapital nicht gewachsen ist." (Kautsky 1899a, 103).

Bernstein's whole argumentation aimed at proving that the polarisation of society into centralised capital (big capitalists) and propertyless wage labourers was not in fact taking place or that it was taking place much more slowly than was usually expected. What Bernstein seemed to be trying to show was that there was still room for small enterprises and middle classes in society. The Marxist doctrine on the ever-increasing polarisation of society could thus be seriously doubted. Kautsky, on the other hand, stressed both the concentration of capital and the parallel increase in wage labourers. Even though small-scale enterprises still existed and even though there were still middle classes side by side with the proletariat and the concentrated capital, the general trend had not changed. There were fewer and fewer chances for a wage labourer to become anything but a wage labourer: the socialist perspective was the only realistic one for the proletariat.

Kautsky was quite clearly able to show many of Bernstein's weak points and the impreciseness of many of the questions he posed.[2] But in a sense the whole polemics might actually be thought rather irrelevant from the point of view of the socialist perspective and the strategy of the social democratic movement – the real issue at stake.

The doctrine against which Bernstein was arguing in his *Voraussetzungen* was the theory of collapse of capitalism. Kautsky was, on the other hand, rejecting the whole

---

[2] According to Colletti the *Antikritik* is one of the best treatises written by Kautsky, only to be compared with his *Die Agrarfrage* (see Colletti 1968, 68).

critique because he thought that it was totally misdirected — neither he nor the Social
Democratic Programme had ever presented any conception of revolution based on the
theory of collapse. In Kautsky's opinion, the idea of a general and final collapse of
capitalism in times of an economic crisis was totally alien to social democracy. Bernstein's critique was based on false assumptions. (See Kautsky 1899a, 42—43.)

Kautsky claimed that Bernstein's mistake was that he understood the nature of the
Marxist conception of the necessary laws of development or economic laws of society in
terms of fatalism.

> "Getreu seiner Uebersetzung von Nothwendigkeit mit Fatalismus erkennt er nur dort eine
> Nothwendigkeit an, wo eine Zwangslage besteht. So wird ihm die marxistische Theorie zur
> Lehre, die ökonomische Entwicklung werde schliesslich eine *Zwangslage* schaffen, in der
> die Menschen gar nicht anders könnten, als den Sozialismus einführen. So und nicht anders
> versteht er die marxistische 'Zusammenbruchtheorie'. Da ist es keine Kunst, sie zu wieder-
> legen." (Kautsky, 1899a, 46).

In Marxism, on the contrary, the socialist revolution is understood to be a result of class
struggle, and not an automatic outcome of economic development. Socialism will not be
established because of a final collapse of capitalism. It will result from the conscious
activity of a mature and revolutionary working class:

> "Diese Theorie sieht in der kapitalistischen Produktionsweise den Faktor, der das Proleta-
> riat in den Klassenkampf gegen die Kapitalistenklasse treibt, der es immer mehr zunehmen
> lässt an Zahl, Geschlossenheit, Intelligenz, Selbstbewusstsein, politischer Reife, der seine
> ökonomische Bedeutung immer mehr steigert und seine Organisation als politische Partei
> sowie deren Sieg unvermeidlich macht, ebenso unvermeidlich aber auch das Erstehen der
> sozialistischen Produktion als Konsequenz dieses Sieges." (Kautsky 1899a, 48).

The above interpretation of Bernstein's critique by Kautsky is very illuminating. One
the one hand, the whole critique seemed to be totally irrelevant because it is based on
the presumed fatalistic idea of collapse. On the other hand, Kautsky admitted that if
the concentration of capital did not take place as predicted by theory, then the whole
Social Democratic Programme would be based on false premises.[3]

The dilemma became once more clear in a critique of Bernstein's *Voraussetzungen*
published by Kautsky in *Vorwärts* in 1899, in which he explicitly stated that the factors
making socialism necessary were as follows:

---

[3]   According to Colletti Bernstein's critique of the conception of collapse in Marxism is — at
least partly — legitimated:

> "Dennoch muss man zugeben, dass durch die Art und Weise, mit der der damalige Marxis-
> mus die Marxsche Theorie auslegte, das in ein 'unvermeidliches *Naturgesetz*' umgewandelt
> wurde, was Marx selbst als *historische Tendenz* bezeichnet hatte. Eine gewaltige Krise
> würde früher oder später grosses Elend hervorrufen, welches die Gemüter gegen das
> System richten und von der Unmöglichkeit überzeugen würde, in der alten Ordnung fort-
> zufahren. Die schwere und verhängnisvolle Wirtschaftskrise würde sich zu einer
> allgemeinen Gesellschaftskrise ausweiten und endlich mit der Machtübernahme durch das
> Proletariat enden." (Colletti 1968, 17).

"Zunahme des Proletariats, der Kapitalkonzentration, der Ueberproduktion, dass sind die Elemente, die zum Sozialismus hindrängen." (Kautsky 1899b: 1).

On the one hand, Kautsky was in this article ready to defend the deductions of Marxism as corresponding to the statistical evidence:

"In Gegentheil, die Zahlen der Statistik stimmen mit den Deduktionen unserer bisherigen Theorie vollkommen überein und bestätigen sie aufs Glänzendste." (Kautsky 1899b: 1).

On the other hand, Kautsky doubted the relevance of such statistical comparison from the revolutionary perspective:

"Ich bezweifle es, dass wir im Stande sind, statistisch berechnen zu können, wann die Gesellschaft für die sozialistische Produktion reif geworden ist. Diese wird ein Produkt nicht bloss der ökonomischen Entwicklung sein, sondern auch der aus ihr hervorgehenden Klassenkämpfe. Sie erfordert eine gewisse Höhe der kapitalistischen Produktion, wie eine gewisse Kraft und Reife des Proletariats." (Kautsky 1899b: 1).

Once again Kautsky was denying Marxism as depending only on the presumed future polarisation or collapse of capitalism. The objective tendencies of capitalism are not as such sufficient, even if necessary, conditions for socialist revolution. In Kautsky's opinion neither Marx nor Engels nor the Social Democratic Programme relied on any such expectations:

"Aber von einer derartigen Taktik, die den Erfolg unserer Bewegung von einer Weltkrise oder einem Weltkrieg, oder einer anderen Weltkatastrophe abhängig macht, die demnächst hereinbrechen soll, ist weder in Deutschland noch sonstwo bei einer sozialistischen Partei etwas zu machen. Der Kampf gegen die Zusammenbruchstheorie in diesem Sinne ist ein Kampf gegen Windmühlen." (Kautsky 1899b: 1).

Bernstein's critique was obviously misdirected, but if it were justified, then the whole Social Democratic Programme would be miscredited:

"Wäre Bernsteins Kritik der Zusammenbruchstheorie begründet, dann erwiesen sich die grundlegenden Sätze unseres Parteiprogrammes als ein einziger grosser Irrthum. Aber nicht sie allein. Wenn die Zahl der Proletarier abnimmt, das Kapital nicht zur Beherrschung der Produktion gelangt, der Markt unabsehbar Ausdehnung fähig ist — was wird dann aus dem Sozialismus selbst?" (Kautsky 1899b: 1).[4]

Bernstein had proposed that the Social Democratic Party reform its programme and dare to appear as what it in reality already was, a democratic party of social reforms. If Bernstein's proposal were accepted, then the party would cease to be what it really was:

---

[4] The same idea had been formulated by Rosa Luxemburg in her critique of Bernstein's *Probleme der Sozialismus:*

"Nimmt man jedoch mit Bernstein an, die kapitalistische Entwicklung gehe nicht in der Richtung zum eigenen Untergang, dann hört der Sozialismus auf, *objektiv notwending zu sein.* Von den Grundsteinen seiner wissenschaftlichen Begründung bleiben dann nur noch die beiden anderen Ergebnisse der kapitalistischen Ordnung: der vergesellschaftete Produktionsprozess und das Klassenbewusstsein des Proletariats." (Luxemburg 1970a (1898—99), 16).

> "Was er ihr vorschlägt, bedeutet aber thatsächlich nichts geringeres, als das sie aufhören soll, zu *sein,* was sie *ist.* Wenn wir Bernstein folgen, werfen wir weit mehr über Bord, als einige blutrünstige Redensarten. Wir werfen dann über Bord nicht nur unsere bisherige Theorie, sondern auch unsere bisherige Praxis, unser Programm und unsere Taktik, unser Endziel und unsere Bewegung, um dafür einen Sozialismus ohne Begründung und ohne bestimmte Abgrenzung von Liberalismus und die Aussicht auf das Wohlwollen des radikalen deutschen Bürgerthums einzutauschen." (Kautsky 1899b: 3).

As a matter of fact, it could be claimed that the result of the dispute between Bernstein and Kautsky was predetermined by the different interpretations of what was understood by them to be the methodology of Marxism, the materialist conception of history. According to Bernstein the materialist conception of history had to be understood as being equivalent to the "Behauptung der Nothwendigkeit aller geschichtlichen Vorgänge und Entwicklungen" (Bernstein 1904, 5). The dominating factors in human society are the productive forces and relations of production. According to Bernstein it would, however, be wrong to emphasise exclusively the role of economic factors in this development. Even ideological factors have a specific effect of their own. This and only this can be the standpoint of modern advanced materialism (and here Bernstein was referring to the authority of old Engels, see Bernstein 1904, 7—8). Even though the economic development of society is still recognised as being the dominant factor, modern historical materialism should not deny the role of other relevant factors either:

> "Aber jedenfalls bleibt die Vielheit der Faktoren, und es ist keineswegs immer leicht, die Zusammenhänge, die zwischen ihnen bestehen, so genau blosszulegen, dass sich mit Sicherheit bestimmen lässt, wo im gegebenen Falle die jeweilig stärkste Triebkraft zu suchen ist." (Bernstein 1904, 9).

Kautsky did not approve of what he understood to be Bernstein's revision of the Marxist conception of history, or its division into an old and a new modern materialism:

> "Die materialistische Geschichtsauffassung ist die Theorie geworden, durch die das Proletariat seine sozialistischen Ansprüche begründet." (Kautsky 1899a, 10).

Kautsky was, however, willing to admit that the theoretical system of Marxism was still in its initial stages (see Kautsky 1899a, 9). It would be a veritable service to Marxism to develop it further. In Kautsky's opinion this would be possible only through a historical study of the development of the economy, by comparing the theory with the relevant historical facts (see Kautsky 1899a, 11).

Bernstein was not, however, doing anything of the kind. He was chiefly discussing the problem in a philosophical, abstract way; as a problem of determinism in history:

> "... eine historische Nothwendigkeit besteht für Bernstein nur dort, wo die Menschen in einer *Zwangslage* sich befinden, wo nicht blos ihr *Wollen* bestimmt motivirt, sondern auch ihr *Handeln* unfrei ist." (Kautsky 1899a, 13).

On the other hand, Bernstein was not only criticising Marx and Engels for their fatalism or determinism, he was also claiming that they were pure voluntarists; they assumed pure will as being the moving power in history via class struggle. On one hand economic determinism, on the other, pure free will. A clear case of a theory of two souls.

In Kautsky's opinion it was not only essential to the materialist conception of history for the factors behind the development of society to be found in the economy, in the relations of production. It was equally important for it to provide a method for analysing which groups and classes in society have an interest in the overthrowing of capitalism:

> "Es sind stets nur ganz bestimmte Klassen, deren Interessen und Neigungen zusammenfallen mit den Bedürfnissen der gesellschaftlichen Entwicklung. Auch diese Interessen und Neigungen können nur erkannt werden durch Erforschung der bestehenden Produktionsweise." (Kautsky 1899a, 17).

This is the scientific method of socialism, the method that is central to scientific socialism.

Kautsky was willing to acknowledge that the materialist conception of history is by no means the only possible scientific one; in principle there are alternatives to it:

> "Wer die marxistische Methode für falsch hält, dem bleiben nur zwei Wege. Er erkennt an, dass die gesellschaftliche Entwicklung eine nothwendige, gesetzmässige ist, aber er leugnet es, dass sie in letzter Linie auf die Entwicklung der Produktionsweisen zurückzuführen ist. Er nimmt an, dass andere Faktoren daneben oder ausschliesslich 'in Rechnung zu ziehen sind'. (...) Von einem wissenschaftlichen Sozialismus könnte erst dann bei dieser Methode die Rede sein, wenn die betreffenden Faktoren ebenso erforscht wären, wie die kapitalistische Produktionsweise im *Kapital,* und dargethan wäre, dass aus ihrem Wirken eine sozialistische Gesellschaft entstehen muss." (Kautsky 1899a, 18).

The second possibility is to totally deny the existence of lawful development in society. In that case scientific knowledge does, however, become impossible:

> "Oder aber, man leugnet überhaupt die Nothwendigkeit und Gesetzmässigkeit der gesellschaftlichen Entwicklung oder wenigstens die Möglichkeit, sie mit den gegebenen Mitteln zu erkennen." (Kautsky 1899a, 18).

If there are no laws in history accessible to scientific knowledge, scientific socialism becomes impossible too; one cannot say anything about the direction of social development and the great social problems of our time:

> "Das schliesst eine sozialistische Bewegung nicht aus, aber ihre Ziele hören auf, etwas anderes zu sein, als aus den Bedürfnissen der Gegenwart entspringende fromme Wünsche. Die Argumente, die Art des Kampfes, alles müsste sich ändern." (Kautsky 1899a, 18).

Kautsky concluded his discussion of Bernstein's critique of the materialist conception of history by claiming that Bernstein seemed altogether to be denying the possiblity of scientific socialism. As a consequence, Bernstein denied the scientific justification of socialism:

> "Sein erbitterter Kapf gegen die historische Notwendigkeit lässt annehmen, er huldige der Anschauung, als sei es überhaupt unmöglich, den Sozialismus wissenschaftlich zu begründen". (Kautsky 1899a, 19).[5]

---

[5]   Rosa Luxemburg summarised the crucial question of the dispute as follows:
"Entweder hat Bernstein in Bezug auf den Gang der kapitalistischen Entwicklung recht,

Bernstein's critique was aimed at questioning the deterministic nature of social development, viz. the role and nature of the economic laws of society (see also Arato 1973—74, 9). The problem with Bernstein's argumentation is that, on the one hand, he was operating on an abstract philosophical level criticising the doctrine of economic determinism, on the other, he was trying empirically to falsify the historical explanations and predictions of Kautsky's theory of capitalism. Thus, he made it relatively easy for Kautsky to defend his Marxist position. Bernstein constructed his theoretical opponent in such a way that Kautsky could deny the relevance of his critique. Marxism was neither a deterministic doctrine, nor did the history of socialism depend on the ever-increasing concentration of capital and the collapse of capitalism.

Still Bernstein's critique was not totally irrelevant after all as evidenced by Kautsky's reaction to it. Kautsky had to admit — at least indirectly — that Bernstein pointed out an important problem in scientific socialism: In what sense is the socialist doctrine and the strategy of the working class based on the idea of the necessary economic development of capitalism?

According to Kautsky it was not the economic development alone that would determine the future of socialism. Neither was it the concentration of capital nor any final and general crisis of capitalism that would give birth to a socialist society, but the increasing strength of a revolutionary working class movement. The dissolution of capitalism and the establishment of a socialist society would, in the final instance, be the outcome of class struggle. Only a revolutionary working class conscious of its historical mission could overthrow capitalism and realise the final goal of socialism.

It can, however, be claimed that Kautsky was unproblematically expecting that the subject of revolution would rather automatically emerge out of the development of capitalism. The political and moral strength of the proletariat was expected to increase parallel to the objective conditions of socialism ripening in the form of concentration and socialisation of production inside capitalism. The wage workers would inevitably come to understand their genuine interests because they did not have any alternative open to them than a socialist revolution — otherwise they would only remain wage workers in a society where their fate was characterised by social and economic misery.

It can be claimed that the conception of immiseration of the working class was the undispensable link between Kautsky's theory of capitalism and his theory of revolution. And, in this respect, Bernstein's critique of Kautsky's determinism was partly justified, even though he was clearly unable to formulate it explicitly. His discussion of determinism and free will in history tended more to confuse the issue than to clarify it and, consequently, his challenge to Kautsky's Marxism remained incomplete.

---

dann verwandelt sich die sozialistische Umgestaltung der Gesellschaft in eine Utopie, oder der Sozialismus ist keine Utopie, dann muss aber die Theorie der 'Anpassungsmittel' nicht stichhaltig sein." (Luxemburg 1970a, 18).

3. THE THEORY OF IMMISERATION, SOCIALIST CONSCIOUSNESS AND THE INTELLECTUALS

Kautsky was quite clearly at his strongest in criticising Bernstein's conceptions about the role of the 'property owners' and the middle classes in society — as can be seen from Kautsky's discussion of the role of the new middle class, which he prefered to call the intellectuals. Bernstein was generally referring to the increase in the number of property owners or people deriving some income from their property — and not from wage labour exclusively — or to small entrepreneurs in different fields of industry. According to Kautsky it would be more valid to discuss the role of intellectuals rather than property owners as the new middle class in modern capitalist society:

> "Hätte Bernstein nichts Weiteres sagen wollen, als dass der Mittelstand nicht ausstirbt, sondern nur an Stelle des alten ein neuer tritt, an Ställe der selbständigen Handwerker und kleinen Kaufleute die 'Intelligenz', so hätten wir ihm das ohne Weiteres zugegeben." (Kautsky 1899a, 128).

Kautsky's concept of the intellectual was very broad. To him an intellectual was any qualified worker representing some kind of organisational function in society. The representatives of free professions were a clear and a rather uninteresting case of intellectuals — as part of the old middle classes. The reason for the increase in the number of middle classes is the transmission of some of the functions of the exploiting classes to specific employed functionaries, qualified wage workers. The broadening of the functions of the modern state and modern enterprises has led to a remarkable increase in these functions. A relatively well-paid group of people with a specially qualified labour power has emerged. It would, however, be a grave misunderstanding to consider the new groups to be identical with the old middle classes. Their position and functions in society are rather different. It would, however, be equally erroneous to regard them as similar to the proletariat in a straightforward way. They resemble the bourgeoisie in their way of life and they have close relations with it in other respects, too. While representing the functions of capital, they assume many of the mental attitudes of the bourgeoisie as well:

> "Auch daraus ergiebt sich ein Gegensatz zahlreicher 'Intelligenzen' gegen das Proletariat." (Kautsky 1899a, 131).

The main characteristic feature of the new middle class stems from its privileged position based on the privilege of education ("der Privilegium der Bildung"). Even though education has become relatively common among the population compared with the period of feudalism, it is still a privilege preserved for a narrow section of the population. Kautsky's most interesting contribution to the analysis of the intellectuals was, however, his analysis of their class position. From this point of view intellectuals do not form any homogeneous class. Their more privileged members are close to the bourgeoisie, their least privileged members are almost proletarian in position. The most interesting group of intellectuals is, however, the increasing middle stratum of the middle class ("die Mittelschichten der Mittelschichten") which is situated between the antiproletarian intellectuals sharing the attitudes of capitalists and the genuinely proletarian intellectuals. This group shares some of the features of both strata in a way similar to the old traditional petit bourgeoisie. There are, however, two important differences; the first being an important advantage from the point of view of the socialist movement:

> "Sie unterscheidet sich von ihm einmal durch ihren weiten geistigen Horizont und ihr geschultes Vermögen abstrakten Denkens. Sie ist jene Bevölkerungsschicht, die am leichtesten dahin kommt, sich über Klassen- und Standenbornirtheit zu erheben, sich idealistisch erhaben zu fühlen über Augenblicks- und Sonderinteressen und die dauernden Bedürfnisse der gesammten Gesellschaft ins Auge zu fassen und zu vertreten." (Kautsky 1899a, 133).

On the other hand the middle stratum of the new middle class presents a feature disadvantageous from the point of view of socialism; it lacks the readiness to fight against capital. Being a relatively small group, without any specific class interest and without a unified organisation, it is not willing to fight for its interests. Moreover, it can easily safeguard its interests even without fighting, while being in a relatively privileged position:

> "Der Klassenkampf ist ihnen verhasst, sie predigen seine Beseitigung oder doch seine Abschwächung. Der Klassenkampf, das ist ihnen die Auflehnung, die Rebellion, die Revolution; sie soll überflüssig gemacht werden durch die soziale Reform." (Kautsky 1899a, 134).

The future social and political development of the new middle class is a genuine problem for the fighting proletariat. Its social position is contradictory by its nature:

> "Sie ganz für das Proletariat in Anspruch zu nehmen wäre übertrieben, aber noch irriger wäre es, sie einfach den 'Besitzenden' zuzurechnen. Wir finden in dieser Schicht in engem Rahmen alle die sozialen Gegensätze vereinigt, die die gesamte kapitalistische Gesellschaft kennzeichnen, wir finden aber auch in diesem Mikrokosmos ebenso wie im gesellschaftlichen Gesammtkörper das proletarische Element in Fortschreiten." (Kautsky 1899a, 135).

The analysis of the new middle class (the intellectuals) is once again characteristic of the whole argumentation presented in Kautsky's anti-critique against Bernstein. Kautsky did not try to deny the importance of all the counter-arguments presented by Bernstein against the thesis of the concentration – or rather polarisation – of society. His aim was more to prove that despite the continued existence and even increase of the middle classes (small property owners, members of the new middle class), their position and functions in society had radically changed due to the development of capitalist relations and the concentration of capital. The groups remaining in-between the proletariat and the bourgeoisie – even if not wholly proletarian in position and consciousness – had important features in common with the proletariat. They were gradually being prole-tarianised.

Summing up the various proletarian elements in modern society, Kautsky came to the conclusion that at least two thirds or even three quarters of the population were already proletarian in character – and hence potential supporters of revolutionary social demo-cracy (see Kautsky 1899a, 186). Even though they were not uniform in their interests, it would in future be possible to unify all the proletarian elements behind the Social Democratic Party and win their support for genuine workers-rule (see Kautsky 1899a, 192–193). All that was needed was skillful and forceful agitation by the party and its representatives. One of the best-known elements in Kautsky's thinking relevant in this respect was his conception of immiseration.

A two-fold tendency towards the represssion and elevation of the proletariat con-stantly operates in capitalist society. The contradiction in the tendency is, however, nothing but an expression of the general contradiction between capitalists and wage workers (see Kautsky 1899a, 115). The growing working class and its organisations are able to fight against increasing exploitation and its effects. Exploitation as such cannot, however, be eliminated in capitalism by an organised working class. The proletariat is able to improve its social position through class struggle, but its moral, rather than economic standing (see Kautsky 1906a, 241). In this respect Kautsky is rather more pessimistic than Engels. In his critical comments on the Party Programme proposal (the *Erfurt Programme*) Engels pointed out that the workers are able to oppose – at least to some extent – the tendency towards increasing misery. They cannot, however, avoid the insecurity characteristic of their existence in capitalism (see MEW 22, 231).[1] As Kautsky formulated it, there exists a constant tendency towards increasing misery in the capitalist society even though many of its effects on the working class have been modified and changed:

> "Also in dem Sinne einer Tendenz, einer auf dem Boden der kapitalistischen Gesellschaft *unausrottbaren Tendenz*, die stets massenhafter sich geltend macht, ist das Wort von der Zunahme des Elends und der Knechtung wie der Empörung vollkommen richtig." (Kauts-ky 1899a, 116).

The fight of the organised working class against exploitation has, however, changed the nature of misery in capitalism. In modern capitalism it would be better to speak about social misery rather than about physical misery:

---

[1] Engels' *Zur Kritik des sozialdemokratischen Programmentwurfs* was originally written in 1891, but it was first published in 1901 in *Die Neue Zeit* (see MEW 22, 594–595; note 196).

> "Aber noch eine andere Auffassung ist mit den Thatsachen vereinbar. Das wort *Elend* kann *physisches* Elend bedeuten, es kann aber auch *soziales Elend* bedeuten. Das Elend in ersterem Sinne wird an den *physiologischen* Bedürfnissen des Menschen gemessen, die allerdings nicht überall und zu allen Zeiten dieselben sind, aber doch bei Weitem nicht so grosse Unterschiede aufweisen, wie die *sozialen Bedürfnisse*, deren Nichtbefriedigung soziales Elend erzeugt." (Kautsky 1899a, 116).

In the physiological sense the Marxist conception of growing misery would obviously be false. In its wider social meaning the concept is still valid:

> "Ist aber die Erhebung der Arbeiterklasse aus dem physischen Elend ein so langsamer Prozess, dann folgt daraus schon ein stetes Wachstum der Zunahme ihres *sozialen Elends*, denn die Produktivität der Arbeit wächst ungemein rasch. Es heisst das nichts Anderes, als das die Arbeiterklasse in steigendem Masse ausgeschlossen bleibt von den Fortsschritten der Kultur, die sie selbst erzeugt, dass die Lebenshaltung der Bourgeoisie rascher steigt als die des Proletariats, dass der soziale Gegensatz zwischen beiden wächst." (Kautsky 1899a, 118).

In the above quotation the growing social misery of the working class could be under-stood as being almost synonymous with the increasing accumulation of capital. Due to the increase in the productivity of labour capital accumulates faster than the total wages in society. The relative share of the national product received by the bourgeoisie is getting bigger. If the struggle against capital is caused by growing misery, and if the growing misery is synonymous with the accumulation of capital in general, then the theoretical implications of this conception are rather devastating.[2] But in Kautsky's opinion the growing misery is also reflected in the increasing number of women and children among the labour force. Social misery is indeed a permanent element of capitalism, as permanent as exploitation, and in countries where capitalism is still only establishing its relations, the misery is even more obvious. In such regions one could even speak of pure physical misery. Hence, Kautsky was able to summarise his discussion of immiseration as follows:

> "Also überall Elend in der kapitalistischen Produktionsweise, eine um so grössere Masse des Elends, je mehr Proletarier vorhanden sind, je mehr Kleinbetriebe vom Kapital degra-dirt oder abhängig gemacht werden, aber auch desto mehr Kampf gegen das Elend, desto mehr Empörung der Arbeiterklasse gegen die kapitalistische Herrschaft." (Kautsky 1899a, 127).

In his *Die Verelendungstheorie − eine hilflose Kapitalismuskritik* Wolf Wagner (1976) discussed the dispute over revisionism mainly as a dispute of the theory of immisera-tion. Wagner is ready to admit that the study of the polemical writings of both Bern-stein and Kautsky does not reveal so many explicit referances to the problem of immi-seration (see Wagner 1976, 23). The dispute seems mainly to concern the theory of the collapse of capitalism. The development of the social position of wage workers was discussed only sporadically. Still, it is easy to agree with Wagner that the concept of

---

[2]   For a discussion of the concept of social misery in Kautsky's thinking see Wagner (1976, 27).

immiseration was perhaps the most important single part of the revolutionary socialist doctrine as presented by Kautsky. It was essential to Kautsky's thinking because it made sense of the general emphasis placed by Kautsky on the future development of the socialist revolutionary consciousness among wage workers.[3] And it was generally understood to be one of the cornerstones of the scientific socialism of Engels and Marx.[4]

To Bernstein's general theoretical argument the fate of the working class was important, too. It was important to show that the worker's position could be improved in capitalism. Bernstein did not, however, primarily discuss the development of the value and price of the labour power. Rather, he tried to show that the devastating consequences of the capital-wage labour relation could already be avoided or at least side-stepped in capitalism by introducing workers' co-operatives and juridical measures by the state and local authorities. The fate of the working class could be improved in spite of capitalism.

In answering Bernstein's critique, Kautsky formulated his revision of the immiseration doctrine — and introduced the concept of social misery discussed above. (Kautsky was of course trying to show that it was no revision after all. According to Kautsky, the *Erfurt Programme* should have been quite understandable to anyone familiar with Marx's work. The misunderstandings were due to an imperfect knowledge of *Capital* (see Kautsky 1899a, 127–128).) In defending the 'Marxist' conception of immiseration against various critics Kautsky gave various definitions of the concept — the growing misery had to be understood as only a tendency (see Kautsky 1899a, 115) — but in its most general meaning it became equivalent to the discrepancy between the growing cultural needs of wage workers and their means of satisfying them. There cannot be any fixed definition of these needs. They are cultural needs because they vary from one

---

[3] In his *Agrarfrage* Kautsky, however, definitely denied that the growing misery of the proletariat was a necessary precondition of its revolutionary aspirations. Improving the position of the proletariat as consumers did not eliminate the necessity for class struggle; on the contrary, it even improved its conditions:

"Der moderne Lohnarbeiter bleibt Proletarier, so lange er nicht im Besitz seiner Produktionsmittel ist, mag er auch als solcher besitzend werden in den Besitz von Schmuck, Möbeln, ja selbst eines Wohnhäuschens kommen. In der Verbesserung seiner Lage als Konsument, weit entfernt, ihn für der proletarischen Klassenkampf untuchtig zu machen, setzt ihn oft in den Stand, diesen um so nachdrücklicher zu führen. Dieser Kampf ist nicht das Produkt seines Elends, sondern das Produkt des Gegensatzes zwischen ihm und dem Besitzer seiner Produktionsmittel. Nicht die Ueberwindung des Elends, selbst wenn sie möglich wäre, sondern nur die Ueberwindung dieses Gegensatzes kann den sozialen Frieden herstellen. Das ist aber nur möglich dadurch, dass die Arbeiterschaft wieder in den Besitz ihrer Produktionsmittel gelangt." (Kautsky 1899c, 306).

[4] Wagner presents a list of the works of Marx supporting the thesis that Marx also shared a conception of immiseration. In Wagner's opinion it does not, however, form a central element of the works of the "mature" Marx (i.e. *Capital*). (See Wagner 1976, 18; note 14; for a discussion of the role of immiseration in Marx's *Capital* see chapter II.4.).

society to another. The growth of cultural needs kept pace with the struggle and organisation of the proletariat. (See Kautsky 1899a, 118.)

The discussion of the Görlitz Party Programme shortly after the war (1921) is even more interesting in this respect. Kautsky defended the *Erfurt Programme* against the revisions in the new programme. According to him (see Kautsky 1968a, 246−249) the doctrine of immiseration could be understood in three different ways: (1) The increase in the share of wage workers was as such part of immiseration; more and more workers were working for capital and under the command of capital. (2) Immiseration was only a tendency, the realisation of which depended on several factors, especially the power of the organised working class. (3) The misery of the wage workers is only a "relative" concept:

> "Dieselbe Lebenslage kann unter verschiedenen historischen Bedingungen das eine Mal als eine günstige, das andere Mal als eine ungünstige empfunden werden." (Kautsky 1968a, 249).

The last formulation is by far the most interesting and at the same time the most problematic. It could be interpreted as proving that Kautsky had adopted a position similar to the concept of 'relative deprivation' in sociology (workers compare their position with that of other groups or classes in society and/or with their own former position and feel deprived if the experience is unsatisfying). This interpretation is not, however, correct. Kautsky represented a position that was, after all, more materialistic.

For Kautsky, as well as for Bernstein, the 'civilising' influence of the struggle of the organised working class and its organisations was enormous; the working class was supposed to develop nothing less than a new and higher sense of morals in its common struggle. And the new cultural needs were going to develop in the common action of the workers, too.[5] The growing sense of solidarity among the workers was an important factor in this development. The organised and educated working class would not be content with its former means of satisfying needs. This is the basis for the different experiences of the same life situation ("Lebenslage") at different times. The conflict between classes would not diminish in power despite the concessions the capitalists were forced to make to an organised working class. New needs were continuously developed in the common action of the working class. Hence, even though Kautsky did not formulate the problem accordingly, he could perhaps be interpreted as having claimed that there is a permanent discrepancy between the value of labour power and the wages actually paid by the capitalists.

Kautsky did not, however, base his ideas of the new conditions of wage workers on any analysis of the possible changes in the production process of capital. (He was not

---

[5]   In an article published in 1907−08, *Verelendung und Zusammenbruch*, Kautsky emphasised the role of immiseration as a factor contributing to the moral and intellectual power of the proletariat:

> "Die grosse Tat von Marx bestand gerade darin, im Elend der Arbeiterklasse nicht bloss die sie degradierenden Seiten zu sehen, sondern auch die sie revoltierenden und damit erhebenden;..." (Kautsky 1907−08b, 550).

actually speaking of any reproduction of the labour power at all, nor did he use the term value of labour power ("der Wert der Arbeitskraft") in this context.) The thesis of growing misery in the *Erfurt Programme* was based on an analysis of the growing use of unskilled labour, the use of women's and children's labour power, the moral dispersion of the working class family, etc. The new needs of the wage workers were not a result of any new 'needs' in the production process of capital (such as the use of skilled labour and the rise in the general level of education; the only factor that is mentioned in this context is the growing intensity of labour). The new needs are produced by the organised class struggle only:

> "So wächst das Proletariat unaufhörlich an Zahl, an sittlicher Kraft, an Intelligenz, an Geschlossenheit, an Unentbehrlichkeit." (Kautsky 1968b (1892), 164).

The class struggle fought by the organised proletariat constitutes a permanent learning process for the workers. That is why Kautsky's vision of the conditions of the socialist revolution included the growing strength of the proletariat, the growing needs of the proletariat, and its growing exploitation and repression by capital.[6]

The theoretical core of Kautsky's theory of capitalism could be summarised as follows: The other side of the concentration and centralisation of capital is increasing proletarisation. Capitalism produces a steadily increasing proletariat. Revolution is not, however, an automatic outcome of the concentration and crisis development of capitalism, it is not caused by any final crisis or collapse of capitalism. It is a conscious deed by the organised socialist working class. In this sense Kautsky was not really the fatalist criticised by Bernstein.[7]

On the other hand, the growth of the revolutionary movement — the subjective factor or agent of revolution — is understood as taking place almost automatically. Kautsky had no doubts about the development of the socialist elements inside the working class. The development of capitalism was a necessary and automatic training

---

[6] In a preface written in 1906 to the Russian edition of *Handelspolitik* Kautsky stated his position without any reservations:

> "Die kapitalistische Produktionsweise bietet zwei Seiten: das Elend des Proletariats und den Reichtum der Kapitalisten. Beide bilden die Vorbedingungen des Sozialismus. Das Elend des Proletariats, seine Ausbeutung und Unterdrückung, erweckt seine Empörung, treibt es sich zu organisieren, gegen Staat und Gesellschaft zu kämpfen, dadurch sich selbst moralisch und intellektuell oft auch physisch zu heben und so jene revolutionäre Kraft zu bilden, die berufen ist, die Gesellschaft umzuwandeln, das Privateigenthum an den Produktionsmitteln in ihr aufzuheben und die Klassenunterschiede zu beseitigen." (Kautsky Nachlass A 48).

[7] In this respect one can agree with Hühnlich's interpretation of Kautsky's conception of socialist revolution: Considerations of the subjective factor are always present in his analysis. But the relationship between the development of the productive forces, or rather of the concentration of capital, and the subjective conditions of revolution, is, after all, a mechanistic one: The development of the revolutionary working class is an automatic process following from the economic development of capitalism. (See Hühnlich 1981, 59–60, 67–68).

ground for the wage workers. It makes them realise that socialism is the only realistic alternative to the 'misery' of capitalism.[8]

In this sense there is some truth in Bernstein's accusation of the fatalistic or rather deterministic − and voluntaristic − nature of Kautsky's theoretical thinking. Scientific socialism is based on the idea of a natural, law-like development of capitalism into two opposite classes, the proletariat and the bourgeoisie, the proletariat growing in "moral and economic strength" and becoming mature to take over the rule of society.

As already pointed out, Bernstein's critique was, however, rather ineffective and Kautsky was able to defend his position against the accusation of fatalism, because Bernstein formulated the problem in terms of the neo-kantian tradition as a problem of the relation between the free will of individuals and the natural necessary laws of development (see Colletti 1968, 36). Bernstein thus did not actually take up the theoretical issue of the constitution of the revolutionary subject. On the one hand he questioned the empirical validity of the economic laws of Marxism, on the other hand the "fatalistic" version of historical materialism.

If the position of Kautsky's *Antikritik* is taken seriously then quite clearly there would not be any problems with the development of revolutionary consciousness among the working class. In other contexts Kautsky did, however, present a conception that would seem to contradict the above one, namely that there are principal limits to the spontaneous consciousness of the wage workers. The wage workers can never develop anything but a limited economic or trade unionistic consciousness all by themselves. They can become conscious of their common economic (wage) interests as opposed to the capitalists and, at their best, learn to understand that these interests must be defended by trade unions in organised common action. The wage workers cannot, however, ever achieve socialist consciousness by themselves. Socialism must be brought into the working class from the outside. Its representative is the socialist party, which is in possession of the scientific theory of the development of capitalism and the socialist strategy based on it. The creators and carriers of this theory are the socialist intellectuals, who represent science in relation to the working class.[9]

---

[8] According to *Videnskab og kapital (Wissenschaft und Kapital)* (1974) the strategic expectations of traditional Marxism are deduced from a theory based on the history of the working class − and thus their character is different from that presented by Marx. They are based not on the analysis of the inner contradictions (or rather form determinations) of capital but rather on the postulated "subjective factor" deduced from the history of the working class. As a consequence, the struggle of the proletariat becomes a struggle of an oppressed class fighting to realise its ideal of a better society. (See *Videnskab og kapital* 1974, 15−16.) In this sense Kautsky's theory is a good example of Marxism.

[9] In the *Erfurt Programme* Kautsky seemed to be representing another kind of position which was not, however, less deterministic. To begin with, it is suggested that in defending their economic interests, workers will inevitably come to state political demands as well (demands such as the demand of free assembly or free association; see Kautsky 1906a, 230−231). Economic struggle will thus inevitably lead to the formation of a political workers' party. Secondly, this party will out of necessity develop into a socialist or social democratic party. In Kautsky's opinion workers

One of the clearest formulations of the relation between the working class movement and scientific socialism was formulated by Kautsky in his pamphlet *Die historische Leistung von Karl Marx. Zum 25. Todestage des Meisters* (1919a (1908)). The difference between trade unionistic consciousness and socialist revolutionary thought as presented by scientific socialism is strictly one of principle:

> "Arbeiterbewegung und Sozialismus sind von Haus aus keineswegs eins. (...) Die urwüchsige Form der Arbeiterbewegung ist die rein ökonomische, der Kampf um Lohn und Arbeitszeit, der zuerst bloss die Form einfacher Ausbrüche der Verzweiflung, unvorbereiteter Emeuten annimmt, bald aber durch *gewerkschaftliche Organisationen* in höhere Formen übergeführt wird." (Kautsky 1919a, 26).

But even the spontaneous common economic interests of the wage workers are by no means obvious. The organisation of the workers into unified trade unions is problematic per se. To begin with, the interests of the workers in various industries are not always identical, they are often even contradictory:

> "Da aber die Gewerkschaft nur die nächsten Interessen ihrer Mitglieder vertritt, steht sie auch nicht ohne weiteres im Gegensatz zur gesamten bürgerlichen Welt, sondern zunächst nur zu den Kapitalisten ihres Berufs." (Kautsky 1919a, 29)

Secondly, organised action by the trade unions can easily lead to a new rift inside the labour movement. There is a widening gap between organised and non-organised workers:

> "So kann die gewekschaftliche Bewegung trotz aller Stärkung einzelner Schichten sogar eine direkte Schwächung des gesamten Proletariats herbeiführen, wenn sie nicht von sozialistischem Geiste erfüllt ist." (Kautsky 1919a, 30).

As a result, a new aristocracy emerges among workers, an aristocracy having no interest in the common cause of the proletariat. Even though trade unions are an important field of recruitment for the socialist movement, left to themselves they easily develop into a force opposing socialism rather than supporting it.

In order to overcome the limitations of the trade union organisation, a wider perspective must be introduced into the worker's movement to make it understand and realise its common historical goals. This can be accomplished only by introducing scientific socialism into the movement. Scientific socialism is not originally a product of the proletariat but of the bourgeois intellectuals taking a proletarian standpoint in their theoretical thinking:

> "Wohl konnte zu sozialistischer Erkenntnis nur ein Mann kommen, der es vermochte, sich auf den Boden des Proletariats zu stellen, von dessen Standpunkt aus die bürgerliche Gesellschaft zu betrachten. Aber es konnte auch nur einer sein, der die Mittel der Wissenschaft beherrschte, die damals noch weit mehr als heute bloss den bürgerlichen Kreisen

---

schooled by machines will come to understand wider social problems and the right nature of class relations will be revealed to them because of the rapid economic development of capitalism (see Kautsky 1906a, 230–231). In his later works Kautsky did not, however, develop these arguments any further.

zugänglich waren. (...) Ueberall aber konnte der Sozialismus zunächst nur aus einem
bürgerlichen Milieu erstehen." (Kautsky 1919a, 27).

Scientific socialism, furthermore, is nothing but a social science having as its starting
point the proletarian position (see Kautsky 1919a, 28). On the one hand, socialist
society can be established only by the power of the working class; the proletariat is able
to liberate itself only through its own action. On the other hand, the social liberation of
man is not possible without scientific socialism:

> "Das vermag es nicht zu erreichen ohne eine sozialistische Theorie, die allein imstande ist,
> das gemeinsame proletarische Interesse in der bunten Mannigfaltigkeit der verschiedenen
> proletarischen Schichten herauszufinden und sie alle zusammen von der bürgerlichen Welt
> scharf und dauernd zu trennen. In dieser Leistung ist jene naive, jeder Theorie bare
> Arbeiterbewegung unfähig, die sich von selbst in arbeitenden Klassen gegen den anwach-
> senden Kapitalismus erhebt." (Kautsky 1919a, 29).[10]

Scientific socialism was developed for the first time by Marx and Engels. According to
Kautsky the socialist theoreticians before them were certainly familiar with the political
economy of their time. They did not, however, accomplish a systematic critique of old
science, and instead used it only to draw conclusions favourable to the proletariat. It
was Marx who for the first time made an independent study of the capitalist mode of
production and proved that it could be understood and analysed much more deeply and
clearly from the standpoint of the proletariat:

> "Nur er, der den Kapitalismus als vorübergehende Form betrachtet, erlaubt es, seine
> besondere historische Eigenart voll zu erfassen." (Kautsky 1919a, 37).

By formulating the scientific laws of capitalism and its historical role the founders of
scientific socialism developed a science far surpassing any of its bourgeois predecessors:

> "Durch diesen Gedankengang haben Marx und Engels die Grundlage geschaffen, auf der
> sich die Sozialdemokratie erhebt, die Grundlage, auf die sich immer mehr das kämpfende
> Proletariat des gesamten Erdkreises stellt, von der ausgehend es seinen glanzvollen Sieges-
> zug angetreten hat." (Kautsky 1919a, 36).

Compared with the socialist perspective as presented by Kautsky in his answer to
Bernstein, the discussion about the limits of spontaneous economic consciousness is
somewhat peculiar. In Kautsky's *Antikritik* − and in the *Erfurt Programme* − the
development of revolutionary consciousness was taken to be a rather self-evident fact,
whereas in the *Historische Leistung* socialist consciousness and perspective are under-

---

[10] It is possible that Kautsky was further developing an idea presented by Marx and Engels in
the *Communist Manifesto*. In the *Communist Manifesto* communists are said to be theoretically
superior to the other masses of the proletariat, having understood the conditions, the development
and the results of proletarian struggle. The next task of the communists − a task shared by all the
other workers' parties − is to develop the proletariat into a class (see MEW 4, 474). There is,
however, an important difference between Marx's, Engels', and Kautsky's formulations of the
problem, respectively: in the *Communist Manifesto* the communists are not claimed to be anything
else but a part of the proletarian mass. (Cf. also Engels' *Die Entwicklung des Sozialismus von der
Utopie zur Wissenschaft* (MEW 19, 208−209).)

stood to be a product of the intellectuals which must be especially incorporated or introduced into the workers' movement.[11] The spontaneous development of the movement is even apt to prevent the development of a unified socialist movement as evidenced by the formation of a new workers' aristocracy. As a matter of fact, the introduction of the socialist theory and perspective is not, however, even now considered to be problematic. The new science of political economy by definition presents the authentic proletarian standpoint. Once the principles of the new science have been taught to the workers, they will readily and naturally adopt the right political conclusions.

On the other hand, the discussion about the new workers' aristocracy − later to be adopted by Lenin in his theory (see pp. 158−159) − also seems somewhat out of place in this connection. If the distinction between economic and socialist consciousness really is one of principle then any rift within the movement caused by a labour aristocracy would seem to be a minor problem compared with the general restrictions of the spontaneous economic interests of the workers.

The postulated distinction between the two kinds of consciousness within the labour movement has very far-reaching consequences for Kautsky's understanding of the role of intellectuals and the Social Democratic Party in relation to the struggle of the workers. Leineweber proposed an interesting formulation of the consequences resulting from the understanding of the socialist science as presenting the authentic proletarian standpoint:

> "... erstens scheint Theorie als die sozusagen natürliche Bewusstseinsform des Proletariats, verliert also ihre Selbständigkeit als Produkt einer eigenständigen Produktionsweise. (...) Zweitens verliert das Proletariat die Selbständigkeit seiner Produktionsweise, indem es keine Erfahrungen, Vorstellungen, Gedanken usw. produziert, die der Theorie entgegenstehen, denn sonst könnten diese nicht ideelle Rückspiegelungen in der Köpfen der Klasse werden. Nur mit Hilfe der Theorie kann und soll sie Einblick gewinnen in die Verlaufsform des Geschichtsprozesses, in dem sie eine Rolle zu spielen hat." (Leineweber 1977, 48−49).

Kautsky's formulation of the problem of socialist consciousness thus has far-reaching consequences both for the understanding of the role of theory and for the role of the proletariat in the socialist movement; representing the authentic proletarian standpoint, theory − and intellectuals − legitimate their leading role in the movement. And in this respect Kautsky's concept of Marxism is representative of the theoretical thinking in the Second International Marxism.

---

[11] Przeworski (1977, 351) explained in an interesting way the evident contradiction in Kautsky's thinking concerning the formation of a revolutionary, socialist working class: Whenever Kautsky stated that the proletariat spontaneously acquires consciousness of its historical mission − and that the party merely assists, supports and participates in the class struggle alongside the working class − he was referring to the situation after the 1890s, whereas the problem of the development of socialist consciousness and the organisation of workers by socialist parties and intellectuals always refers to the situation around 1848 before the organised working class movement had come into being. The character of Kautsky's *Historische Leistung* as a "Festschrift" paying homage to Marx evidently supports Przeworski's thesis. But the ambivalence still remains: Kautsky did not seem to recognise it, and he never tried to explicate it in similar terms as Przeworski.

4. SOCIALISM AS SCIENCE

Kautsky's argument that the socialist perspective and scientific socialism are brought into the labour movement from outside by bourgeois intellectuals who have taken the proletarian standpoint seems to display an ambivalence, namely that the intellectuals[1] are able to develop scientific socialism precisely because they do not have a clear class position of their own. As a result, they do not only represent higher learning and scientific knowledge, they also have a specific capacity for abstract thinking. And it seems to be their classless position which endows them with a wider perspective in their thinking:

> "Die Intelligenz unterscheidet sich jedoch von diesen beiden Klassen durch ihren weiteren geistigen Horizont, durch ihr besser geschultes Vermögen abstrakten Denkens und durch den Mangel einheitlicher Klasseninteressen." (Kautsky 1894—95a, 76).

Concrete interests in the daily struggle make it impossible for the other classes in society to understand the general laws of social development, the specific subject matter of scientific socialism.[2]

On the other hand, Kautsky seems to believe that the modern proletariat is the only rightful heir to bourgeois culture ("Bildung"). A wage worker has no use for scientific knowledge in improving his social and economic position. He cherishes scientific knowledge for its own sake, like an ancient philosopher:

> "Eine der auffallendsten Erscheinungen der heutigen Gesellschaft ist der *Wissensdurst des Proletariats*. Während alle anderen Klassen ihre Mussezeit so geistlos als möglich todtzuschlagen suchen, strebt das Proletariat mit einer wahren Gier nach Bildung. (...)

---

[1] In referring to the intellectuals as creators and producers of scientific socialism Kautsky was clearly using the concept in a narrower sense than when talking about intellectuals as the new middle class having some organisational functions in capitalism. He did not, however, explicitly discuss the different uses of the concept, and he did not therefore make any distinction between critical intellectuals and the intellectuals as a social class.

[2] According to Leineweber (1977, 58), Kautsky's theoretical discussion of the social position of intellectuals was the first Marxist contribution to a class theory of "intelligentsia". It is interesting to note that Karl Mannheim's famous concept of 'socially unattached intelligentsia' (freischwebende Intelligenz) is clearly a further extrapolation of Kautsky's ideas. The classless position of intellectuals is the central theme of Mannheim's theory of intelligentsia in *Ideology and Utopia* (1960 (1936), 136—146). There is, however, an important difference between Kautsky and Mannheim, viz. in Mannheim's thinking intellectuals — although situated between classes — do not constitute a new middle class (see Mannheim 1960, 139).

Und dieser Drang nach Wissen ist ein völlig interesseloser. Dem Arbeiter an der Maschine kann das Wissen nicht helfen, sein Einkommen zu erhöhen. Wenn er die Wahrheit sucht, so sucht er sie um ihrer selbst willen, nicht um irgend eines materiellen Gewinnens halber. Darum beschränkt er sich auch nicht auf ein einzelnes, kleineres Gebiet: sein Blick richtet sich aufs Ganze; die ganze Welt will er begreifen. Die schwierigsten Räthsel locken ihn am meisten, mit Vorliebe wendet er sich Fragen der Philosophie, der Metaphysik zu, es hält oft schwer, ihn aus den Wolken wieder auf die Erde herabzubringen." (Kautsky 1906a, 174).

The proletariat is the inheritor of the philosophical spirit of the ancient aristocracy because it is interested in the most general and abstract problems of the world for the sake of pure knowledge. Kautsky's argument is similar to that used in connection with the intellectuals: they, too, have a wider spiritual horizon. And science — the great science — is something that deals with the general and necessary development of the world and society in particular. The specific interests and needs of the various groups of population are often a hindrance to a correct understanding of these general tendencies and laws.

Scientific socialism has a double role in relation to the proletariat: to make it recognise its common goals and general interests, and to make it possible for the proletariat to reach these goals with maximum efficiency. It is, however, not legitimate to draw any ideals from scientific knowledge.[3] In this respect Kautsky made a rather clear neo-kantian distinction between values and science:

"Auch die Sozialdemokratie als Organisation des Proletariats in seinem *Klassenkampf* kann das sittliche Ideal, kann die sittliche Empörung gegen Ausbeutung und Klassenherrschaft nicht entbehren. Aber dies Ideal hat nichts zu suchen im *wissenschaftlichen* Sozialismus, der wissenschaftlichen Erforschung der Entwicklungs- und Bewegungsgestze des gesellschaftlichen Organismus zum Zwecke des Erkennens der *notwendigen* Tendenzen und Ziele des proletarischen Klassenkampfes. (...) Die Wissenschaft hat es stets nur mit dem Erkennen des Notwendigen zu tun. Sie kann wohl dazu kommen, ein Sollen vorzuschreiben, aber dies darf stets nur als eine Konsequenz der Einsicht in das Notwendige auftreten." (Kautsky 1906b, 141–142).[4]

---

[3] For a discussion of the neo-kantian impact on Marxism and Kautsky and Bernstein especially, see Colletti 1968, 36–40. The distinction between "Sachurteile" and "Werturteile" is crucial in the neo-kantian tradition. It is characteristic in this respect that Karl Vorländer, who in his *Kant and Marx* (1911) proposed to unite und supplement historical materialism with Kant, approvingly referred to Kautsky's conception of ethics and science (see Vorländer 1924).

[4] In discussing the limits of science and scientific knowledge Kautsky also made a distinction between individual and mass phenomena. Only the latter can become the object of scientific study and knowledge:

"... das Gebiet der Wissenschaft reicht nur so weit, wie das Gebiet der erkennbaren *Notwendigkeit*. Wo diese aufhört, hört auch die Wissenschaft auf. Ihre Grenzen werden täglich erweitert, aber so weit sind wir noch nicht, das Willen des *Individuums* in der Gesellschaft wissenschaftlich ergründen, dass heisst, es als Notwendigkeit erkennen zu können. Bloss die gesellschaftlichen *Massenerscheinungen* können wir wissenschaftlich Untersuchung unterwerfen." (Kautsky 1900–01, 358).

It is, however, somewhat unclear whether this distinction is thought to be one of principle or whether it is a practical limitation due to the present stage of the development of science.

Science cannot ascribe any ideals or goals to action; it can, however, reveal the direction of development and, hence, the necessary outcome of history.[5] In this sense it can be of assistance in showing that some goals of action are impossible to achieve (i.e. wage workers have no other realistic alternative but socialist society to liberate them from the exploitation of capital). Hence, the unifying role of science is based on the recognition of the laws of development of society:

> "Ohne sozialistische Theorie vermögen sie die Gemeinsamkeit ihrer Interessen nicht zu erkennen, stehen die einzelnen Proletarierschichten einander fremd, mitunter sogar feindlich gegenüber." (Kautsky 1919a, 29).

It is, indeed, easier for someone not directly involved in the daily struggle to recognise the wider perspective of development:

> "Aber man kommt mit diesen persönlichen Erkenntnissen nicht weit, wenn man die dauernden Interessen einer Klasse und ihre Zukunftsaufgaben erkennen will (...) Das ist nicht möglich ohne gesellschaftliche Erkenntnis, die am tiefsten dort reicht, wo sie mit den Methoden und Hilfsmitteln der Wissenschaft gesucht und gewonnen wird. Die persönliche Erfahrung des 'Praktikers' reicht dazu niht aus." (Kautsky 1916–17b, 108–109).

Apart from its role as a unifying force, science can function as a guideline in the struggle for socialism, i.e. only with the help of science is the proletariat able to reach its historical goals with the maximum efficiency and minimum use of energy:

> "Nur die *Erkenntnis* des gesellschaftlichen Prozesses, seiner Tendenzen und Ziele vermag dieser Verschwendung ein Ende zu machen, die Kräfte des Proletariats zu konzentrieren, sie in grossen Organisationen zusammenzufassen, die durch grosse Ziele vereinigt werden und planmässig persönliche und Augenblicksaktionen den dauernden Klasseninteressen unterordnen, die ihrerseits wieder in den Dienst der gesamten gesellschaftlichen Entwicklung gestellt sind. Mit anderen Worten, die Theorie ist der Faktor, der die mögliche Kraftentfaltung des Proletariats aufs höchste steigert, indem er dessen durch die ökonomische Entwicklung gegebenen Kräfte aufs zweckmässigste gebrauchen lehrt und ihrer Verschwendungen entgegenwirkt." (Kautsky 1909b, 37).

Because the proletariat does not realise its own power in the present society, the analysis of the development of society and the class position of the proletariat is a necessary step on the way to the establishment of proletarian power.

The proletariat is in a more fortunate position than the earlier revolutionary classes in history.[6] Its science is the most developed form of knowledge. The new science was

---

[5]   Kautsky's discussion of science as revealing the necessity in history was certainly influenced by Engels' conception of freedom and necessity in *Anti-Dühring* (see MEW 20, 264). According to Engels, in socialism men will consciously make use of the laws governing the development of society. For Engels, then, socialism does not abolish the natural laws of society, but will be equal to the conscious utilisation of these laws in the interest of man:

> "Die Gesetze ihres eignen gesellschaftlichen Tuns, ... werden dann von den Menschen mit voller Sachkenntnis angewandt und damit beherrscht." (MEW 20, 264).

[6]   Cf. also:

> "Aber das Schweineglück der Sozialdemokratie rührt daher, dass sie das Glück hat, eine Theorie zu besitzen, die sie besser als jede andere im Labyrinth der modernen Gesellschaft

developed from the proletarian standpoint, yet to Kautsky the proletarian and the scientific standpoint are identical, because the proletariat represents progress in history. In this sense its general interests are identical to the interests of the whole of society:

"Es hat aber noch nie eine Partei gegeben, welche die gesellschaftlichen Tendenzen ihrer Zeit so tief erforscht und so genau begriffen hätte, wie die Sozialdemokratie. Das ist nicht ihr Verdienst, sondern ihr Glück. Sie hat es zu verdanken, dass sie auf den Schultern der bürgerlichen Oekonomie steht, welche die erste wissenschaftliche Untersuchung gesell-schaftlicher Zusammenhänge und Zustände unternahm ..." (Kautsky 1906a, 142).

The revolutionary proletariat is the rightful heir to this theoretical aspiration, which is dying out with the increasing conservatism and reactionary nature of the bourgeoisie (see Kautsky 1902−03a, 730). The proletariat must and can base its whole action and struggle on scientific knowledge of the laws of society. In this very sense the proletarian standpoint is the scientific one, and the proletariat the inheritor of the scientific world outlook of the bourgeoisie.

The scientific perspective is synonymous with the recognition of the objective neces-sary laws of society, and the recognition of these necessities is identical to the general proletarian interest:

"Und diese Ausblicke sind auch nicht Erwartungen von Zuständen, die bloss kommen *sollen*, die wir bloss *wünschen* und *wollen*, sondern Ausblicke auf Zustände die kommen *müssen*, und notwendig sind. Allerdings notwendig nicht in dem fatalistischen Sinne, dass eine höhere Macht sie von selbst uns schenken wird, sondern notwendig, unvermeidlich in dem Sinne, wie es unvermeidlich ist, dass die Erfinder die Teknik verbessern, dass die Kapitalisten in ihrer Profitgier das ganze wirtschaftliche Leben umwälzen, wie es unver-meidlich ist, dass die Lohnarbeiter nach kürzeren Arbeitszeiten und höheren Lohnen trachten, dass sie sich organisieren, dass sie die Kapitalistenklasse und deren Staatsgewalt bekriegen, wie es unvermeidlich ist, dass sie nach der politischen Gewalt und den Umsturz der Kapitalistenherrschaft trachten. Der Sozialismus ist unvermeidlich, weil der Klassen-kampf, weil der Sieg des Proletariats unvermeidlich ist." (Kautsky 1906b, 144).

The scientific interest is not, however, identical to the specific interests of the wage workers, and the proletariat cannot come to know the social necessities all by itself in its practical political action. It presupposes that the proletarian science − a new positive

---

zurechtweisst, und ihrem Wollen stets dieselbe Richtung gibt, welche die der notwendigen gesellschaftlichen Richtung ist, indes das Wollen unserer Gegner in entgegengesetzter Richtung geht. Darum erweist sich unser Wollen schliesslich immer als unwiderstehlich und das Wollen unserer Gegner als fruchtlos." (Kautsky 1905−06, 859)

But the socialist theory does not only point out the direction of social development, it is also able to predict the coming situation awaiting the Social Democratic Party:

"Aber unsere sozialistische Theorie zeigt uns nicht bloss die allgemeine Richtung der Entwicklung, sie bietet uns auch die Möglichkeit, in jedem gegebenen Moment die zunächts kommenden Situationen und deren Erfordernisse mit grösserer Sicherheit voraus-zusehen, als es sonst möglich wäre, uns für sie zu wappnen und sie aufs rascheste und energischte auszunützen." (Kautsky 1905−06, 859).

science more scientific than its predecessors — is developed.[7] Socialism is inevitable, but only on condition that its inevitability is understood by the proletariat; the problem is not, however, unsolvable since the proletariat will inevitably come to understand this inevitability. It has no other alternative. Once the development of society towards greater concentration and polarisation is understood and recognised, the interests of the proletariat become identical to the demands of progress in society, and the coalition of science and proletariat is accomplished.

Kautsky's comment (1909a) on the discussion about Mach and Machism — a discussion very lively among Marxists of his time, as shown also by Lenin's *Materialism and Empirio-criticism* (Lenin 1967) — is typical both of his willingness to avoid any disputes which would endanger the unity of the party and which — in his opinion — are also totally irrelevant from the point of view of social theory and practical politics. To Kautsky Marxism was essentially a positive science of society and of history and it did not include any specific theory of knowledge. Even though materialism is characteristic of Marxism, questions of the theory of knowledge are irrelevant to Marxism, and the stand adopted by a Marxist on these questions is exclusively a private matter for every individual member of the party.

The main task of the proletariat is to learn Marxist theory of capitalism and the materialist conception of history, and especially to recognise the immediate tasks in its own country:

> "Der Marxismus will dem Proletariat die Einsicht in die Bedingungen, den Gang und die allgemeine Resultate der proletarischen Bewegung beibringen, wie das Kommunistische Manifest sagt." (Kautsky 1909b, 452).

Compared with these main truths of Marxism, the theoretical clarity about different versions of the theory of knowledge is of secondary importance.[8]

---

[7] Cf. also:

> "Eine aufsteigende Klasse, die zu voller Gleichberechtigung und freier Entfaltung nicht im Rahmen der Gesellschaft kommen kann, in der sie erswächst, muss danach trachten, sobald sie einigermassen zum Selbstbewusstsein gekommen ist, an Stelle der bestehenden Gesellschaftsform eine andere, ihren Interessen angepasste, zu setzen. Sie kann sich aber dies Ziel nicht setzen, ohn eine Theorie der ganzen Gesellschaft zu entwickeln. Der Character dieser Theorie hängt von dem Stande des allgemeinen und ihres besonderen Wissens ab;..." (Kautsky 1902—03a, 729)

Leineweber has suggested an interesting interpretation of such a conception of scientific socialism. The classless socialist science anticipates the future classless society:

> "Er (der Theoretiker — J.G.) ist ideell dort, wo der Proletarier reell hinstreut, ohne es zu wissen." (Leineweber 1977, 70).

[8] In this respect Lenin's position could be characterised as a total antithesis. In his opinion questions concerning the theory of knowledge are of immediate interest to the party. Il'enkov (1980) accordingly interpreted the importance of Lenin's *Materialism and Empirio-criticism* mainly from the point of view of the political line of the Russian Social Democratic Party: the main result of Lenin's critique of Mach's theory of knowledge is that a Menshevik having a false conception of the strategy of the party but a right position in the theory of knowledge is less dangerous than a Bolshevik representing a Machist theory of knowledge.

5. THE CAPITALIST LAW OF APPROPRIATION: KAUTSKY'S INTERPRETATION OF KARL MARX'S ECONOMIC THOUGHT

One would expect that the phenomenon of revisionism would have had something to do with the question of the dual nature of consciousness of the working class. Revisionism however, never was a serious theoretical problem to Kautsky. He could cherish illusions that the theoretical authority and the programme of the party were not seriously challenged by revisionism because, in his opinion, revisionism had not so far presented any alternative scientific theory endangering the role of Marxism in the movement. As a matter of fact, it had not presented any theory at all. In this respect it could better be compared with the historical school of national economy (see Kautsky 1902–03a, 727–728). On the other hand, one would expect Kautsky to have wondered why the proletariat, in his opinion already a decisive majority in the developed capitalist countries, had not been ready to take over state power. The only explanation offered by him was that the proletariat was not yet ripe for its historical mission.

As regards Germany Kautsky's optimism in this respect, shared by Engels (see MEW 22, 524), was understandable. During the relatively short period since the abolition of the socialist law, the party had succeeded quite well in the parliamentary elections. The final victory was only a question of time. Minor setbacks could be explained by concrete political conditions. In England, however, the situation should have been theoretically more challenging. The increase of the proletariat and its organisation into trade unions had tended to weaken the revolutionary spirit of the labour movement. As a matter of fact, in England — as was already pointed out by Engels (see MEW 19, 200–201) — there had not been any genuinely revolutionary movement of importance, but only socialist workers inspired by various utopian ideals.

However, Kautsky never developed any theoretical explanation for the phenomenon of revisionism or reformism inside the party and trade unions. He clearly understood revisionism as only a singular event in the development of Social Democracy and did not analyse it at all in the wider context of emerging reformist tendencies in the labour movement. In 1902 Kautsky could (in *Die drei Krisen des Marxismus*) already state that the newest crisis in Marxism, the challenge posed by revisionism, had been overcome and had not left any permanent effect on Social Democracy:

> "Vor allem hat sie die Haptsache, den *praktischen Marxismus*, fast völlig unberührt gelassen, was auch begreiflich ist." (Kautsky 1902–03a, 727).

This crisis did not have any real reasons: it was caused exclusively by the personal reaction of certain persons. Thus it did not leave any permanent traces and

> "...nicht einmal zu einer grundsätzlichen Revision unserer Programme hat es die jüngste Krisis des Marxismus bisher gebracht... "(Kautsky 1902–03a, 727).

In an article written shortly after the Dresden Party Congress in 1903 Kautsky could triumphantly announce that "the declarations and votes in Dresden signify the burial of theoretical revisionism *as a political factor*" (Kautsky 1902–03d, 814).

Finally, in an article dedicated to the 70th anniversary of Bernstein in 1920, the former opponent of Bernstein could even afford to give Bernstein credit for having discussed the new problems posed by imperialist politics and economic prosperity and connected with the relations of Social Democracy with radical bourgeois parties (Kautsky 1920, 45–46). At the same time Kautsky, nevertheless, preserved his old position intact, and stated that the development of capitalism had subsequently made the problems posed by Bernstein obsolete:

> "Die Frage der Richtigkeit der Marxschen Prognose hörte auf, eine Rolle zu spielen, als der Imperialismus aus seinem ersten Stadium in sein zweites trat und an Stelle der Prosperität und steter gewekschaftlicher Erfolge die rasch wachsende Teuerung und die Stagnation des gewerkschaftlichen Kampfes trat, gleichzeitig aber auch die Rüstungslasten sich beängstigend mehrten und die Gefahr des Weltkrieges immer bedrohender aufstieg." (Kautsky 1920, 47).

The problems posed by Bernstein were thus understood to have been connected only with a specific economic conjuncture of capitalism. Even according to Kautsky's own conception, reformism was, however, a natural feature of the labour movement in its initial stages of development. Without the political guidance of the party provided with a socialist theory the labour movement could never become conscious of its genuine interests. Obviously Kautsky believed that once the labour movement was politically organised and the proletariat had adopted the essentials of scientific socialism, reformism could not any more gain any permanent footing in the movement. Revisionism was only a temporary indiscretion on the part of some party intellectuals caused by ignorance and insufficient knowledge of the wider perspectives of social development.

There are several explanations as to why the proletariat cannot attain a general and common class consciousness in its economic struggle scattered throughout Kautsky's work (petit bourgeois traditions and remnants, labour aristocracy, etc.), but the main obstacle is clearly one of principle: there are limits of principle to economic consciousness that can never be overcome automatically. In this respect Kautsky's dualism is rather devastating. Political consciousness and the struggle for power − whether inside parliament or outside it − have practically nothing to do with the daily interests of the

wage workers, yet the labour movement is supposed to develop automatically and out
of necessity into a revolutionary political party. The mediator is the Social Democratic
Party in possession of the scientific socialism and the right strategy. The best form of
political struggle in this respect is parliamentary politics. Electoral compaigns have an
important organisational function. They are the best means of organising the proletariat
of the whole country into common action. (See Kautsky 1911a, 137.)

Theoretically Kautsky's conception of the economic vs. socialist consciousness of the
wage workers and the political consequences drawn from it are deeply rooted in his
interpretation of Karl Marx's 'economic thought'. Kautsky's book *Karl Marx' Oekonomische Lehren* (which was written in co-operation with Bernstein and under the guidance of Engels; see Steenson (1978, 66)) was originally published in 1887. It could be
argued that at least in some of its basic interpretations *Karl Marx' Oekonomische
Lehren* presents the core of the Marxism of the Second International; the fundamental
aspects of this interpretation were shared by most theoreticians of the time.

The basic idea behind the Kautskyan interpretation of *Capital* was the historical
character of its economic theory; *Capital* is basically a presentation of the historical
development of capitalism, the most important part of which is the presentation of the
historical law of capital accumulation. Kautsky is quite explicit in his interpretation in
this respect. In the preface to his book he formulated the task of his presentation not
only as a popularisation ("Gemeinverständlichung") of *Capital*, but also in an important sense as a further development of Marx's economic thought (see Kautsky 1906c,
X—XII).

According to Kautsky, Marx's *Capital* is often said to be very difficult to understand
and hard to read. In Kautsky's opinion this complaint is totally misplaced. The presentation in *Capital* is superior in its beauty and clarity; its style is classical. And yet it
must be admitted that many a reader has found it very difficult to understand. The
presentation should not, however, be made responsible for the many misunderstandings. Economics is by its very nature a difficult field of study; society is such a complicated formation. The part of economic science which Marx called 'vulgar economics' is
easy enough to understand for anyone familiar with the business transactions of everyday life. A knowledge of everyday business life is not, however, sufficient for the study
of Marx's critique of political economy. The theory presented in *Capital* can be compre-
hended only when the relevant historical and contemporary facts are known:

> "Das Verständnis des *Kapital* von Marx, welches in der Form einer Kritik der politischen
> Oekonomie ein neues historisches und ökonomisches System begründet, setzt dagegen
> nicht nur ein gewisses historisches Wissen, sondern auch die Erkenntnis der Thatsachen
> voraus, welche die Entwicklung der Grossindustrie bietet. Wer nicht die Thatsachen min-
> destens theilweise kennt, aus denen Marx seine ökonomischen Gesetze abgeleitet, dem
> wird der Sinn dieser Gesetze allerdings dunkel bleiben, der mag über Mystizismus und
> Hegelianismus klagen. Die klarste Darstellung wird ihm nichts nützen." (Kautsky 1906c,
> IX—X).

Knowledge of the relevant historical facts is, however, problematic, because Marx himself did not – for some odd reason – always present them in *Capital*.[1] The chapters on big industry ("grosse Industrie") carefully present the relevant historical facts, whereas they clearly are missing at the beginning of *Capital*. And Kautsky takes it upon himself to supplement the presentation in this respect:

> "Die Aufgabe lag einestheils darin, den Leser auf die Thatsachen aufmerksam zu machen, die den theoretischen Ausführungen zu Grunde liegen. Dies war namentlich nothwendig im ersten Abschnitt. Marx hat auf diese Thatsachen meist selbst hingewiesen, aber oft nur mit Andeutungen, die in der Regel übersehen wurden. An anderen Stellen musste sich der Verfasser erlauben, auf die Thatsachen auf eigene Verantwortung aufmerksam zu machen. Dies gilt namentlich in ersten Paragraphen des erstes Kapitels. Es konnte sich in vorliegender Arbeit nur um Hinweise handeln. Eine ausführliche Darstellung der dem *Kapital* zu Grunde liegenden Thatsachen würde nicht nur den zugemessenen Raum, sondern auch die Kräfte des Verfassers weit übersteigen; eine solche hiesse nichts geringeres, als eine Entwicklungsgeschichte der Menschheit von der Urzeit zu verfassen. Das *Kapital* ist ein wesentlich historisches Werk." (Kautsky 1906c, X–XI).

The main shortcomings in the presentation of *Capital* are to be found in the chapters dealing with commodity and money. According to Kautsky, Marx analyses in these chapters a specific historical stage of production called simple commodity production. He does not, however, present the necessary historical facts in relation to this mode of production. The presentation of these facts is – in his own opinion – Kautsky's main contribution to the further development of Marx's economic thought.

According to Kautsky, Marx's abstract-theoretical presentation of simple commodity circulation is easier to comprehend and clearer when understood as the description of a specific historical stage of production. The simple commodity production is a mode of production based on private ownership of the means of production and the exchange of products in the market. Every producer is the owner of his own means of production and subsistence and, hence, the products of his labour. The right of property is based on the labour of every commodity producer. Even though Kautsky set out to present the missing historical facts supporting the postulated existence of simple commodity production, he was quite obviously at great pains to try to find anything that really existed in history. The manufacturing period of capitalism dates back to the mid-16th century in Europe. Consequently, simple commodity production should already have existed in the Middle Ages. (See Kautsky 1906c, 144.) On the other hand, Kautsky

---

[1] In a letter to Werner Sombart in 1895 Engels formulated the task of the further development of Marx's *Capital* in terms similar to those employed by Kautsky. In discussing the problematic nature of value in capitalism (in a "developed system of exchange of commodities") Engels stated that in capitalism value is hidden as opposed to the immediate value of undeveloped exchange. It would, thus, be a veritable service to the further development of Marx's theory of value to present the necessary mediating steps of the historical process of transformation from the still undeveloped exchange of commodities into capitalism, from the immediate value to the hidden value of commodities – a process, in Engels' opinion, not presented by Marx in *Capital*. (See MEW 39, 428–429; see also Himmelmann (1978, 306) who interpreted Engels as requiring a positive verification of Marx's theory of value.)

accepted Marx's conception of the products of labour taking the form of a commodity only under developed capitalistic relations — at least in general.[2]

The emphasis on the historical interpretation of *Capital* has important consequences for Kautsky's conception of the production relation in capitalism. In simple commodity production the right of property is based on one's own labour. The appropriation of alien labour — and its products — is only possible when the law of equal exchange of commodities (exchange of equal values) is respected. This form of appropriation is, however, reversed as soon as the capitalist mode of production is introduced:

> "Akkumulation von Mehrwert heisst Aneignung unbezahlter Arbeit zum Behuf erweiterter Aneignung unbezahlter Arbeit. Welch' ein Widerspruch gegen die Grundlagen des Waarenaustausches! Wir haben gesehen, dass der Waarenaustausch ursprünglich einerseits das Privateigenthum des Waarenproduzenten an seinem Produkt bedingt und andererseits den Austausch gleicher Werthe, so dass keiner in den Besitz eines Werthes gelangen konnte ausser durch eigene Arbeit oder durch Hingabe eines gleichen Werthes. Jetzt finden wir als Grundlagen der kapitalistischen Produktionsweise auf der einen Seite die Trennung des Arbeiters vom Produkt seiner Arbeit; Derjenige, der das Produkt erzeugt und Derjenige, der es besitzt, sind nun zwei verschiedene Personen; und auf der anderen Seite finden wir die Aneignung von Werth ohne Hingabe eines gleichen Werthes, den *Mehrwerth*. (...) Diese Verkehrung der Grundlagen der Waarenproduktion in ihr Gegentheil erfolgte jedoch nicht im *Widerspruch* mit ihren Gesetzen, sondern auf *Grundlage* derselben." (Kautsky 1906c, 225—226).

Kautsky's formulation of the historical transformation of the law of appropriation is rather difficult to interpret. It is, however, quite obvious that taken together with the strong emphasis on the historical character of Marx's theory of capitalism, a specific conception of the wage labour-capital relation follows from it. Projekt Klassenanalyse has in the book *Kautsky. Marxistische Vergangenheit der SDP?* (1976) made a comparison of Kautsky's Marxism with Marx's critique of political economy in *Capital*. According to Projekt Klassenanalyse Kautsky made an elementary theoretical mistake in his interpretation. Kautsky did not understand the theoretical position of the presentation of simple commodity circulation in *Capital*. According to him the circulation of commodities shows that alien labour can be appropriated only when one's own labour is given as an equivalent in exchange. Before being able to appropriate alien labour, one must appropriate the product of one's own labour outside the relations of exchange. And this original appropriation of one's own product can only take place as an appropriation of nature's products, a relation which is socially undetermined. As a consequence, Kautsky postulated the existence of a specific historical stage of production, simple commodity production, preceding capitalism:

---

[2]   "Erst wenn kapitalistisch produzirt wird, produzirt also der *einzelne Waarenproduzent* (der Kapitalist) in der Regel mit gesellschaftlich nothwendiger Durchschnittsarbeit, und er muss es thun. Erst unter der kapitalistischen Produktionsweise kommt das Gesetz des Waarenwerthes zur vollen Entfaltung." (Kautsky 1906c, 149).

> "So entsteht aus den Erscheinungsformen der Warenzirkulation der Schluss, der einfachen Warenzirkulation unterliege eine entsprechende einfache Warenproduktion, in der Arbeit und Eigentum am Produkt der Arbeit nicht getrennt sind. (...) Es ist also sein Verständnis der einfachsten ökonomischen Formen der bürgerlichen Gesellschaft, welches ihn beständig zu einer These über deren historische Genesis zwingt, die zugleich durch das zur Untermauerung angeführte historische Material widerlegt wird." (Projekt Klassenanalyse 1976, 23).

Kautsky failed to understand the specific character of the capital relation as an indirect or mediated relation of domination and serfdom ("Herrschaft und Knechtschaft") because of his historical conceptualisation of simple commodity production. Consequently, in his thinking there is no necessary relation between the appropriation of surplus value and the exchange of equivalents. He recognised the capital relation only as a relation of exploitation of surplus value, as a relation in which the producers are subordinated under the products of their own labour and in which they are faced by capital as an alien force. He failed to recognise the other side of the relation, viz. the formal equality of a wage worker and a capitalist:

> "Er sieht nicht, dass die Verwandlung von Arbeit in eine den Arbeitern feindliche Macht Vermittlungsglieder einschliesst, die zwar die Arbeitar beständig wieder zur Unterwerfung unter die Gesetze des Kapitals zwingen, sie aber zugleich in Verhältnisse versetzen, worin sie scheinbar dem Kapitalisten gleichgestellt sind. Diese durch die kapitalistische Produktionsweise selbst erzeugten verkehrten Formen hält er für historisch überholt, ohne Grundlage in der kapitalistischen Produktionsweise selbst." (Projekt Klassenanalyse 1976, 27).

The most serious confusion in Kautsky's interpretation is that he seemed to understand the capital relation as a direct relation of exploitation which can obviously be experienced by wage workers as such, whereas the freedom and equality of the commodity owners are something belonging exclusively to the world of simple commodity production preceding capitalism. They are a remnant of an earlier mode of production. His conceptualisation of the consciousness of the proletariat was, consequently, contradictory. Even though the relation of exploitation seemed in his understanding to result from an immediate and direct violation of the original rule of property, Kautsky was forced to postulate a limit in principle to the consciousness of the wage worker. The capitalistic reality is not revealed to the wage worker after all. Spontaneous class struggle is often even something actually opposed to the socialist cause:

> "Und für Kautsky steht der Klassenkampf solange im *Gegensatz* zum Sozialismus, wie die Arbeiter auf sich selbst gestellt sind in ihrem Bemühen, für die Widersprüche der kapitalistischen Produktionsweise eine Lösung zu finden." (Projekt Klassenanalyse 1976, 47).

Kautsky did not consider it necessary to seek a theoretical mediator between the existence of the wage worker as a free and equal commodity owner and his role as a producer of surplus value.

> "Mit dem Satz, das Proletariat könne von sich aus nicht zu sozialistischem Bewusstsein gelangen, ist für den Widerspruch im Bewusstsein des Proletariats scheinbar eine Lösung gefunden." (Projekt Klassenanalyse 1976, 47).

According to Projekt Klassenanalyse Kautsky's attempt to solve the problem of the formation of socialist consciousness with the help of the auxiliary theoretical construction of the dual nature of consciousness immediately lead to further problems. If socialist consciousness is not a result of the immediate experience of exploitation, then it must be introduced into the labour movement from outside. The proletariat cannot develop the "proletarian standpoint" all by itself; it is left to the science of socialism to develop it. But the main precondition for scientific socialism is the adaptation of the proletarian standpoint. A real *circulus vitiosus* seems to be the result of Kautsky's reasoning:

> "Das erst wissenschaftlich zu Begründende wird ihm zur Voraussetzung der Wissenschaft." (Projekt Klassenanalyse 1976, 53−54).

As has already been pointed out, science is produced not by the proletariat but by the intellectuals. The position of the intellectuals is, on the other hand, contradictory. They are both above the classes, and must consequently be treated with suspicion by the socialist party, and at the same time they − or at least those of them who have adopted the proletarian standpoint − are the producers and developers of socialist theory and abstract knowledge. In the second role they are irreplaceable to the party. (See Projekt Klassenanalyse 1976, 56.)

Projekt Klassenanalyse's interpretation of Kautsky's Marxism is in most respects adequate. It could, however, be claimed that in some respects Kautsky's interpretation of *Capital* in *Karl Marx' Oekonomische Lehren* was more complicated. There are clearly many formulations which directly support Projekt Klassenanalyse's main thesis, especially in the preface to the work, in which Kautsky explicates his historical conception of *Capital*. On the other hand, some of Kautsky's formulations seem to suggest that he was, after all, more conscious of the theoretical problems involved in the relation between the laws of commodity circulation and capitalist production.[3] Kautsky was, for instance, obviously aware that the laws of commodity exchange are preserved intact even during capitalist production, and that the capitalist and wage worker meet at the market as commodity owners with equal rights:

> "Wie immer aber auch das System der Lohnzahlung sein möge, stets stehen Arbeiter und Kapitalist einander unter normalen Verhältnissen gegenüber wie zwei Waarenbesitzer, die gleiche Werthe gegenseitig austauschen. Das Kapital bewegt sich jetzt nicht mehr im Widerspruch gegen die Gesetze der Waarenzirkulation, sondern auf Grund dieser Gesetze. Arbeiter und Kapitalist stehen sich als Waarenbesitzer, also als *freie* und *gleiche* voneinander persönlich unabhängige Personen gegenüber; sie gehören als solche zur selben Klasse, sie sind *Brüder*. Arbeiter und Kapitalist tauschen *gleiche* Werthe gegen einander aus: das Reich der Gerechtigkeit, der Freiheit, Gleichheit und Brüderlichkeit scheint also mit der Herrschaft des Lohnsystems angebrochen, das tausendjährige Reich des Glückes und Friedens. Der Jammer der Knechtschaft und der Tyrannei, der Ausbeutung und des Faustrechts liegt hinter uns." (Kautsky 1906c, 67−68).

---

[3] Kautsky even explicitly stated that in capitalism we are not dealing with the exchange of commodities, but with the circulation of commodities presupposing the existence of money (see Kautsky 1906c, 60).

Despite the recognition of the "empire of freedom" within the capital relation, Kautsky's position seems to be quite ambivalent in this respect. The ideas of freedom and equality seem to be more a form of falsification performed by the bourgeois theoreticians than a real manifestation of the relation between capital and wage labour (see Kautsky 1906c, 68). As soon as the sphere of production is substituted for the field of circulation, this falsification should become appearent to everyone (see Kautsky 1906c, 71). The same ambivalence is present in Kautsky's discussion of the transformation of the form of appropriation. The new form of appropriation is, according to Kautsky, based on the old one, but in Kautsky's historical interpretation it is unclear in which sense. On the one hand, the appropriation of surplus value does not violate the rules of commodity circulation (see Kautsky 1906c, 59—63), on the other hand, the laws of commodity production are transformed into their opposites. In a similar way the recognition of the commodity form becoming the general form of labour's products only in developed capitalism (see Kautsky 1906c, 5) did not lead Kautsky to problematise his conception of simple commodity production. This ambivalence of Kautsky's thinking could be interpreted as resulting from the specific character of *Karl Marx's economic thought*. On the one hand, Kautsky simply presented Marx's central ideas in a condensed form paraphrasing Marx; on the other hand, he also developed Marx's theory following his own interpretation of its shortcomings.[4]

The main result of Projekt Klassenanalyse's interpretation of *Karl Marx' Oekonomische Lehren* in any case remains valid: In Kautsky's conceptualisation of *Capital* there is no need to problematise the specific character of capital relation as a relation of both exploitation and equality. The equality and freedom of commodity producers belong to an earlier mode of production, simple commodity production, whereas in capitalism the relation between capital and wage labour is basically a relation of exploitation. (For a discussion of Marx's analysis of the problem see chapter II.2.)

At the very end of his study *Karl Marx' Oekonomische Lehren* Kautsky formulated his socialist perspective in a way that shows the similarity between his conception and that of Friedrich Engels:

> "So drängt alles nach einer Lösung des Widerspruchs, der in der kapitalistischen Produktionsweise verkörpert ist, des Widerspruchs zwischen dem gesellschaftlichen Charakter der Arbeit und der überkommenen Aneignungsform der Produktionsmittel und Produkte." (Kautsky 1906c, 264—265).

Further:

> "Man erkennt auch den einzigen Weg, der für die Fortentwicklung der Gesellschaft übrig bleibt: die Anpassung der Aneignungsform an die Produktionsweise, die Besitzergreifung

---

[4]   Kautsky even emphasised the importance of the chapter on the fetish character of a commodity in *Capital:*

> "Das Kapitel über 'den Fetischcharacter der Waare und sein Geiheimnis' erscheint uns daher als eines der wichtigsten des *Kapital,* dem jeder Leser dieses Buches besondere Aufmerksamkeit schenken sollte." (Kautsky 1906c, 15).

He did not, however, draw any further conclusions from it.

der Produktionsmittel durch die Gesellschaft, die vollendete, rückhaltlose Durchführung der vom Kapital nur halb durchgeführten Verwandlung der Produktion aus Einzelproduktion in gesellschaftliche Produktion." (Kautsky 1906c, 267).

The conception of the basic contradiction of capitalism in terms of the contradiction between the private form of appropriation and the social character of production or means of production was first formulated by Engels in his *Anti-Dühring* (MEW 20).[5] Kautsky's reading of *Capital* as a historical presentation with a strong emphasis on the transformation of the form of appropriation quite clearly goes back to *Anti-Dühring*.[6] Engels formulated the basic contradiction as follows:

"Produktionsmittel und Produktion sind wesentlich gesellschaftlich geworden. Aber sie werden unterworfen einer Aneignungsform, die die Privatproduktion einzelner zur Voraussetzung hat, wobei also jeder sein eignes Produkt besitzt und zu Markte bringt. Die Produktionsweise wird wieder dieser Aneignungsform unterworfen, obwohl sie deren Voraussetzung aufhebt. In diesem Widerspruch, der der neuen Produktionsweise ihren kapitalistischen Charakter verleiht, *liegt die ganze Kollission der Gegenwart bereits im Keim.*" (MEW 20, 252).

This contradiction is the specific capitalistic form of the general contradiction between the means of production and the relations of production; it shows how big capitalist industry is faced with the limits set by the very capitalist mode of production (see MEW 20, 251).

During an earlier historical stage of simple commodity production there could be no question of the ownership of the products of labour. Every producer was the owner of his own means of production and the right of property was based on one's own labour. The development of capitalism, does, however, transform the means of production used in big workshops and manufacture into "such means of production which are already social in reality".

Engels continues:

"Aber die gesellschaftlichen Produktionsmittel und Produkte wurden behandelt, als wären sie nach wie vor die Produktionsmittel und Produkte einzelner. Hatte bisher der Besitzer der Arbeitsmittel sich das Produkt angeeignet, weil es in der Regel sein eignes Produkt und fremde Hülfsarbeit die Ausnahme war, so fuhr jetzt der Besitzer der Arbeitsmittel fort, sich das Produkt anzueignen, obwohl es nicht mehr *sein* Produkt war, sondern ausschliesslich Produkt *fremder Arbeit.* So wurden also die nunmehr gesellschaftlich erzeugten Produkte angeeignet nicht von denen, die die Produktionsmittel wirklich in Bewegung gesetzt und die Produkte wirklich erzeugt hatten, sondern von *Kapitalisten.*" (MEW 20, 252).

The contradiction between the social character of production and the private form of appropriation also reproduces itself as a contradiction between the planned organisation

---

[5] For a more detailed discussion, see Gronow 1975.

[6] For Engels' historicising interpretation of Marx's *Capital* and its influence on the theory of capitalism of the Marxists of the Second International see also Paul 1978, 44−58. For a further discussion see chapter II.3.

of production in a single factory and the anarchy of the market. All the main contradictions in capitalism can be deduced from this basic one. They become apparent during periods of violent crises, in which

> "...die Produktionsweise rebelliert gegen die Austauschweise, die Produktivkräfte rebellieren gegen die Produktionsweise, der sie entwachsen sind" (MEW 20, 258).

On the one hand, an overproduction of products and means of production, on the other an oversupply of workers. The contradiction has developed into "absurdity". (Cf. Kautsky 1906c, 263).

There is a clear difference between the formulation of the basic contradiction of capitalism by Engels and Marx's conception of capitalistic appropriation. Marx takes up the problem of appropriation in the chapter dealing with the transformation of surplus value into capital.

As soon as the labour power of the wage worker is bought using capital produced during an earlier capital relation (surplus value is tranformed into capital), the form of appropriation is reversed even though the relation between the capitalist and wage labourer still follows the principle of equal exchange of commodities, and even though the worker is paid the value of his labour power. The role of the original relation, the exchange of equivalents has, however, changed, since the exchange now belongs to the realm of appearance:

> "...indem erstens der gegen Arbeitskraft ausgetauschte Kapitalteil selbst nur ein Teil des ohne Äquivalent angeeigneten fremden Arbeitsproduktes ist und zweitens von seinem Produzenten, dem Arbeiter, nicht nur ersetzt, sondern mit neuem Surplus ersetzt werden muss" (MEW 23, 609).

The relation of exchange between the capitalist and the worker becomes a relation belonging to the realm of appearance in the process of circulation. It becomes a mere form, alien to its contents ("blosse Form, die dem Inhalt selbst fremd ist und ihn nur mystifiziert" (MEW 23, 609)):

> "Der beständige Kauf und Verkauf der Arbeitskraft ist die Form. Der Inhalt ist, dass der Kapitalist einen Teil der bereits vergegenständlichten fremden Arbeit, die der sich unaufhörlich ohne Äquivalent aneignet, stets wieder gegen grösseres Quantum lebendiger fremder Arbeit umsetzt. Ursprünglich erschien uns das Eigentumsrecht gegründet auf eigne Arbeit. (...) Eigentum erscheint jetzt auf Seite des Kapitalisten als das Recht, fremde unbezahlte Arbeit oder ihr Produkt, aus Seite des Arbeiters als Unmöglichkeit, sich sein eignes Produkt anzueignen. Die Scheidung zwischen Eigentum und Arbeit wird zur notwendigen Konsequenz eines Gesetzes, das scheinbar von ihrer Identät ausging." (MEW 23, 609–610).

The form of appropriation and the right to property is reversed in capitalism even according to Marx, but Marx is very careful to stress that the capitalist form of appropriation is still based on the equal exchange of commodities — not only as a historical precondition but as a condition permanently present in capitalism. Even though the capitalist form of appropriation seems to contradict the original laws of commodity circulation, it does not exclude them: it is based on them. The whole secret of the capitalist form of appropriation is already inherent in the following formulation:

> "Das Gesetz des Austausches bedingt Gleichheit nur für die Tauschwerte der gegeneinander weggegebenden Waren. Es bedingt sogar von vornherein Verschiedenheit ihrer Gebrauchswerte und hat absolut nichts zu schaffen mit ihrem Verbrauch, der erst nach geschlossnem und vollzognem Handel beginnt." (MEW 23, 611).

Taken as such, Marx's formulation of the transformation of the law of appropriation seems to be quite similar to that of Engels and Kautsky. There is, however, an important difference, viz. Marx does not comprehend this transformation as consisting of any contradiction – not to speak of the basic contradiction of capitalism. The real content of the wage labour-capital relation is the appropriation of alien labour in the form of surplus value, but its form is the exchange of equivalents. This form is alien to its content and mere appearance ("Schein"), but still a form that is preserved intact even in capitalism.

While formulating the fundamental contradiction of capitalism as if there were a contradiction between the form and content of capital relation, Engels seems to be regressing into an almost moralising critique of capitalism. To Marx the whole discussion of the capitalist form of appropriation is only a means of summarising the results of his analysis of surplus value production: capital relation is, as a matter of fact, a relation in which former objectified alien labour is exchanged for a larger amount of future alien labour. Even though the law of exchange of equivalents is respected in the selling and buying of labour power, the result of the transaction is the exploitation of surplus labour. The law of appropriation is thus only another expression of the economic laws of capitalism. It summarises the analysis of the production of surplus value from the point of view of the right of property, and its critical point is directed against the bourgeois economics. The bourgeois society is not the real world of liberty and equality, as propagated by the science of economics, but a world of exploitation and repression. The right of property is based not on the appropriation of one's own labour, but on that of alien labour. The "Schein" of bourgeois society is thus revealed.

In criticising Engels' conception of appropriation the context of his presentation should, however, be kept in mind. Engels was analysing those elements of capitalism which anticipated socialism, even though he rather unfortunately tried to deduce all the basic contradictions – and even economic crises – from the transformation of the form of appropriation. While discussing the social character of production – production as actually social in character – Engels was obviously trying to analyse the conditions of socialism already developed inside capitalism. Marx was criticising capitalism immanently (for a discussion of Marx's immanent critique see chapter II.1.) Engels' theory of capitalism in *Anti-Dühring* ideally anticipates socialism, a classless society where all the contradictions of capitalism have been overcome. The same element of anticipation was also included in the corresponding formulations in Kautsky (1906c, 161–163). More often, however, Kautsky formulated the contradiction in terms of the contradiction between the organised character of production and the anarchic character of the market.[7] The establishment of socialism is thought to imply the transformation of the total national production into a single big firm or cooperative factory with a conscious and planned organisation of production by the state (see Kautsky 1906a, 117 and 119).

The crucial problem in Kautsky's theory of capitalism was not the interpretation of the law of appropriation as such but the interpretation of Marx's *Capital* as an essentially historical presentation of the development of capitalism. For Kautsky the core of Marxism was composed of the laws of accumulation and concentration of capital, which also included the conception of the inevitable proletarisation of the majority of the population. The difference between the formulations of Engels and Kautsky was rather one of minor emphasis. The interpretation of Marx's economic thought as being fundamentally a presentation of the historical laws of development of capitalism was already implicit in Engels' thinking, too.

The socialist perspective connected with increasing capital concentration was a direct consequence of this interpretation. In a sense, the independent producer owning his own means of production represents in Kautsky's thinking the simple commodity production historically preceding capitalism in which the right of property was still based on one's own labour. The big enterprise produced by capital concentration represents the capitalist form of appropriation. Continuous capital concentration proves that there is no return to the bourgeois paradise of natural rights. (See Kautsky 1906a, 111—113.) The task of the party and the intellectuals (or rather party intellectuals) is to make the growing proletarian masses realise the irreversible nature of this development.

---

[7] Cf. also:

"Das wirtschaftliche Getriebe der heutigen Produktionsweise wird immer mehr ein so verwickelter und empfindlicher Mechanismus, dass sein ungestörter Fortgang mehr und mehr davon abhängt, dass alle seine unzähligen Rädchen genau ineinander greifen und ihre Schuldigkeit thun. Nie bedurfte eine Produktionsweise so sehr der planmässigen Regelung, wie die heutige. Aber das Privateigenthum macht es unmöglich, Plan und Ordnung in dieses Getriebe zu bringen. (...) Je mehr der Grossbetrieb sich entwickelt, je grösser die einzelnen Betriebe werden, desto mehr wird die wirtschaftliche Thätigkeit innerhalb eines jeden derselben eine geregelte, nach einem bestimmten, genau erwogenen Plane bis ins Kleinste geordnete. Aber das Zusammenwirken der einzelnen Betriebe mit einander bleibt der blinden Triebkraft der *freien Konkurrenz* überlassen. (...) Man nennt das 'Auslese der Besten im Kampf ums Dasein'." (Kautsky 1906a, 63—64).

6. THE CENTRALISATION OF CAPITAL AND MONOPOLY FORMATION

In analysing Kautsky's theoretical conceptions about the centralisation of capital and the formation of monopolistic associations and restrictions of competition, it should be remembered that Kautsky never developed any very systematic theoretical ideas about monopoly capital — or about imperialism (see also Kraus 1978, 57–58). His formulations are scattered as smaller or larger remarks throughout most of his work, and they are, furthermore, usually connected with rather practical political questions and disputes (the policies of the Social Democrats against the war and restrictive tariffs). Care should be taken in analysing Kautsky's position out of context. There are, however, certain basic ideas and problems that recur throughout his writings. The differences of emphasis caused by the different contexts of discussion should, however, also be kept in mind.

One of the earliest analyses of the formation of monopolies and their effects can be found in *Das Erfurter Programm*. The new restrictions on competition which became visible and important during the last quarter of the 19th century were a result of the centralisation of capital and the decreasing rate of profit. The rate of profit had a tendency to decrease in the long run because the organic composition of capital grew; the share of variable capital became smaller in comparison with the share of constant capital. Following Marx's presentation of the problem Kautsky argued that the long-term tendency of the rate of profit — and the rate of interest — to decrease could take place simultaneously with an increase in the rate of exploitation. Kautsky remarked that the rate of profit is, furthermore, negatively affected by increasing state expenditure and land rent subtracted from the surplus value produced by industrial capital. The new restrictions of competition at the market are an attempt to compensate the decreasing rate of profit. The monopolistic associations — or the various forms of their existence (cartels, trusts, syndicates, etc.) — are able to price their commodities above their real value by restricting competition and the supply of products. Hence, they are able to get higher gain in the form of extra profit. The formation of big nation-wide cartels is the most recent and visible form of this development. (See Kautsky 1906a, 76–78).

The restrictions of competition and the formation of cartels are made possible by the centralisation of capital. There are fewer and fewer independent firms operating on a

certain market. The centralisation of capital has reduced the number of firms on many
an important market to a handful of big enterprises co-operating with each other:

> "Wo es zur Kartellirung kommt, da bilden die verschiedenen Betriebe, die sich verbinden,
> thatsächlich nur *einen* Betrieb unter *einer* Leitung, sehr oft werden sie auch formell einer
> einheitlichen Leitung unterstellt." (Kautsky 1906a, 79).

Such cartels can already be found in certain important fields of production, especially in
the production of raw materials (steel and coal cartels).

In his article *Der imperialistische Krieg* Kautsky stated that the motive force behind
capitalist production is always the appropriation of extra or maximum profit. Every
single capitalist tries to make more profit than his competitors. In general, the extra
profit is based on the fact that the firm has a more advantageous position either on the
market or in the production process:

> "Nie war das Kapital mit dem Durchschnittsprofit zufrieden, stets strebte jeder Kapitalist
> nach besonderen Extraprofiten. Man kann sie erreichen entweder durch eine besonders
> günstige Stellung auf dem Markt, beim Einkaufen oder Verkaufen oder durch eine beson-
> ders günstige Stellung im Produktionsprozess." (Kautsky 1916–17a, 475).

The advantages in the production process are due to more advance means of production
and higher productivity of labour, which make it possible to increase exploitation. As
soon as the new methods of production became generalised, there is no extra profit to
be appropriated. Such is, however, the case only during free competition. As soon as
monopolies or cartels have been introduced and free competition gives way to restrictions of competition the situation changes. Cartellisation and monopoly formation is
promoted by the economic policy of the state functioning in the interests of big capital:

> "Dagegen ändert sich die Situation, sobald an Stelle der Konkurrenz das Monopol tritt.
> Und dafür kommt die Zeit im Fortgang der kapitalistischen Entwicklung. Diese zentrali-
> siert nicht nur die Kapitalien immer mehr in wenigen Hände; Unternehmerverbände,
> Aktiengesellschaften, Banken bewirken die Zentralisierung der *Leitung* und *Beherrschung*
> der Kapitalien noch weit rascher als die Zentralisierung des *Eigentums* an ihnen. So
> erwächst in den Staaten fortgeschrittener kapitalistischer Industrie das Regime der grossen
> Monopole und die Beherrschung der Staatsgewalt durch sie." (Kautsky 1916–17a, 477).

As a result, a new method of acquiring extra profits is introduced. The monopolies are
able to reach an advantageous position at the market with the help of state power —
through colonial policy and high import tariffs:

> "Wiedersuchen die grossen Kapitalisten eine monopolistische günstige Stellung auf dem
> Markt zu gewinnen mit Hilfe der Staatsgewalt: einerseits durch *Schutzzölle*, die die äussere
> Konkurrenz auf dem inneren Markt schwächen, die Unternehmer-Organisationen erleich-
> tern und diesen die Kraft geben, auf dem Weltmarkt Schleuderkonkurrenz zu üben.
> Andererseits durch *Kolonialpolitik*, die Angliederung agrarischer Gebiete als direkte Kolo-
> nien oder als Vasallenstaaten an den Industriestaat und Monopolisierung dieser Länder als
> Absatzgebiete, Rohstoffquellen und Anlagestätten für exportiertes Kapital." (Kautsky
> 1916–17a, 477).

In his writings on imperialism (imperialism was not yet explicitly discussed in the *Erfurt Programme*, see however Kautsky 1906a, 99—100) Kautsky analysed monopolistic extra profits almost exclusively in terms of a new state policy. Imperialism is essentially a new method of securing extra profits for the big cartels and monopolies. The extra profits are due to the restrictions of competition organised by the bourgeois state in the form of restrictive tariffs and colonial policy. According to Kautsky, monopoly profits are thus essentially politically mediated. In this sense the discussion of monopolies and cartels is closely connected with a discussion of the world market and the orientation of national capitals and states towards changing international competition. Imperialism is a political method of guaranteeing higher profits for the big capitals.[1]

In *Handelspolitik und Sozialdemokratie* (1911b (1901)) Kautsky stated that the industrial crises in 1873 marked the end of free trade as bourgeois ideal:

> "Gewiss, nach wir vor blieb die freie Konkurrenz unter dem Privateigentum an den Produktionsmitteln das beste Mittel, Nachfrage und Angebot, Konsum und Produktion wenigstens vorübergehend in Einklang zu bringen und die Interessen der Konsumenten am besten zu wahren." (Kautsky 1911b, 38).

At the same time as the ideology of free trade was being discredited, the centralisation of capital made the appropriation of extra profits possible in a new way:

> "Wenn der moralische Bankerott der freien Konkurrenz den *Wunsch* erregte, an ihre Stelle das private Monopol für die Unternehmer einzelner Gewerbe zu setzen und ihnen eine Ausnahmestellung zu sichern, in der sie durch ihre überlegene Kraft sich Extraprofite erpressen konnten, so bot die fortschreitende Konzentration der Kapitalien die Möglichkeit dazu." (Kautsky 1911b, 38).

Historically the cartels developed simultanously with the new system of restrictive tariffs. They represented the specific interests of a small group of capitalists at the cost of the general public ("Allgemeinheit"):

> "Die Grundlage der freien Konkurrenz ist wenigstens der Idee nach Freiheit und Gleichheit von Käufern und Verkäufern, Unternehmern und Arbeitern. Die Idee des Kartells ist von vornherein die Privilegierung einzelner Unternehmergruppen, die auf das gewaltsameste und rücksichtsloseste ihre Ueberlegenheit auf dem Markte wie in der Werkstatt zur Geltung bringen." (Kautsky 1911b, 39).

If the restrictive tariffs are a political method of increasing the profits of the big capitals organised into cartels, they are essentially a result of the political power of the cartel magnates. Despite their political power the cartels are not, however, able to solve all the problems of capital accumulation; on the contrary, they only lead to the sharpening

---

[1] One can agree with Rainer Kraus that Kautsky's theory of the formation of cartels and monopolies was rather unsystematic and fragmentary. According to Kraus, Kautsky explained the formation of monopolies mainly by the strong position of finance capital; consequently monopolies are sometimes understood to be atavistic phenomena at the time of increasing industrialisation (see Kraus 1978, 128).

of both the international and national contradictions of capitalism. In the last instance, world war is the necessary outcome of cartel politics (see Kautsky 1911b, 94).

Because of the restrictions of competition and production, cartels are faced with the chronic problem of overproduction. Growing exports are the only possible means of solving this problem. The cartels must export their commodities in an ever increasing amount. There must always be new foreign markets open for their products. On the other hand, the cartels are permanently faced with the problem of cheap raw materials. Both the problems are − at least ostensibly − solved by colonial policy. Colonies offer both a market for the industrial products of cartels and a source of cheap raw materials and foodstuffs. If all the industrial countries follow the interests of the cartels in their foreign economic policy and introduce restrictive tariffs, then naturally the development will out of necessity lead to increasing competition for non-industrial markets and the annexation of colonies. Colonialist competition is the inevitable result of this new economic policy. Consequently, as Kautsky predicted, the conflicts between industrial states become intensified and world war is the logical outcome (see Kautsky 1911b, 90−94). As will be shown later in this study (see pp. 85−89), Kautsky came to modify the results of his analysis. In his later writings there are other alternatives open to capitalism than war and barbarism or socialism.

7. IMPERIALISM AND THE RELATION BETWEEN INDUSTRIAL AND AGRARIAN COUNTRIES

The problem of external markets for industrial products is, however, even more deeply rooted in capitalist commodity production. According to Kautsky, capitalism is constantly in need of new markets to swallow the increasing amount of commodities produced by the industrially developed countries. Capitalism has a permanent tendency towards overproduction. Overproduction − or rather underconsumption − is the basis of the relation between the industrial and the agrarian countries, which is an essential part of Kautsky's thinking on modern capitalism − and his theory of imperialism and ultra-imperialism.

The reasons behind the conception of general overproduction are not altogether clear: why cannot all industrial commodities be absorbed by the consumers of the industrial countries? In this sense Kautsky seemed to be sharing a conception widely accepted by the Marxists of the Second International. On the most abstract level the problem of overproduction seems to be a result of the very nature of capitalism as the production of surplus value.

In her *Accumulation of Capital* (1963 (1913)) Rosa Luxemburg formulated the problem facing the accumulation of capital in a most pronounced manner: the accumulation of capital faces the difficulty of principle of realising its surplus product. The continuous accumulation of capital would − according to Luxemburg − require a continuous and increasing demand for commodities. And this demand cannot be satisfied within a capitalist economy. Luxemburg takes as the starting point of her analysis of the conditions of the accumulation of capital the relation between the two departments of production in capitalism as formulated in the reproduction schemes of the second volume of Marx's *Capital*. Maintaining the right proportion between the two departments of production, Department I producing the means of producing and Department II producing the provisions or consumer goods, is as such a permanent problem in capitalism, because there is no predetermined plan for maintaining the right proportion. In principle it is still possible for accumulation to continue as long as the right proportion is maintained, and no necessary economic collapse can be deduced from the relative development of these two departments of production; still, there is a permanent problem of effective demand in capitalism:

"Here we must ask first of all: what is the starting point of accumulation? That is the approach on which we have to investigate the mutual dependence of the accumulative process in the two departments of production. There can be no doubt that under capitalist conditions Department II is dependant on Department I in so far as its accumulation is determined by the additional means of production available. Conversely, the accumulation in Department I depends upon a corresponding quantity of additional consumer goods being available for its additional labour power. It does not follow, however, that so long as both these conditions are observed, accumulation in both departments is bound, as Marx's diagram makes it appear, to go on automatically year after year. The conditions of accumulation we have enumerated are no more than those without which there can be no accumulation. There may even be a desire to accumulate in both departments, yet the desire to accumulate plus the technical prerequisites of accumulation is not enough in a capitalist economy of commodity production. A further condition is required to ensure that accumulation can in fact proceed and production expand: The effective demand for commodities must also increase. Where is this continually increasing demand to come from, which in Marx's diagram forms the basis of reproduction on an ever increasing scale?" (Luxemburg 1963, 131−132).

According to Luxemburg this increasing demand can result from the consumption of neither the capitalists nor the workers. A necessary and obvious precondition for accumulation is precisely that at least some of the commodities representing surplus value are not consumed by the capitalists but are on the contrary accumulated. Workers cannot possibly absorb these commodities either, because the purpose of capitalism is not to increase the demands and needs of the wage workers. Even though Luxemburg did not explicitly refer to the conception of the wage worker as being principally an underconsumer while producing a surplus value, her discussion of the problem in fact led to the acceptance of this premise.

The conclusion drawn from the discussion is, nevertheless, that the realisation of surplus value is altogether impossible within a pure capitalist economy:

"Realisation of the surplus value outside the only two existing classes of society appears as indispensable as it looks impossible. The accumulation of capital has been caught in a vicious circle." (Luxemburg 1963, 165).

And if the commodities representing surplus value cannot be realised within the capitalist economy, the only alternative left is that − if they are to be realised at all − they must be realised outside it:

"Seeing that we cannot discover within capitalist society any buyers whatever for the commodities in which the accumulated part of the surplus value is embodied, only one thing is left: foreign trade." (Luxemburg 1963, 135−136).

But not even foreign trade is the final solution to the problem as foreign trade cannot simply be directed at other capitalist countries, which also face the same problem of lacking demand. The only possible extra demand for commodities can, then, come from a non-capitalist economy and non-capitalist areas and countries.

"It requires as its prime condition ... that there should be strata of buyers outside capitalist society. (...) The decisive fact is that the surplus value cannot be realised by sale either to workers or to capitalists, but only if it is sold to such social organisations or strata whose own mode of production is not capitalistic." (Luxemburg 1963, 351−352).

Thus the accumulation of capital constantly requires the existence of either non-capitalist societies or other non-capitalist social strata:

> "The solution envisaged by Marx lies in the dialectical conflict that capitalism needs non-capitalist social organisations as the setting for its development, that it proceeds by assimilating the very conditions which alone can ensure its own existence." (Luxemburg 1963, 366).

So long as there are non-capitalist markets for the commodities produced in capitalism, accumulation can proceed. Once capitalist production has been established in all the remaining areas and fields of production, accumulation must come to an end, and the final collapse of capitalism will result:

> "As soon as this final result (the establishment of capitalist production in all the countries of the world − J.G.) is achieved − in theory, of course, because it can never actually happen − accumulation must come to a stop. The realisation and capitalisation of surplus value becomes impossible to accomplish. (...) For capital, the standstill of accumulation means that the development of the productive forces is arrested, and the collapse of capitalism follows inevitably, as an objective historical necessity. This is the reason for the contradictory behaviour of capitalism in the final stage of its historical career: imperialism." (Luxemburg 1963, 417).

Imperialism is the necessary outcome of the problems facing the accumulation of capital, and Luxemburg associated imperialism with all the features later to become familiar in the theories of imperialism of both Kautsky and Lenin: export of capital in the form of international loans, protective tariffs, increasing armaments and militarism, colonial policy, annexation of colonies by the major capitalist states. In earlier capitalism "peace, property and equality" prevail − at least in principle. In imperialism they are superseded by other principles:

> "Its predominant methods are colonial policy, an international loan system − a policy of spheres of interest − and war. Force, fraud, oppression, looting are openly displayed without any attempt at concealment, and it requires an effort to discover within this tangle of political violence and contests of power the stern laws of the economic process." (Luxemburg 1963, 452).

Kautsky's analysis of the necessary conditions for the accumulation of capital resembled that of Luxemburg's in many respects.[1] It may be claimed that according to Kautsky, too, the wage workers are always "overproducers" because they are producing a surplus value and surplus product. There cannot possibly be an effective demand for the surplus product by the wage workers. Furthermore, the luxury consumption of the

---

[1]   Kautsky actually formulated the dilemma of capitalist accumulation and the relation between industrial and agrarian production before Luxemburg's *Accumulation of Capital* (see Kautsky 1911b (1901)). It is not known whether Luxemburg's analysis was directly influenced by Kautsky. At least one can assume that the idea was prevalent among the Marxists at that time.

capitalists cannot satisfy the necessary extra demand. The wage workers are by definition thus overproducers and underconsumers. As a result, overproduction is a permanent curse of capitalism:

> "Neben den periodischen Krisen, neben der zeitweisen Ueberproduktion mit der darauf-
> folgenden zeitweisen Werthvernichtung und Kraftvergeudung entwickelt sich aber immer
> stärker die *dauernde (chronische) Ueberproduktion* und die *dauernde Kraftvergeudung.*"
> (Kautsky 1906a, 98).

Markets expand much more slowly than production. Hence, it is impossible for capitalism to develop its productive forces maximally:

> "Die Zeiten des wirtschaftslichen Aufschwungs werden immer kürzer, die Zeiten der
> Krisen immer länger, namentlich in alten Industrieländern, wie England und Frankreich."
> (Kautsky 1906a, 100−101).

In more concrete terms, overproduction is explained by the limitless need for the
accumulation of capital and the permanent revolution in the means of production. Since
production increases much faster than the number of employed wage workers, it becomes more and more difficult for the capitalists to realise their products on the home
market:

> "Die wachsende Produktivität der Arbeit vermehrt nicht bloss den Mehrwert, der den
> Kapitalisten zufällt, sie vermehrt auch die Menge der Waaren, die auf den Markt gelangen
> und von den Kapitalisten abgesetzt werden müssen. Mit der Ausbeutung wächst auch die
> Konkurrenz, der erbitterte Kampf aller Unternehmer gegen alle Unternehmer." (Kautsky
> 1906a, 85).

The rapid growth of production and the accumulation of capital in industry are made
possible by the development of the modern loan system and the constant supply of free
workers on the labour market. There do not seem to be any natural limits to the
increase of production.

    Even in Kautsky's analysis of capitalism there is the permanent danger that the
proportional relations between the different sectors of production will be disturbed.
The relation between the sectors producing the means of production and the means of
consumption is especially important. If the right relation is not maintained, there will be
serious disturbances in the market. The problem is that the proportional relations are
constantly changing due to improvements in the technical and social relations of production. Equilibrium is achieved only through continuous disturbances and changes in
prices and volumes of production (see Kautsky 1913−14, 910).

    According to Kautsky, there is, however, an even more serious problem in capitalism
connected with the establishment of the right proportional relations between the industrial and agrarian products and sectors. Whereas a non-capitalist mode of production is a
necessary precondition for the realisation of the surplus value in Luxemburg's conception, there is in Kautsky's analysis a further difficulty connected with the relation
between agrarian and industrial production due to differences in the rate of accumula-

tion in these departments. The expansion of industrial production is always possible. Agricultural production is, however, always faced with natural limits — even in its capitalistic form (see Kautsky 1913—14, 914). There are still other reasons why it cannot expand at the same rate as industry:

> "Die Proportionalität zwischen beiden Gruppen ist unter allen Umständen notwendig, sie unterliegt aber stets der Gefahr, durchbrochen zu werden. Einmal durch die Landflucht, die der Landwirtschaft Arbeitskräfte nimmt und der Industrie zuführt, und dann durch das Wachstum der Intelligenz und der Technik in den Städten, wodurch die Produktivität der Industrie leicht gesteigert wird. Das Produkt der Industrie hat also die Tendenz, rascher zu wachsen als das der Landwirtschaft, weil die Zahl der Produzenten und die Menge des Produkts pro Produzent in jener schneller zunimmt als in dieser." (Kautsky 1913—14, 912).

Industrial production is forced to accumulate and find an ever increasing demand for its products:

> "Er muss jetzt seine Produktion unter allen Umständen immer weiter ausdehnen, und wenn die Nachfrage nach ihnen nicht von selbst in gleichem Masse steigt, muss er alle Kräfte aufwenden, diese Nachfrage künstlich zu vergrössern, den Markt zu erweitern. Die intensität der industriellen Konkurrenz ist eine Folge davon, dass der Drang und die Möglichkeit zur Akkumulation von Kapital und zur Erweiterung der Produktion in der Industrie weit grösser sind als in der Landwirtschaft; aus einer Folge wird diese Triebkraft ihrerseits zu einer der mächtigsten Ursachen, jenen Unterschied zwischen Industrie und Landwirtschaft zu vergrössern." (Kautsky 1913—14, 916).

On the other hand, agricultural production is — in a rather trivial sense — a necessary basis for all economic enterprise as we cannot go on living for a single moment without the products of agriculture. If industrial production is to increase continuously, an increase in agricultural production and population is also demanded. The agricultural sector must produce the raw materials and the foodstuffs consumed by industry and the industrial wage workers on an ever larger scale. But what is even more important, it must also be ready to buy the surplus produce of industry which is not consumed by the industrially active population (see Kautsky 1913—14, 916).

Kautsky's main problem is, consequently, how to establish the right balance between agriculture and industry if the accumulation of capital is much faster in industry than in agriculture. The solution is the constant expansion of the agrarian areas and regions in the capitalist market:

> "Die kapitalistische Akkumulation kann in der Industrie nur dann ungehindert vor sich gehen und sich frei entfalten, wenn sie das landwirtschaftliche Gebiet, das ihr als Lieferant und Abnehmer dient, beständig erweitert..." (Kautsky 1913—14, 916).

If the agrarian areas do not constantly expand, there will be an oversupply of industrial products and an overdemand for agrarian products. As a consequence, capital accumulation will be seriously hindered and disturbed. Capitalism has tried to solve the problem by imperialism or colonial policy.

The expansion of the market and the resources of raw materials was possible for Britain with a policy of free trade so long as she was the main industrial country in the world. As soon as other European countries developed their capitalist production and introduced protective tariffs to be able to compete with Britain, an international system of restrictive tariffs − and imperialism − was born. (See Kautsky 1913−14, 917−918.)

The main determinant of imperialism is thus the contradictory relation between the industrial and the agrarian countries ("Entscheidend wird für den Imperialismus der Gegensatz zwischen industriellen und agrarischen Gebiet") as summarised by Kautsky in his booklet *Nationalstaat, imperialistischer Staat und Staatenbund* (1915a, 15). In the same pamphlet − later to become famous as a polemical target of Lenin's *Imperialism as the highest stage of capitalism* − Kautsky referred to his article *Der Imperialismus* − already referred to earlier − published in *Die Neue Zeit* in 1913−14 as the best presentation of his conception of imperialism. The concept of imperialism is defined as follows:

> "Dies Wort (imperialism − J.G.) wird heute auf Schritt und Tritt gebraucht, aber je mehr man darüber spricht und diskutiert, desto unbestimmter wird es, was natürlich jede Verständigung erschwert. Heute sind wir schon so weit, dass man unter Imperialismus alle Erscheinungen des modernen Kapitalismus zusammenfasst, Kartelle, Schutzzölle, Finanzherrschaft ebenso wie Kolonialpolitik. In diesem Sinne gefasst, ist der Imperialismus natürlich wie Lebensnotwendigkeit für Kapitalismus. (...) Fassen wir das Wort nicht in dieser Allgemeinheit, sondern in seiner historischen Bestimmtheit, die in England ihren Ursprung nahm, dann bezeichnet es nur eine besondere Art politischer Bestrebungen, die allerdings durch den modernen Kapitalismus verursacht werden aber mit ihm nicht zusammenfallen." (Kautsky 1913−14, 908−909).

Imperialism is consequently not to be understood as being synonymous with modern capitalism in general but as a specific form of capitalist rule which is, by all means, caused by the economic development of capitalism but is not identical to it. Imperialism is a necessary companion of capitalism − if the modern conditions are taken as given:

> "Der Imperialismus ist ein Produkt des hochentwickelten industriellen Kapitalismus. Er besteht in dem Drange jeder industriellen kapitalistischen Nation, sich ein immer grösseres *agrarisches* Gebiet zu unterwerfen und anzugliedern, ohne Rücksicht darauf, von welchen Nationen es bewohnt wird." (Kautsky 1913−14, 909).[2]

Imperialism is also necessary for the proletariat, insofar as it is interested in the rapid development of capitalism and its productive forces. (See Kautsky 1915a, 17.)

However, Kautsky firmly believed that imperialism as a method of guaranteeing high profits is doomed to fail in the end; imperialistic policies based on the export of capital and protective tariffs cannot be continued eternally. There is a natural limit to the further development of imperialism. As soon as all the agrarian areas have been divided

---

[2]   In this respect Luxemburg's characterisation of imperialism resembles Kautsky's definition, as well:

> "Imperialism is the political expression of the accumulation of capital in its competitive struggle for what remains still open of the non-capitalist environment." (Luxemburg 1963, 446).

among the industrial nations, the expansion of imperialism comes to a natural end, and
the only way open for further development is — an open trade war:

> "Es wachsen Kapital und Arbeit im eigenen Lande, es wächst die Zahl der konsumieren-
> den Industrieländer, indes die der Agrarländer sich verringert. Bald werden diese, soweit
> sie noch frei, völlig aufgeteilt sein, und dann gibt es zur weiteren Ausdehnung des monopo-
> lisierten Gebiets nur noch *einen* Weg: nicht mehr den Kampf zwischen Industriestaat und
> Agrarstaat, sondern den blutigen Kampf der grossen Industriestaaten, also den Welt-
> krieg." (Kautsky 1911b, 94).

The final result of the analysis proves that there are thus only two alternatives facing
capitalism and imperialism: socialism or world war:

> "Der *Weltkrieg* ist nur eine Alternative des heutigen, seinem Zusammenbruch ent-
> gegeneilenden Welthandelssystems; die andere ist die *sozialistische* Gesellschaft." (Kautsky
> 1911b, 94).

Even though Kautsky considered imperialism to be a specific political method — and
not an economic necessity — of industrial states based on the annexation of agrarian
regions and protective tariffs, the only possible alternative to its violent and reactionary
tendencies seems to be socialism. The establishment of socialism is shown to be even
more necessary during imperialism because in the last instance imperialism restricts the
development of productive forces in its centres and therefore shows that capitalism has
become obsolete (see Kautsky 1911b, 53; Kautsky 1915a, 79—80).

At the same time Kautsky thought that capitalism, however, developed towards
greater elasticity. It is able to transform itself faster according to new emerging needs of
production due to the greater role of science in production and most of all to the
centralisation of capital (see Kautsky 1915a, 20). The greater elasticity of capitalism
does not, however, necessarily guarantee better chances for its future existence and
development — an idea common in revisionism. The contradiction between the propertyless masses and the big capital owners has, on the contrary, become intensified.
Political catastrophy will be the inevitable outcome of the economic development of
capitalism, but because of its greater elasticity, a general economic catastrophe can still
be avoided:

> "Die wachsende Elastizität und Anpassungsfähigkeit des Kapitalismus ermöglicht es nicht,
> dass er ins Unendliche wächst und besteht, sondern bloss, dass selbst eine Verschiebung
> der Machtverhältnisse der Klassen, die so weit geht, dass sie zu einer politischen und
> sozialen Katastrophe wird, nicht auch eine ökonomische Katastrophe werden muss, dass
> sich der Uebergang vom Kapitalismus zum Sozialismus ohne ökonomischen Zusammen-
> bruch vollstehen kann." (Kautsky 1915a, 20—21).

Allowing for the growing elasticity of capitalism due to capital concentration and technical efficiency it is not plausible to claim that imperialism can be overcome only
through the overcome of capitalism itself. Kautsky firmly believed that it is both possible and necessary to oppose imperialism even during the rule of capitalism. Imperialism
is, after all, only a question of power, not an economic necessity:

"Und nur eine Frage der Macht, nicht aber der ökonomischen Notwendigkeit ist der Imperialismus. Er ist nicht nur nicht notwendig für das kapitalistische Wirtschaftsleben, seine Bedeutung dafür wird vielfach masslos überschätzt." (Kautsky 1915a, 22).

There are alternative ways of developing capitalism − alternatives more beneficial to the working class and all the propertyless masses, as well.

8. IMPERIALISM AND ITS ALTERNATIVES

Colletti saw the merit of Bernstein's critique of Marxism as a response to the new developments of capitalism largely neglected by Engels and Kautsky and other theoreticians at the turn of the century. Because of his sensitivity to these new features of capitalism, Bernstein would be nearer to Lenin's and Hilferding's generation of Marxists than to Kautsky's and Plechanow's:

> "Aktiengesellschaften, Entwicklung von Kartellen und Trusts, Trennung von 'Besitz' und 'Kontrolle', zunehmende Sozialisierung der 'Produktion', 'Demokratisierung des Kapitals' usw., sind Themen, die in Bernsteins Abhandlungen grosse Bedeutung haben und gleichzeitig im *Finanzkapital* von Hilferding und im *Imperialismus* von Lenin zu finden sind: die treffendsten Antworten auf Bernstein sind deshalb in diesen Schriften zu finden." (Colletti 1968, 25).

It may, however, be added that these new phenomena – especially trusts and cartels – became the subject for discussion among other Marxists, as well, including Kautsky, at the beginning of the century. Among Marxists they became part of an analysis of the new features of modern capitalism, called imperialism.

Hans-Holger Paul pointed out that it was Parvus (Alexander Helphand) who was the first Marxist to conduct a special analysis of the transformations in the conjunctural development of capitalism due to imperialism:

> "So hatte Parvus als erster hinsichtlich der Analyse der weltwirtschaftlichen Zusammenhänge, der Beurteilung der konjunkturellen Entwicklung, des weltweiten Wirtschaftsaufschwungs und der Zyklität der Krisen die wesentlichen theoretischen Bestimmungen geliefert, die im grossen und ganzen von Kautsky und Rosa Luxemburg übernommen wurden und Eingang in die parteioffiziellen Erklärungen der deutschen Sozialdemokratie fanden." (Paul 1978, 146; see also Parvus 1897; 1895–96; 1900–01a, b; 1901).

Some of the main ideas of Kautsky were already present in one of his earliest articles on imperialism, *Deutschland, England und Weltpolitik* (1900): In the first stage of imperialism the colonies functioned as "Absatzmärkte" for industrial products.[1] In the new

---

[1] In the following Kautsky's first article on imperialism *Ältere und neuere Kolonialpolitik* (1897–98) is not discussed. John. H. Kautsky (1961, 111–118) characterised this period of Kautsky's thinking as 'Schumpeterian' (colonial policy was explained by the influence of the remnants of precapitalist expansionism of states) as opposed to his later industrial or capitalist explanations of imperialism. Only the 'industrial' explanations of imperialism will be discussed here.

present stage of imperialism the export of capital becomes the decisive motive force for the acquisition of colonies:

> "Neben dem Warenexport entsteht der Kapitalexport; nicht mehr handelt es sich allein darum den wachsenden Warenüberschussen Absatzgebiete zu sichern, sondern auch darum, der wachsenden Kapitalvermehrung neue Anlagemärkte, neue Bethätigungsfelder zu eröffnen." (Kautsky 1900:2).

Colonies and colonial trade are more profitable to finance − resulting from the increasing connections between moneyed and industrial capital[2] − than to industrial capital:

> "So sicher es ist, dass Englands und Deutschlands Industrie aufeinander angewiesen sind und dass eine Stockung in den Handelsbeziehungen beider Länder die schwersten Rückschläge auf ihre industrielle Entwicklung haben muss, so sicher ist andrerseits, dass das Finanzkapital vielfach andre Interessen und Bedürfnisse hat, wie das Industriekapital. − Dagegen hat das Finanzkapital einen durchaus monopolistischen Character, sein Bestreben ist sich Monopole auf die Exploitation gewisser Gebiete zu sichern." (Kautsky 1900:2).

Even though industrial capital can profit from imperialism, the costs incurred by imperialistic methods are even higher. The only fraction of capital really benefiting from imperialism is, then, finance capital:

> "Was von den Kolonialgründungen, von der modernen Expansionspolitik allein wirklichen Nutzen hat, ist das Finanzkapital, das ja selbst von dem Misserfolgen der Kolonialverwaltungen und den durch diese hervorgerufenen Aufwendungen und Anleihen zu Kolonialzwecken noch Vorteile zieht." (Kautsky 1900:2).

Export and import tariffs and their consequences are the main interests in Kautsky's earliest analysis of imperialism and imperialistic methods of government. In *Die Handelsverträge und der Zolltariff* written in 1903 Kautsky stated that a high rate of tariffs is not in the interests of industry. The abolition of industrial tariffs would clearly increase the productivity of the home industry and lower its production costs. Imperialistic customs policy and its consequence, colonialism, were also seen to be the main factors favouring militarism and the armaments race. The best method of fighting imperialism is to oppose high import and export tariffs. Imperialism is a result of the economic policy of the state and there is no effective direct method of opposing it. Military strikes propagated by the party's left wing have generally proved ineffective (see Kautsky 1904−05, 368−370).

In the third part (*Werttheorie und Kolonialpolitik*) of a series of articles called *Die Nutzen der Kolonien für die Arbeiter* (1907a) Kautsky already presented a line of argumentation later to become central to his theory of imperialism. According to Kautsky there are in principle two possible ways of developing capitalism. The first is

---

[2]   Rainer Kraus (1978, 59) pointed out that in the earlier articles on imperialism in particular Kautsky used the parallel terms of finance capital and high finance (hohe Finanz), and only after the publication of Hilferding's *Finanzkapital* in 1910 the term finance capital more systematically.

essentially based on the repression of the working class, the second on a continuous increase in the productivity of labour. The most important difference is, however, that whereas the first method is in general disadvantageous to economic development, and thus also to the future perspective of establishing socialism, the second method effectively promotes general economic development and thus the present conditions and the future possibilities of socialism, too:

> "Ein moderner kapitalistischer Staat hat nur die Wahl zwischen zwei Wegen: die eine davon besteht darin, das Proletariat mit allen Mitteln zu unterdrücken. Gelingt ihm das, dann sinkt mit der Intelligentz und Kraft seiner Arbeiter auch die Produktivität ihrer Arbeit, geht seine Konkurrenzfähigkeit zurück, schwindet sein gesellschaftlicher Reichtum, geht er völligem Bankrott entgegen. Der andere Weg geht darin, dass der Staat die ökonomische Entwicklung möglichst zu fördern, sein Proletariat intellektuell und physisch zu heben sucht. Zu diesem Falle entwickelt er mit dessen Kraft und Selbstbewusstsein auch den Drang nach Befreiung von seinem Jo h nach Beherrschung des Staates. Dann wächst die Produktivität der Arbeit, wächst der gesellschaftliche Reichtum, wachsen Macht und Anschein des Staates in der Welt, *wachsen aber gleichzeitig innerhalb des Staates Macht und Ansehen des Proletariats, dann reift rasch die Staat des Sozialismus.* Unterdrückung der Arbeit und Bankrott — rasches Wachstum des Reichtums und Sozialismus: keinen anderen Ausweg gibt es für den Kapitalismus, denn die Arbeit ist die Quelle aller Werte." (Kautsky 1907a:3).

The development of the productive forces is the crucial question in evaluating the role of imperialism and its advantages and disadvantages for the proletariat:

> "Die Entwicklung der Produktivkräfte, über die die Menschheit verfügt, ist für das Proletariat von äusserster Wichtigkeit. (. . .) Wir müssen also untersuchen, wie die Kolonialpolitik auf die Entwicklung der Produktivkräfte der Menschheit wirkt." (Kautsky 1907b, 22).

Just as there are two possible alternatives of developing capitalism, so there are two methods of colonial policy itself. According to Kautsky there are in principle two kinds of colonies: labour colonies and colonies of exploitation.[3] The first are favourable to the working class and to the development of the productive forces in general. The labour colonies are a 'gewaltiger Hebel' of human development, even though it must immediately be added that the aborigines are sometimes unjustly treated in them. By labour colonies Kautsky seemed to mean areas of settlement which are favourable and suited for the emigration of white people and which consequently have a chance of developing an industry of their own. (See Kautsky 1907b, 24—26.)

---

[3]   In a letter to Kautsky in 1882 (MEW 35, 356—358) Engels made a rather similar distinction between colonies populated by European people and colonies occupied by European states but populated mainly by aborigines. According to Engels the strategy of the socialist parties should take into account the respective differences in the situation of these colonies. Colonies presently populated by Europeans should all become independent, whereas those populated mainly by the natives should be taken over by the European proletariat and only then — even though as soon as possible — can they look towards their independence.

By the end of the last century all the possible areas open for European settlement had already been taken into use and populated by Europeans. The new colonial policy emerging in the 1880s was of an altogether different type. It was based on the crude exploitation of non-European population and areas of the world, and its total effect on the development of mankind was negative. The new colonial areas were used exclusively to find profitable fields of investment for the surplus capital which could not be profitably invested in the home market. (See Kautsky 1907b, 34–35.)

The new colonial policy thus marked the beginning of an era in which capitalism had become an obstacle to the future development of productive forces – Kautsky's main criterion in evaluating progressive or regressive states of society. It would not be true to say that capitalism has become totally ineffective in developing productive forces, but imperialism does concretely prove that there is another possible way of organising production, in which the development of productive forces would be more effective than in capitalism. Capitalism has become a hindrance to the development of productive forces. (See Kautsky 1907b, 35.)

In this new era of capitalism technical development is no longer a decisive factor in guaranteeing the appropriation of extra profits; on the contrary, extra profits are best achieved by restricting competition, made possible by the centralisation and re-organisation of capital, by the formation of trusts, cartels, etc. The formation of cartels and trusts directly promotes militarism while leading to a policy of high customs tariffs. Only socialism would open up a new era in the development of productive forces. In other words, socialism in the only alternative to imperialism:

> "Die Überwindung des Militarismus ebenso wie die des Kartell- unde Trustsystems ist eben heute nur noch möglich durch den Sozialismus." (Kautsky 1907b, 38).

In the two articles *Sozialismus und Kolonialpolitik* (1907b) and *Sozialistische Kolonialpolitik* (1908–09) Kautsky analysed the economic factors leading to imperialism in a way that was later to become common in Lenin's theory on imperialism. First, the formation of monopolies is the decisive factor promoting imperialistic policies:

> "Der Drang nach dem *Monopol*, dass heisst nach gewaltsamer Vertreitung der *Konsumenten*, um die *Konsumenten* beliebig schröpfen zu können, war bei der staatlichen Kolonialpolitik noch mehr beteiligt als der Drang nach gewaltsamer Beraubung der *Produzenten. Das sind die wahren Triebfedern der Kolonialpolitik.*" (Kautsky 1908–09, 38).

Second, besides the formation of monopolies and the direct exploitation of consumers, the export of capitals is another important feature of imperialism. There is overproduction of both surplus value and of commodities in the developed capitalist countries due to the increase in productivity in industry and the increasing exploitation of the workers:

> "Ehedem waren die Ausbeutungskolonien in erster Linie in Betracht gekommen als Lieferanten von Kapital, das ihnen in den verschiedensten Formen entzogen wurde. Heute dagegen ist in den kapitalistischen Ländern die Produktivkraft der Grossindustrie und die Ausbeutung der Arbeiterklasse so enorm entwickelt, dass sie kolossale Ueberschüsse –

Mehrwerte − liefert, von denen ein grosser Teil wieder als neues, zusätzliches, 'akkumu-liertes' Kapital verwendet wird. (...) Wohl bleiben die Austachelungen der Konkurrenz und des Profits bestehen, aber die Produktion findet immer wieder ihre Grenzen am Markt. Wenn die kapitalistische Produktionsweise die Produktivät in der Erzeugung der Massengüter aufs höchste steigert, so beschränkt sie gleichzeitig den Massenkonsum der Arbeiter, die diese Güter produzieren, auf ein minimum, produziert also einen immer grösseren Ueberschuss von Massengütern für den persönlichen Konsum, der ausserhalb der Arbeiterklasse verkauft werden muss." (Kautsky 1907b, 35).

Exporting commodities is typical of the earlier stages of capitalism, exporting capital becomes a dominating developing force in colonialism:

"Mit anderen Worten, die Kapitalisten exportieren da ihre Produkte nicht als *Waren*, zum *Verkauf* an das Ausland, sondern als *Kapital* zur Ausbeutung des *Auslandes*." (Kautsky 1907b, 39).

Investments in foreign countries are, on the other hand, risky, and these risks are minimised when the countries to which capital is exported become direct colonies of the country exporting capital. Colonial policy further promotes militarism and increases armaments (Kautsky 1907b, 42).

In *Handelspolitik und Sozialdemokratie* (1911b (1901)) Kautsky for the first time developed his conception of the relation between agrarian and industrial countries − already discussed earlier (see chapter I.7.) − as the decisive cause of imperialism. The uneven development of the different sectors of capitalism is promoted to being the decisive factor creating imperialism and colonialism and leading to the application of imperialistic methods of government by the developed capitalist countries.

In *Handelspolitik und Sozialdemokratie* Kautsky further concretely identified im-perialism with a specific political method, customs policy; economic development leads to the centralisation of capital and the formation of trusts and cartels. High tariffs are in the economic interests of cartels. On the other hand, export and import tariffs are favourable to the formation of trusts and cartels. They are, thus, both the cause and the effect of the centralisation of capital:

"Die ganze ökonomische Entwicklung drängt die Kapitalisten zu Kartellen und Trusts. Nirgends aber gedeihen diese so leicht und gut, wie unter der Herrschaft des Schutzzolls; je höher dieser desto mehr können sie ihre Macht entfalten und ausnutzen. "(Kautsky 1911b, 39).

Protective tariffs further promote policies of repression, the annexation of colonies and trade wars. They are all essential companions to the "Schutzzöllesystem" (see Kautsky 1911b, 17).

In a way reminiscent of Lenin's and Luxemburg's discussion of imperialism Kautsky identified policies of violence with the monopolisation of capital and the formation of cartels. Violence is the essence of a cartel system:

"Gewalttätigkeit ist das Wesen der Kartellwirtschaft; mit gewaltsamen Mitteln suchen die Kartelle ihre Gegner niederzuwerfen und niederzuhalten; zunächst nicht mit Flinten und

Kanonen, aber mit den gewaltsamsten Mitteln des ökonomischen Kampfes. Das gilt natür-
lich nicht nur gegenüber den Konkurrenten und Konsumenten, sondern auch gegenüber
den Arbeitern." (Kautsky 1911b, 40).

Further:

"So erwächst an Stelle des Geistes des Freihandels ein Geist der Gewaltsamkeit in der
industriellen Bourgeoisie." (Kautsky 1911b, 41).

The prime purpose of the system of protective tariffs is not to promote industrial
development at home or to prevent its regression, but to raise the price of industrial
products and to sell them on the home market at a higher price than abroad (Kautsky
1911b, 43). The export of capital is another immediate result of this system. When the
customs barrier in the countries to which commodities are exported becomes high
enough and exporting of commodities becomes more difficult, it is more profitable to
establish industry and invest capital in foreign countries direct. As a consequence, the
development of productive forces in foreign countries is promoted while home industry
degenerates (see Kautsky 1911b, 48). Kautsky summarised the result of his analysis as
follows:

"Entwicklung der Industrie des Auslandes auf Kosten derjenigen des Inlandes, dass ist die
Signatur des neuen Schutzzolls zu dem der Merkantilperiod." (Kautsky 1911b, 48).

Even though Kautsky admitted (see Kautsky 1911b, 53) that protective tariffs are still
beneficial to some restricted groups of capitalists, seen from the wider perspective of
the realisation of socialism, the main problem of the system of protective tariffs lies in
its negative consequences for the development of productive forces:

". . . und gleichzeitig ist der Schutzzoll ein Mittel geworden, die ökonomische Entwicklung
zu hemmen; der für das Proletariat wie für die Gesamtgesellschaft günstige Zustand der
kapitalistischen Produktionweise ist aber der ihrer rascheren Entwicklung. Der Schutzzoll
ist also in jeder Beziehung ein Mittel geworden, die dem Proletariat günstigen Seiten der
kapitalistischen Gesellschaft zu beengen und die ihm ungünstigen zu entfalten. "(Kautsky
1911b, 71).

As a result of his analysis of imperialism and its causes, Kautsky could state that the
working class is the only social class which represent the general interest of the nation,
an interest interpreted as the most effective development of productive forces; at the
present stage of capitalism capitalists only represent their own specific interests as a
small fraction of society (see Kautsky 1911b, 55). This result also proves that the system
of protective tariffs cannot be opposed as such; a change in imperialist policy presupposes a general struggle against any form of capitalist exploitation. Increasing exploitation and the system of protective tariffs go hand in hand. The whole system of capitalism has to be opposed in order to improve the living conditions of wage workers (see
Kautsky 1911b, 78).

In the various articles and pamphlets written shortly before and during the First
World War Kautsky explicated and developed his conception of imperialism. Now, −

contrary to his earlier analysis — imperialism was seen to be the result of only one possible line of development of capitalism which can — at least in principle — be followed by another kind of development of capitalism. In the article *Der Imperialismus* (1913–14) the alternative to imperialism is called ultra-imperialism — reached via the extrapolation of the economic tendencies of capitalism and the centralisation of capital in particular. In the writings *Die Internationalität und der Krieg* (1915b) and *Nationalstaat, imperialistischer Staat und Staatenbund* (1915a) Kautsky's position had already changed. The alternative to imperialism was now the democratic union of states based on free trade and just trade treaties.[4] Whereas the first alternative is characteristically only a continuation of the negative tendencies and features of imperialism — a kind of extrapolation of the economic tendencies inherent in modern capitalism, and as such to be opposed by the proletariat and its organisations, the second alternative, characterised by Kautsky as a democratic union of states, is favourable both from the point of view of the proletariat and also of vast sectors of the population including industrial capitalists. Thus by introducing the idea of the union of democratic states, Kautsky proposed a critique of modern imperialism which did not necessarily have as its counterpoint a socialist society — as was the case in the earlier articles. There is another alternative open to capitalism, too, and in principle it would be possible to win the support of various groups in society for a programme aiming at the realisation of this alternative. The idea of a positive alternative to imperialism thus also has a direct impact on the strategic alternatives of Social Democracy as it, in principle, would seem to be possible to organise a 'democratic front' against imperialism.

The concept of ultra-imperialism is extrapolated from the analysis of the economic development of capitalism. The analysis of the different possibilities or different methods of enlarging production and the accumulation of capital also formed the basis for the analysis of ultra-imperialism. In this respect the article *Der Imperialismus* only repeated Kautsky's earlier statements. As already has been pointed out, in his analysis there were natural limits to the development of agrarian production (see Kautsky 1913–14, 914–15). Due to the different rates of increasing production in agriculture and industry there is a further problem of the permanent overproduction or oversupply of industrial products which can be solved only by continuously expanding the market for industrial products.

The export of industrial products to agrarian areas is, however, faced with the immediate problem of competion from other industrial countries:

> "Der Wunsch, dem entgegenzuwirken, wird für die kapitalistischen Staaten ein neues Motiv, sich die agrarische Gebiete direkt — als Kolonie — oder indirekt — als Industrie zu entwickeln, um sie zu zwingen, sich ganz auf die agrarische Produktion zu beschränken. Dies die wichtigsten Wurzel des Imperialismus, der den Freihandel abgelöst hat. (Kautsky 1913–14, 919).

---

[4] This alternative was already mentioned in the *Erfurt Programme* (1906a, 122) but Kautsky did not refer to it any more in his early writings on colonial policy.

Imperialism is thus a necessary consequence of international competion on industrial markets: the only means of guaranteeing the further realisation of a country's industrial products on the international market is to conquer and annex colonies.

So far Kautsky's reasoning in *Der Imperialismus* merely seemed to repeat an argumentation already presented in other writings. Kautsky did not, however, stop his argumentation at this stage. For he formulated a further proposal. The question of possible alternatives to imperialism was actualised:

> "Bildet er nun die letzte mögliche Erscheinungsform der kapitalistischen Weltpolitik oder ist noch eine andere möglich? Mit anderen Worten: Bietet der Imperialismus die einzige noch mögliche Form, den Wechselverkehr zwischen Industrie und Landwirtschaft innerhalb des Kapitalismus auszudehnen? Das ist die Frage." (Kautsky 1913—14, 919—920).

According to Kautsky there are two sides of any imperialistic policy. The first is connected with the production and import of raw materials and foodstuffs. This problem is an essential element of imperialism. Its solution presupposes the repression of local colonial populations (see Kautsky 1913—14, 920). The other side of imperialism is the sharpening of contradictions between industrial states themselves and the increase in militarism closely connected with it. And the only consequent end-result of this development is world war:

> "Aber der Imperialismus hat noch eine andere Seite. Das Streben nach Besetzung und Unterjochung der agrarischen Gebiete hat starke Gegensätze zwischen den kapitalistischen Industriestaaten hervorgerufen, Gegensätze die bewirken, dass das Wettrüsten, das ehedem nur eines der Landrüstungen war, nun auch eines der Seerüstungen wurde und die es in letzter Linie verursacht haben, dass der schon lange prophezierte Weltkrieg nun zur Tatsache geworden ist." (Kautsky 1913—14, 920).

The outbreak of world war has since become an established fact. It is only a logical consequence of the tendencies present in imperialism. It cannot, however, be claimed that the only alternative open to imperialism, once peace has been restored, is the continuation of the present methods of economic development; at least in principle there is another solution open to the future development of capitalism. The continuation of the present violent and repressive tendencies of imperialism is not the only alternative to capitalism:

> "Eine *ökonomische* Notwendigkeit für eine Fortsetzung des Wettrüstens nach dem Weltkrieg liegt nicht voraus, auch nicht vom Standpunkt der Kapitalistenklasse selbst, sondern höchstens vom Standpunkt einiger Rüstungsinteressen." (Kautsky 1913—14, 920).

Because the whole capitalist system is, in fact, threatened by the sharpening of the present contradictions in imperialism, it is in the interests of the very capitalists to prevent the collapse of capitalism:

> "Umgekehrt wird gerade die kapitalistische Wirtschaft durch die Gegensätze aufs äusserste bedroth. Jeder weitgehende Kapitalist muss heute seinen Genossen zurufen: Kapitalisten aller Länder, vereinigt euch." (Kautsky 1913—14, 920).

A continuation of the present policy of imperialism would obviously lead to early bankruptcy of the whole capitalist economy. Kautsky's main thesis was that this bankruptcy can in principle be prevented, and there are in fact such tendencies already present in modern caitalism which make its prevention possible; imperialism is basically the result of the centralisation of capital, the formation of cartels and trusts, and immense groupings of finance capital.

This very same centralisation of capital does, on the other hand, make it possible for imperialism to overcome its economic contradictions as the concentration of capital enters a completely new stage as soon as it reaches the whole international market. International cartels take the place of competing national capitalists. Most of the devastating results of international competition can then be overcome, and a new stage of imperialism, ultra-imperialism, is reached:

> "Die wütende Konkurrenz der Riesenbetriebe, Riesenbanken und Milliardäre erzeugte den Kartellgedanken der grossten Finanzmächte, die die kleinen schluckten. So kann auch jetzt aus dem Weltkrieg der imperialistischen Grossmächte ein Zusammenschluss der stärksten unter ihnen hervorgehen, der ihrem Wettrüsten ein Ende macht." (Kautsky 1913–14, 921).

Considering the economic tendencies of capitalism only it is thus possible to think that imperialism will reach a new stage; it should, however, be recognised that ultra-imperialism is only an economic possibility; it is possible that increasing political opposition to imperialism will overthrow capitalism even earlier, and that the working class will be able to establish a socialist society even before the stage of ultra-imperialism has been reached.

The concept of ultra-imperialism is an extrapolation of the economic tendencies of capitalism and of the centralisation of capital. It is at least possibly to think that the formation of cartels, now taking place so rapidly at national level exclusively, will in the near future also take place on the international market, and as a consequence international competition, which is at present leading to increasing contradictions between individual imperialistic states, will come to an end. It will be just as necessary for the working class to oppose ultra-imperialism as it is to fight the present imperialism, but ultra-imperialism would, in one respect, be more favourable to the majority of the people: it would not endanger world peace:

> "Vom rein ökonomischen Standpunkt ist es also nicht ausgeschlossen, dass der Kapitalismus noch eine neue Phase erlebt, die Übertragung der Kartellpolitik auf die äussere Politik, eine Phase des Ultraimperialismus, den wir natürlich ebenso energisch bekämpfen müssten wie den Imperialismus, dessen Gefahren aber in anderer Richtung liegen, nicht in der des Wettrüsten und der Gefährdung des Weltfriedens." (Kautsky 1913–14, 921).

There would, anyhow, be a natural limit to the development of ultra-imperialism, too, because industrial production can be increased only insofar as the supply of raw materials and the demand for its products increase, in other words, insofar as agrarian markets also expand:

"Rein ökonomisch betrachtet kann er sich weiterentwickeln, solange es der wachsenden Industrie der alten kapitalistischen Staaten möglich ist, eine entsprechende Ausdehnung der landwirtschaftlichen Produktion hervorrufen, was freilich mit der zunehmenden Grösse des jährlichen Wachstums der Industrie der Welt und der steten Verkleinerung des noch unerschlossenen agrarischen Gebiets immer schwieriger wird." (Kautsky 1913–14, 921).

In the end, even ultra-imperialism would thus be faced with the problem of the natural limits of agrarian production and agrarian markets. Even though a general, international cartel would solve some of the main economic problems of imperialism and prolong its survival, it would not eternalise capitalism in general; neither would it make the perspective of socialism obsolete.

The idea of ultra-imperialism developed by Kautsky shortly after the outbreak of war is especially interesting because of its connection with the wider debate on the future destiny of capitalism at the beginning of the century. In his *Das Finanzkapital* Rudolf Hilferding (1968) introduced – as has already been discussed earlier – the concept of a general cartel which is reached by extrapolation of the economic tendencies of capital, as well. According to Hilferding the formation of a general cartel would definitely transform the economic laws of capitalism. The only remaining problem or contradiction would be the conflict over the distribution of the national product. A general cartel would thus assume the role of the regulator of market relations in capitalism. This idea of a general cartel or ultra-imperialism was also widely discussed by Lenin, who principally accepted the future perspective of the development of a general cartel, though with some important reservations (according to him a general cartel is abstractly thinking a logical consequence of the economic tendencies in capitalism, but still it would be both economically and politically impossible for capitalist economy to develop into one single general cartel). (See in more detail pp. 110–111.)

It is not, however, altogether clear whether ultra-imperialism really would, even in Kautsky's opinion, be a realistic alternative to imperialism. Earlier, in another context, Kautsky seemed to deny quite explicitly the possibility of the emergence of an international cartel which would abolish competition.[5] In criticising Bernstein Kautsky had, on the other hand, long before the publication of Hilferding's *Finanzkapital* already acknowledged the theoretical possibility of the further development of the centralisation of capital into a cartel economy (see Kautsky 1899b:1).

It is, however, more important to note that the idea of an international general cartel is in a sense a logical conclusion of Kautsky's understanding of the historical development of capitalism: such an ultra-imperialism would be economically totally possible;

---

[5]   "Eine Regelung der Produktion durch die Kartelle setzt vor Allem voraus, dass sie alle wichtigen Produktionszweige umfassen und auf *internationaler Grundlage* aufgebaut sind, über sämtliche Länder der kapitalistischen Produktionsweise sich erstrecken. Bisher giebt es kein einziges internationales Kartell in einem der für das ganze Wirtschaftsleben massgebenden Industriezweige. (...) Marx hat schon mehr als fünfzig Jahren bemerkt, dass nicht nur die Konkurrenz das Monopol schafft, sondern durch das Monopol die Konkurrenz." (Kautsky 1906a, 94–95).

politically it would, however, be faced with such contradictions that the future development of capitalism in the direction of ultra-imperialism is actually highly improbable.[6]
Ultra-imperialism − as well as imperialism − are forms or methods of realising the
interests of finance capital (or big capital magnates). Ultra-imperialism and the establishment of a nation-wide general cartel, too, would reveal the exploitative nature of
capitalism in such a direct, crude form that people would not for a moment endure it.

The concept of ultra-imperialism is probably Kautsky's best-known formulation of
the future destiny of capitalism. It was, however, only presented in the article *Der
Imperialismus*. *Der Imperialismus* was, in fact, only Kautsky's first attempt to reformu-
late the stategy of Social Democracy after the outbreak of war. The outbreak of war
concretely proved that the strategy aimed at preventing world war was ineffective and
obsolete. In his writings published during the war, Kautsky still tried to defend the
strategy of the International before the war, and revised it to meet the new demands
and changing conditions. In his later writings he seems to have abandoned the idea of
ultra-imperialism, its place as a positive alternative to imperialism being taken by the
conception of a union of democratic states.

In the booklet *Nationalstaat, imperialistischer Staat und Staatenbund* (1915a) Kautsky
presented a new solution, a reorganisation of post-war international economic relations
which would prevent the development of any future contradictions and hostilities and
would guarantee the further development of capitalism, a development more favourable to the working class, as well. The alternative to imperialism as proposed by him
was a democratic union of states based on a common trade treaty and free trade. This
new proposition respected the criteria of democracy of nations and their right to self-
determination:

"Die Demokratie und die mit ihr eng verbundene Idee des Nationalstaates fordern, das der
Statusquo *nicht geändert werde ohne Zustimmung der davon betroffenen Bevölkerungen.*"
(Kautsky 1915a, 14).

------

[6] Even a general cartel including the whole production of a nation could not possibly survive
its political contradictions:

"... dass die Tendenz der kapitalistischen Produktionsweise dahin geht, die Produktionsmittel, welche das Monopol der Kapitalistenklasse geworden sind, in immer weniger und
weniger Händen zu vereinigen. Diese Entwicklung läuft schliesslich darauf hinaus, dass die
gesamten Produktionsmittel einer Nation, ja der ganzen Weltwirtschaft, das Privateigenthum einer einzelnen Person oder Aktiengesellschaft werden, die darüber nach Willkür
verfügt; dass das ganze wirtschaftliche Getriebe zu einem einzigen ungeheuren Betrieb
zusammengefasst wird, in dem Alles einem einzigen Herrn zu dienen hat, einem einzigen
Herrn gehört. Das Privateigenthum an den Produktionsmitteln führt in der kapitalistischen
Gesellschaft dahin, dass Alle besitzlos sind, einen Einzigen ausgenommen. (...) In der That
wäre ein Zustand, wie der hier geschilderte, ebenso ungeheuerlich wie unmöglich. Es wird
und kann nie dazu kommen. Denn die blosse Annäherung an diesen Zustand muss die
Leiden, Gegensätze und Widersprüche in der Gesellschaft zu einer solchen Höhe treiben,
dass sie unerträglich werden, dass die Gesellschaft aus ihren Fugen geht und zusammen-
bricht, wenn der Entwicklung nicht schon früher eine andere Richtung gegeben wird."
(Kautsky 1906a, 83−84).

Even though the solution is new, Kautsky's analysis of the causes of imperialism followed the arguments mainly presented earlier: The decisive cause of imperialism is the
opposition between agrarian and industrial regions. The agrarian regions which industrial states are trying to annex are primitive and underdeveloped. They have not, furthermore, reached the stage of democracy, because the material conditions of democracy have not yet been developed (see Kautsky 1915a, 15). There is, in fact, thus a
civilising influence in imperialism, viz. the development of the productive forces in
colonies and of the ensuing material conditions for democracy is the historical task of
imperialism. Thus imperialism is by nature not altogether reactionary.

According to Kautsky, imperialism is an economic necessity under the present conditions of capitalism, and it has also been acknowledged as such by the proletariat. The
working class in the industrial countries is interested in the most effective development
of the productive forces, and it suffers mostly under a degenerating phase of capitalism
(see Kautsky 1915a, 17). It is true that the elasticity and adaptability of capitalism
increases during imperialism as production becomes scientific and is revolutionised. It
would, however, be wrong to associate this fact with any increased ability of capitalism
to outlast its present stage (see Kautsky 1915a, 20−21).

No economic catastrophe that would of necessity lead to the final overthrow of
capitalism can therefore be expected − a thought to be understood as a general critique
of economic determinism. The overthrow of capitalism will not be an automatic result
of economic development, it will result out of political struggle.

The most important explanation of imperialism presented in *Nationalstaat, imperialistischer Staat und Staatenbund* is the thought that even though imperialism is a consequence of the economic tendencies of capitalism, it is by no means a necessary result of
these tendencies − a thought also presented in other writings:

> "...dann wird man nicht mehr ohne weiteres aus der Tatsache, dass der Imperialismus
> seine starken ökonomischen Triebkräfte im Kapitalismus findet, einfach schliessen, er sei
> unvermeidlich, so lange die kapitalistische Produktionsweise bestehe, und es sei ein Un-
> sinn, ihm innerhalb dieser Produktionsweise widerstehen zu wollen." (Kautsky 1915a, 21).

The increasing export of means of production instead of intustrial products in general is
a tendency of great importance (see Kautsky 1915a, 24). The new maxim of capital is to
try to sell as much as possible and to buy as little as possible, and when every state
favours this kind of policy, the conflicts are ready at hand. The centralisation of capital,
the combination of finance with industrial capital and the changing patterns of foreign
trade are, in fact, tendencies that will remain intact as long as capitalism prevails. On
the other hand, the methods used by the state to promote these tendencies − colonialism and imperialistic expansion − are not as such unavoidable (see Kautsky 1915a, 22).
Even at present there are modern examples of another approach to these problems.
There already exist unions of states of another kind (the United States of America and
South Africa or the "Burenrepublik"), which concretely prove that there is at hand
another method that is both effective and possible:

"Imperialistische Bedürfnisse haben an seiner Bildung sicher mitgewirkt, aber die Land-erwerbungen, auf denen er sich aufbaut, wurden, mit Ausnahme der Burenrepublik, ein Jahrhundert von der Aera des Imperialismus vollzogen, und der enge Zusammenhang dieses Bundes wurde allen Beteiligten zum Bedürfnis gemacht durch das Gegenteil dieser Methoden, durch die Anziehungskraft der Demokratie und, was hier gleich gesagt sei, durch die des Freihandels des Mutterlandes." (Kautsky 1915a, 41).

The imperialistic methods of expansion are by no means the most effective ones, and industrial capital in particular can profit more from other methods. Its commodities can be more effectively exported under the conditions of free trade not restricted by im-perialistic customs policy (see Kautsky 1915a, 70). The best method for guaranteeing the export of commodities and the import of raw materials would be an effective treaty between all industrial states, as a result of which their mutual trade would all but resemble free trade (see Kautsky 1915a, 73). Such treaties would, according to Kauts-ky, be the most effective guarantee of peace and economic development in the future:

"Der Staatenbund und nicht der Nationalitätenstaat, auch nicht der Kolonialstaat, dass ist die Form für die grossen Imperien, deren der Kapitalismus bedarf, um seine letzte, höchste Form zu erreichen, in der das Proletariat sich seiner bemächtigen wird." (Kautsky 1915a, 75).

Kautsky's favourite thought of the two possible ways of developing capitalism was repeated intact in this writing as well. The first method is based on the most rapid development of the productivity of labour and productive forces. The second method is based on the increasing direct and violent exploitation of labour. The first method is to be preferred, because it promotes the cause of socialism and the interests of the work-ing class in general:

"Die Möglichkeit liegt darin, dass es verschiedener Arten gibt, den Kapitalismus zu för-dern. (...) Zur ersten Methode gehört die Einführung neuer Maschinen, besserer Organisa-tionsformen der Produktion und des Betriebs, Erfahrung niedriger durch höherer Be-triebsformen, von Kleinbetrieb durch Grossbetrieb, Bau- oder Verbesserung von Verkehrsmitteln, höhere Bildung und physische Kräftigung der Arbeiter, wissenschaftliche Gestaltung des Produktionsprozesses. "(Kautsky 1915a, 78).

The first method could also lead to greater suffering among the vorking class, but it still creates better potential for its emancipation.

It is, however, impossible simply to choose between the two methods according to the preference of the working class. The actual choice between the methods is made by power. As long as finance capital and its allies and representatives are in power, the second method will prevail and the development of capitalism will be limited. The task of the working class is to fight for the adoption of the first method and to win the support of other sections of the population for this common cause through propaganda and agitation. It should be remenbered that this 'people's front' is potentially a very conclusive one. Even the industrial capitalists can, at least in principle, be included in it. And because the adoption of imperialistic policy is purely a question of power, it can at any time be replaced by more democratic and peaceful methods of foreign trade:

> "Und darum muss dem Imperialismus gegenüber dasselbe gelten, was den Lohnherabset-
> zungen, der Verlängerung der Arbeitszeit, der Erhöhung der Lebensmittelpreise durch
> Steuern und Zölle u.s.w. gegenüber gilt − entschiedne Bekämpfung, nicht um den ökono-
> mischen Fortschritt zu hemmen, sondern um die Kapitalistenklasse zu zwingen, die Ver-
> grösserung ihres Profits, die Ausbeutung ihres Ausbeutungsgebiets, Vermehrung der Aus-
> fuhr industrielle Produkte, der Einfuhr von Lebensmitteln und Rohstoffen nicht mehr
> durch die nächstliegenden und bequemsten Methoden des Imperialismus, sondern durch
> die freilich mehr Geist erfordenden Methoden der Demokratie und des freien Verkehrs zu
> suchen, die dem ökonomischen Forstscritt die weitesten Bahnen eröffnen, dabei aber auch
> das Proletariat physisch, geistig, politisch kräftigen." (Kautsky 1915a, 80).

Nothing would, in Kautsky's opinion, be a greater mistake than to think that the
materialist conception of history makes it impossible to fight against imperialism. To
oppose imperialism is, on the contary, the most important and immediate task of the
whole working class today (see Kautsky 1915a, 80).

The strategy of the Social Democrats in opposing imperialism could be compared
with their attitude towards technical progress in capitalism. The motive force of capitalism is profit, but there are always different methods of promoting this goal. The Social
Democrats should not, for instance, oppose technical progress as such − the introduction of new machines, the centralisation of capital, the scientific organisation of work,
etc. − even though it is in the interests of capital accumulation. While increasing the
rate of exploitation and surplus value, technical progress due to the accumulation of
capital is also beneficial to the working class. Technological progress improves both the
conditions of revolutionary socialism and the material position of the wage workers. It
is the task of the Social Democrats to guarantee that the workers get their share of the
benefits of capital accumulation. In this sense the Social Democrats are able to combine
the fight for socialism with the fight for the improvement of the position of the working
class in capitalism:

> "Auf diese Weise löst die Sozialdemokratie den anscheinenden Widerspruch ihrer histori-
> schen Aufgabe, bekämpft und fördert sie gleichzeitig den Kapitalismus. "(Kautsky 1915a,
> 79).

The result of Kautsky's analysis of imperialism could be summarised as follows: There
are two methods for promoting the economic expansion of modern capitalism. One is
imperialism, the other is the expansion of free trade and the establishment of varying
degrees of international political and economic association. Both methods fulfill the
functions of capital expansion and aim at solving the problems of permanent overproduction. The first method, based on restrictive tariffs and colonial policy, will sharpen
the contradictions between nations and further militarism and militant policy. It is also
undemocratic because it is based on the repression of both the colonial people and the
working class at home. Hence it does not promote the struggle for socialism. The
second method is that of international economic associations. It is both democratic and,
furthermore, more advantageous for the rapid economic and technological development
of capitalism. This method is also antimilitaristic and the only possibility of avoiding
devastating world war in the future.

There seems to be an interesting paradox in Kautsky's thinking. Even though imperialism is caused by the economic development of capitalism, imperialism is at the same time disadvantageous to its further development even from the point of view of capital accumulation. Why, then, is it the prevalent form of capitalist expansion? Kautsky's answer was simple: imperialism is a pure question of power (see Kautsky 1915b, 22). To understand imperialism we must, consequently, analyse the power relations in modern capitalism and the economic interests of the different power groups. Theoretically the analysis is relatively clear. Imperialism is supported by and is exclusively in the interests of the big capital magnates, finance capital. The rest of the nation − with the exclusion of the big land owners − does not have any direct economic interests in the future of imperialism; all the people are − at least potentially − opponents of imperialism. The role of power in Kautsky's analysis becomes even more accentuated because imperialism is not actually even in the economic interests of the industrial capitalists; in the last instance it does not even effectively promote the industrial development and technological progress of the nation and the accumulation of capital.

In adopting the idea of the central role of finance capital in modern capitalism Kautsky was able to determine the only genuine supporters of imperialism, the representatives of finance capital. There is a major difference between the economic interests of industrial and finance capital as such. Industrial capital is a supporter of peace and democracy. From a historical perspective it was interested in restricting the economic power of the absolutist state − and its political goal is saving in fiscal policy and state expenditure. Industrial capital is not interested in restrictive tariffs on raw materials and foodstuffs because they are apt to raise the costs of production. Industrial tariffs are accepted only in cases of industrial backwardness. (See Kautsky 1915a, 23.)

The political and economic orientation of finance capital is totally different:

> "Das Finanzkapital dagegen, die Klasse der grossen Geldverleiher und Bankiers, neigt zur Förderung der absoluten Staatsgewalt, nach gewalttätiger Durchsetzung ihrer Ansprüche nach Innen und Aussen. Es hat eine Intresse an grossen Staatsausgaben und Staatsschulden (...) Es steht auf gutem Fuss mit dem grossen Grundbesitz und hat gegen dessen Begünstigung durch agrarische Zölle nicht einzuweden." (Kautsky 1915a, 23).

Economic development has brought finance capital into power. With the introduction of the joint stock companies the biggest industrial capitalists have been united with finance capital. The close relation between industrial and money capital is a characteristic feature of imperialism (see Kautsky 1915a, 22):

> "Damit werden die grössten und stärksten Teile des industriellen Kapitals mit dem Geldkapital vereinigt, zugleich aber auch ihre Verständigung mit dem grossen Grundbesitz angebahnt. Trusts und die Zentralisation der Grossbanken treiben diese Entwicklung auf die Spitze." (Kautsky 1915a, 23).

Because of the union of industrial and money capital, the political interests of finance capital become the general interests of the ruling class:

> "Die staatlichen Tendenzen des Finanzkapitals wurden jetzt zu allgemeinen Tendenzen der gesamten ökonomisch herrschenden Klassen der kapitalistisch fortgeschrittenen Staaten. Das ist das Kennzeichen der heutigen Periode, die man als die imperialistische bezeichnet." (Kautsky 1915a, 23).

Thus, Kautsky concluded that the united industrial and finance capital is the new power block supporting imperialism, which lends further support to the thesis that imperialism really is only a pure question of power; it is the result of the economic and political domination of finance capital, domination not only in relation to the "people" but also within the capitalist class as such. Finance capital has forced the industrialists to adopt imperialist policy even though it is not even beneficial to future industrial developments.

In his last article on imperialism *Der imperialistische Krieg* (1916—17a) written during the war Kautsky again repeated many of the arguments presented in most of his earlier writings. According to him, it is important to understand that even though the war was in fact of an imperialistic nature, it could not be explained by the economic factors of imperialism exclusively. And what is even more important, imperialism would not be at all necessary for the future development of capitalism. And Kautsky repeated his former arguments about imperialism being only one possible method of appropriating extra profit — the motive force of every single capital — and even though the appropriation of extra profits is the decisive motive force of capitalism which will remain in power as long as capitalism prevails, there are also other ways of guaranteeing the effective appropriation of profits, and accumulation of capital (see Kautsky 1916—17a, 475). Imperialism is only a question of power, in the very same sense as the determination of the length of the normal work day.

The big capitalists try to reach a monopoly position on the international market with the support of their state by establishing both protective tariffs and colonies. And it is this very policy that is called imperialism. It would not be at all necessary for the future of capitalism:

> "Sie ist nicht eine Notwendigkeit für den Fortgang der industriellen Produktion unter der Herrschaft des Kapitalismus, sondern nur eine der Methoden der Gewinnung von Extraprofit. Durch ihre Bekämpfung und Einschränkung wird die Industrie ebensowenig gehemmt wie durch einen Normalarbeitstag." (Kautsky 1916—17a, 477).

Kautsky did not tire of repeating that imperialism is purely a question of power, and that the future of imperialism is accordingly decided by the respective power of its opponents and adherents. Imperialism does not, furthermore, characterise the policy of all the capitalist countries. It is only characteristic of the big capitalist states (see Kautsky 1916—17a, 482). Imperialism thus is, and in this respect Kautsky is consequent in all his writings, only a specific economic policy of capitalism which — by all means — is influenced by the economic development of capitalism (the centralisation of capital, the domination of finance over industrial capital, the problem of industrial and raw material markets, and the problem of overproduction and underconsumption). It is not, however, totally determined by these economic tendencies or factors. Both the problem of markets and of the appropriation of extra profits can be solved through means and methods other than imperialism.

The main strategic conclusion drawn by Kautsky from his analysis is, then, that it is both rational and possible to oppose the use of imperialistic methods in capitalism. The only possible alternatives open to capitalism are not socialism or war (or socialism or barbarism), there is also another alternative open for the further development, an alternative which would be democratic by its nature and more effective in promoting the development of productive forces.

There is an interesting shift in emphasis in Kautsky's thinking on modern capitalism revealed in comparing the *Erfurt Programme* and the writings on imperialism in the beginning of the century with the studies written during the war. In the earlier writings the formation of cartels is connected with the problem of the decreasing rate of profit, and the introduction of tariffs and colonial policy is explained by overproduction and the realisation problems of cartels. The general contradiction between industrial and agrarian production was further emphasised by Kautsky as an explanation of imperialism. These explanations were preserved intact in the later writings, as well; but now the political power of the finance capital was understood to be the basic factor promoting imperialism. In Kautsky's later writings colonial policy and imperialism were explained as being adopted mainly because they are in the central interests of the cartels, or rather finance capital. Both the explanations are, however, easy to combine. In the earlier discussion the explanation of the source of extra profit was essentially a political one, as well; cartels are able to appropriate high profits due to the economic policy of the bourgeois state including annexation of colonies and high import tariffs. The state is a political instrument in the hands of big cartels and the finance capital.

Kautsky always seemed to think and even wanted to emphasise that imperialism is only one of the several possible alternatives or methods of the economic policy of the state — a method guaranteeing the profits of centralised capital or high finance. According to Kautsky, imperialism is mainly a political method for coping with the problem of the relation between industrial and agrarian countries and the overproduction in general inherent in capitalism. In this sense it is a result of the economic development of capitalism, and it includes policies of protective tariffs and regional expansion in the form of colonies. There are strong economic interests in modern capitalism supporting imperialist policies: protective tariffs, raw material resources and colonial markets are in the interests of the monopolistic capital associations as a means of securing extra profits and continuous accumulation of capital. There are, however, other alternatives which are more favourable to the development of capitalism and the future of the working class in capitalism, too.

In Kautsky's analysis imperialism then is more of an exception in the development of capitalism caused by a rather specific and historically exceptional constellation of political and economic forces in the developed capitalist countries during the last decades of the 19th century. It is by no means the necessary outcome of the economic development

of capitalism in Europe. There are other politically and economically superior alternatives open to capitalism besides imperialism. The future of imperialism is only a question of power.

Ever since the publication of Kautsky's main writings on imperialism he has been
criticised for his characterisation of imperialism as only one possible alternative to the
future development of capitalism. An early and perhaps the best known critique came
from Lenin, who criticised him for his exclusively political definition of imperialism (see
next chapter; see also Kraus 1978, 210). In this respect one can agree with John H.
Kautsky's interpretation of Karl Kautsky's theory of imperialism as presented in his
article on A. Schumpeter and Karl Kautsky:

> "Whether Kautsky inclined to the Schumpeterian 'pre-industrial' or the Hilferdingian 'in-
> dustrial' explanation of imperialism certain elements of his thought remained constant; it
> was banking capital rather than industrial capital in its pure form that was a driving force, if
> not the driving force, of imperialism; ... and finally, imperialism was merely one possible
> form of the general and inevitable phenomenon of industrial expansionism into agrarian
> areas and hence was not necessary to capitalism." (John H. Kautsky 1961, 118).

The same argument was presented even more forcefully by Rainer Kraus:

> "Der Grundzug der Kautskyanischen Imperialismustheorie besteht seit den achtziger
> Jahren des vorigen Jahrhunderts in dem Versuch, die Haltlosigkeit nahezu aller
> Argumente für eine koloniale Expansion, soweit sie ihre Notwendigkeit für das ökonomi-
> sche Ueberlegen der bürgerlichen Gesellschaft präjudizieren, nachzuweisen." (Kraus 1978,
> 171).

Even though Kautsky did not simply think of imperialism as being an atavism in
capitalism caused by the precapitalist remnants in society, and even though Kautsky's
theory is not in this respect identical to J.A. Hobson's, Joseph Schumpeter's and Emil
Lederer's conceptions as claimed by Gottschalch (see 1962, 89), it is, however, true,
that Kautsky understood imperialism as being more of an exception in the normal
development of capitalism. Imperialism is both a permanent problem caused by the
unequal development of industrial and agrarian production and a politically avoidable
problem to be eliminated as soon as the power of finance capital could be eliminated.

9. IMPERIALISM AS THE LAST STAGE OF CAPITALISM

As already stated earlier, Kautsky's conception of imperialism resembled that of Lenin's in many respects. To both of them imperialism is a consequence of the centralisation and monopolisation of capital and the formation of cartels and trusts. The centralisation of capital is, further, a necessary feature of capitalism. Another characteristic feature of imperialism is the power and domination of finance capital over industrial capital, and the importance of the export of capital compared with the export of commodities. Kautsky's emphasis of the role of protective tariffs did not, on the other hand, figure in Lenin's analysis — a fact already indicating that Kautsky, more than Lenin, analysed imperialism as a concrete historical form of the economic policy of the state. Neither did the idea of the difference and conflict between agrarian and industrial countries and production explain the annexation of colonies and their economic importance to Lenin — even though it was mentioned by Lenin, as well. For Kautsky, this difference was the most important single cause of imperialistic policy. The main and decisive difference is, however, that whereas Kautsky understood imperialism as a specific political method of guaranteeing the profits of capital, Lenin also considered imperialism as being a specific and necessary stage in the economic development of capitalism.

To Lenin the future of capitalism was by nature necessarily violent; it represented the repression of the people and led to the stagnation of productive forces and repressive methods of government. In the analysis of imperialism of both Kautsky and Lenin there was, however, one more important common characteristic: power is the new decisive factor in imperialism and relations of power and dominance replace relations of a purely economic character in imperialism.

In defining imperialism as the monopolistic phase of capitalism Lenin did not yet differ essentially from Kautsky's analysis. Neither Kautsky nor Lenin discussed in any great detail the nature of the transformation of free competition into monopolistic competition. They simply stated that monopolistic competition — to a certain extent — takes the place of free competition and that this transformation is made possible by the centralisation of capital — at least in the internal market. It must nevertheless be admitted that Lenin discussed the relation between free competition and monopolistic competition in more detail than Kautsky. To Kautsky the monopolistic organisations were simply the most influential power organisations in a society realising their interests in state policy. Kautsky did not formulate any explicit conception of competition in capitalism.

According to Lenin, monopoly is the economic essence of imperialism. This definition must, however, be complemented by a list of other defining characteristics of imperialism:

> "And so (...), we must give a definition of imperialism that will include the following five of its basic features: 1) the concentration of production and capital has developed to such a high stage that it has created monopolies which play a decisive role in economic life; 2) the merging of bank capital with industrial capital, and the creation, on the basis of this 'finance capital', of a financial oligarchy; 3) the export of capital as distinguished from the export of commodities acquires exceptional importance; 4) the formation of international monopolist capitalist associations which share the world among themselves; and 5) the territorial division of the whole world among the biggest capitalist powers is completed." (Lenin SW 1, 745–746).

Having presented the above list, Lenin was ready to formulate a 'more complete' definition of imperialism:

> "Imperialism is capitalism at the stage of development at which the dominance of monopolies and finance capital is established; in which the export of capital has acquired pronounced importance; in which the division of the world among the international trusts has begun, in which the division of all territories of the globe among the biggest capitalists has been completed." (Lenin SW 1, 746).

Immediately after presenting his own 'definition' of imperialism, Lenin criticised Kautsky's conception. According to Lenin, Kautsky made two grave mistakes in his analysis of imperialism. To begin with, Kautsky's conception of imperialism was restricted to a certain specific political method of capitalist states. The second mistake was that Kautsky emphasised imperialism as being equivalent to the method of annexation of colonies. Kautsky's definition of imperialism as a specific political form or method of capitalist states was as such correct, but in Lenin's opinion incomplete. Kautsky forgot that imperialism is essentially reactionary and violent by nature. At least in this respect Lenin's critique of Kautsky was, however, misdirected. On several occasions Kautsky stated explicitly that imperialism is reactionary and violent in character. Lenin's critique of the economic causes of imperialism as formulated by Kautsky was, however, more adequate. According to Lenin, Kautsky was mistaken in indentifying the causes of imperialism with the complex and problematic relation between industrial and agrarian capital. Imperialism cannot be adequately characterised as representing the interests of industrial capital in enlarging the market for its products; the dominating form of capital in imperialism is finance capital. Furthermore, the annexation of agrarian areas or countries as colonies of industrial states is not as such typical only of imperialism. Imperialism is, on the contrary, characterised by the struggle for hegemony over industrial countries, as well (see Lenin SW 1, 746–748).

Kautsky's main failure in analysing imperialism was, however, that in distinguishing between political and economic factors in imperialism he claimed that there is possibly another kind of policy in modern capitalism which would satisfy the interests of industrial capital as well as imperialism and which would not be violent and reactionary in character (see Lenin SW 1, 748). Lenin's conclusion in his critical analysis of Kautsky's conception of imperialism was that Kautsky had become a reformist and an enemy of Marxism:

> "The result is a slurring over and a blunting of the most profound contradictions of the latest stage of capitalism, instead of an exposure of their depth; the result is bourgeois reformism instead of Marxism." (Lenin SW 1, 748–749).

The main target of Lenin's critique was, however, Kautsky's concept of ultra-imperialism. Lenin did in principle admit that the economic development of capitalism would lead to the formation of one single worldwide trust. On one occasion Lenin even referred to the possible formation of a super-monopoly (see Lenin SW 1, 728). But such a prophecy would be totally devoid of interest (see Lenin SW 1, 750). Compared with the actual development of the world economy at the beginning of the century, the conception of ultra-imperialism could, furthermore, be shown to contradict the actual state of affairs. Kautsky's conception was, after all, dangerous. It lent support to the legitimation of imperialism in emphasising the possibility of a non-contradictory development of capitalism. According to Kautsky, capitalism can develop without crises; in reality, imperialism sharpens these contradictions and increases the occurrence of crises in capitalism (see Lenin SW 1, 750):

> "Are not the international cartels which Kautsky imagines are the embryos of 'ultra-imperialism' (...) an example of the division *and the redivision* of the world, the transition from peaceful division to non-peaceful division and vice versa?" (Lenin SW 1, 751–752).

And further:

> "Finance capital and the trusts do not diminish but increase the differences in the rate of growth of the various parts of the world economy. Once the relation of forces is changed, what other solution of the contradictions can be found *under capitalism* than that of *force?*" (Lenin SW 1, 752).

As Lenin stated, it is exactly the characterisation of imperialism as only one specific and possible form of the politics of a capitalist state which does not pay any attention to the fact that imperialism is a necessary consequence of the development of capitalism which marks the main difference between their conceptions.[1] Lenin did not furthermore

---

[1]   This major difference in the interpretations of the essential nature of imperialism was already explicitly formulated by Karl Radek in the article *Zum unseren Kampf gegen den Imperialismus:*

> "Die Grundlage aller Differenzen in unserem Verhältnis zum Imperialismus bildet *die Frage nach seinem Charakter.* Was ist der Imperialismus, welches ist sein Verhältnis zur kapitalistischen Entwicklung überhaupt, zur weltwirtschaftlichen Expansion im Beson-

approve of Kautsky's 'deduction' of imperialism from the different conditions of industrial and agrarian production. On the other hand, he did not pay attention to the fact that Kautsky repeatedly mentioned both monopolisation and the dominance of finance capital as the main causes of imperialism, too. The main target of his critique was quite obviously and repeatedly not so much the fact that Kautsky did not understand the economic 'essence' of imperialism (imperialism as monopolistic capitalism). Kautsky was to be criticised mainly because his analysis led to the dangerous conclusion that imperialism can develop into a new stage of peaceful and non-aggressive capitalism. It is exactly this conclusion that made Kautsky's conception essentially a reformist one, to be criticised as such.[2]

On the other hand there is, in fact, not such a big difference between Lenin and Kautsky in their evaluation of the consequences of imperialism for the future of capitalism. According to both of them, imperialism leads to the application of violent methods in politics and militarism at home and in foreign relations. In Lenin's opinion:

> "...domination, and the violence that is associated with it, such are the relationships that are typical of the 'latest phase of capitalist development'." (Lenin SW 1, 694).

Democratic methods of government are displaced by repressive and reactionary ones, economic competition as the regulatory principle of capitalism is displaced by the power and dominance of finance capital. Imperialism further leads to the stagnation of productive forces and the sharpening of crisis development both internationally and nationally. Lenin's conception of the consequences of imperialism for the economic progress of capitalism did not either markedly differ from Kautsky's corresponding formulations. Kautsky would accept all the conclusions drawn by Lenin, as well:

> "As we have seen, the deepest economic foundation of imperialism is monopoly. This is capitalist monopoly, i.e. monopoly which has grown out of capitalism and which exists in the general environment of capitalism, commodity production and competition, in permanent and insoluble contradiction to this general environment. Nevertheless, like all monopoly, it inevitably engenders a tendency of stagnation and decay. Since monopoly prices are established, even temporarily, the motive cause of technical and, consequently, of all other progress disappears to a certain extent and, further, the *economic* possibility arises of deliberately retarding technical progress." (Lenin SW 1, 754).

---

deren? Ist er *die* auswärtige Politik des krachenden Kapitalismus oder *eine* der noch jetzt möglichen Formen der kapitalistischen Machtentfaltung?" (Radek 1911–12, 194). Radek's own answer to the question is obvious:
> "Der Imperialismus ist *die einzig mögliche Weltpolitik der jetzigen kapitalistischen Epoche.*" (Radek 1911–12, 199). Socialism is the only alternative to imperialism: "Sozialismus oder Wüten des imperialistischen Bandes" (Radek 1911–12, 239).

[2] For a modern Marxist-Leninist evaluation of the elements of both genuine Marxism (read: Marxism-Leninism) and revisionism in Kautsky's thinking about imperialism, see Braionovič 1982, 181–188; see also Braionovič 1979, 208–219).

Kautsky's most serious mistake — according to Lenin — was, however, in imagining that capitalism would develop more rapidly and more effectively if free competition were re-established and it were not restricted by monopolies or finance capital. Lenin claimed that even though it might be presupposed that capitalism would develop more rapidly under the conditions of free competition, this presupposition is completely abstract. Kautsky forgot that the very development of capitalism necessarily gives rise to the permanent monopolisation and centralisation of capital:

> "And monopolies have *already* arisen — precisely *out of* free competition! Even if monopolies have now begun to retard progress, it is not an argument in favour of free competition, which has become impossible after it has given rise to monopoly." (Lenin SW 1, 765).

In other words, Kautsky did not understand that the process of monopolisation is an unavoidable result of capitalist development and as such an irreversible process. And because of this mistake, Kautsky became a reactionary and a reformist (see Lenin SW 1, 765).

In Lenin's analysis imperialism was not only the necessary consequence of capitalist development, it was also the immediate predecessor of socialism. There is no other alternative to imperialism but socialism, and on the other hand, the preconditions for socialism practically ripen in imperialism. These conclusions are already included in the very definition of imperialism as monopoly capitalism:

> "This in itself determines its place in history, for monopoly that grows out of the soil of free competition, and precisely out of free competition, is the transition from the capitalist system to a higher socio-economic order." (Lenin SW 1, 772—773).

Imperialism is thus the immediate transitory stage from capitalism to socialism which determines its place in human history:

> "From all that has been said in this book on the economic essence of imperialism, it follows that we must define it as capitalism in transition, or, more precisely, as moribund capitalism." (Lenin SW 1, 775—776).

The development of capitalism into imperialism was thus argued by Lenin to be an inevitable and irreversible consequence of the economic development of capitalism. The contradictions of capitalism are furthermore accentuated in imperialism. According to Lenin, the relations of private property which are preserved intact even in imperialism no longer correspond to its relations of production:

> "Production becomes social, but appropriation remains private." (Lenin SW 1, 693).

Thus Lenin seemed to round off his argumentation of the consequences of imperialism following Engels' formulation of the basic contradiction of capitalism. But in Lenin's analysis this basic contradiction took a new form and was even accentuated in imperialism. Due to the monopolisation of production "the social means of production remain the private property of a few" (Lenin SW 1, 693), even fewer than before. And in imperialism the contradiction between private appropriation and socialisation of pro-

duction becomes even more accentuated as the contradiction between "formally recognised free competition" and the factual "monopolistic competition". As a consequence
"the yoke of a few monopolists on the rest of the population becomes a hundred times
heavier, more burdensome and intolerable" (Lenin SW 1, 693). In imperialism the
basic contradiction of capitalism is developed to its utmost form, and, consequently, the
relations of private property must give way to a socialisation of the means of production
which recognises that the means of production are, in fact, already in capitalism, social
means of production.

10. THEORETICAL SOURCES OF KAUTSKY'S AND LENIN'S STUDIES ON IMPERIALISM

Lenin formulated his conception of imperialism as a specific stage of capitalism for the first time in his *The War and Russian Social-Democracy* of 1914 (see Lenin SW 1, 657–663; see also Vasilevskij 1969, 89). Before this, at the end of the previous and in the beginning of the present century, Lenin had, however, already studied the concentration of capital and the production and the influence of monopolies in capitalism. The problem of transformation of crisis development was also the subject of study in these writings. According to Lenin, it is continuously claimed that monopolies can change the development of crises but forgotten that they cannot totally eliminate them. The same question figures in many of Lenin's later writings. He also published articles on finance capital, worldwide syndicates and the mutual links between monopolies and state. (See Leontev 1969.)

In 1915 Lenin published his *Socialism and War*, which already included a formulation of all the basic characteristics of imperialism mentioned in *Imperialism as the Highest Stage of Capitalism*: imperialism is the highest stage of capitalim, which became the dominating form of capitalism at the end of the last century; the concentration of capital led to the increasing power of syndicates and cartels in various fields of industry; organised capitalists divided almost the whole globe among themselves and subsumed it under finance control and exploitation; free trade and competition were transformed into monopoly; the export of capital became important in international trade; from a former liberator of nations capitalism was transformed into their oppressor (see Lenin CW 21, 301; see also Rozental 1973, 141–142). In writing his work on imperialism Lenin set out to reveal the "economic essence" of imperialism — and this economic essence was shown to be the monopoly.

Lenin's study of imperialism was a part of a large and wide interest in the emerging new phenomena of capitalism studied and analysed by Marxists and non-Marxists scholars and theoreticians. There are, however, four works on imperialism which influenced Lenin's own conception more than others: Rudolf Hilferding's *Das Finanzkapital*, Rosa Luxemburg's *Die Akkumulation des Kapitals*, Karl Kautsky's *Nationalstaat, imperialistischer Staat und Staatenbund* (and other writings by Kautsky, e.g. *Der Imperialismus*) and J. Hobson's *Imperialism*. These studies influenced Lenin's theoretical conceptions

more or less directly.[1] The idea of the importance of the export of capital and of rentier
states stems from Hobson. Luxemburg and Kautsky figured more as negative examples
for Lenin, to be criticised for their mistakes. Lenin's relation with them was highly
polemical. Luxemburg's analysis of imperialism, which was well known among Marxists
in the beginning of the century, was not referred to in Lenin's study but it is known
from other sources (Lenin's notebooks on imperialism) that Lenin regarded Luxemburg's theory as false and that he planned to write a separate analysis to prove it. (See
Leontev 1969, 87.)

The importance of capital export exceeded the importance of the export of commodities in both Lenin's and Kautsky's analysis of imperialism. To Lenin the role of capital
export was even more important than to Kautsky; the fact that capitalist states become
rentier states and live on the rents received from profitable investments in colonies is
one of the main characteristics of imperialism. As already pointed out, Lenin relied
heavily on Hilferding's *Das Finanzkapital* in his analysis of imperialism; both the problem of foreign markets and export of capital was discussed excessively by Hilferding.
He, however, paid more attention than Lenin to the emergence of new protectionism in
international economic relations (see Hilferding 1968, 421–430; see also Hilferding
1902–03). Lenin's idea of the rentier state stemmed – as readily acknowledged by him
– from another main work on imperialism of the time, Hobson's *Imperialism* (1948),
published for the first time in 1902.[2] It is not known whether Kautsky was acquainted
with Hobson's theory, but his emphasis on the role of capital export in imperialist
relations is an indicator of the fact that the main ideas of imperialism were shared by
many of the theoreticians of the time. The export of capital is in various theories of
imperialism also an important factor explaining the stagnation of productive forces and
economic development in general. When capital is exported, it is not invested in domestic industry and thus industrial development degenerates.

According to Hobson the basic facts about modern capitalism are the following:

> "Whatever figures we take, two facts are evident. First, that the income derived as interest
> upon foreign investments enormously exceeded that derived as profits upon ordinary ex-
> port and import trade. Secondly, that while our foreign and colonial trade, and presumably
> the income from it, were growing but slowly, the share of our import values representing
> income from foreign investments was growing very rapidly." (Hobson 1948, 53).

---

[1]   In the beginning of his *Imperialism as the Highest Stage of Capitalism* Lenin referred to
Hobson and Hilferding as the main inspirators of his theory of imperialism (see Lenin SW 1, 684).
[2]   The factors mentioned by Lenin leading to the increase and necessity of export of capital are,
in fact, a combination of both Hobson's and Kautsky's theories of imperialism. Despite his critique
of Kautsky's analysis of the relation between the industrial and agrarian areas and production,
Lenin, in fact, mentioned the slow increase of agrarian production as one of the factors leading to
imperialism via overproduction:

> "... if capitalism could develop agriculture, which today is everywhere lagging terribly
> behind industry, if it could raise the living standards of the masses, who in spite of the
> amazing technical progress are everywhere still half-starved and poverty-stricken, there
> could be no question of a surplus of capital." (Lenin SW 1, 723).

According to Hobson the only people to benefit from the new colonial markets are the finance capitalists, or as he prefers to call them, the investors. The manufacturers and trading classes do not benefit from "aggressive imperialism":

> "Aggressive Imperialism, which costs the taxpayer so dear, which is of so little value to the manufacturer and trader, which is fought with such grave incalculable peril to the citizen, is a source of great pain to the investor who cannot find at home the profitable use he needs for his capital, and insists that his government should help him to profitable and secure investment." (Hobson 1948, 55).

The main cause of imperialism and of the export of capital was that "the power of production far outstripped the actual rate of consumption" (Hobson 1948, 75). During free competition an increase in production leads to the lowering of prices, whereas monopolies and trusts are able to maintain high prices and both limit consumption and collect high profits. This is a cause of action which "at once limits the quantity of capital which can be effectively employed and increases the share of profits out of which fresh savings and fresh capital will spring" (Hobson 1948, 76). Trusts and combinations of capital cannot invest their profits inside the trusted industry:

> "Everywhere appear excessive powers of production, excessive capital in search of investment. (...) It is this economic condition of affairs that forms the taproot of Imperialism." (Hobson 1948, 81).

It is thus not industrial progress as such which causes the export of capital and imperialism, but the maldistribution of consuming power. The general overproduction is caused by saving, which is explained by a distribution of income which does not follow according to needs. Profits and interests from imperialism are excessive elements of income which have no 'legitimate raison d'être' and no proper place in the normal economy of production and consumption. Thus there is a remedy for imperialism ready at hand: if all the classes could convert their needs into an effective demand for commodities, there would not be any excessive capital and consequently, neither, any fight for foreign markets. And consequently there would not be any need for imperialism, either (see Hobson 1948, 82–87). If the power of consumption of the population could be increased, the export of capital would become unnecessary, as would the fight for foreign markets.

Unless the power exercised by trusts and cartels over foreign policy is made ineffective, capitalism will necessarily become parasitic, militaristic and undemocratic — all features of imperialism also analysed by Lenin and Kautsky. According to Hobson, "the whole struggle of so-called Imperialism upon its economic side is towards a growing parasitism" (Hobson 1948, 107). Imperialism also leads to increasing military expenditure and endangers the maintenance of peace (see Hobson 1948, 138). Imperialism has a tendency from democracy to reaction because representative institutions do not function in an empire:

> "The antagonism with democracy drives to the very roots of Imperialism as a political principle". (Hobson 1948, 145).

Even according to Hobson, imperialism is repressive by nature, and its repressiveness stems from its very economic nature:

> "Finally, the spirit, the policy, and the methods of Imperialism are hostile to the institu-
> tions of popular self-government, favouring forms of political tyranny and social authority
> which are the deadly enemies of effective liberty and equality." (Hobson 1948, 152).

The final verdict on imperialism by Hobson was a moral one:

> "It is the besetting sin of all successful states, and its penalty is unalterable in the order of
> nature". (Hobson 1948, 368).

Imperialism is an expression of the lower instincts of man, of the animal struggle for existence which prevents the cultivation of higher inner qualities of both man and nation (see Hobson 1948, 368).

The relation between Lenin's conception of imperialism and Hobson's was very similar to the relation between Lenin and Kautsky. Lenin adopted practically all the results of the analysis but did not approve of its consequences. Lenin even directly compared Hobson with Kautsky: neither accepted the economic necessity of imperialism and referred to democratic methods of government as a remedy. But in one respect Hobson was more honest than Kautsky. Hobson was a democratic liberal and did not pretend to be anything else. He was consequent in recommending a liberal policy against imperialism. Kautsky pretended to be a real Marxist but in fact committed the sin of revisionism. And an honest liberal is always better than a false Marxist, at least one knows where everybody stands (see Lenin SW 1, 763–765).

According to Lenin, Hobson's analysis of imperialism as basically caused by a redistribution of income by trusts and combinations of capital was thus in principle correct, but the conclusions drawn from it were wrong. Eliminating imperialist politics by increasing the power of consumption of the population is only a liberal's dream, and doomed to failure. The 'iron law' of imperialism, of which monopoly is the economic essence, does not permit any alternatives to imperialism and its consequences, war and barbarism, apart from socialism – an alternative also formulated by Kautsky at an earlier stage of the development of his conception of imperialism. Whereas Kautsky's theory of imperialism remained essentially the same in practically all his writings on the subject, the strategic conclusions drawn from it varied and it is the strategic conclusions that were the main target of Lenin's critique.

Most important and, at the same time, most problematic is Lenin's relation to Hilferding's *Das Finanzkapital*. *Das Finanzkapital* was perhaps the most influential Marxist study on modern capitalism published before the First World War and it gave rise to wide debate. It is not known to what extent *Das Finanzkapital* influenced Kautsky's ideas on imperialism.[3] Kautsky's article devoted to the presentation and critique of *Das*

---

[3]   The theoretical influence of Kautsky and Hilferding on each other has been evaluated differently by different authors. John H. Kautsky – perhaps not an impartial observer – stated that

Finanzkapital published in *Die Neue Zeit* in 1910 did not discuss Hilferding's study in any detail. It is true that Kautsky (1910−11, 771) criticised Hilferding's conception of money (in a similar way to Lenin in his notebooks on imperialism; see Lenin CW 39, 334), but otherwise he presented Hilferding's ideas more or less uncritically, and devoted the major part of the review to a presentation of his own ideas about the development and explanation of crises in modern capitalism. It is, anyhow, quite certain that Lenin adopted the concept of finance capital and the merger of industrial with finance capital from Hilferding's work, and it is also rather probable that Kautsky's discussion of the role of finance capital in imperialism was influenced by Hilferding's work. It is further quite probable that Kautsky's idea of ultra-imperialism was an extrapolation of Hilferding's discussion about the general cartel which Kautsky reformulated concerning international relations; an idea also discussed in detail by Lenin. Thus, it could perhaps be claimed that *Das Finanzkapital* was the most important theoretical work discussing the development of modern capitalism during the Second International, a fact explicitly acknowledged by Kautsky. Kautsky characterised *Das Finanzkapital* as the fourth volume of *Das Kapital* (see Kautsky 1910−11, 883).

Hilferding had become an acknowledged Marxist even before the publication of *Das Finanzkapital* in taking part in the theoretical discussion concerning the transformation problem or the relation between values and prices in Marx's *Capital* actualised by the publication of the third volume of *Capital* in 1894 (see Hilferding 1973b (1904)). The essential elements of the idea of a "Generalkartell" or of an organised capitalism were first formulated by Hilferding in an article *Der Funktionswechsel des Schutzzolles* as early as 1903:

> "... dass das Kapital in seinem Hunger nach Profit das, was es auf dem ursprünglichen Wege der Ausbeutung der Proletarier einer Fabrik... nicht mehr erreichen kann, auf eine andere Art zu erreichen sucht: durch die Unterwerfung der gesamten Bevölkerung unter die *organisierte* Macht des Kapitals. Die Organisation der Arbeiterklasse tritt die Organisation der Kapitalistenklasse geschlossen gegenüber." (Hilferding 1902−03, 275).

The organised capitalist class − organised in cartels and trusts − transforms the state into a tool of exploitation. This new form of exploitation is readily recognised as such by every single member of the proletariat, and the proletariat is forced to make an end to this exploitation by occupying the state power:

> "Die Kapitalistenklasse ergreift unmittelbar, unverhüllt, handgreiflich Besitz von der staatlichen Organisation und macht sie zum Werkzeug ihrer Exploitationsinteressen, in einer Weise, die auch dem letzten Proletarier fühlbar wird. (...) Die offenkundige Besitznahme

---

"Hilferding owed a significant debt to Kautsky's influence" (John H. Kautsky 1961, 114). Steenson (1978, 174) claimed that Kautsky was influenced by Hilferding's study. Kraus seemed to agree with John H. Kautsky in claiming that it is a fact that Karl Kautsky did influence and even initiate many of the thoughts later formulated by Hilferding (see Kraus 1978, 68). The problem may perhaps be fairly safely solved by assuming influences in both directions and by assuming that the ideas expressed both by Kautsky and by Hilferding were shared by many a Marxist of the period.

des Staates durch die Kapitalistenklasse zwingt unmittelbar jedem Proletarier das Streben nach Eroberung der politischen Macht auf als dem einzigen Mittel, seiner Exploitation ein Ende zu setzen." (Hilferding 1902—03, 280).

This new organisation of capitalism is an immediate predecessor of socialism. The socialisation of production has been completed, not in the interests of the social totality, but in order to increase exploitation of this totality to the utmost:

> "Es ist direkte Vorstufe der sozialistischen Gesellschaft, weil es ihre vollständige Negation ist: bewusste Vergesellschaftung aller in der heutigen Gesellschaft vorhandenen wirtschaftlichen Potenzen, aber eine Zusammenfassung nicht im Interesse der Gesamtheit, sondern um den Grad der Ausbeutung der Gesamtheit auf eine bisher unerhörte Weise zu steigern." (Hilferding 1902—03, 281).

In this article Hilferding was still mainly interested in the new features of trade policy explained by the new organisational forms of capital. The most important feature in this respect is the changing function of protective tariffs. From a protection against foreign competition, they are transformed in the hands of the cartels into a method of eliminating competition on both the domestic and the international market in order to obtain higher prices (see Hilferding 1902—03, 276—277). Increasing contradictions of capitalism are the necessary consequence of the policies of the cartels, and the new colonial policy is a further consequence of this system (see Hilferding 1902—03, 278—279).

Shortly after the publication of Lenin's *Imperialism* some of his commentators pointed out that Lenin did, in fact, only present Hilferding's ideas in a more popular form.[4] Even a spurious study of Lenin's work on imperialism is enough to prove that there are many ideas common to both works. Lenin seemed to adopt some of the main ideas about monopoly, finance capital and cartels rather directly from Hilferding. Lenin's first list of the contents of *Imperialism* follows almost point by point the contents of Hilferding's *Das Finanzkapital* (see Lenin CW 39, 201—202; at this stage he planned exclusively to write a critique of Kautsky). The order of the chapters in the final version of the study was already different as the discussion of banks was preceded by a study of monopolisation and the concentration of capital.

Lenin regarded Hilferding as a Marxist scholar and presented almost no theoretical critique of his ideas. In his notebooks on imperialism Lenin gave only a short list of the contents and a summary of the book without any further comments. (See Lenin CW 39, 333—338.) It is, however, known that Lenin considered Hilferding's theory of money incorrect ("According to Hilferding money enters into exchange without value", Lenin CW 39, 334; cf. Kautsky's analogous critique), but he did not develop this critique any further. In *Imperialism* Lenin criticised Hilferding for defining finance capital without taking into account the fact that the formation of finance capital presupposes the existence of monopolies. Shortly after the above comment Lenin did, however, admit

---

[4] Horowitz is a modern commentator of the same opinion (see Horowitz 1970). Cf. also Gottschalch (1962, 142): "Von den marxistischen Imperialismustheoretikern steht Lenin Hilferding am nächsten."

that Hilferding did, in fact, analyse the concentration of capital and the formation of cartels before discussing finance capital (see Lenin SW 1, 710–711). Lenin's critique was thus rather formal, dealing with the order of presentation and not the analysis as such.

According to Hilferding, the characteristic features of modern capitalism are those acts of concentration which, on the one hand, emerge as the substitution of free competition by cartels and trusts and, on the other hand, as the close liaisons between industrial and bank capital. It is this relation between industrial and bank capital which gives the capital the form of "finance capital, which is its highest and most abstract form of appearance" (Hilferding 1968, 17).

According to Hilferding:

> "Ein immer wachsender Teil des Kapitals der Industrie gehört nicht den Industriellen, die es anwenden. Sie erhalten die Verfügung über das Kapital nur durch die Bank, die ihnen gegenüber den Eigentümer vertritt. Andrerseits muss die Bank einen immer wachsenden Teil ihrer Kapitalien in der Industrie fixieren. Sie wird damit in immer grösserem Umfang industrieller Kapitalist. Ich nenne das Bankkapital, also Kapital in Geldform, das auf diese Weise in Wirklichkeit in industrielles Kapital verwandelt ist, das Finanzkapital. Den Eigentümern gegenüber behält es stets Geldform, ist von ihnen in Form von Geldkapital, zinstragendem Kapital, angelegt und kann von ihnen stets in Geldform zurückgezogen werden. In Wirklichkeit aber ist der grösste Teil des so bei den Banken angelegten Kapitals in industrielles, produktives Kapital (Produktionsmittel und Arbeitskraft) verwandelt und im Produktionsprozess fixiert. Ein immer grösserer Teil des in der Industrie verwendeten Kapitals ist Finanzkapital, Kapital in der Verfügung der Banken und in der Verwendung der Industriellen." (Hilferding 1968, 309).

Even though banks have always functioned in capitalist production as mediators of money capital, finance capital only comes into being with the foundation of joint stock companies and the coming into being of fictive capital (see Hilferding 1968, 301).

Lenin accepted Hilferding's definition of finance capital with a slight difference of emphasis: finance capital is monopolised capital and the centralisation of bank capital is also its precondition:

> "The concentration of production; the monopolies arising therefrom; the merging or coalescence of the banks with industry – such is the history of the rise of finance capital and such is the content of that concept." (Lenin SW 1, 711)

The foundation of joint stock companies makes it possible to mobilise and centralise capital for the disposal of industrial capital. At the same time, banks become owners and controllers of industrial enterprises. The above analysis was accepted by Kautsky in all its essentials.[5]

---

[5]   In a review of Hilferding's Finanzkapital Kautsky approvingly referred to Hilferding's conception of finance capital:
> "Dem Finanzkapital gehört die kapitalistische Zukunft. Dieses bedeutet aber sowohl im internationalen Konkurrenzkampf wie im inneren Klassenkampf die brutalste und gewalttätigste Form des Kapitals." (Kautsky 1910–1911, 769).

In his study Hilferding stated that, in principle, there are no obstacles or limits to the formation of cartels. Thus the concentration of capital will finally lead to the formation of one single general cartel:

> "Vielmehr ist eine Tendenz zu stetiger Ausbreitung der Kartellierung vorhanden. Die unabhängigen Industrien geraten, wie wir gesehen haben, immer mehr in Abhängigkeit von kartellierten, um schliesslich von ihnen annektiert zu werden. Als Resultat des Prozesses ergäbe sich dann ein Generalkartell. Die ganze kapitalistische Produktion wird bewusst geregelt von einer Instanz, die das Ausmass der Produktion in allen ihren Sphären bestimmt. Dann wird die Preisfestsetzung rein nominell und bedeutet nurmehr die Verteilung des Gesamtprodukts auf die Kartellmagnaten einerseits, auf die Masse aller anderen Gesellschaftsmitglieder andrerseits. (...) Das Kartell verteilt das Produkt." (Hilferding 1968, 321−322).

The regulation and distribution of production by finance capital will finally substitute the specific role and nature of value as the regulator of production and distribution in capitalism. A society governed by a general cartel would be a consciously regulated society which would, however, still retain its antagonistic nature. The formation of a general cartel would, in fact, be economically if not politically possible:

> "An sich wäre ein Generalkartell ökonomisch Denkbar, das die Gesamtproduktion leitete und damit die Krisen beseitigte, wenn auch ein solcher Zustand sozial und politisch eine Unmöglichkeit ist, da er an dem Interessengegensatz, den er auf die äusserste Spitze treiben würde, zugrunde gehen musste. Aber von den einzelnen Kartellen eine Aufhebung der Krisen erwarten, zeigt nur von der Einsichtlosigkeit in die Ursache der Krisen und den Zusammenhang des kapitalistischen Systems." (Hilferding 1968, 402−403).

It is not difficult to find formulations in Lenin's work on imperialism to support the interpretation that he accepted Hilferding's theoretical conceptions and even the idea of an all-powerful general cartel and a general bank consciously directing the total production and distribution. Lenin did particularly seem to trust the capacity of the banks to direct and govern the production and distribution of products:

> "These single figures show perhaps better than lengthy disquisitions how the concentration of capital and the growth of bank turnover are radically changing the significance of the banks. Scattered capitalists are transformed into a single collective capitalist. When carrying the current accounts of a few capitalists, a bank, as it were, transacts a purely technical and exclusively auxiliary operation. When, however, this operation grows to enormous dimensions we find that a handful of monopolists subordinate to their will all the operations, both commercial and industrial, of the whole of capitalist society; for they are enabled ... first, to *ascertain exactly* the financial position of the various capitalists, then to *control* them, to influence them by restricting or enlarging, facilitating or hindering credits, and finally to *entirely determine* their fate, determine their income, deprive them of capital, or permit them to increase their capital rapidly and to enormous dimensions, etc." (Lenin SW 1, 700−701).

In the foreword to Bucharin's *Imperialism and the World Economy* Lenin presented most explicitly his own conception of the possibility of the formation of an international general cartel or ultra-imperialism. His conception seemed to follow Hilferding's formulation of the question:

> "Can it be denied, however, that a new phase of capitalism, is 'imaginable' in the abstract *after* imperialism, namely, ultra-imperialism? No, it cannot. Such a phase can be imagined. But in practice this means becoming an opportunist, turning away from the acute problems of the day to dream of the unacute problems of the future. (...) There is no doubt that the trend of development is *towards* a single world trust absorbing all enterprises without exception and all states without exception. But this development proceeds in such circumstances, at such a pace, through such contradictions, conflicts and upheavals — not only economic but political, national, etc. — that inevitably imperialism will burst and capitalism will be transformed into its opposite *long before* one world trust materialises, before the 'ultra-imperialist', world-wide amalgamation of national finance capitals takes place." (Lenin CW 22, 107).

In the above characterisation of the possibility of the formation of a general trust there is, however, one important difference from Hilferding's conception. For Lenin emphasised that there are not only political contradictions, as claimed by both Hilferding and Kautsky, which prevent the establishment of a general world-wide trust and transform capitalism into its opposite, socialism, before the stage of ultra-imperialism is reached, but even economic contradictions. Both Hilferding and Kautsky seemed to think that such a development would — at least in principle — be economically possible. According to Lenin, such thinking is abstract. On the other hand, even the context of Kautsky's argumentation should be kept in mind. He was arguing against the idea of the realisation of socialism as a result of purely economic collapse. Actually, Lenin's critique of the conception of ultra-imperialism was not all that different from Kautsky's own ideas. Even to Kautsky — one could claim — the idea of ultra-imperialism was an abstract possibility reached through an extrapolation of the economic tendencies present in capitalism which would thus actually be prevented by many possible intervening counterfactors.

The main difference between Lenin's and Hilferding's conceptions of monopolist or finance capital sprang from the differences in their analysis of the nature of competition between capitals and the transformation of free competition into monopolistic competition. Kautsky did not explicitly discuss the problem of the nature of competition and of changes in competition caused by the monopolisation of capital. To him monopolies or, more concretely, cartels and trusts made possible by the centralisation of capital seem to function simply as powerful groups of influence dictating the direction of the economic policy of the state. Monopolistic extra profits are furthermore appropriated through the utilisation of the favourable position guaranteed by the economic policy of the state through tariffs or colonial annexations. In this respect both Lenin's and Hilferding's analyses in particular were more detailed and interesting. According to Hilferding, cartels are born out of certain limitations of competition due to the centralisation of capital and the changing composition of industrial capital.

Hilferding's conception of the changing form of competition can be summarised as follows (see Hilferding 1968, 246—281). The motive force of every single capital is to acquire extra profit higher than the average. During the reign of free competition extra profit is made possible only by higher productivity and technical innovations. The competition of capitals results in an objective tendency, the formation of a general or average rate of profit. The realisation of this tendency does, however, presuppose that there are no obstacles to competition restricting the free flow of capital from one field of industry to another. But because such obstacles are, in fact, a necessary outcome of the development of capitalism, capitalism based on free competition is transformed into monopolist capitalism. An increase in the productivity of labour necessarily leads to an increase in the share of fixed capital. Consequently, the amount of capital which is needed to start new production in a specific field increases, too. This last factor does not, however, according to Hilferding, prevent as such competition between capitals and the inflow of new capital into fields with high productivity and high profits. Associations of capital and joint stock companies come into being at the same time as individual production units grow thus making it possible to mobilise capital in even larger quantities. The inflow of new capital is thus not the main problem facing capital due to the increase of the organic composition of capital. It is, on the contrary, the outflow of capital which becomes difficult and all but impossible from those fields in which the share of fixed capital is especially high. Consequently, the rate of profit becomes low in these fields. It is relatively easy to mobilise new capital into these fields but difficult to withdraw old capital from them. Thus if there were no counteracting factors in operation, the biggest capitals would paradoxically show the lowest rate of profit. Capital once invested can, according to Hilferding, only stop functioning when it loses its value completely in bankruptcy and the closing down of factories.

New obstacles to capital mobility thus lead to a diminishing rate of profit at both ends of the production scale. Both in big industry, in which the share of fixed capital is high, and in the technically backward small-scale industry, profits tend to be lower than average. The formation of cartels is the immediate result of the low rate of profit in industries with a high rate of fixed capital. Because of the increasing competition, all such capitals are threatened by devaluation, and thus the formation of cartels controlling the whole industry is in the interests of all the capitals functioning in that field. In abolishing competition cartels make it possible for firms to acquire a higher profit than average. Cartels are, furthermore, especially in the interests of the big banks which have invested capital in various firms operating in certain industries. They are in danger of losing their capital if free competition is allowed to continue.

Hilferding's argumentation about the reasons and causes favouring cartel formation is especially interesting because he was almost the only one among the Second International Marxists to discuss theoretically and to explicate the reasons leading to the transformation of the laws of competition in modern capitalism. Neither Lenin nor Kautsky developed any detailed conception of their own about the causes and effects of the formation of cartels and monopolies. They were merely content to state that the formation of monopolies is the immediate result of the concentration of capital. It is, anyway, true that Lenin did discuss more specifically the problem of the transformation of the laws of competition due to the formation of monopolies – a problem almost totally neglected by Kautsky. But not even Lenin developed his argumentation any further. He merely stated that monopolies partially displace free competition and introduce the factor of power into economic relations. And the reason why free competition is subsumed is that monopolies are able to appropriate higher profits than average. Hilferding's argumentation located the factors abolishing free competition in the technical properties of invested capital in production. According to Hilferding's analyses capital becomes immobilised because it is concretely 'fixed' in the immobile means of production. In this sense there is a resemblance between both Hilferding's and Kautsky's reasoning: Kautsky found that the decisive factor giving rise to imperialism is the natural limits of agricultural production which make it impossible to enlarge production in agriculture as rapidly as in industry.

Further interpretation of Lenin's concept of imperialism and monopoly capitalism is hindered by the fact that Lenin was ambiguous in discussing the transformation of free competition into monopolistic competition. He seemed to think that monopolies are born out of the concentration of capital, and due to the small number of firms operating in a certain field of production they are able to share the markets among themselves. The strengthening of finance capital is a further consequence of the concentration of both banking and industrial capital (see also Kraus 1978, 128). Lenin tended to think that in imperialism monopolistic competition does not function as an objective and coercive law in relation to the individual capitals in the same sense as free competition does; monopolistic competition is a result of conscious acts on behalf of the individual capitalists or cartels. In other words, the anarchy of production is substituted for a conscious regulation of production. (For a discussion of the relation between competition and monopoly in Lenin's theory of imperialism see Jordan 1974b, 220–231.)

Despite the ambiguous nature of Lenin's conception of competition it can be argued that he obviously did not understand the role of competition in capitalism in the same sense as Marx. According to Marx competition realises the inner laws of capital. More specifically, competition realises the inner laws of capital as outer laws of coercion in relation to individual capitals (see MEW 23, 286 and 355; see also Marx s.a., 617). Furthermore, free competition is in a specific sense the adequate form of realisation of the productive process of capital (see Marx s.a., 543-544; see also Jordan 1974a, 139). In the third volume of *Capital* Marx discussed more concretely the way in which free competition realises both a production price and an average rate of profit in every field of production. Thus every single capital is but an aliquent part of the total social capital. Marx's presentation and analysis of competition does not, on the other hand, include any analysis of the concrete modes of competition or 'price competition', the determination of market prices, and the fluctuation of prices due to demand and supply.

The difficulty in interpreting Lenin's theory of imperialism stems from the fact that, on the one hand, Lenin seemed to think that somehow monopolies displace free competition but still do not abolish competition altogether. They only substitute it for another kind of competition. On the other hand, monopolistic competition takes place alongside free competition; monopolies operate "under formally recognised free competition" (Lenin SW 1, 693; see also Jordan 1974b, 220−231). There are consequently two possibilities in interpreting Lenin's theory: Either monopolistic competition takes place alongside free competition and is not changing the role of competition as an objective regulatory principle in capitalism functioning behind the backs of its actors. In this case monopolistic competition would be a historically specific and concrete form of competition influencing the determination of market prices and profits only in certain fields of production. There would not necessarily be any continuous monopolisation of production, and monopoly would not be the single decisive feature of modern capitalism. Or if monopolistic competition, in fact, transforms the laws of functioning of capitalism, and even if not abolishing competition altogether (a possibility suggested by Hilferding and Kautsky but, on the other hand, denied by Lenin) introduces power and dominance as the decisive new determinators of the mutual relations of producers, then capitalism really is transformed into a new stage of monopoly capitalism. The conception of monopoly capitalism would then characterise a capitalism fundamentally different from the old 'capitalism of free competition'. Lenin's emphasis on monopoly capitalism as the highest and last stage of capitalism and his analysis of the transformation of relations of free competition into relations of power and dominance seem to lend support to the thesis that the second interpretation corresponds better to the core of Lenin's theory of imperialism.

Hilferding's *Das Finanzkapital* can be criticised for the same ambiguity as Lenin's theory of imperialism. According to Schimkowsky, instead of regarding monopolistic competition as only a specific concrete and historical form of competition, Hilferding was led to absolutise the obstacles in the way of mobilising capital and also to overemphasise the influence of the formation of cartels. Consequently Hilferding's finance capital is not capitalism any more. And in Hilferding's analysis above all relations of dominance take the place of competition between capitals. (See Schimkowsky 1974b.) Schimkowski's interpretation of Hilferding's *Das Finanzkapital* is interesting but somewhat too restricted; it could namely be claimed that Hilferding did not only not understand the role of competition in the same sense as Marx did in *Capital,* he did not analyse competition either in any serious sense.

Hilferding, in fact, only analysed the sphere of circulation in capitalism − as pointed out by many critics (see Kautsky 1910−1911, 767, who does not, however, draw any further conclusions from his critical comment; see also Gottschalch 1962, 103 and Leontev 1969, 80−81); in Hilferding circulation comes first, production second. As Cora Stephan has pointed out Hilferding tended to comprehend the production process as a technical work process, and hence in his analysis capital relation only exists as a relation within circulation (see Stephan 1974, 140). This restriction becomes very apparent in Hilferding's analysis of competition. Hilferding did not actually analyse the competition between capitals producing commodities; competition is restricted to the competition between money or loan capitals.

Competition predominantly consists of money capital being transferred from one field of industry into another, and the obstacles preventing the mobilisation of capital are technical due to the technical composition of capital invested. There did not, furthermore, exist in Hilferding's analysis any market value or cost price which would be the result of competition between different capitals and industries, and it is not the production price which realises an average rate of profit in every industry. The amount of capital disposable at a certain period is simply mobilised according to the rentability or according to the amount of profits, in different fields of industry. Profits are then — under free competition — simply divided between the capitals according to their size. The following statement by Hilferding about the role of joint stock companies is characteristic of this conception:

> "Die Mobilisierung des Kapitals lässt natürlich den Produktionsprozess unberührt. Sie berührt nur das Eigentum, schafft nur die Form für die Übertragung des kapitalistischen fungierenden Eigentums, die Übertragung von Kapital als Kapital, als Profit heckende Geldsumme. Da sie die Produktion unberührt lässt, ist diese Übertragung in der Tat nur Übertragung der Eigentumstitel auf den Profit. (...) Die Sphäre, in der der Profit produziert wurde, ist ihm gleichgültig. Der Kapitalist macht nicht eine Ware, sondern er macht in einer Ware — Profit. (...) Denn die Mobilisierung des Kapitals lässt die wirkliche Bewegung des Kapitals zur Ausgleichung der Profitrate unberührt." (Hilferding 1968, 252).

Karl Kautsky would in all probability undersign many of the reservations about the possibility of the total regulation of production and distribution in capitalism made by Lenin. Kautsky emphasised in many contexts that monopolies do not by any means lead to the abolition of crises and the uneven development of capitalism.[6] Even though there is a moment of regulation inherent in monopoly capitalism and imperialism — and in this sense they do, in fact, anticipate socialism — monopolies do not abolish the market forces in operation. After all, the main difference between Lenin's and Kautsky's conceptions of imperialism is, then, that Lenin understood imperialism to be the last stage of capitalism and a necessary consequence of its economic development, emphasising all its consequences: stagnation, repression, and direct domination by the monopolies are characteristic features of imperialism which also show its place in history. According to Lenin, monopoly is the economic essence of imperialism and the formation of monopolies and finance capital is an irreversible process having the stagnation of economic development and the repression of the working class as its direct consequences. According to Kautsky, on the other hand, some of the consequences of the monopolisation and centralisation of capital and of the formation of finance capital could in fact be avoided even in capitalism: protective tariffs, annexations of agrarian areas and countries as colonies, undemocratic methods of government, etc. could be replaced by more democratic and even more effective methods once a union of democratic states had been established. The above conclusion was characteristic of Kautsky's

---

[6]   According to Kautsky it is a "ridiculous hope" to assume that the cartels and trusts could "regulate production and thus deal with the crises" (see Kautsky 1907—08a, 114).

"reformism" and in this sense Lenin's critique that Kautsky was a reformist was justified.

On the other hand, Lenin's accusation of Kautsky seems to be unjustified as Kautsky
was consistent in his theoretical positions, and it is impossible to find any crucial
changes in his theoretical position. His conception of the democratic union of states as a
realistic alternative to imperialism is quite understandable. It is a direct continuation of
his conception of parliamentary democracy as the ideal struggling ground for socialism
during a transformation period of the society (see chapter I.12.). According to him the
conditions for socialism do, indeed, ripen in capitalism, but the subjective and objective
conditions for socialism, interpreted as the growth of productive forces and the development and organisation of the proletariat, respectively, develop most effectively during
democratic and not during imperialist rule. A socialist revolution is unavoidable, and it
will take place as soon as its conditions are ripe – and the best indicator of these
conditions is the balance of power in a parliament. The context for Kautsky's conception of imperialism is the ripening of the conditions for socialism. Imperialism is a
method of government unfavourable to the proletariat and to the establishment of
socialism. The maintenance and continuation of the methods of imperialism are in the
interests of only a small fraction of finance capitalists. The development of both proletarian organisations and of productive forces will proceed under more favourable
conditions once the methods of imperialism, protective tariffs and annexations of
foreign territories are abolished. The only possible alternatives to capitalism are not,
accordingly, imperialism or socialism. Another alternative open to capitalism is the
democratic union of states.

To Kautsky imperialism is not the necessary last stage of capitalism immediately
preceding socialism, even though the centralisation of capital and the elements of the
regulation of production introduced by monopolies are immediate preconditions for
socialism already developing inside capitalism. According to Lenin, on the other hand,
imperialism is the immediate predecessor of socialism, from which there is no return
either to any previous or to any future stage of capitalism. The centralisation and
socialisation of production in the form of monopolies concretely prove that the private
mode of appropriation of capital has become obsolete. It must give way to a "higher
mode" of production. This, then is the main difference between the "renegade" Kautsky and the "revolutionary" Lenin – a difference which lies not so much in the evaluation of the causes and effects of imperialism as in the evaluation of the historical role of
imperialism as such.

11. IMPERIALISM AS THE TRUTH ABOUT CAPITALISM

In Kautsky's analysis of imperialism the economic relations of capitalism are transformed into pure relations of power. Monopolistic profits are made possible either by artificially high prices of commodities or interests on investments exported to foreign colonies or dependent countries. The state is a political instrument in the hands of finance capital, and its economic policy favours cartels and trusts, and finance capital. In Kautsky's reasoning imperialism is, furthermore, a pure question of power. The accentuated role of power in Kautsky's thinking about imperialism resulted from the seemingly paradoxical thesis that imperialism is a product of the economic development of capitalism and yet not an economic necessity in developed capitalism (in fact, imperialism is disadvantageous even from the point of view of capital accumulation). Once imperialism is understood to be a result of a relation of power, the thesis becomes theoretically non-contradictory. There are different methods for coping with the problems facing the accumulation of capital, of which imperialism is only one possible alternative, and the choice between different methods is made by the factual power constellation in society.

Kautsky's analysis of imperialism has in the preceding discussion been shown to be two-sided: On the one hand, imperialism is found to be determined by the natural qualities of the different sectors of production. The relations between industrial and agrarian countries are determined by the natural obstacles of the development of agrarian production; industrial overproduction is a result of natural − and not of any specific social − limits of agrarian production. As such the contradiction causing imperialism would not seem to be solvable at all. There are only different methods for coping with it, of which imperialism is only one possible, although historically prevalent method. And the different methods of coping with overproduction are shown to be dependent on the power relations in society. On the other hand, in Kautsky's analysis imperialism is a result of the centralisation of capital, of the formation of trusts and cartels, and of finance capital which both increase the problems of overproduction of commodities and capital and are able to regulate production. Being especially powerful groups of capital, big, centralised capitalists also force the capitalist state to apply imperialistic methods in its politics.

In analysing Kautsky's conception of the law of capitalist appropriation it was argued that he understood the capital-wage labour relation essentially as a relation of direct exploitation. To him, freedom and equality were essentially characteristics of an earlier mode of production, simple commodity prodution, in which the appropriation of commodities and private property were consequently based on the labour of every producer, whereas in capitalism the right to property is based on the appropriation of alien labour and its products. Consequently, Kautsky did not comprehend the capital relation as being a specific socially mediated relation of exploitation recognising the (formal) freedom and equality of commodity producers, but as being a relation of unequal exchange based on direct dominance and power.

It could thus be claimed that Kautsky's theory of imperialism was a logical result of his concept of capital; as a matter of fact, it is in imperialism that the true nature of capitalism is revealed and becomes visible to everyone. In imperialism the relations of production are in fact replaced by relations of power and dominance. Finance capital is understood to exploit not only wage workers but all consumers and even other producers by artificially increasing the prices of products and lowering the prices of raw materials. This new method of appropriation of profits is based on political power exercised through the state by finance capital; it is furthermore based on direct repression and violence both at home and abroad. Imperialism reveals the exploitative nature of capitalism at its clearest. Instead of from the capital labour relation monopolistic profits predominantly result from the unequal exchange of commodities or from the distribution of the whole national product in the interests of cartels and finance capital. There cannot, consequently, be any talk of even the illusions of freedom and equality between the exploiters and the exploited.

As has already been pointed out, there are important similarities and differences between Lenin's concept of imperialism and Kautsky's. Lenin did not emphasise the relation between agrarian and industrial countries in his analysis, even though he referred to it as one of the reasons for overproduction. While emphasising monopoly as the economic essence of imperialism, he understood imperialism mainly as a result of the centralisation of capital and the formation of finance capital transforming the functioning of the laws of competition in capitalism. There are not, therefore, any natural or technical conditions for production influencing the rise of imperialism − unless one understands the increasing amount of capital necessary for production to be such a condition. There is an interesting ambivalence in Lenin's thinking which becomes explicit in his critique of Bucharin: On the one hand, imperialism does not transform the functioning of capitalist laws from bottom to top and consequently does not represent a totally different mode of production. There is more concrete evidence of this in Lenin's analysis of the monopolistic competition taking place side by side with free competition; free competition is not totally abolished by monopolies. The denial of the possibility of the development of capitalism into a general cartel or into ultra-imperialism is a further indicator of this fact. On the other hand, these reservations did not seem to have much influence on Lenin's general analysis of the functioning and consequences of imperialism. Even Lenin constantly referred to the economic power and dominance of monopolies as the source of their extra-profits. Monopolies maintain artificially high prices and exploit the whole nation. Their foreign investments bring them a highly profitable interest and through them other nations are exploited, too. Monopolies further lead to the stagnation of the productive forces. They also represent repression and violence in their own country and in international relations, and are undemocratic by their very nature. Even to Lenin, then, imperialism became practically synonymous with an economic system violating the rules of commodity exchange, the equality and freedom of the commodity owners; imperialism is essentially based on a forced distribution of the surplus product of the whole hemisphere determined by the power of the big capital magnates.

Moishe Postone and Barbara Brick, in a totally different context discussing Pollock's theory of 'state capitalism', gave a general characteristic of what they understood to be the essence of traditional Marxism. In the conceptions of traditional Marxism the relations of production are basically identified with the relations of distribution (see Postone & Brick 1982, 630; see also Linder 1973, 74):

> "The ultimate concern of this theory, then, is the historical critique of the mode of distribution." (Postone & Brick 1982, 631).

Socialism is simply understood to be a mode of distribution more appropriate to the industrial mode of production — the centralisation and concentration of production has given rise to new possibilities for centralised planning and for overcoming private property. This interpretation of Marxism further takes in an understanding of industrial production essentially as a technical process, a labour process that is not intrinsically socially determined (see Postone & Brick 1982, 630−631).

Postone's and Brick's characterisation of traditional Marxism seems to be especially fitting to the theories of imperialism of the Second International. Capitalism is fundamentally analysed as a process of distribution — monopolistic profits basically have their source in the sphere of circulation, and not in production. Hilferding states this explicitly: the remaining antagonism of the new capitalism is an antagonism of distribution. The characterisation of traditonal Marxism as understanding the production process as a technical labour process is also an adequate one; one could even claim that the technical prerequisites for the production process play an even more important role in these theories as the technical or even natural properties of production are understood to be the main cause of monopolisation and imperialism. This is most clearly the case in Kautsky's and Hilferding's theories of modern capitalism but even to Lenin the new technical conditions of production were among the reasons behind the formation or coming into being of trusts and cartels (cf. also Linder 1973, 74).

The conception of capitalism inherent in the theories of imperialism has serious consequences for the strategic conclusions drawn from it and especially for the understanding of the role of democracy in capitalism. The most obvious consequence is connected with the analysis of the formation of revolutionary consciousness and a revolutionary subject. Once again Kautsky presented the problem in a most consistent manner. Since his theory excluded a categorical mediation between the exploitation of surplus value and the exchange of commodities as equivalents on the market, he was forced to adopt a dual conception of consciousness. On the one hand, the exploitative nature should be obvious to the proletariat − and, in imperialism, to the rest of the population as well − and the economic development of capitalism is expected to lead automatically to the formation of a revolutionary subject, a revolutionary working class. On the other hand, the economic interests of the wage workers are not immediately identical with the wider socialist perspective. There is thus a major difference between the economic, or − to use Lenin's expression − trade-unionistic, and the socialist consciousness of the proletariat. The socialist intellectuals, representing scientific social-ism, and the socialist party are a necessary link connecting socialism with the labour movement. The Social Democratic Party is the representative of scientific socialism possessing the right knowledge about the socialist goal of social development. As will be seen in more detail later on, Lenin followed Kautsky's formation of the problem in practically all the essentials.

One would expect the analysis of imperialism to have led Kautsky and Lenin to problematise their conceptions about the formation of revolutionary consciousness and of a revolutionary subject − if not otherwise, then at least as a problem of the relation between the theory and programme of the party and the political reality of modern capitalism. As a theoretical question the problem did not, however, exist for them any more. When analysis of the capital relation was substituted by analysis of exploitation by finance capital mediated through the state, the antagonism between workers and capitalists was substituted by the antagonism between the rest of the people and a finance oligarchy. As a consequence, exploitation should become obvious and visible to everyone, as proved most obviously by the case of a general cartel − which, in a sense, is a logical conclusion of Kautsky's and Lenin's reasoning: capitalism, in the form of a general cartel or a handful of big capitalists could not possibly survive, because its exploitative nature would be developed to absurdity. Hence, it really is surprising how anyone could expect imperialism to survive while it is in the interest of a negligible fraction of the population only, the tiny fraction of finance capitalists. The realisation of socialism should self-evidently be in the interests of all the people.

As in the case of his earlier analysis, Kautsky referred to auxiliary explanations in order to save his conception of the people as the potential opponent of imperialism. From the point of view of their economic interests it is relatively easy to show that the various middle-class groups − intellectuals, farmers, the old petit bourgeoisie − have no direct economic interests in supporting imperialism. The case of the proletariat should even be more obvious. Its interests are clearly and directly opposed to those of finance capital. Kautsky claimed that the situation is, however, complicated because the supporters of imperialism have strong instrument of power at their disposal and there-fore they are able to influence large segments of the population both economically and ideologically (see Kautsky 1915a, 21). In Lenin's work on imperialism the rise of a labour aristocracy similarly explained the reformist tendencies in the labour movement;

certain groups of workers have been bought over by the imperialists. (In Lenin's earlier thinking the problem was tackled with the dual theory of consciousness (see p. 159).)

A second important problem of the theories of imperialism and the conception of capitalism in general is in this respect the question of democracy, both as to its role in the strategy of the Social Democratic Party and in its relation to capitalism and socialism. In this respect it becomes even more obvious that imperialism reveals the truth about capitalism. Since imperialism is essentially determined by the relations of power and dominance, democracy and imperialism are mutually exclusive. Imperialism does not only prove that the bourgeoisie has betrayed its former ideals of democracy and freedom, imperialism is undemocratic by its very nature. A form of exploitation mediated more or less directly by the capitalist state could not possibly go on within a state having a democratic constitution. The realisation of a parliamentary democracy and the guarantee of the political rights of all the people would automatically result in the establishment of the power of the proletariat. The fight for democracy thus factually becomes identical with the fight for socialism.

In Kautsky's conception of political democracy and its role in the struggle for socialism this standpoint is formulated most explicitly. But one could also claim that despite Lenin's vehement critique of Kautsky's conceptions of democracy and dictatorship of the proletariat, his own analysis of democracy did not differ all that markedly from Kautsky's. In Lenin's analysis democracy is something totally external to bourgeois society.

12. PARLIAMENTARY DEMOCRACY
AND REVOLUTIONARY TACTICS

In his book *Negative Integration und revolutionäre Attentismus* Dieter Groh (1973) characterised the politics of German Social Democracy before the First World War as a combination of revolutionary attentisme and negative integration. The Social Democrats did continuously speak of revolution and understand their politics as inherently revolutionary, but in practical politics they concentrated on parliamentary politics and reformist tactics. The revolutionary spirit did, however, have an important function. It satisfied the revolutionary aspirations and hopes of the supporters and members of the party and, at the same time, remained harmless in its practical consequences, or contributed to the integration of the Social Democratic Party into the Wilhelminian German 'Reich'. The propaganda of revolution did also distinguish the party from other political forces and thus emphasise the specific role of the party in German politics. At the same time the results of the parliamentary elections were interpreted by the leaders of the party to prove that the Social Democrats would in the very near future gain a majority in parliament and become a dominating and decisive force in German politics.

Revolutionary attentisme had as its precondition an evolutionist conception of social development and history, a conception of the law-like development of bourgeois society towards the pending downfall of capitalism and the introduction of socialism. Socialism was regarded as a necessary outcome of the economic development of capitalism and thus the socialist revolution was expected to be an unavoidable and an almost automatic outcome of this development. All the Social Democrats had to do was to wait and be ready for the moment to take over political power in the state.

Karl Kautsky was the main theoretical representative of this "centrist" conception of the ripening of the revolutionary conditions within capitalism, and August Bebel was his counterpart in practical politics and in the leadership of the party. The expectation of the coming revolution had as its counterpart an orientation towards reformist politics in all practical issues — long before this revisionism was to become an acknowledged force inside the party and an independent fraction within it. One could even claim that the socialist law introduced by Bismarck in 1876 forced the Social Democrats to concentrate on parliamentary politics by depriving them of other means of political activity, and it was thus an important precondition for the centrist conception of a revolutionary strategy:

> "Der den revolutionären Attentismus zugrundeliegende Revolutionsbegriff der deutschen Sozialdemokratie war von vornherein und nicht erst unter dem Einfluss des Revisionismus im Vergleich zum Marxschen auf das objektive Moment reduziert, was von Marx nicht verhindert und von Engels sogar gefördert war. Im Gegensatz zu Lassalle, der seinen Anhängern eingeschärft hatte, sie sollten, wenn er vom allgemeinen Wahlrecht spreche, Revolution verstehen, sprach die deutsche Sozialdemokratie seit den 70er Jahren zwar dauernd von Revolution, meinte aber damit nur die von den steigenden Wähler- und Mitgliederziffern indizierte und von der ökonomischen Entwicklung garantierte 'naturgeseztliche' oder 'naturnotwendige Entwicklung zum Sozialismus'." (Groh 1973, 57).

The revolution was expected to be almost a natural-like event which was to be realised more or less regardless of the aspirations of an acting subject:

> "Eine Entwicklung, die man durch Agitation und Organisation fördern konnte, denn revolutionärer Klimax im 'Zusammenbruch' der bürgerlichen Gesellschaft und des Staates aufgrund historisch-ökonomischer Gesetze und weitgehend unbeeinflusst durch den Willen der handelnden Individuen erreicht werde. Da der Revolution ein historisches Subjekt mehr und mehr abhanden kann, trat sie in Gestalt eines Naturereignisses auf." (Groh 1973, 57).

Dieter Groh's interpretation of the political role of the German Social Democratic Party and its concept of revolution was closely related to an earlier interpretation by Erich Mathias. In his article *Kautsky und der Kautskyanismus* published in 1957 Mathias analysed the function of the German Social Democratic Party before the First World War and Kautsky's theoretical contribution to the self-understanding of the party in specific. In his analyses Kautsky's concept of Marxism was seen to be a logical continuation of the traditional understanding of socialism by Marxists functioning under the socialist law in Germany. This conception was a consequence of a strict respect for legality and legal procedures in society: "An unserer Gesetzlichkeit werden unsere Feinde zugrunde gehen" was a typical slogan of the party leadership during the socialist laws (see Mathias 1957, 156). One of the reasons explaining this self-understanding of the Marxism of the Second International was Engels' and even Marx's own evaluation of the role of the emerging mass parties in Europe and specifically in Germany since the 1860s. Kautsky developed his own interpretation of Marxism in close collaboration with Engels, who never criticised the understanding of Marxism by Kautsky and Bernstein, his close friends and collaborators in the late '80s and early '90s:

> "Engels war sich der Grenzen der Rezeptionsfähigkeit seiner Schüler nicht bewusst, die sich dem Marxismus auf dem Wege über den als Filter wirkenden *Anti-Dühring* genährt hatten, der ohnehin nur die Partikel des ursprünglichen Systems passieren liess, die sich nahtlos in das naturwissenschaftliche Weltbild der neuen Generation einzufügen schienen." (Mathias 1957, 157).

In his preface to Marx's *Klassenkämpfe in Frankreich*, written in 1895 and regarded as his testament, Engels had declared that "die Kampfweise von 1848 ist heute in jeder Beziehung veraltet. . ." (MEW 22, 513). This statement was interpreted both by Bernstein and Kautsky as proving that the period of revolutionary upheavals was over;

revolutions by small minorities were definitely outdated (sec Mathias 1957, 158). There was, however, an important difference in the interpretations of Kautsky and Bernstein. Whereas Bernstein was eager to interpret Engels' text as proving that revolutions were unnecessary in general and only damaging to the cause of Social Democracy, Kautsky did not draw the corresponding conclusions. In his understanding, the new ideas in Engels' preface only legitimated the parliamentary tactics of the party. The coming revolution was to be committed by a parliamentary majority, but still the introduction of socialism was a question of a revolutionary takeover. Socialism could not be realised through a gradual growing into a democratic and righteous society.

According to Engels, the parliamentary democracy already established in England and America opened up new possibilities for the workers' movement; it opened up an era of peaceful transitation to socialism. Even in Germany the old style of revolution had become obsolete and the conditions for its realisation had changed:

> "Denn auch hier hatten sich die Bedingungen des Kampfes wesentlich verändert. Der Rebellion alten Stils, der Strassenkampf mit Barrikaden, der bis 1848 überall die letzte Entscheidung gab, war bedeutend veraltet." (MEW 22, 519).

The German workers were to be given the merit for two important achievements: first, they had organised a disciplined and strong party, and second, they had made effective use of general franchise:

> "Die deutschen Arbeiter hatten aber zudem ihrer Sache noch einen zweiten grossen Dienst erwiesen nedem dem ersten, der mit ihrer blossen Existenz als die stärkste, die disziplinierteste, die am raschesten ausschwellende sozialistische Partei gegeben war. Sie hatten ihre Genossen aller Länder eine neue, eine der schärfsten Waffen geliefert, indem sie ihnen zeigten, wie man das allgemeine Stimmrecht gebraucht." (MEW 22, 518).

General franchise had become an effective new method in the struggle for socialism and it was expected to become all the more important. In this struggle the German Social Democrats had proved to be of special importance, having become the avantgarde of international Social Democracy:

> "Was aber auch in anderen Ländern geschehen möge, die deutsche Sozialdemokratie hat eine besondere Stellung und damit wenigstens zunächst auch eine besondere Aufgabe. Die zwei Millionen Wähler, die sie an die Urnen schickt, nebst den jungen Männern und den Frauen, die als Nichtwähler hinter ihnen stehen, bilden die zahlreichste, kompakteste Masse, den entscheidenden 'Gewalthaufen' der internationalen proletarischen Armee. (. . .) Ihr Wachstum geht so spontan, so stetig, so unaufhaltsam und gleichzeitig so ruhig vor sich wie ein Naturprozess. (. . .) Dies Wachstum ununterbrochen in Gang zu halten, bis es dem gegenwärtigen Regierungssystem von selbst über den Kopf wächst, . . . das ist unsere Hauptaufgabe." (MEW 22, 524).

The impressive increase in social democratic votes in Germany had made a strong impression on Engels. Only a few years earlier he had expressed strong doubts about a possible democratic development in Germany. In his critique of the first draft of the Erfurt Programme in 1891 Engels had written:

"Man kann sich vorstellen, die alte Gesellschaft könne friedlich in die neue hineinwachsen in Ländern, wo die Volksvertretung alle Macht in sich konzentriert, wo man Verwassungs- mässig tun kann, was man will, sobald man die Majorität des Volkes hinter sich hat: in demokratischen Republiken wie Frankreich und Amerika, in Monarchien wie England, wo die bevorstehende Abkaufung der Dynastie tagtäglich in der Presse besprochen wird und wo diese Dynastie gegen den Volkswillen ohnmächtig ist. Aber in Deutschland, wo die Regierung fast allmächtig und der Reichstag und alle andern Vertretungskörper ohne wirkliche Macht, in Deutschland so etwas proklamieren, und noch dazu ohne Not, heisst das Feigenblatt dem Absolutismus abnehmen und sich selbst vor die Blösse binden." (MEW 22, 234).

It is no surprise that Kautsky was even more enthusiastic about the increasing support for the party in the elections than Engels — and from this it was but a short way to Bernstein's absolutisation of parliamentary politics. The Erfurt programme adopted by the party in 1891 was widely regarded as genuinely revolutionary and Marxist. Engels, whose critique was cautiously published for the first time in *Die Neue Zeit* in 1901 seems to have accepted the draft of the programme in general and only criticised certain details (see MEW 22, 225—240). According to Mathias the Erfurt programme should be understood rather as a programme of an inherently reformist party than as a revolution- ary manifesto. The revolutionary expectations were mainly reduced to the natural and necessary development of capitalism and supported — it may be added — by the expectation of the parliamentary majority shortly to be achieved. Once the majority of the seats in parliament were in the hands of the socialists, revolution would be easy. At the same time, the increase in the number of supporters for the party gave reason for the party to operate more cautiously. Bebel expressed this idea in the very meeting that approved the new Erfurt programme in the following words: a party which has millions of supporters must operate more carefully than a sect which is without importance and without responsibility (see Bebel 1891—92, 57). Increasing support and membership also brought with it the danger of an increasing segmentation of the party (see Mathias 1957, 160—162).

According to Mathias, Kautsky's evolutionary conception of Marxism and its practi- cal conclusions were well in accordance with the official party ideology of its time, as was already shown by Kautsky's theoretical foundation of the Erfurt programme. Kautsky's leading position can already be deduced from *Ein sozialdemokratischer Kathekismus* (1893—94) published in *Die Neue Zeit* in 1893. The legend about the revolutionary Kautsky and his turning into a revisionist after the First World War can thus be seriously doubted. In the social democratic catechism the Social Democratic Party is characterised as a revolutionary party which does not, however, prepare a revolution ("eine revolutionäre, nicht aber eine Revolutionen machende Partei" (cit. in Kautsky 1909b, 44)). The revolutionary goal principally accepted by the party in its programmes seems to be of no practical importance:

"Wir wissen, dass unsere Ziele nur durch eine Revolution erreicht werden können, wir wissen aber auch, das es ebensowenig in unserer Macht steht, diese Revolution zu machen, als in der unserer Gegner, sie zu verhindern. Es fällt uns daher auch gar nicht ein, eine

Revolution anstiften oder vorbereiten zu wollen. Und da die Revolution nicht von uns willkürlich gemacht werden kann, können wir auch nicht das mindeste darüber sagen, wann, unter welchen Bedingungen und in welchen Formen sie eintreten wird." (Kautsky 1909b, 44; see also Mathias 1957, 163).

According to Kautsky it is impossible to predict the nature of the future "decisive" struggles:

"...ob sie blutige sein werden, ob die physische Gewalt eine bedeutende Rolle in ihnen spielen oder ob man sie ausschliesslich mit den Mitteln ökonomischer, legislativer und moralischer Pression ausfechten wird." (Kautsky 1909b, 45).

All we can say is that in the last instance the final goal is guaranteed by the objective economic development of capitalism. Despite this uncertainty it is, however, more probable that the peaceful means of struggle will be dominant in the future revolutionary upheavals of the proletariat. The probability of the application of peaceful methods is increasing all the time because both the importance of the democratic institutions and the knowledge about economic and political development are increasing (see Kautsky 1909b, 45−46). In conclusion, the Social Democrats have to do everything in their power to prevent all kinds of provocation:

". . .alles vermeiden, ja bekämpfen, was eine zwecklose Provokation der herrschenden Klassen wäre, was deren Staatsmännern einen Anhaltspunkt gäbe, um die Bourgeoisie und deren Anhang in sozialistenfresserische Tollhäuslerei zu treiben." (Kautsky 1909b, 48).

Revolutionary enthusiasm is at present, however, even more important than ever. Revolutionary enthusiasm is the great moving force of a socialist movement. There is, however, a danger connected with the increasing strength and importance of the party: it becomes difficult to balance immediate tasks with the more important and decisive ones. It becomes difficult not to lose the future perspective, and to maintain the consciousness about the Social Democrats as a party of revolutionary struggle, as a party waging war against the bourgeois social order. The conclusion drawn by Kautsky from the above discussion is somewhat amazing:

"Wir könnten die friedliche Entwicklung nur gefährden durch allzu grosse Friedlichkeit." (Kautsky 1909b, 51).

In other words, one must continuously speak of revolution in order not to have to make one.

According to Mathias the main question in the discussion about the role of different methods of revolution did not concern actual parliamentary or reform politics. Kautsky's main problem was to integrate the different factions inside the party and to unify them into one organisation despite their practical and tactical differences. Thus the official ideology of the party made it possible to maintain the fiction of the revolutionary character of a unified party. The fiction of the revolutionary nature of the party was an essential element of the politics of integration. As a consequence, revolutionary

Marxism is transformed into an undialectic theory of evolution, which trusts the objective relations and forces of development to realise socialism (see Mathias 1957, 167):

> "Im Grunde sind ihre ideologischen Positionen auch in der Zeit der leidenschaftlichsten Kämpfe nichts als Momente ein und derselben Revisionsbewegung, die bereits mit der beginnenden Marxismusrezeption während des Sozialistengesetzes anhebt und von dem Krypto-Revisionismus des Erfurter Programms zum offenen Revisionismus fortschreitet, der in der offiziellen Partei-Ideologie und auch bei Kautsky erst in der Weimarer Republik zum Durchbruch kommt, obgleich es auch jetzt noch nicht gelingt, die Kluft zwischen Idelogie und Praxis zu schliessen." (Mathias 1957, 168).

According to Mathias the real controversy (between Kautsky and Bernstein or between revolutionary and revisionist Marxism) in no way concerned the right interpretation of Marxism. The real reason why Kautsky and Bebel opposed revisionism inside the party was that it seemed to contradict the revolutionary aspirations and hopes of the masses, and not that it contradicted the practical political and tactical aims of the party. A revolutionary programme was important for the party because it guaranteed the integrity and unity of the party. As Kautsky had formulated it:

> "Auf die Einheitlichkeit der Taktik beruht die Einheit der Partei, und wo jene verloren geht, geht auch diese bald in die Brüche." (Kautsky 1899a, 3).

According to Kautsky revolutionary Marxism as presented by the party had proved victorious against Bernstein's revisionism — Bernstein's critique had brought about practically no changes in the party tactics or programme. Kautsky was convinced of the inadequacy of Bernstein's attempts to revise the programme and defended the revolutionary nature of Social Democracy, which did not, in any case, have any consequences in practical politics. In Kautsky's opinion revolution was not to be understood as a forthcoming great social upheaval but rather as a goal that must be postulated and proved theoretically. Having made the concept of revolution rather empty of meaning — it was only a question of tactics — Kautsky was ready to conclude:

> "Tatsächlich ist, gerade durch ihre theoretische Basis, nichts anpassungsfähiger, als die Taktik der Sozialdemokratie." (Kautsky 1899a, 166).

Kautsky was even willing to admit that there was not actually any great divergence of opinion among the disputants. Both were, in fact, aiming at social and democratic reforms. It is, however, important to discuss the final goal because it is closely connected with the question of the organisation and propaganda of a modern political party (see Kautsky 1899a, 184). Bernstein's main mistake was not that he defended a reformist turn in practical politics. His mistake was that he totally abandoned the thought of revolution. (See Kautsky 1914, 39.)

According to Mathias' interpretation, Kautsky never abandoned the idea of a socialist revolution and the dictatorship of the proletariat as the final goal of the Social Democratic Party but he interpreted the idea in a sense that, in fact, transformed revolution into a peaceful development of capitalism into socialism and got rid of its

dangerous connotations (see Mathias 1957, 171). The position was − according to
Mathias − typical of the parties of the Second International:

> "Diese Haltung war charakteristisch für die Parteien der II. Internationale, die sich der
> besonderen Arbeiterinteressen annahmen und im übrigen in den grossen Fragen der prak-
> tischen Politik mit der liberalen bürgerlichen Demokratie durchaus übereinstimmten. Ge-
> tragen von dem echten und starken Klassenbewusstsein der europäischen Arbeiterschaft
> dieser Zeit, war es ihnen jedoch ein Bedürfnis, die Sonderstellung der sozialistischen
> gegenüber allen anderen Parteien zu betonen." (Mathias 1957, 173).

The politics of careful balance characterized as centrist which was presented in practice
by the leadership of the party and by Kautsky in theory became more obvious after
1910. But it did not at this stage lead to a formation of clear factions of right, left and
centrist wings inside the party. This centrist politics satisfied both the needs of the party
as a democratic and reformist party of opposition and the aspirations of the radical
section of its membership. (See Mathias 1957, 179−180.) One of the consequences of
the centrist strategy was an emphasis on the organisation as the connecting link between
the everyday practice of the party and the final goal of socialism (see Mathias 1957,
184). The organisation was to be preserved intact and strengthened by all means, and
every increase in the strength of the organisation was interpreted as a real increase in its
power. The passive waiting for revolution was legitimated either by the argument that
the workers' organisation was not yet strong enough, or by the opposite argument that
the organisation, being already strong, should not be endangered by any revolutionary
adventures, the possible risks of which could not be calculated in advance. (See Mathias
1957, 183.)

Kautsky's position in the lively discussion about the role of a mass strike was typical
of this cautious and passive expectation of the outbreak of revolution. Kautsky could
proudly state that as early as 1891 he was the only Marxist in Germany to defend the
use of a political mass strike as a means of achieving important political goals; on the
other hand, he immediately hurried to add that "solange sich die gegebenen Verhältnisse nicht ändern, ein Massenstreik in Deutschland nicht möglich ist" (Kautsky 1914,
298). In the same context Kautsky both defended the electorial struggle as the greatest
possible mass action of the proletariat, and considered the elections an effective safety
valve which could prevent a dangerous explosion (see Kautsky 1914, 276).

In Kautsky's opinion, then, both radical demands and mass actions could in a similar
way endanger the development of the organisation and the achievement of the final
goal.The final struggle for power should thus be postponed until a nonpredictable
future. It would in any case take place of necessity. Kautsky's position − shared by the
party leadership − was summarised by Mathias as follows:

> "Im ungestörten Fortgang des passiven Prozesses der sich steigernden faszinierenden
> Stimmzahlen − nicht in der Realisierung der von der Partei repräsentierten Macht − ist für
> die Parteiinstanzen die Lösung selbst der drängendsten Probleme der Zeit beschlossen."
> (Mathias 1957, 192).

The combination of the ideology of integration and seemingly revolutionary vigour outlined by Mathias could be documented in more detail even in Kautsky's *Der Weg zur Macht* (1909b). Constant worry about the revolutionary adventures endangering the future of the party and socialism are expressed throughout Kautsky's booklet. The transformation of capitalism into socialism was supposed to be guaranteed by the objective processes of development, the growing into socialism:

> "Von zwei Seiten aus wachsen wir hinein: einmal durch die Entwicklung des Kapitalismus, durch die Konzentration des Kapitals. (. . .) Heute sind wir bereits so weit, dass Banken und Unternehmerorganisationen den grössten Teil der kapitalistischen Unternehmungen der verschiedensten Nationen beherrschen und organisieren. So wird die gesellschaftliche Organisierung der Produktion immer mehr vorbereitet." (Kautsky 1909b, 24).

The centralisation of capital and property is, however, only one aspect of the growing into socialism. Kautsky was quite well aware of the dangers of objectivism, and he never got tired of emphasising the role of the subjective factor as the other side of development. Fortunately, there was another side to the same process, namely a continuous increase in the proletariat and the increasing power of the workers' organisations:

> "Die Vorbereitung des Sozialismus durch die Kapitalkonzentration ist indes nur die eine Seite des Hineinwachsens in den Zukunftsstaat. (. . .) Mit der Zunahme des Kapitals wächst auch die Zahl der Proletarier innerhalb der Gesellschaft. Sie werden deren zahlreichste Klasse. Und gleichzeitig wachsen ihre Organisationen." (Kautsky 1909b, 25).

According to Kautsky reformists acknowledge the objective process of transformation of capitalism into socialism. They do not, however, acknowledge the other component of this process:

> ". . .das Wachstum, das sie beschreibt, ist nicht das Wachstum eines *einzigen* Elementes, sonder *zweier* Elemente, und zwar zweier sehr *gegensätzlichen* Elemente: Kapital und Arbeit." (Kautsky 1909b, 25).

Kautsky was eager to point out that this transformation does not take place without the conscious action of the proletariat. Human will is an essential element in social change and history; the growing into socialism cannot be an unconscious process (see Kautsky 1909b, 33). Class struggle results from the antagonistic will of the representatives of the social classes (see Kautsky 1909b, 34). Will is thus in the last instance the basic motive force of the whole social process. Consciousness played an important role in Kautsky's thinking in another sense, too. Increasing consciousness of the nature of economic processes also makes it possible for the proletariat to use its power more economically and effectively, and to save its resources:

> "Nur die *Erkenntnis* des gesellschaftlichen Prozesses, seiner Tendenzen und Ziele vermag dieser Verwendung ein Ende zu machen, die Kräfte des Proletariats zu konzentrieren, sie in grossen Organisationen zusammenzufassen, die durch grosse Ziele vereinigt werden und

planmässig persönliche und Augenblicksaktionen den dauernden Klasseninteressen un-
terordnen, die ihrerseits wieder in den Dienst der gesamten gesellschaftlichen Entwicklung
gestellt sind. Mit anderen Worten, die Theorie ist der Faktor, der die mögliche Kraftentfal-
tung des Proletariats auf höchste steigert, indem er dessen durch die ökonomische Entwicklung gegebenen Kräfte auf zweckmässigste gebrauchen lehrt und ihrer Verschwendung
entgegenwirkt." (Kautsky 1909b, 37).

While the conditions for socialism are ripening inside capitalism, the future destiny of
the society is simultaneously determined by the relations of power between capital and
wage labour. In Kautsky's opinion in a developed capitalist state — as in England or
Germany — the proletariat already has the power necessary to take over the government of the state and the economic conditions already exist for the transformation from
the private to the socialist ownership of property. Only one problem remains: the
proletariat is in principle powerful but it does not yet recognise its own social power,
the consciousness of the working class is not sufficiently developed:

"Aber was dem Proletariat fehlt, ist das Bewusstsein seiner Kraft." (Kautsky 1909b, 38).

The task of the party is to assist the proletariat to become conscious of its real power.
This can be done through theoretical schooling, but even more effectively through
exemplary actions:

"Ihre Erfolge im Kampf gegen den Gegner sind es, wodurch die Sozialdemokratie dem
Proletarier seine Kraft am deutlichsten demonstriert und dadurch sein Kraftgefühl am
wirksamsten hebt." (Kautsky 1909b, 38).

Thus, the consciousness and theoretical knowledge of the proletariat is a decisive precondition for a successful socialist revolution, and it is the task of the party both to
assist in the development of this consciousness and to decide when the consciousness
and the feeling of power are sufficiently developed to accomplish the great historical
mission.

Even though nothing definite can be said about the nature of the coming struggles it
can be predicted that peaceful methods will be more important than violent ones. In the
future the proletariat will have better opportunities for making use of economic, political and moral means of resistance than of directly violent ones (see Kautsky 1909b,
45). Kautsky did admit that it is also true that sometimes democratic institutions have a
tendency to pacify the social struggle in a bourgeois society. Sometimes they are even
said to pacify the class struggle completely. This, however, is not true. But the new
methods available do make it possible for the proletariat to economise its efforts:

"Die Demokratie kann die Klassengegensätze der kapitalistischen Gesellschaft nicht be-
seitigen, und deren notwendiges Endergebnis, den Umsturz dieser Gesellschaft, nicht auf-
halten. Aber eins kann sie: sie kann nicht die Revolution, aber sie kann manchen ver-
frühten, aufsichtslosen Revolutionsversuch verhüten und manche revolutionäre Erhebung
überflüssig machen. Sie verschafft Klarheit über die Kräfteverhältnisse der verschiedenen
Parteien und Klassen; sie beseitigt nicht deren Gegensätze und verschiedet nicht deren

Endziele, aber sie wirkt dahin, die aufstrebenden Klassen zu hindern, dass sie sich jeweilen an die Lösung von Aufgaben machen, denen sie noch nicht gewachsen sind, und sie wirkt auch dahin, die herrschenden Klassen davon abzuhalten, Konzessionen zu verweigern, zu deren Verweigerung sie nicht mehr die Kraft haben. Die Richtung der Entwicklung wird dadurch nicht geändert, aber ihr Gang wird steter, ruhiger." (Kautsky 1909b, 46).

It is rather characteristic that in the same context of discussion Kautsky proposed to name the Paris Commune, generally regarded as the great heroic revolutionary up-heaval of the proletariat, as a warning example of a struggle in which the proletariat clearly was not yet ready to take power into its hands (see Kautsky 1909b, 46). Kautsky warned the workers' movement that its enemy, the ruling class, was all but waiting for a confrontation in which it could destroy the whole proletarian organisation. The pro-letariat was, according to Kautsky, already conscious enough of these dangers, and it could postpone the decisive struggle until it really was strong enough to win. it (see Kautsky 1909b, 47−48). There is a danger in Kautsky's cautious strategy which he was ready to admit, namely it might seem that the Social Democrats are no longer a party of revolution at all. This loss of revolutionary enthusiasm could endanger the achievement of its future goals. It may further sound paradoxical that even though Kautsky was continuously eager to warn the working class movement of revolutionary adventures of all kinds, he nevertheless stated that the time was actually already ripe for a revolution:

"Und es kann nicht mehr von einer *vorzeitigen* Revolution reden, wenn es aus dem gegebenen staatlichen Boden so viel Kraft gesogen hat, als ihm zu entnehmen war, wenn eine Umgestaltung dieses Bodens zu einer Bedingung seines weiteren Aufstiegs darf." (Kautsky 1909b, 97).

In his book *Karl Kautsky und der Marxismus der II. Internationale* Reinhold Hühnlich (1981) defended Kautsky and his pamphlet *Der Weg zur Macht* as representing genuine revolutionary Marxism and criticised Mathias' earlier interpretation of the ideological role of Kautskyanism. According to Hühnlich, *Der Weg zur Macht* is not restricted to a specific theory of revolution and can consequently be read as a representative document of Second International Marxism. It also includes elements of a theory of imperialism and a description of the latest developments in capitalism. The alternative of war or socialism as presented at the end of the booklet is a final proof that Kautsky is not a reformist (see Hühnlich 1981, 157). There is, furthermore, a new contribution to the discussion of the subjective conditions of Social Democratic action in Kautsky's book, one of its main theses being the convergence of economic and political struggle under imperialism (see Hühnlich 1981, 159). Hühnlich, however, admits that Kautsky did not in fact analyse the subjective conditions of revolution in detail; neither did he analyse the role of the different factions inside the working class and their corresponding interests. The only explanation given for the emerging reformist movement inside the party is the petit bourgeois origins of the workers and changing economic conjunctures (see Hühnlich 1981, 161).

According to Hühnlich, Kautsky's position definitely cannot be characterised as a

reformist one — with an overtone of verbal radicalism — because he emphasised parliamentary action not only as aiming at reforms but also as an important factor in the
development of a revolutionary consciousness. Neither did he neglect the importance of
action by the proletariat taking place outside parliament:

> "Die Politik der Sozialdemokratie steht somit gerade auch in den sogenannten politischen
> Tagesfragen immer unter der Perspektive des sozialistischen Endziels, was den revolu-
> tionären Charakter der Partei ausmacht." (Hühnlich 1981, 162).

Hühnlich did not accept Mathias' interpretation of *Der Weg zur Macht*, especially
because in his opinion Mathias did not pay any attention to the wider contexts of the
book. Kautsky's slogan "wir sind revolutionäre, nicht aber eine Revolutionen
machende Partei" cannot be intepreted as exemplifying Kautsky's verbal radicalism. In
the chapter under discussion Kautsky was essentially criticising on the one hand fatalistic and on the other hand voluntaristic conceptions of socialism, and no conclusions can
be drawn about either Kautsky's attentisme or reformism (see Hühnlich 1981, 163).

Der Weg zur Macht argued not only that the general conditions for revolution and
socialism are present at the moment but also for the immediate actuality of revolution
(see Hühnlich 1981, 165). Thus there cannot be any talk of a premature revolution, as
proved by the political situation since the 1890's. Furthermore, the possible outbreak of
war would only function as a catalyser of revolution. This thesis should be enough to
prove that Kautsky was a representative of the genuine left wing of Social Democracy
and not a reformist after all. According to Hühnlich Kautsky cannot be accused of
attentisme either, because he was not satisfied with expecting a revolution to start; he
also formulated a consequent democratic programme of action. The democratisation of
the German Reich was supposed to lead to a transformation stage of the society, and
even more important, Kautsky emphasised the role of non-parliamentary action (mass
strikes, May Day demonstrations, etc.) as important forms of struggle. Kautsky's position was consequently not defensive but offensive. It proposed offensive methods of
struggle and did not only emphasise the role of organisation and enlightenment. Hence,
Kautsky's position cannot be characterised as representing negative integration (see
Hühnlich 1981, 165–167).

Hühnlich does, however, admit that there is one weak point in Kautsky's argumentation concerning the future society and state: Kautsky understood the dictatorship of the
proletariat in purely political terms and his defence of the revolutionary process remained mainly negative.Kautsky did not recognise the task of crushing the bourgeois
state machinery; neither did he discuss in which way the state machinery could be
transformed from an organ of capitalists into one of the propertyless, from an organ of
repression into one of emancipation. This weakness was, however, shared by all the
other representatives of the Second International and Kautsky should not be criticised
for it alone (see Hühnlich 1981, 168). In Hühnlich's analysis Kautsky thus genuinely
represented the left wing within the Social Democratic theoretical spectrum, and he
cannot be identified as an ideologist of integration and attentisme.

Hühnlich's defence of Kautsky and Kautskyanism is justified to the extent that the context of argumentation in *Der Weg zur Macht* should really be taken into account. If Kautsky had only presented his idea of the revolutionary nature of the Social Democratic Party in this context, Hühnlich's defence of Kautsky would be well-grounded. The conception presented in *Der Weg zur Macht* can, however, be discussed in the wider context of Kautsky's thinking, and in this context Mathias' argumentation is more convincing: no one is actually denying that Kautsky did continuously speak of the ripening conditions for revolution and fundamentally identified himself as a revolutionary Marxist. Neither will anyone deny that at least in principle Kautsky defended non-parliamentary methods of struggle and understood the role of parliament as an organ making the revolutionary transformation possible. It is more the strange combination of revolutionary vigour and cautiousness in practical politics that caused Mathias and Groh to interpret Kautsky's position in terms of negative integration and revolutionary attentisme.[1] Hühnlich is, of course, right in emphasising that Kautsky did present some kind of a democratic action programme stressing both parliamentary reforms and the role of demonstrations which were supposed to support the demands for reforms. Reforms were, furthermore, supposed to increase the strength of the proletarian organisations and to function as a measure of this very same strength. And, of course, Kautsky considered socialism as the final goal of the workers movement and studied its conditions. A revolutionary period was opening up; the workers should, on the other hand, be careful not to take the initiative into their own hands under the pretext of endangering their organisation and present achievements. The organisation is both an indicator and an instrument of the power of the workers' movement, the strength of which is not, however, realised in practical politics. The democratic action programme is evaluated by the criterion of strengthening the organisation, and all the demands and achievements are measured by this criterion. Kautsky certainly was a revolutionary in demanding the socialist revolution, but the only connection between the immediate tasks of the movement and its final goal is provided by the organisation; once the organisation is sufficiently developed the socialist revolution will be realised.

---

[1] Salvadori reminded that there were other more influential historical factors contributing to the integration of Social Democracy into bourgeois society than the theoretical position represented by Kautsky, but even Salvadori does not deny Mathias' general interpretation:

> "We have seen that a cautious conclusion was typical of Kautsky, who theorized the inevitability of escalating social conflict in general historical terms, yet constantly retreated to a passive *attentisme* when it came to the concrete conjuncture in Germany." (Salvadori 1979, 90).

It may be that Mathias had a tendency to interpret Kautsky's work as a direct factor leading to the integration of Social Democracy into the bourgeois state. It seems more reasonable, however, to read Mathias as claiming that Kautsky's scientific socialism was only an expression and perhaps the most prominent expression of the dilemma facing a growing revolutionary mass party at the turn of the century.

Until then, all political demands and achievements must serve this very purpose. It is this idea which Mathias called organisational patriotism.[2]

Kautsky's discussion of parliamentary democracy and struggle in other contexts can be used to give further support to Mathias' thesis — despite the fact that Mathias did not exceedingly analyse Kautsky's conception of democracy and parliament and its role in Kautsky's theory of revolution.

Parliamentary democracy was understood by Kautsky as having a twofold role in the socialist strategy. On the one hand, it formed the ideal training ground for the development of the proletarian organisation and party, it was essential for the development of consciousness, too. On the other hand, parliament functioned as an indicator of the strength of political parties in society, it showed when the time was ready for a socialist revolution or, in other words, when the proletariat formed the majority of society. Even though Kautsky by no means greatly denied the importance of mass action or demonstrations and their propagation for agitationary purposes, he warned against their premature use; their use could lead to provocation — before the Social Democrats could be sure of winning the final struggle which, once again, was best shown by their success in elections. Even though Kautsky did not at this stage regard parliamentary politics as the exclusive form of proletarian political activity, he did regard it as its principal form of activity. Parliamentary democracy was not yet synonymous with proletarian rule in general — as it was practically to become after the Russian Revolution in 1917 — but it constituted the institution within which the final struggle was to be solved. It was also the institution through which the working class was to exercise its political power.

Mathias was not the first to point out Kautsky's position as representing attentisme and leading to integration — even though the terms were not used. In a discussion of the role of the general strike — a discussion which was very vivid after the first Russian Revolution in 1905 — Anton Pannekoek characterised Kautsky's position in very similar terms. Pannekoek claimed that Kautsky neglected the importance of mass actions as promoters of revolution. And Kautsky's answer to the critique was also characteristic of his position. In a series of articles published in *Die Neue Zeit* in 1912—13 Pannekoek analysed the basic difference of opinions as follows:

> "Die Frage, *wie das Proletariat die demokratischen Grundrechte bekommt*, die ihm bei genügenden sozialistischen Klassenbewusstsein die politische Herrschaft in die Hand

---

[2]   It is not difficult to find enthusiastic statements about the role of organisation in Kautsky's writings:

> "Der Proletarier sieht sein Glück nicht in der Grösse und Macht seiner eigenen Persönlichkeit, sondern in der Grösse und Macht der Organisation, welcher er angehört." (Kautsky 1904—05, 345).

And further:

> "Durch die Entwicklung seiner Organisation schreitet er siegreich vorwärts. Organisation heisst aber nichts anderes als Unterordnung des einzelnen unter eine Gesamtheit, Einschränkung seiner persönlichen Freiheit." (Kautsky 1904—05, 345).

liefern, ist die *Grundfrage unserer Taktik*. Wir vertreten die Auffassung, dass sie der herrschenden Klasse nur durch Kämpfe abgezwungen werden können, in denen sie ihre ganze Macht gegen das Proletariat ins Feld führt und ihre ganze Macht also vernichtet werden muss. Eine andrere Auffassung wäre diese dass die herrschende Klasse sie freiwillig gibt." (Pannekoek 1912—13, 365)

Kautsky's mistake was that he did not represent either of these conceptions. He seemed to think, on the contrary, that the final takeover of political power was something altogether different from the practical politics of the Social Democrats:[3]

> "Wir haben aus seinen Äusserungen geschlossen, dass er sich die Eroberung der Herrschaft als eine einmalige Niederwerfung der Macht des Feindes denkt, als einen Akt ganz anderer Natur als alles, was bis dahin, als Vorbereitung zu dieser Revolution, die Tätigkeit des Proletariats bildet." (Pannekoek 1912—13, 365).

Further, Pannekoek accused Kautsky of restricting the activity and initiative of the masses on the pretext of strengthening the organisation and the power potential of the party. Pannekoek's accusation thus closely resembled that of Mathias'. According to Pannekoek Kautsky's reasoning was faulty and led to unbearable conclusions. The masses do not transfer part of their energy and their revolutionary willpower to an organisation, the proletarian party, in order to diminish it. On the contrary, the party should represent the general will and power of the proletariat, and as such, it should strengthen and not diminish the total power of the proletarian movement:

> "Was die Massen dabei an Initiative und spontaner Aktionskraft verlieren, ist kein wirklicher Verlust, sondern kommt an einer anderen Stelle in anderer Form als Initiative und Aktionskraft der Partei wiederum zum Vorschein: es findet gleichsam eine Transformation der Energie statt." (Pannekoek 1912—13, 373).

Kautsky misunderstood the relation between the party and the masses. He wanted to restrict the power and activity of the masses in order to strengthen the power and activity of the party. The result could only be the opposite:

---

[3]   Rosa Luxemburg's discussion of a mass strike can also be understood as a critique of the party leadership, Kautsky included:

> "Der Massenstreik, wie ihn uns die russische Revolution zeigt, ist nicht ein pfiffiges Mittel, ausgeklügelt zum Zwecke einer kräftigen Wirkung des proletarischen Kampfes, sondern er ist *die Bewegungsweise der proletarischen Masse, die Erscheinungsform des proletarischen Kampfes in der Revolution*. (...) Der Massenstreik ist vielmehr die Bezeichung, der Sammelbegriff einer ganzen jahrelangen, vielleicht jahrzehntelangen Periode des Klassenkampfes." (Luxemburg 1970b (1906), 168—169).

And further:

> "Bei dem deutschen aufgeklärten Arbeiter ist das von der Sozialdemokratie gepflanzte Klassenbewusstsein ein *theoretisches, latentes: ...* In der Revolution, wo die Masse selbst auf dem politischen Schauplatz erscheint, wird das Klassenbewusstsein ein *praktisches, aktives.*" (Luxemburg 1970b, 194). "Sechs Monate einer revolutionären Periode werden an der Schulung dieser jetzt unorganisierten Massen das Werk vollenden, das zehn Jahre Volksversammlungen und Flugblattverteilungen nicht fertigzubringen vermögen." (Luxemburg 1970b, 195).

"Würde die Partei es als ihre Aufgabe betrachten, die Massen solange als es nur geht von Aktionen zurückzuhalten, so bedeutete die Parteidisziplin den Verlust an Initiative und spontaner Aktionskraft der Massen, einen *wirklichen* Verlust, statt eine Transformation der Energie. *Dann bedeutete die Existenz der Partei eine Schmälerung der revolutionären Kraft des Proletariats, statt ihre Stärkung.*" (Pannekoek 1912–13, 373).

Kautsky's answer to Pannekoek's critique was typical. On the one hand he wanted to defend himself as being a radical revolutionary. He agreed with Pannekoek on the importance of actual struggle in increasing the activity and power of the revolutionary organisation:

"Das heisst wir stimmen auch darin überein, dass wir beide annehmen, die proletarischen Machtorganisationen seien Kampfesorganisationen, die sich in Kampfe bewähren, durch den Kampf wachsen und gedeihen." (Kautsky 1912–13, 438).

The only difference between the disputants as understood by Kautsky was that whereas Pannekoek was ready to endanger the organisation even in struggles without the guarantee of success, Kautsky was willing to risk the organisation only insofar as success war certain:

"Aber Pannekoek versteht darunter den *Kampf im allgemeinen* ich nur den *erfolgreichen* Kampf. Er meint, der Geist, der die Organisation beherrsche, ist die Hauptsache, und der werde durch jeden Kampf angestachelt, ob er Sieg bringe oder Niederlage." (Kautsky 1912–13, 438–439).

Even though Kautsky did not explicitly state it, the logical conclusion was that since one never can be sure of the results of a struggle in advance — at least not until the proletariat forms the majority of the population and proves its power in parliamentary elections — one should restrain from any struggle that might endanger the integrity and organisation of the party. Participation in political struggles and the presentation of one's own demands to other political forces is only justifiable insofar as it supports the organisational growth of the workers' party.

Kautsky's position in the discussion about the use of mass strike as a weapon was also typical. He warned the party not to use this weapon recklessly — as he thought Panne-koek was suggesting:

"Unsere Partei hat unzweideutig erkennen lassen, dass sie nicht geneigt ist, bei jeder Gelegenheit zum Massenstreik zu greifen." (Kautsky 1912–13, 445).

Kautsky did not in principle deny the use of mass strike or other mass actions as a weapon. But he trivialised the whole question and stated that it was self-evident that mass actions belong to the arsenal of the party:

"Heute von unserer Partei Massenaktionen fordern, heisst einfach fordern, dass sie das Selbstverständliche tut, dass sie sich bewegt." (Kautsky 1912–13, 445).

Kautsky's and Pannekoek's debate on the general strike showed Kautsky's twofold position rather clearly: on the one hand he was all too ready to accept the use of a mass action as a political weapon, but on the other hand he made the point harmless by stressing, first, that care should be taken not to use it recklessly, without the certainty of success, and second, that there was not in fact any real disagreement between him and Pannekoek on the subject. Kautsky had, in fact, always approved of the use of mass strike as a political method. Then Pannekoek's defence of the use of mass actions did not, in fact, add anything new to the tactics of Social Democracy. They had always been part of the agitation and propaganda of the party. Kautsky was, then, on the one hand revolutionary, while on the other he denied the actuality and possibility of political action aiming at a revolution. There could hardly be a clearer manifestation of revolutionary attentisme.

In his pamphlet *Die Internationalität und der Krieg* (1915b) Kautsky explicitly discussed the new situation caused by the World War and its consequences for the International. Kautsky was not willing to admit that the outbreak of war would indicate bankruptcy for the policy of the International. On the contrary, the theory of Social Democracy had, in fact, been verified. Marxists had predicted the necessary outcome of the war as a consequence of the imperialist politics of the major powers. If the politics recommended and propagated by the Marxists had been adopted, war could have been avoided. Thus the Social Democrats had been right from the very beginning. (See Kautsky 1915b, 6.)

Kautsky did not, however, only try to legitimate the strategy and theoretical conclusions of Social Democracy; he even tried to make them more adequate under the present conditions. The most important new idea was included in the proposal that Social Democrats do not necessarily have to condemn war in general; there are just wars, wars that can be defended and supported by the Social Democrats. Everything depends on the motives of the participants in the war:

> "Anders sieht die Sache, wenn man bei der Parteinahme ausgeht nicht vom *Interesse des eigenen Staates*, sondern von dem der *Gesamtheit des Proletariats der Welt* und sich fragt: wessen Sieg bietet für den Fortschritt unserer Sache nicht nur im eigenen Staate, sondern in der Welt, bessere Aussichten?" (Kautsky 1915b, 8).

Thus one could say that a class standpoint acts as the criterion for just or unjust wars.

Kautsky's position in relation to the strategy of the International was very characteristic: On the one hand the politics of the International were in fact correct even before the war, and they proved to be correct even during the war. On the other hand, the International could not play any active role opposing the war once it had been declared. The International was basically an instrument of peace, not one of war. Kautsky's position was thus paradoxical: the International was in the possession of the right theory and strategy, which, however, proved altogether ineffective:

> "Das heisst, sie ist kein wirksames Werkzeug im Kriege, sie ist im *Wesentlichen ein Friedensinstrument*. Und Zwar in doppeltem Sinne. Sie kann ihre volle Kraft nur entfalten im Frieden. Und so weit sie ihre volle Kraft entfalten mag, wirkt sie stets für den Frieden." (Kautsky 1915b, 38).

Thus there did not seem to be any chance of opposing the war once it had been declared. The International was at its strongest during peace; and indeed, it was the best instrument for maintaining peace, but paradoxically not suited to opposing war (see Kautsky 1915b, 39).[4]

The International was a "Friedensinstrument" which is in principle able to function only during peace, opposing the preparations for war. Because opposing a war seems to be doomed to failure, it should be possible to further differentiate the strategy and to take a stand on questions of war in a differentiated way. According to Kautsky it was thus justified to defend one's own nation against an alien aggressor which demands the annexation of the areas of one's own country. A distinction should thus be made between a defence war and a war of aggression. And he came to the conclusion that a defence war always is justified.

Kautsky, however, clained that the peace efforts of Social Democracy are not at all futile even if they are unable to prevent or stop a war. They have in any case an immense propagandistic effect:

> "Aber welches immer auch bei der Festsetzung der Friedensbedingungen der augenblick-liche praktische Erfolg eines Friedensprogramms der Internationale sein mag, sein dauern-der, propagandischer Erfolg muss auf jeden Fall ein gewaltiger sein, um so mehr, je tiefer und allgemeiner das Friedensbedürfnis nach dem Kriege sein wird und je deutlicher die Politik der Internationale als die einzige erscheint, die Welt vor einem neuen Kriege zu bewahren. Gerade durch unsere Internationalität werden wir dann unsere grössten Erfolge erzielen, und gerade dadurch wird auch ein jeder von uns das Gedeihen seiner Nation am meisten sichern und fördern." (Kautsky 1915b, 40).

Participation in and active support of the war effort by the Social Democrats can, in principle, then be in accordance with a major opposition to any war and a striving for permanent peace. One of the reasons for this is that it is not possible to oppose a war directly — a position already presented by Kautsky earlier — it is first necessary to abolish the economic and political causes of war, and then the war itself becomes unnecessary:

> "Tun wir das, dann wird die Parteinahme im Krieg die Internationale nicht hinder, einig und geschlossen ihre grossen historischen Aufgaben zu erfüllen: Kampf für den Frieden, Klassenkampf im Frieden." (Kautsky 1915b, 40).

As the above discussion makes evident, Kautsky's main position and argument concern-ing the questions of war and peace was in line with his more general strategic position

---

[4] In discussing Kautsky's attitude to the danger of war and to the possibility of preventing the outbreak of war in general Pannekoek formulated Kautsky's position as follows:

> "Kautsky stellt den Gegensatz auf: nur wenn wir herrschen, ist die Kriegsgefahr beseitigt; solange der Kapitalismus herrscht, wird der Krieg nicht absolut zu verhindern sein. (...) übersieht Kautsky den *Prozess der Revolution,* worin durch das aktive Auftreten des Pro-letariats die eigene Macht allmählich aufgebaut wird, die Herrschaft des Kapitals stück-weise abbröckelt." (Pannekoek 1911−12, 616).

characterised by Mathias as a combination of revolutionary vigour and practical cautiousness or as a combination of revolutionary attentisme and negative integration by Groh. In principle, Kautsky criticised both the economic and political causes of imperialism and condemned imperialism outright as a policy of war and violence. The only permanent solution to the contradictions of capitalism causing imperialistic policies and increasing armaments, was the alternative proposed by the Social Democrats, namely the realisation of socialism. On the other hand, no practical means were proposed for preventing the outbreak or preparations for war.

The above discussion of Kautsky's position as it came into appearance in different contexts seems thus to support Mathias' thesis. Steenson defended Kautsky against accusation of 'quietism' by claiming that "Kautsky's position was not quietistic; he urged constant, vigorous participation in various endeavours, was particularly forceful in his demands for political activity, and argued that theoretical work was an integral part of socialist practice" (Steenson 1978, 153). And further:

> "His view of the party was that it was revolutionary in its opposition to the state and its aim for the future, but not 'revolution-making' because aggressive action not in accordance with objective conditions (that is, the strength of the German state) would only end in disaster." (Steenson 1978, 154).

Even though one were to agree with Steenson that the objective conditions of revolution were in fact lacking in Germany and that Kautsky's cautiousness was only dictated by his sense of political realism, Steenson's argument does not solve the problem originally posed by Mathias; it was the paradoxical combination of revolutionary vigour and practical cautiousness that was pointed out by Mathias.

In this respect Lichtheim's empathetic assesment of the role of Kautsky's thinking comes closer to the point. The very starting point of Lichtheim's analysis is the seemingly paradoxical situation in the German Social Democratic movement: at the very moment when the German Social Democratic Party had factually transformed itself into a radical-democratic opposition movement (after the abolition of the anti-socialist legislation in 1890) it — by adopting the Erfurt programme in 1891 — proclaimed its undying antagonism to bourgeois society (see Lichtheim 1964, 260). Consequently there was a widening gap between the theoretical analysis and the practical demands facing the party. In Lichtheim's opinion the great merit of Kautsky's thinking consisted of this very paradox: he provided an essentially reformist party with a revolutionary programme without, however, altering the practice of the party. There is a real paradox in Kautsky's thinking and in the situation facing the movement, but "the seeming paradox of an essentially pacific and gradualist movement equipped with a revolutionary doctrine loses much of its bewildering aspect when viewed against the background of Bismarckian and Wilheminian Germany" (Lichtheim 1964, 260). It was Kautsky's identification of the dictatorship of the proletariat and the socialist revolution with a democratic parliament having a socialist majority that solved the paradox. In retrospect, one could even agree with Lichtheim's assesment that "Kautsky was the theorist of the democratic revolution that occurred in Central Europe at the end of the war" (Licht-heim 1964, 270).

The most plausible explanation for Kautsky's cautiousness is that in his opinion not the objective conditions but the subjective factor was lacking in Germany and in Europe in general. The proletariat was unripe to accomplish a socialist revolution. The assumption of the unripe proletariat makes it sensible to emphasise the role of theore-tical training and to demand the strengthening of party organisation — both tasks that could not be accomplished without a revolutionary doctrine. The seeming paradox in Kautsky's thinking becomes understandable once the role of the subjective factor is recognised. The socialist party must in principle be a revolutionary party. Otherwise it would not be able to organise a revolutionary proletariat. But it is of equal importance that the party should not try to make an untimely revolution and provoke its oppo-nents; and a revolution is untimely — per definition — insofar as the proletariat is not ready to make it.

As Steenson pointed out, there was in Kautsky's theory of revolution a clear disctinc-tion between political and social revolution (see Steenson 1978, 8—9). By first accom-plishing a political revolution the proletariat will later be able to realise a social one. Kautsky did not, however, problematise the relation between these two types of revolu-tion. The political revolution was largely equal to the establishment of a parliamentary democracy with a Social Democratic majority. In this respect one can agree with Lichtheim's formulation of Kautsky's position:

> "As he saw it, the Socialist movement had in the meantime shed its Blanquist tendencies and become democratic, without for that reason ceasing to be revolutionary. Its rise to power necessarily implied a complete alteration in the class struggle, and this to Kautsky was what 'the revolution' meant, (. . .). This accomplished, democracy could be relied upon to do the rest." (Lichtheim 1964, 268).

Kautsky's idea of a socialist revolution and growing into socialism was thus closely connected with his conception of parliamentary democracy and parliamentary politics — a question discussed extensively neither by Mathias nor by Hühnlich in this context. The question of democracy, however, first made Kautsky's position understandable in a broader context. In *Parlamentarismus und Demokratie* (1911a) originally published in 1893 Kautsky criticised different forms of direct democracy and defended parliamentary democracy as the only adequate form of exercise of proletarian power. In this article Kautsky clearly formulated a position which he defended in various contexts later on during his career. Parliamentary democracy is — according to him — the ideal form of exercising political power and it suits the purposes of the proletariat as well. Parliamen-tary activity also guarantees the best possible growing ground for a proletarian organisa-tion.

The Social Democrats have, in fact, become the only genuine representative of democracy since liberals have deceived the cause of democracy. In the article *Was nun?* Kautsky wrote:

"An ein Wiederaufleben des Liberalismus ist nicht mehr zu denken, die Demokratie kann
nur noch durch die Sozialdemokratie erobert werden; . . ." (Kautsky 1902–03c, 398).

Social Democrats are, furthermore, the only real representatives of general social progress:

"So sehen wir jetzt, dass seine Klasseninteressen das Proletariat zum entscheidensten und
heute bereits alleinigen Verfechter des gesellschaftlichen Fortschritts machen." (Kautsky
1902–03b, 273).[5]

The general progress of society is in the interests of the working class, whereas the
capitalists only represent their specific interests:

"Statt dessen zeigt es sich, dass auch in der Handelspolitik die Interessen der Arbeiter und
die der Kapitalisten immer mehr auseinandergehen; es zeigt sich aber auch, dass dabei
immer mehr die Arbeiterinteressen mit denen der ökonomischen Entwicklung der gesamten Nation zusammenfallen, indessen die der Kapitalisten immer mehr zu Sonderinteressen
einzelner Cliquen werden, die die weitere Entwicklung der Gesamtheit schädigen."
(Kautsky 1911b, 55).[6]

This evaluation of specific vs. general interests was based on an analysis of the transformation of the capitalism of free competition into monopolistic capitalism governed
by trusts and cartels introducing restrictioins on trade and competition.

In 1915 Kautsky issued a warning to the critics of parliamentarism. It was — according to him — easy to criticise but difficult to make use of a parliament:

"So entwickelte sich die moderne Demokratie, deren wesentliche Merkmale der Parlamentarismus, die Presse und grosse, das ganze Bereich des Staates umfassende Parteior-
ganisationen bilden. Nichts leichter, als an diesen Institutionen Kritik zu üben, nichts
unmöglicher, als sie in der modernen Demokratie auszuhalten." (Kautsky 1915a, 8).

Even though the Social Democrats are fighting for democracy, they are not simply
bourgeois democrats; parliamentary democracy is not their final goal, but neither is it

---

[5] Cf. Kautsky in *Agrarfrage:*
"Mit anderen Worten: die soziale Entwicklung steht höher als die Interessen des Proletariats, und die Sozialdemokratie kann proletarische Interessen nicht schützen, die der
sozialen Entwicklung im Wege stehen. Im Allgemeinen kommt das freilich nicht vor. Die
theoretische Basis der Sozialdemokratie bildet ja gerade der Erkenntnis, dass die Interessen der sozialen Entwicklung und die des Proletariats zusammenfallen, dass dieses daher
die berufene Triebfeder der letzteren ist." (Kautsky 1899c, 318).
Earlier, capitalists represented the general interests of society; now their role was inherited by the
proletariat:
"Das Klasseninteresse des Proletariats war stets insofern zusammengefallen mit dem
allgemeinen gesellschaftlichen Interesse, als es die *Zukunft* der Gesellschaft re-
präsentierte." (Kautsky 1919b, 8).
[6] It is interesting to note that in this respect Kautsky came to the same conclusion as Adam
Smith in stating that a progressive development of society is favourable to workers but not to the
capital owners (see Kautsky 1911b, 71; see also Smith 1970, 357–358).

only a mean to achieve a certain end. It is true that democracy makes it possible to achieve the final goal, socialism, but it is also an essential element of this very final goal:

> "Das Proletariat als unterste Klasse im Staate kann gar nich anders zu seinem Rechte kommen als durch die Demokratie. Nur teilen wir nicht die Illusionen der bürgerlichen Demokratie, als sei das Proletariat schon zu seinem Rechte gekommen, wenn es die Demokratie errungen hat. Diese bildet erst den Boden, auf dem es sich sein Recht erkämpft. In der Demokratie hört der proletarische Emanzipationskampf nicht auf, er nimmt nur andere Formen." (Kautsky 1915a, 11).

Democracy is, further, closely connected with the idea of a national state. The ideas of both democracy and national state presuppose that the opinion of the majority of the population is taken into account before any social changes are introduced:

> "Die Demokratie und die mit ihr eng verbundene Idee des Nationalstaats fordern, dass der Statusquo *nicht geändert wurde ohne Zustimmung der davon betroffenen Bevölkerungen.*" (Kautsky 1915a, 14).

The idea of parliamentarism as the basic instrument of proletarian power was not by any means new to Kautsky. A similar argumentation can already be found in the *Erfurt programme.*[7] In the hands of the bourgeoisie, a parliament is destined to remain an instrument of the bourgeoisie, but as soon as the working class takes part in parliament, its nature is changed. It is no longer exclusively a bourgeois instrument of political power. In *Parlamentarismus und Demokratie* the same idea was expressed even more explicitly: a parliament can just as well function as an instrument of the dictatorship of the proletariat as of the bourgeoisie (see Kautsky 1911a, 121). And a democratic state is, furthermore, the ideal field of struggle for the fighting proletariat:

> "Das kämpfende Proletariat hat so viel vertrauen zur gesellschaftlichen Entwicklung, viel Vertrauen zu sich selbst, dass es keinen Kampf fürchtet, auch nicht den mit der Über- macht; es verlangt nur nach einem Slachtfeld, auf dem es sich frei rühren kann. Der demokratische Staat bietet dieses Schlachtfeld; dort kann der letzte Entscheidungskampf zwischen Bourgeoisie und Proletariat am ehesten ausgefochten werden." (Kautsky 1911a, 125).

In order to fight an organised state power the proletariat must likewise be organised. And organisation is favoured by a parliament to which the proletariat has access. Election campaigns are the best means of organising and uniting the proletariat despite its different occupations and places of residence:

---

[7]   "Die Arbeiterklasse hat also nur keine Ursache, dem Parlamentarismus fern zu bleiben, sie hat alle Ursache, überall für die Kräftigung des Parlaments gegenüber der Staatsverwal- tung und für die Kräftigung ihrer Vertretung im Parlament aufs Entscheidenste thätig zu sein. Neben dem *Koalitionsrecht* und der *Pressefreiheit* bildet das *allgemeine Stimmrecht* eine *Lebensbedingung* für die gedeiliche Entwicklung des Proletariats." (Kautsky 1906a, 225). .

"Die Wahlkämpfe zu diesem Parlament und die Anteilnahme an den Kämpfen in diesem Parlament erweisen sich als mächtige Mittel, das Proletariat des ganzen Landes, ohne Unterschied des Berufs oder des Wohnortes, zu einheitlichem Tun, zu einem geschlossenen Körper zusammenzufassen, der den arbeitenden Massen das Maximum an Kraft verleiht, das sie unter den gegebenen Verhältnissen zu entwickeln vermögen." (Kautsky 1911a, 137).

In conlusion it could be said that in Kautsky's analysis parliamentary democracy is an important institution in a twofold meaning: it is both the ideal arena for struggle and the ideal arena for developing the organisation of the proletariat. But it is also an essential element of the dictatorship of the proletariat, interpreted as rule by the majority, without violating the rights of the minority.

In an article published in *Vorwärts* (1899b: 3) Kautsky criticised the definition of democracy proposed by Bernstein. Bernstein proposed to translate democracy as the nonexistence of any class rule, as a state of society in which no class has a privilege over the others or the whole of society. This definition is not, however, adequate. According to Kautsky, even in democratic states there is class rule:

"Bernstein identifiziert die Abwesenheit von politischen Privilegien mit Abwesenheit von Klassenherrschaft. Haben wir jetzt in demokratischen Staaten nicht ebenso eine Klassenherrschaft, wie in nicht demokratischen, ja mitunter eine noch grössere? Was Bernstein mit Abwesentheit von Klassenherrschaft sagen wollte, war offenbar nichts anderes, als Gleichberechtigung aller Volksgenossen." (Kautsky 1899b: 3).

This definition is not, however, complete at all. In Kautsky's opinion there is another more important side of democracy than equality of rights of the people:

"Zur Gleichberechtigung muss die *Unterwerfung der Regierung unter den Volskwillen* kommen, sollen wir von Demokratie reden können. Diese Seite der Demokratie hat Bernstein ganz ausser Acht gelassen, und doch wird sie praktisch für uns immer wichtiger." (Kautsky 1899b: 3).

The development of democracy has in recent years led to the equality of rights of citizens and general franchise, including the working class.[8] This is not, however, enough. The control of the governmental institutions by the people is the decisive question. Without this control, there cannot be any democracy. Even though Kautsky did not say so explicitly, the precondition for the control of the government by the

---

[8] As pointed out by Pannekoek, Kautsky's eagerness to defend parliamentarism as a means of realising socialism was somewhat out of place in Germany, where the very democratic rights were strongly restricted:

"Wenn *Parlamentarismus und Demokratie* herrschen, wenn das Parlament über die ganze Staatsgewalt und die Volksmehrheit über das Parlament gebietet, würde der politisch-parlamentarische Kampf, dass heisst die allmähliche Gewinnung der Volksmehrheit durch Parlamentspraxis, Aufklärung und Wahlkampf, den graden Weg zur Eroberung der Staatsgewalt bilden. Aber diese Vorbedingungen fehlen; sie sind nirgends vorhanden und am wenigsten in Deutschland. Sie müssen erst durch Verfassungskämpfe, durch die Eroberung des demokratischen Wahlrechtes vor allem, hergestellt werden." (Pannekoek 1911–12, 245).

people was the achievement of the majority in parliament – which on the other hand presupposed equality in the political rights of the people. Thus there was not after all such a great difference between Kautsky's and Bernstein's conceptions of democracy.

Kautsky's conception of parliamentary democracy seemed to undergo a definite change after the First World War and the Russian Revolution. Closer study of his writings during this period does, however, show that the change was not, after all, a crucial one.[9] Now Kautsky did not only state that a democratic state is an ideal institution for the purposes of the proletariat to measure and increase its power potential and also to exercise it. A centralised parliament elected by the people in a free election is also the ideal form of proletarian government. The dictatorship of the proletariat established in Soviet Russia and propagated by Lenin and others as the real democratic state of the proletariat is in reality only a caricature of democracy. The only real change in Kautsky's conception of democracy was, after all, that whereas he earlier rather unproblematically approved of the dictatorship of the proletariat and characterised the future state as representing it, he now fought the Russian dictatorship with democracy. The difference was not, however, so big, because even before this he had identified the dictatorship of the proletariat with parliamentary democracy and democratic methods of government. Dictatorship was equal to rule by a proletarian majority in parliament. In *Terrorismus und Kommunismus* Kautsky made his position quite clear:

> "In der Tat, seitdem Marxismus die sozialistische Bewegung beherrscht, dies bis zum Weltkrieg fast bei jeder ihrer bewussten grossen Bewegung vor einer grossen Niederlage bewahrt geblieben, und der Gedanke, sich durch eine Schreckenherrschaft durchzusetzen, war aus ihren Reihen vollständig verschwunden. Viel trug dazu bei der Umstand, dass in derselben Zeit, in der der Marxismus die herrschende sozialistische Lehre wurde, die Demokratie sich in Westeuropa einwurzelte und dort begann, aus einem Kampfobjekt eine feste Basis des politischen Lebens zu werden. Damit wurde nicht nur die Aufklärung und Organisation des Proletariats erleichtert, sondern auch seine Einsicht in die ökonomischen Bedingungen sowie in die Kraftverhältnisse der Klassen vermehrt, dadurch phantastischen Abenteuern vorgebeugt, und zugleich der Bürgerkrieg als Methode des Klassenkampfes ausgeschaltet." (Kautsky 1919c, 100).

---

[9]   After 1918 Kautsky's energies were primarily devoted to an ideological polemic against Bolshevism (see Salvadori 1979, 251). According to Salvadori,

> "Kautsky could be accused of immobility, but not of having abandoned the fundamental lines of his conception of the revolutionary process, the dictatorship of the proletariat, and the socialist state". (Salvadori 1979, 253).

In *Die Erhebung der Bolschewiki* (1917) written shortly after the Russian Revolution Kautsky only was

> "reaffirming his classical point of view: defence of universal suffrage and political democracy on the one hand, insistence on the role of socialists in bringing the social weight of the toiling masses to bear within political democracy and representative institutions on the other hand." (Salvadori 1979, 224).

In other words:

> "Capitalist development, proletarian strength and democracy together constituted the preconditions for a new socialist regime." (Salvadori 1979, 229).

Democracy is an ideal form of government because it makes it possible and necessary for different classes and individuals to formulate their own interests as the general interest of society and rationally to evaluate the arguments and propositions presented by every party and member of society:

> "Die beste Bildungsmöglichkeit wird ihnen gegeben in der Demokratie, zu deren wesentlichsten Einrichtungen völlige Freiheit der Diskussion und der Mitteilung von Tatsachen gehört, die aber auch für jede Partei und Richtung den Zwang mit sich bringt, um die Seele des Volkes zu ringen, die jedes Mitglied der Volksgemeinschaft in die Lage versetzt, die Argumente aller Seiten zu prüfen und sich dadurch zu einer Selbständigkeit des Urteils durchzuarbeiten. Endlich verleiht die Demokratie dem Kampf der Klassen seine höchsten Formen. Denn in ihr wendet sich jede Partei an die Gesamtheit der Bövelkerung. Jede verficht bestimmte Klassenintressen, ist aber gezwungen, jene Seiten dieser Interessen hervorzukehren, die mit den allgemeinen Intressen des gesamten Gemeinwesens zusammenhängen." (Kautsky 1919c, 118).

Kautsky acknowledged that even in democracy there is an element of coercion as well, but this coercion represents the will of a majority against a minority. During the transformation of capitalism into socialism the proletariat, which as the majority has taken over state power, must exercise its power in the form of coercion against the class of capitalists. This kind of coercion does, however, have nothing in common with the dictatorship of the proletariat as propagated by Lenin in Russia.[10] The democratic exercise of power by the majority also guarantees the rights of the minority — as Kautsky had already stated.

> "Dass *diese Art Zwang* mit der Demokratie unvereinbar ist, wiederlegt Lenin mit keinem Wort, er sucht sie annehmbar zu machen durch ein Taschenspielerkunststück, indem er aus dem Zwang, den die grose Masse auf die einzelnen Kapitalisten ausüben muss, um den Sozialismus herbeizuführen, und der mit der Demokratie sehr wohl vereinbar ist, schlankweg schliesst, jeder Zwang, die von irgendwem in der Absicht ausgeübt wird, den Sozialismus herbeizuführen, sei vereinbar mit der Demokratie, auch wenn er die Allmacht einzelner Personen gegenüber der Masse bedeute." (Kautsky 1919c, 124).

Lenin had misunderstood the idea of democracy in identifying it with its opposite, the dictatorship of some individuals over the rest of the population.

Kautsky did accept that workers' soviets ("Arbeiterräte") can play a limited role in exercising proletarian power in a period of transformation. They are not, however, suitable to take the place of parliamentary democracy in socialism.[11] Only a centralised

---

[10]   According to Salvadori:
> "For Kautsky, the counterposition of councils to parliament masked the design of a dictatorship by a minority, disguised in the formula of a democracy distinct from parliamentary sovereignty, branded as bourgeois." (Salvadori 1979, 237).

[11]   In Kautsky's opinion the workers' soviets can play a central role during the socialisation of production (see Kautsky 1919b, 11). But in the same speech socialisation is mainly seen to contribute to the unity of the proletarian organisation:
> "Die Einigung des Proletariats ist die Hauptsache — Sozialisierung, ist am ehesten geeignet, die proletarische Massen zu einigen. Sie ist schon deshalb in den Vordergrund zu schieben." (Kautsky 1919b, 15).

parliament is able to represent the interests of the totality of the wage workers. The soviets, on the contrary, can only represent — at their best — the limited interests of the industrial workers in big industry (see Kautsky 1919c, 151).

The communists in Russia claim that democracy is exclusively a form of the bourgeois exercise of power. This is not, however, true. Democracy understood as including general franchise does not in any way belong to the rule of the bourgeoisie. It was the proletariat who first fought for the general right to take part in elections, and the bourgeoisie was opposed to it (see Kautsky 1919c, 152).

Democracy is thus the only constitutional form suitable for a higher form of society, a socialist society, and democracy is the form in which higher forms of social life can become a reality:

> "Die Demokratie ist die einzige Methode, durch die jene höheren Lebensformen hervorgearbeitet werden können, die der Sozialismus für den Kulturmenschen bedeutet." (Kautsky 1919c, 152).

According to Kautsky, dictatorship belongs (exclusively) to an asiatic form of socialism. Such a socialism could also be called tartar socialism (see Kautsky 1919c, 152). The line of argumentation presented by Kautsky in other writings dealing with the Russian Revolution was in general similar to that outlined above (see Steenson 1978, 207). Kautsky claimed that democracy is not by any means compatible with dictatorship, not to speak of a higher form of democracy, socialist democracy. In *Die Diktatur des Proletariats* (1918) Kautsky explicitly stated that it is impossible to think of socialism without democracy:

> "Sozialismus als Mittel zur Befreiung des Proletariats ohne Demokratie ist undenkbar." (Kautsky 1918, 5).

In this writing Kautsky formulated in a compact form his central idea of the essential role of democracy both in the struggle for socialism and in socialism too:

> "Die Demokratie bildet die unerlässliche Grundlage für den Aufbau einer sozialistischen Produktionsweise. Und nur unter den Wirkungen der Demokratie erlangt das Proletariat jene Reife, derer es bedarf, um den Sozialismus durchführen zu können. Die Demokratie endlich bietet den sichersten Gradmesser für seine Reife." (Kautsky 1918, 19–20).

Socialism cannot be realised in a country in which the proletariat constitutes only a small minority, as is the case in Russia. One cannot expect such a country to be ripe for the introduction of socialism. And democracy is necessary for the ripening of the subjective conditions for socialism. Only fanatics would deny this basic proposition. The majority of both the German and the international proletariat is — according to Kautsky — ready to accept it (see Kautsky 1918, 63).

It is understandable that Kautsky continuously connected socialism with democracy. He seemed to think that the proletariat already constituted the absolute majority of the population both in Germany and in other developed capitalist countries. In *Terrorismus und Kommunismus* the proletariat is already said to form nine tenths of the total population (see Kautsky 1919c, 151). And the economic development is supposed to guarantee not only the increase in the absolute number of the proletariat but also the revolutionary consciousness and the will for socialism. As has already been pointed out democracy was, however, not only a tactical question to Kautsky. There are more important reasons for him to support democracy; the rights of minorities must be respected in socialism, as well.

One would expect Kautsky to discuss more systematically the problem of the development of revolutionary consciousness and to give some explanation why a socialist revolution has not yet taken place despite the overwhelming majority of the proletariat in the population. Why is the proletariat not yet ripe enough?

Kautsky's comments on this problem were, however, rather scattered and unsystematic. From time to time he referred to the petit bourgeois origins of the proletariat and the formation of a workers' aristocracy as factors preventing the development of revolutionary consciousness. For Kautsky, the problem was always reduced to a question of time: it is only a question of time when the majority of the population will adopt the cause of socialism as its own.

Despite the great hopes placed in the proletariat Kautsky on various occasions discussed the relation of the different groups or classes of the population to socialism and the possibility of a "Bundnispolitik" (politics of alliance). The possibility of a coalition government was denied in principle by Kautsky; the major contradiction of interests in society makes such a coalition impossible (see Kautsky 1909b, 12). The problem of winning support from other groups of society for the Social Democratic programme and cause was mainly discussed in connection with the problem of the changing nature of capitalism and imperialism. The foundation of cartels and the introduction of high tariffs had aroused expectations among Social Democrats of the formation of new anticapitalistic groups. Kautsky could, however, already, write in *Der Weg zur Macht* in 1909 that these expectations had not been fulfilled:

> "Manche von uns erwarteten, die Kartelle und Ringe der Kapitalisten abenso wie die Zollpolitik würden die Mittelschichten, die darunter so sehr litten, in unsere Reihen führen. Tatsächlich ereignete sich das Gegenteil. Die Agrarzölle und Unternehmerverbände kamen gleichzeitig auf mit den Gewerkschaften. So sahen sich die *Handweksmeister* gleichzeitig von allen Seiten bedrängt." (Kautsky 1909b, 85).

As a result of the development of trade unions, many former supporters of the proletarian party became its direct opponents. Further development of colonialism even increased the contradictions between the different groups in society:

> "In den Grosstaaten wird die Feindschaft der mittleren Klassen gegen das Proletariat noch vermehrt durch die gegensätzliche Stellung in der Frage des Imperialismus und der Kolonialpolitik. Wer nicht auf dem Boden des Sozialismus steht, diesen ablehnt, dem bleibt, will er nicht verzweifeln, gar nichts anderes übrig als der Glaube an die Kolonialpolitik. Sie ist die einzige Aussicht, die der Kapitalismus seinen Verfechtern noch zu bieten hat." (Kautsky 1909b, 87).

It would also be wrong to promise small proprietors a different future from that factually reserved for them due to the iron law of economic development.[12] Their future is to become wage workers, too, and the Social Democrats cannot, even for agitationary purposes, offer them any other alternative or try to prolong their existence as small proprietors (see Kautsky 1899c, 320). The small proprietors are thus bound to become the natural enemies of the Social Democrats, even though the alternative offered to them by the Social Democrats is objectively the best possible one as they are offered the prospect of becoming workers in socialist industry and of being saved from becoming wage workers in capitalism.

The development of imperialism would, however, also seem to offer new possibilities for agitating new groups to join the ranks of social democracy. Petit bourgeoisie, intellectuals and peasants do not objectively have any interests of their own in imperialism. And even industrial capitalists do, in principle, favour democracy and oppose the increase in state expenditure caused by imperialism (see Kautsky 1915a, 21−23). There would seem to be a new opposition emerging against the big magnates of financial capital and agrarian exploitators by the rest of the people. (Kautsky 1911b, 78). Despite the acknowledgement of this potential opposition against imperialism, Kautsky was forced to admit that in practice the class of wage workers is the only consistent opponent of capitalism. And the only alternative left to those who do not wish to support Social Democracy is imperialism.

The same position as regards the potential support to be expected from the petit bourgeoisie that characterises Kautsky's later writings can already be found in the Erfurt Programme: Social Democrats have no right to fight for the immediate interests of proprietors, however small and poor they may be, because Social Democrats cannot oppose the general, necessary economic development. Such an attempt would be doomed to failure (see Kautsky 1906a, 254). They can, however, improve the position of peasants and petit bourgeoisie as consumers. Such an attempt would furthermore favour the general development of society and the cause of socialism:

> "Je besser deren Lage als Konsumenten, je höher ihre Lebenshaltung, je grösser ihre leiblichen und geistigen Ansprüche, je grösser ihre Einsicht, desto eher werden sie aufhören, den Kampf gegen den Grossbetrieb vermittelst der *Hungerkonkurrenz* führen zu wollen, desto eher werden sie das hoffnungslose Ringen aufgeben und die Reihen des Proletariats verstärken: (...) Sie werden direkt in die Reihen der kämpfenden, 'begehrlichen', zielbewussten Proletarier eintreten und damit deren Sieg beschleunigen." (Kautsky 1906a, 259−260).

One should not, however, expect too much of this support of non-proletarian groups for the cause of socialism. The only secure and sincere recruites of Social Democracy

---

[12]   Kautsky chiefly denied any support for small proprietors of any kind:
"A social democratic agrarian programme for the capitalist mode of production is an absurdity." (Kautsky 1894−95b, 617).
According to Salvadori (1979, 55), in Kautsky's opinion "any reform that conflicted with the laws of capitalist development would remain without real effect".

come from the ranks of the proletariat. As stated by Kautsky in the Erfurt Programme, only the proletariat has nothing to lose in the present society:

> "Aber bisher sind die einzig ergiebigen Rekrutierungsgebiete der sozialistischen Armeen nicht die Klassen Derjenigen gewesen, die noch etwas, wenn auch vielleicht nicht viel, zu verlieren hatten, sondern Derjenigen, die 'nichts zu verlieren haben, als ihre Ketten, die eine Welt zu gewinnen haben'." (Kautsky 1906a, 182).

13. THE QUESTION OF DEMOCRACY AND DICTATORSHIP: LENIN'S CRITIQUE OF KAUTSKY THE RENEGADE

Kautsky was first accused by Lenin of being a renegade of Marxism after the Russian Revolution. Until then Lenin, like many others, had regarded Kautsky as a real and genuine Marxist. The best-known and most vehement criticism of Kautsky was first introduced by Lenin after Kautsky's direct and unconditional critique of the Russian Revolution and Lenin's conception of the dictatorship of the proletariat. Lenin's critique reached its utmost vehemence after the publication of Kautsky's *Die Diktatur des Proletariats* in 1918. Kautsky had become a 'renegade of Marxism'. In *The Proletarian Revolution and the Renegade Kautsky* (Lenin SW 3) Lenin criticised Kautsky's conception of democracy and the dictatorship of the proletariat (cf. also Trotsky 1921).

The socialist character of the Russian Revolution and the dictatorship of the proletariat was the main target of critique in Kautsky's *Die Diktatur der Proletariats*. The relation between dictatorship and democracy was understood both by Lenin an Kautsky to be the main question (see Lenin SW 3, 45). The analysis of these two methods of government was the main idea in Kautsky's pamphlet. Kautsky's interpretation of Marx's concept of the dictatorship of the proletariat was, in Lenin's opinion, totally false, even though Kautsky tried to defend his own position as a genuine Marxist interpreter by claiming that Marx did not understand the dictatorship of the proletariat as a form of government but rather as a specific state of affairs or condition, a mediating state between a bourgeois and real proletarian government (see Lenin SW 3, 47–48 and 50). Lenin thought that Kautsky's attempt was merely ridiculous. His main mistake was that he did not make any distinction between democracy in general and bourgeois democracy in particular; he did not even pose the question about the class character of bourgeois democracy. According to Lenin democracy always functions in favour of one particular class. (See Lenin SW 3, 46).

In Lenin's opinion Kautsky understood only one question correctly: dictatorship means that one class in society is deprived of its political rights, and during proletarian dictatorship this class is the bourgeoisie. Kautsky was, however, at the same time mistaken in claiming that proletarian dictatorship is equivalent to a dictatorship exercised by a small group of persons depriving the rest of society of its democratic rights.

The dictatorship of the proletariat is, on the contrary, equal to the most perfect democracy of the working class and other poor elements in society. Revolutionary proletarian dictatorship is equal to power which has been won in class struggle and which is maintained and exercised even violently against the bourgeoisie. It is a power not bound by any laws. (See Lenin SW 3, 52).

According to Lenin the whole idea of Kautsky's discussion of democracy and dictatorship seemed to be that Kautsky tried to conceal the essential difference between a violent and a peaceful transition to socialism. Kautsky opposed any use of violence in revolution:

> "Kautsky has in a most unparalleled manner distorted the concept of dictatorship of the proletariat, and has turned Marx into a common liberal; that is, he himself has sunk to the level of a liberal who utters banal phrases about 'pure democracy', embellishing and glossing over the class content of *bourgeois* democracy, and shrinking, above all, from the use of *revolutionary violence* by the oppressed class. By so 'interpreting' the concept 'revolutionary dictatorship of the proletariat' as to expunge the revolutionary violence of the oppressed class against its oppressors, Kautsky has beaten the world record in the liberal distortion of Marx. The renegade Bernstein has proved to be a mere puppy compared with the renegade Kautsky." (Lenin SW 3, 54).

Lenin did not tire of repeating that proletarian democracy is a million times more democratic than any form of bourgeois democracy. This essential fact was misunderstood by Kautsky because he never faced the question of the class character of democracy, a question separating a real Marxist from a liberal trying to pose as a Marxist. Soviet Russia is the most democratic country in the world, its workers and proletarian peasants have the right to make use of the freedom of assembly, the freedom of press and the right to elect their own representatives in state institutions, and these rights are not only formal rights — as in a bourgeois democracy. The material conditions for their realisation are namely present in Soviet Russia. (See Lenin SW 3, 58—59). This simple fact should prove that a soviet democracy really is a democracy for the poor and in this sense crucially different from any formal democracy which only makes it possible for the rich to use the democratic institutions in their own interests.

Kautsky did not think it possible for the soviets to become a new representative state institution, even though he accepted their role as oganisers and agitators of the working class. In Lenin's opinion Kautsky's position was, however, strange. He acknowledged that the proletariat has a right to wage war against capital which is repressing and subordinating it and the whole nation. On the other hand he did not approve of the ideal proletarian institutions, the soviets, becoming a real state power. Kautsky's position was thus one of a petit bourgeois afraid of class struggle and its logical conclusion, a socialist state power (see Lenin SW 3, 70).

Lenin's critique against Kautsky could be summarised as follows: Kautsky did not understand the nature of the dictatorship of the proletariat in general and its Russian variant in particular. In demanding the maintenance and introduction of democratic institutions in their bourgeois form Kautsky revealed that he did not understand that democracy is always equivalent to the exercise of the power of one class over another, and that the dictatorship of the proletariat is in reality the most democratic form of exercising state power; it is true that capitalists and the big agrarian proprietors are deprived of their democratic rights. The political rights of workers and poor peasants are in fact more comprehensive than ever. Despite his critique Lenin did not, in principle, deny the possibility of establishing socialism without depriving the bourgeoisie of their former democratic rights – even though he thought of it more as an exception. In certain developed countries with long traditions of political freedom and democracy parliamentary democracy could be maintained even during the transitionary period, which would under these circumstances be more peaceful (see Lenin SW 3, 52 and 66).

Lenin's most famous writing concerning the question of the socialist state, *The State and Revolution* was similar in its argumentation. He defended the 'Marxist' conception of the dictatorship of the proletariat against the liberal ideas of Kautsky:

> "The theory of the class struggle, applied by Marx to the question of the state and the socialist revolution, leads as a matter of course to the recognition of the *political rule* of the proletariat, of its dictatorship, i.e. of undivided power directly backed by the armed force of the people. The overthrow of the bourgeoisie can be achieved only by the proletariat becoming the *ruling class*, capable of crushing the inevitable and desperate resistance of the bourgeoisie, and of organising *all* the working and exploited people for the new economic system. The proletariat needs state power, a centralised organisation of force, and organisation of violence, both to crush the resistance of the exploiters and to *lead* the enormous mass of the population – the peasants, the petty bourgeoisie, and semi-proletarians – in the work of organising a socialist economy." (Lenin SW 2, 285).

A real Marxists recognises the necessity of the dictatorship of the proletariat. The proletariat has to crush the repressive state machine, a task which is in the interets of both the working class and the peasants:

> "On the other hand, he (Marx – J.G.) stated that the 'smashing' of the state machine was required by the interests of both the workers and the peasants, that it united them, that it placed before them the common task of removing the 'parasite' and of replacing it by something new." (Lenin SW 2, 296).

To Marx the Paris Commune was the primary example of this 'new organ', taking the place of the old state machine (see Lenin SW 2, 29).

Once the state machine is substituted by the new organ, a specific power organisation becomes unnecessary. The people recognise the oppressor and can effectively keep it in control (see Lenin SW 2, 298). The process of the withering away of the state can begin. The withering away of the state is also made possible by the simplification of the functions of the state apparatus once its repressive functions become obsolete:

> "Capitalist culture has *created* large-scale production, factories, railways, the postal service, telephones, etc., and *on this basis* the great majority of the functions of the old 'state power' have become so simplified and can be reduced to such exceedingly simple operations of registration, filing and checking that they can be easily performed by every literate

person, can quite easily be performed for ordinary 'workmen's wages', and that these functions can (and must) be stripped of every shadow of privilege, of every resemblance of 'official grandeur'." (Lenin SW 2, 299).

The dying away of the state is a theme that was not discussed in Kautsky's writings even though Lenin did not explicitly criticise him for this neglect. There is not, however, such a great difference between Lenin's and Kautsky's conceptions of the future socialist state. According to Kautsky a centralised state is needed even in socialism for the organisation of production. Lenin's conception was rather similar, as was revealed by his characterisation of the future state. In Lenin's *The State and Revolution* the postal service is mentioned as the ideal example of the future socialist state:

"To organise the *whole* economy on the lines of the postal service so that the technicians, foremen and accountants, as well as *all* officials, shall receive salaries no higher than 'a workman's wage', all under the control and leadership of the armed proletariat − this is our immediate aim. This is the state and this is the economic foundation we need. This is what will bring about the abolition of parliamentarism and the preservation of representative institutions. This is what will rid the labouring classes of the bourgeoisie's prostitution of these institutions." (Lenin SW 2, 304).

The metaphor of the postal service was not at all that different from Kautsky's characterisation of the future state; to Kautsky as well as to Lenin it was the modern industrial factory which already had solved the problems of technical efficiency and planning that functioned as the model of the future state (see Kautsky 1906a, 114−123).

There was, however, an important difference between Lenin's and Kautsky's conceptions. In *The State and Revolution* Lenin's conception of democracy was almost directly opposed to that of Kautsky's. According to him, bourgeois democracy is always equal to government by a minority:

"In capitalist society, providing it develops under the most favourable conditions, we have a more or less complete democracy in the democratic republic. But this democracy is always hemmed in by the narrow limits set by capitalist exploitation, and consequently always remains, in effect, a democracy for the minority, only for the propertied classes, only for the rich. Freedom in capitalist society always remains about the same as it was in the ancient Greek republics: freedom for the slave owners. Owing to the conditions of capitalist exploitation, the modern wage slaves are so crushed by want and poverty that 'they cannot be bothered with democracy', 'cannot be bothered with politics'; in the ordinary, peaceful course of events, the majority of the population is debarred from participation in public and political life." (Lenin SW 2, 333).

Lenin's understanding of the class character of democracy seemed mainly to be based on an analysis of the factual social position of the different classes. Democracy is a formal principle. It does not pay attention to the fact that members of the working class and other poor classes of society are factually deprived of all the means of exercising power, whereas capitalists have all the necessary economic and political means at their disposal; they can even influence the opinions of the people by these means. To this fact Kautsky did not pay much attention; to Lenin democracy is a formal principle and democratic institutions — a general franchise, free press and freedom of assembly — are really insufficient to guarantee the realisation of the interests of the majority in society. There is, however, one important argument in Kautsky's analysis which was not at all commented on by Lenin: in Kautsky's opinion the working class has one important resource of power and influence at its disposal, organisation, and the power represented by an organisation is best increased within democratic institutions. Lenin did not seem to acknowledge that the power of mass organisations would increase in democracy; Kautsky put all his hopes in them. This fact also partly explains Kautsky's 'ultra-democratism'.

Despite the evident differences in Kautsky's and Lenin's analysis, there are in fact some presumptions common to both of them. These similar premises are more evident in Lenin's earlier writings about the nature of the future revolution. In 1905, during the first Russian Revolution, Lenin's position was very close to that of Kautsky's. The immediate task of the revolution was understood to be the establishment of a democratic state with all the modern democratic institutions. A democratic revolution was thus the immediate task, a socialist one would follow later. In *Two Tactics of Social Democracy in the Democratic Revolution* Lenin wrote without reservation:

> "Whoever wants to reach socialism by any other means than that of political democracy, will inevitably arrive at conclusions that are absurd and reactionary both in the economic and political sense." (Lenin SW 1, 468).

Democracy is also necessary for the organisation and development of the consciousness of the proletariat. Lenin's conception was similar to that of Kautsky's in one more respect: according to both of them it is mainly the task of the proletariat to realise a bourgeois revolution, because the bourgeosie is neither willing nor capable of realising this task. A bourgeois revolution is, then, paradoxically more in the interests of the proletariat:

> "And from this conclusion, among other things, follows the thesis that *in a certain sense* a bourgeois revolution is *more advantageous* to the proletariat that to the bourgeoisie." (Lenin SW 1, 486).

The development of democracy is, like the general development of capitalism, favourable to the proletariat in general — a proposition regularly to be found in Kautsky's writings. Lenin had, then, really the right to claim that he had always presented the Social Democratic ideas of Kautsky and Bebel. There was not, in fact, any major difference between Lenin's and Kautsky's conceptions at this stage.[1] Lenin even criti-

---

[1]   Lenin's bitter reaction to Kautsky's critique of the Russian Revolution becomes understandable when one keeps in mind that to Lenin as well as to other Bolsheviks, Kautsky had been the main theoretical authority of Social Democracy. In the preface to *The Development of Capitalism in Russia* Lenin (CW 3, 27), for instance, referred to Kautsky's *Agrarfrage* as the most noteworthy contribution to recent economic literature since the publication of the third volume of *Capital*.

cised the idea of 'revolutionary communes' because it did not make any distinction between a democratic and a socialist revolution:

> "It is, however, precisely for this very reason that the slogan of 'revolutionary communes' is erroneous, because the very mistake made by the communes known to history was that of confusing the democratic revolution with the socialist revolution. On the other hand, our slogan — a revolutionary democratic dictatorship of the proletariat and the peasantry — fully safeguards us against this mistake. While recognising the incontestably bourgeois nature of a revolution incapable of *directly* overstepping the bounds of a mere democratic revolution our slogan *advances* this particular revolution and strives to give it forms most advantageous to the proletariat; consequently, it strives to make the utmost of the democratic revolution in order to attain the greatest success in the proletariat's further struggle for socialism." (Lenin SW 1, 519).

There is, however, one important difference between Lenin's and Kautsky's opinion. To Kautsky the difference between a democratic — or more generally between a political and a social revolution — was more on of degree. Socialism and social revolution will automatically follow as soon as Social Democrats have a majority in parliament. Lenin, on the other hand, made a sharp distrinction between a democratic and a socialist state and revolution. Before the Russian Revolution Kautsky continuously defended the idea of the dictatorship of the proletariat against revisionists, but his conception of dictatorship remained devoid of content or was equal to the majority rule in parliament (see also Lichtheim 1964, 269). According to Lenin, the democratic state has to be followed by the dictatorship of the proletariat representing a totally different form of state, and finally, in communism, the state is supposed to wither away.

The apparent contradiction in Lenin's conceptions of 1905 and 1917–18 has been pointed out by many critics. The contradiction is a real one, even though Lenin could claim that his idea of the two phases of revolution had remained intact in 1917; the February Revolution was the expected democratic-bourgeois revolution and the October Revolution was the following socialist one. According to Lenin the development of capitalism had been so rapid in Russia that a socialist revolution could follow the democratic one almost immediately. They both took place within one single year:

> "Beginning with *April* 1917, however, long before the October Revolution, that is, long before we assumed power, we publicly declared and explained to the people: the revolution cannot now stop at this stage, for the country has marched forward, capitalism has advanced, ruin has reached fantastic dimensions, which (whether one likes it or not) *will* *demand* steps forward, to *socialism.* For there is *no* other way of advancing, of saving the war-weary country and of *alleviating* the sufferings of the working and exploited people." (Lenin SW 3, 104).

And further:

> "It was the Bolsheviks who strictly differentiated between the bourgeois-democratic revolution and the socialist revolution: by carrying the former through, they opened the door for the transition to the latter. This was the only policy that was revolutionary and Marxist." (Lenin SW 3, 114–115).

Now, in 1917, there was not any more such a big difference between the two revolutions; they could only be separated by using the criterion of the preparedness and willingness of the proletariat:

> "The attempt to raise an artificial Chinese wall between the first and second, to separate them by *anything else* than the degree of preparedness of the proletariat and the degree of its unity with the poor peasant, means to distort Marxism dreadfully, to vulgarise it, to substitute liberalism in its place." (Lenin SW 3, 105).

In referring to the degree of preparedness of the working class as the decisive criterion for the actuality of revolution Lenin was arguing along the line of his previous analysis and following Kautsky's analysis. But it could still be doubted whether Lenin had previously meant that the schooling of the proletariat in the class struggle within a democratic state really could be substituted by 'one single revolutionary day' or some months of actual revolutionary struggles.

In addition to the question of democracy and dictatorship the controversy between Lenin and Kautsky about the Russian Revolution concentrated on the problem of the present stage of development of capitalism – and of Russia in particular. The class structure of different capitalist states was considered to be an essential indicator of the ripening of the conditions for socialism. In the opinion of Kautsky the majority of the population consisted undoubtedly of the proletariat in all the developed countries, and this fact proved the conditions for socialism to be ripe in those countries. Lenin posed the problem in a similar way. The main question in his analyses both before and after the Russian Revolution was the relation of the proletariat to the two other big classes in Russia, the peasants and different factions of the petit bourgeoisie. Even Lenin acknowledged that the proletariat represented only a small minority in Russian society, even though in his early empirical study of the development of capitalism in Russia he had come to the conclusion that the situation of the poor peasant, due to the introduction of capitalistic market relations in the countryside, was starting to resemble more and more the situation of the proletariat (see Lenin CW 3). In Lenin's analysis small peasants and propertyless farm workers were also the main allies of the proletariat in the coming democratic and socialist revolutions. It was in the interests of these classes to oppose the bourgeois state apparatus which was exploiting the vast majority of the population. The future destiny of revolution was essentially linked with the future of the proletariat, small peasants and farm workers.

Kautsky never acknowledged that the interests of the peasants could be similar to those of the real proletariat or wage workers. Soviet Russia was nothing but a "Bauern-republik", or a form of tartar socialism. In analysing the future tasks of revolution, even Lenin had to admit that the main problem facing the young socialist state was the reaction of the petit bourgeoisie. In his *The Tasks of the Proletariat in Our Revolution* written on the 10th (25th) of March, 1917, Lenin in fact characterised Russia as the most petit bourgeois country in Europe. The proletariat represented only a negligible part of the population and both its organisations and socialist consciousness were rather weak (see Lenin SW 2, 27).

In *"Left-wing" Communism — an Infantile Disorder* (written in 1920) Lenin finally stated that the immediate task of the revolution was the liquidation of all petit bourgeois elements in society (Lenin SW 3, 339). Petit bourgeoisie is not mainly dangerous and harmful because of its opposition to socialism. The main danger lies in the fact that it continously nourishes capitalistic tendencies in society:

> "Unfortunately, small-scale production is still widespread in the world, and small-scale production *engenders* capitalism and the bourgeoisie continuously, daily, hourly, spontaneously, and on a mass scale. All these reasons make the dictatorship of the proletariat necessary, and victory over the bourgeoisie is impossible without a long, stubborn and desperate life-and-death struggle which calls for tenacity, discipline, and a single and inflexible will." (Lenin SW 3, 339).

The final abolition of all classes in society is not yet accomplished by destroying capitalists and landlords; all the small-scale producers (or elements of the petit bourgeoisie) must be abolished simultaneously. They cannot, however, simply be destroyed and expurgated, they must be transformed and educated to become different kinds of people. The existence of a petit bourgeoisie is a constant danger to the proletariat and socialism because it constantly nourishes individualism and destroys the necessary discipline of the proletariat. In order to oppose individualism, a proletarian organisation with iron discipline is needed. The necessity for a centralised and disciplined party as the ideal form of proletarian emancipatory organisation is — even after the illegal phase of the struggle was over — thus deduced by Lenin from the minority position of the proletariat in Russian society; a conclusion which in Kautsky's opinion proved the undemocratic and unsocialist character of this revolution. Proletarian dictatorship meant, according to Lenin:

> "a persistent struggle — bloody and bloodless, violent and peaceful, military and economic, educational and administrative — against the forces and traditions of the old society. The force of habit in millions and tens of millions is a most formidable force. Without a party of iron that has been tempered in the struggle, a party enjoying the confidence of all honest people in the class in question, a party capable of watching and influencing the mood of the masses, such a struggle cannot be waged successfully. It is a thousand times easier to vanquish the centralised big bourgeoisie than to 'vanquish' the millions upon millions of petty proprietors; however, through their ordinary, everyday, imperceptible, elusive and demoralising activities, they produce the *very* results which the bourgeoisie need and which tend to *restore* the bourgeoisie. Whoever brings about even the slightest weakening of the iron discipline of the party of the proletariat (especially during its dictatorship), is actually aiding the bourgeoisie against the proletariat." (Lenin SW 3, 357).

In this statement Lenin actually seemed to be acknowledging Kautsky's critique of the Russian Revolution and proletarian dictatorship. If Soviet Russia actually is a petit bourgeois country, and if socialism can be victorious only by suppressing millions and millions of peasant and small-scale proprietors, Soviet Russia really is shown to be a case of a peasant state or tartar socialism prophesied by Kautsky. The revolution will triumph only at the cost of the majority of the population, the petit bourgeoisie and the peasants, violating their real interests, as acknowledged by Lenin's idea of the necessity for iron discipline inside the party. The interests of the proletariat will be realised only through a disciplined organisation.

Petit bourgeoisie was not, however, in Lenin's opinion the only problem of the socialist revolution. The very core of the proletariat, the organised workers and their immediate interests, posed a serious threat to the party and the proletarian dictatorship. Lenin claimed that even the most organised part of the proletariat, represented by the trade unions, had everywhere caused serious splits inside the proletariat and its movement. Trade unions, in fact, only represent specific interests of specific groups of workers, and not the general interest of the proletariat:

> "The trade unions were a tremendous step forward for the working class in the early days of capitalist development, inasmuch as they marked a transition from the workers' disunity and helplessness to the *rudiments* of class organisation. When the *revolutionary party of the proletariat*, the *highest* form of proletarian class organisation, began to take shape (and the Party will not merit the name until it learns to weld the leaders into one indivisible whole with the class and the masses) the trade unions inevitably began to reveal *certain* reactionary features, a certain craft narrow-mindedness, a certain tendency to be non-political, a certain inertness, etc." (Lenin SW 3, 362).

In the more developed European countries the reactionary features of trade unions are even more developed. In Russia trade unions have traditionally been the main supporters of mensheviks, as well. In western countries mensheviks (read: revisionists and reformists) have an even more pronounced position in the trade unions. There is a reactionary faction of trade union workers in the West:

> "...there the *craft-union, narrow-minded, selfish, case-hardened, covetous, and petty-bourgeois labour-aristocracy, imperialist-minded, and imperialist-corrupted,* has developed into a much stronger section than in our country." (Lenin SW 3, 363).

Lenin was paradoxically faced with a two-fold opposition: both the petit bourgeoisie and peasants (the vast majority in Russia) and the organised and skilled workers (a small but influential minority) oppose the bolsheviks and their policy. The only supporters of the bolshevik party then are the poor unskilled workers.

The reasons given by Lenin for the revisionistic tendencies inside the working class were rather superflous and they closely resembled those analysed by Kautsky. Workers organised in trade unions have certain specific economic interests which can be in contradiction with the general political goal of the proletariat as determined by scientific socialism and a proletarian party. The workers' aristocracy, a specific faction of the working class, is able to gain privileges from capitalists, especially during the stage of imperialism: a monopolistic bourgeoisie is able to buy the support of skilled workers and bribe them with economic privileges.

As a conclusion from the above discussion, Lenin stated that it was easier to start a revolution in Russia than in other European countries. On the other hand, in Russia it was much more difficult to complete the revolution (see Lenin SW 3, 374).

The threat posed by petit bourgeoisie in socialism was understood by Lenin to be a strategic problem, namely how to overcome its opposition and prevent the further development of capitalistic tendencies in Russia. The problem of the revisionistic tendencies within the working class is, however, a more important one. If Lenin's analysis of the possible supporters of the party is correct, then the conflict between the specific economic interests and the general political interests of the proletariat remains unsolved. One would almost naturally expect the oldest and most organised sectors of the proletariat to be the most vehement supporters of socialism, and not its opposers. The problem is connected with Lenin's general analysis and conception of the development of the socialist consciousness of the workers. In this respect Lenin's position was very similar to that of Kautsky. According to both Lenin and Kautsky the consciousness developing spontaneously among wage workers could only be trade-unionistic. A real socialist consciousness must be brought into the workers' movement from outside:

> "The history of all countries shows that the working class, exclusively by its own effort, is able to develop only trade union consciousness, i.e., the conviction that it is necessary to combine in unions, fight the employers, and strive to compel the government to pass necessary labour legislation, etc." (Lenin SW 1, 122).

The principal problem facing Lenin was then the following: if the wage workers can never spontaneously develop a genuine socialist consciousness, and the party is the only representator of a genuine socialist consciousness, where does the socialist idea come from in the last instance? Both Lenin and Kautsky answered the question similarly: the idea and goal of socialism is the result of scientific socialism, a theoretical knowledge represented by intellectuals. Scientific socialism then is a theory of socialist revolution, its necessity and the social conditions leading to it, and only insofar as wage workers are willing to accept the conclusions of scientific socialism as an adequate expression of their own interests and aspirations as wage workers they are qualified to represent the general interests of the proletariat and the final goal of socialism.

As has already been pointed out in analysing imperialism, democracy seems to be either a principle incompatible with or alien to capitalism (Kautsky), or a principle which is only contingent to capitalism and does not have any rooting in the social relations of bourgeois society (Lenin). For both Kautsky and Lenin the proletariat is the only genuine representative of democracy in capitalism. The bourgeoisie – once an adherent of democracy in its fight against feudalism – has become reactionary and more or less directly represses any democratic aspirations in society. A democratic revolution would then be in the interests of the proletariat exclusively, and it would furthermore lead more or less immediately to a socialist revolution, too. In the case of Kautsky, this position is quite evident. For Kautsky the establishment of democracy would in the end inevitably lead to the establishment of a socialist state. Once the proletariat has become the majority in a society and, consequently, in a parliament, too, it would accomplish a socialist revolution using the state institutions at its disposal.

A capitalist society having a democratic constitution and a proletarian majority would, in fact, not be able to survive for any length of time. Democracy thus has nothing to do with the social relations of a bourgeois society; it is a pure question of power and the ideal constitution for the proletariat to exercise its power in society (see also Kraus 1978, 202).

Lenin continuously accused Kautsky of representing a formal conception of democracy and forgetting the class character of bourgeois democracy. Even though he undersigned Kautsky's idea of democracy as the most suitable training ground for the proletarian organisations and as the best means of organising the working class in his earlier writings, in the writings written after the Russian Revolution, democracy is no longer understood to be relevant to the proletarian struggle. Lenin claimed to be taking into account the factual position of classes in society. In capitalism the bourgeoisie has all the political and economic means of power at its disposal; consequently, only it can effectively make use of the democratic institutions and exercise its power through them. Parliamentary democracy is only a formal principle which does not pay attention to the factual social position of the different classes in a bourgeois society. The proletariat does not possess the factual means to make use of its democratic rights — freedom of the press, general franchise, freedom of assembly — even under a democratic constitution. Only the establishment of a dictatorship of the proletariat would deprive the bourgeoisie of its factual political power and establish the genuine political rights of the proletariat. In this sense, the dictatorship of the proletariat, while realising the power and interests of the majority exploited in capitalism, represented to Lenin real and genuine democracy; it is more democratic than the formal bourgeois parliamentary democracy.

To Lenin, then, a state is always essentially an instrument at the disposal of the ruling class — a class possessing the factual economic and political resources of power in society — and in capitalism the state will always represent the interests of its ruling class, the bourgeoisie, notwithstanding its possible democratic constitution. Democracy as such has nothing to do with the bourgeois society and parliamentary democracy has nothing to do with real democracy. A bourgeois democracy is bourgeois and a proletarian democracy is proletarian, depending on the factual power position of the classes. To Kautsky, democracy simply meant the exercise of the power of a majority in a society, and once the proletariat has become a majority it will be able to exercise its power through a parliament and transform the society into a socialist one. Democracy is thus in the interests of the proletariat; the bourgeoisie represents violence and reaction in society. Either democracy is thus a principle opposed to bourgeois society (Kautsky), or it is a purely formal principle, the class character of which will depend on the factual power position of the classes (Lenin). The main difference between Lenin and Kautsky is that whereas they both thought that a bourgeois state always is an instrument of power in the hands of its ruling class, the bourgeoisie, Kautsky thought that socialism could only flourish in a society having a democratic constitution and, furthermore, that parliamentary democracy is the ideal form of the future socialist state. Lenin — even though not principally denying the possibility of a socialist revolution using democratic institutions — thought of it more as an exception.

As was pointed out by Steenson (1978, 9–10) and Lichtheim (1964, 264) Kautsky certainly was a radical democrat by conviction. There is, however, one feature in Kautsky's thinking that makes his strong adherence to parliamentary democracy understandable. Kautsky made a clear distinction between political and social revolution. It was the political revolution which first made the further social revolution, understood as comprising mainly of the socialisation of large-scale production by the state, possible. In analysing the future socialist revolution, Kautsky seemed mainly to be discussing the first political phase of this revolution, which was then often not practically related to the wider social tasks of the ensuing socialist revolution. It was furthermore Kautsky's strong reliance on the development of the power of the proletarian organisations which formed the necessary connecting link between democracy and socialism.

As was already pointed out at the end of the discussion of Kautsky's and Lenin's theories of imperialism, capitalism was understood by the Second International Marxists as mainly being a mode of production based on the exploitation of surplus value and the distribution of the whole national product on behalf of the capitalists. The capital-wage labour relationship was basically analysed as a relation of direct exploitation, and the specific character or form of the social relations in a bourgeois society, e.g. the relation between equal and free commodity producers, emphasised by Marx, was largely neglected. Similarly, in their analyses, democracy had nothing to do with the specific social relations of commodity producers in capitalism or with the freedom and equality of the commodity exchangers, wage workers included. The conceptions of imperialism represented by these Marxists are a further consequence of this basic understanding of the nature of capitalism. Imperialism was, in fact, understood both by Kautsky and Lenin as being a specific mode of distribution based on the direct appropriation of a part of the national product by big cartel magnates and finance capitalists who are exploiting the rest of the people. Thus freedom and equality are principles which do not even formally belong to an imperialist society. Imperialism, which was explicitly stated to be violent and reactionary, is based on the appropriation of monopoly profits which do not stem from any relation of production but from a forced distribution of the national — and international — product to the benefit of finance capital. Imperialism is essentially characterised by an accentuating antagonism of distribution.

To the theoreticians of imperialism, capitalism seems to be all but a short historical phase between an earlier mode of production, that of simple commodity production, and a following mode of production, that of imperialism. Classical capitalism — capitalism of free competition — was understood as having been transformed into imperialism according to its own economic laws of development, and thus is was only a short interregnum between simple commodity production and imperialism. And if there is any freedom and equality of commodity producers at all, they seem to belong exclusively to the stage of simple commodity production. As soon as capital relation and wage labourer come into being in society, capitalism inevitably develops towards in-

creasing centralisation and monopolisation of production and thus leads to the exploitation of all the producers and consumers in society by centralised finance capital. For the
bourgeoisie, then, democracy is only a tactical weapon in its fight against feudalism and
absolutism; a capitalism standing on its own is by its nature violent, reactionary and
undemocratic.

PART II

MARX'S MARXISM

1. THE IMMANENT CRITIQUE AND THE NATURAL RIGHTS THEORY

In a recent contribution to the discussion of Marx's concept of critique and method of presentation ("Kritik und Darstellung"), Georg Lohmann (1980) explicated different levels or principles of critique in Marx's *Capital* and his critique of political economy in general. According to Lohmann there is a fundamental difference between two principles of critique in Marx's *Capital* − the immanent and the transcending critique. The first form of critique is called immanent because bourgeois society is criticised with its own normative standards. The equality and freedom of the commodity producers is shown to be a mere appearance ("reiner Schein") of the surface of that society, the sphere of commodity circulation preventing the exploitation of surplus value and surplus product from becoming visible. The title of property to the products of labour is not, in fact, as thought by classical political economy, based on one's own labour but, on the contrary, on the appropriation of alien labour and its products. The right to private property is nevertheless, even in a bourgeois society, legitimated by the right to one's own labour and its products. The second form of critique is based on the experiences and the normative standards of those living under capitalism. Its standards and norms are those of the participants, actual social movements and forces of resistance. It takes its standards and principles from the arguments and declarations of the actual movement of emancipation under capitalism.

Only the immanent critique can be presented systematically and conceptually ("begrifflich"); the transcending critique presupposes a form of presentation which is fragmentary and narrative. Marx's combination of presentation and critique in *Capital* follows the principle of immanent critique, whereas the elements of transcending critique are imbedded as fragments in the presentation and in the so-called historiographic-narrative parts of *Capital*.

Basically, the immanent critique is a critique of the fundamental suppositions of the modern natural rights theory as presented especially by John Locke and classical political economy with Adam Smith and David Ricardo as its leading representatives. Lohmann did not anyhow notice, that even the transcending critique does, in a specific manner, criticise the basic legitimatory argument of the scientific self-understanding of the bourgeois society, viz. the possibility of human existence and the general well-being of the individual, including the wage worker, as a product of the accumulation of capital.

It can be argued that Marx was thus implicitly criticising the fundamental legitimatory argument of classical political economy, according to which the economic laws, while functioning 'invisibly', behind the backs of private subjects, guarantee 'the greatest happiness of the greatest number'. Marx's critique, as presented most systematically in the chapter in *Capital* on the general law of capitalist accumulation, was later to become an essential and important part of the theory of capitalism of the Second International Marxism which emphasised the growing misery of the working class in capitalism as an essential element of its theory of revolution.

In the beginning of his article Lohmann presented two 'programmatic theses' about the systematic structure of *Capital:*

> "Meine erste Interpretationsthese lautet: Der systematische Aufbau des 'Kapitals' folgt durchgehend dem Programm einer *immanenten Kritik* an der naturrechtlichen (Locke-schen) Selbstdarstellung der bürgerlichen Gesellschaft. Die zweite These lautet: In der Durchführung dieser immanenten Kritik wird eine den naturrechtlichen Rahmen transzen-dierende Kritik entwickelt, deren normativer Masstab in den historiographischen Passagen des Kapitalbuches impliziert ist. Erst der spezifische Zusammenhang beider Kritiktypen bezeichnet die Systematik der *Kritik* der politischen Ökonomie. Diese ist danach durch-gängig Kritik, d.h. jede Interpretation geht fehl, die aus ihr eine 'positive Theorie' (z.B. deskriptive Ökonomi) isolierend herausholen will, oder sie als ganz so versteht." (Lohmann 1980, 237).

One of the problems in interpreting the conceptual or theoretical structure of Marx's presentation in *Capital* is the methodological demand of uniting presentation and criti-que (see Lohmann 1980, 237; cf. also MEW 29, 550). Marx's presentation in this respect followed Hegel's well-known dictum, according to which the presentation in-cludes the critique of the object presented. When something is conceptually compre-hended, it is related to its very idea or concept ("Idee oder Bergiff"). The critical presentation is identical to bringing something to its concept of essence ("wesenmässi-ger Begriff"). Comprehending thus includes critique, or rather it means judging the perfection of something or its correspondence to its concept (see Lohmann 1980, 240).

The main problem in Hegel's Logic — according to Lohmann — is that Hegel had to affirm in the presentation that which is negated in the critique.[1] Following Theunissen in his interpretation of Hegel's *Wissenschaft der Logik* Lohmann made the following distinction between presentation and critique in Hegel's Logic: the presentation aims at the truth explicated as communicative freedom, the critique has falsehood as its object; the falsehood is understood, first, as not yet truth and, second, as totally false, as appearance ("Schein") (see Lohmann 1980, 240; Theunissen 1978, 87). Such a com-bination of presentation and critique is possible only when the standard of critique is included in the object of presentation. Such a critique is, therefore, characterised as immanent.

---

[1]   In this respect Lohmann followed Theunissen's interpretation:
    "Was nämlich die Logik Hegels, sofern sie Kritik ist, negiert, dass muss sie als Darstellung affirmieren." (Theunissen 1978, 88).

The object of Marx's presentation was the inner relation of bourgeois society. It had to be presented in such a manner that it included its necessary form of appearance ("Schein") without being reduced to a mere appearance-likeness ("Scheinhaftigkeit") – the fate of the vulgar economy as criticised by Marx. According to Lohmann the constitution of this inner relation or order of bourgeois society is the classical theme of the modern natural rights theory (Hobbes, Locke, Rousseau). The systematic starting point for all of these modern conceptions is the concept of self-preservation or of survival (see Lohmann 1980, 242–243).

According to Lohmann (1980, 243–244) the starting point for Locke's conception of the state of nature is the self-preservation of the individual. Every individual has a right to self-preservation by using the necessary means of support. He is, however, entitled to these products only so long as his own self-preservation does not endanger the self-preservation of others. The appropriation of the products of nature is mediated by labour. Just as every man is the sole owner of his own body, so is he the owner of the labour of his body and the work of his hands. The products are freed from the state of nature by mixing labour with them so that something of the worker's own is added to them. From this thesis two further conclusions are drawn. These main axioms of Locke's natural rights doctrine are: (1) only labour can create a title to property, and (2) the different values of objects are based on labour used in appropriating them from the original state of nature.

Both the freedom and self-preservation of the individual are thought to be secured by the natural right to private property. It furthermore secures the autonomy and independence of the individual. Under such circumstances the property of another individual can only be appropriated by mutual consent through exchange of goods. The original rules and conditions prevailing in the original state of nature are, however, endangered by the introduction of durable goods (gold and silver). Once common consent has been reached, money may be used as a means of exchanging goods. In the original state of nature nobody is allowed to own more that he or his dependants can dispose of privately. Thus, the tacit consent of the participants to introduce money in relations of barter threatens to imbalance the relation in the first state of nature characterised by the non-existence of money by encouraging a desire to appropriate more than is privately consumed. The accumulation of money capital and landed property made possible by the introduction of money presented by durable goods endangers everybody's natural right to private property and his self-preservation, and the corresponding rights of freedom and equality. To guarantee these rights a social contract constituting a state power was postulated by Locke (see Lohmann 1980, 44).

According to Lohmann, the re-interpretation of the state of nature by the post-Lockean political economy further harmonised the Lockean concept by introducing the conception of a commercial or bourgeois society, the functioning of which is governed by immanent economic laws guaranteeing – invisibly – the realisation of the common interest of commodity producers. At the same time the principles of Locke's state of nature remain valid even for this 'natural society' (freedom of the individual, the rightful appropriation of property by means of one's own labour and mutual exchange, and the equality of every individual as private property owner (see Lohmann 1980, 244–245).

Marx characterised the "exchange of exchange values" (commodities) as the "productive, real basis of all freedom and equality" (Marx s.a., 156). For Marx the relation of exchange did not, however, constitute the inner relation of bourgeois society. Very generally speaking, Marx's critique of the natural rights theory and the political economy was — according to Lohmann — concentrated on the following idea: the real inner relation has to be sought in the relation of appropriation, i.e. production. In classical political economy this inner relation is analysed as the determination of value by labour time; the value of commodities which makes the exchange of commodities possible and is the integrative aspect of the constitution of society, is reduced to its immanent genesis, labour time. This reduction is, however, valid and possible only under the conditions postulated by the natural rights theory. At the same time, the relations of exchange prevent the relations of production from appearing as the 'truly general' inner relation of society; value appears in a specific value form (see Lohmann 1980, 246).

According to Lohmann, Marx was in his critique of political economy interested in this very difference between the integrative and genetic aspect of the constitution of bourgeois society. He found the classical political economy praiseworthy because of its analysis of the constitution of bourgeois society (hence, its classicity) but criticised it for its lack of comprehension of the relation between the integrative and genetic aspects of society:

> "So stimmt sie (die klassische politische Ökonomie — J.G.) mit der Lockeschen Konzeption des Selbstverständnisses der bürgerlichen Gesellschaft überein: allein die integrierende Character der Konstitution (Austausch der Waren) erscheint als derjenige, der den gesellschaftlichen Zusammenhang herstellt, während der genetische Character (Aneignung durch eigene Arbeit) nur als Voraussetzung für diesen Zussammenhang erscheint, der in der Bereich der Privatsphäre fällt." (Lohmann 1980, 246).

Marx's presentation was by nature immanent while understanding its object from the perspective of the appearing and appeared relation and it consequently followed the process of the constitution of its object. The immanent presentation was systematic in structure. It begins with the abstract and conceptual image of the whole and develops this image during the course of presentation into a concrete and differentiated thought totality ("konkreter und differenzierter Gedankentotalität"). While doing this the presentation does not presuppose anything more than the bourgeois self-understanding does: the whole is only a realisation of the principles of the Lockean state of nature. Thus, the normative demands of freedom and equality are simultaneously presupposed, the demands which are claimed to be realised by society. In following this process of constitution, the realisation of the promise of freedom and equality is criticised (see Lohmann 1980, 247).

The immanent critique thus finds the standards of its critique in the very object of its study. It can formally 'take over' the normative standards of bourgeois society as explicated in the classical manifestation of its self-understanding; the classical political economy. These normative standards are formal principles of freedom and equality, and the right to private property based on one's own labour. In classical political economy these standards are supposed to be universally valid, for all members of society. The task of the immanent critique is, firstly, to prove the inadequacy and formal character of these normative standards and, secondly, by showing the self-contradictory nature of the system, it is shown to be determined as a negative totality; it does not fulfill its own principles which is equivalent to it being untrue. The immanent critique has now reached the point where it no longer 'understands' its object. It becomes evident that the whole object is in contradiction to its own normative standards, and consequently it cannot be measured with these standards any more (see Lohmann 1980, 248). Only when it is possible to show that the standard of the immanent critique is a necessary standard of the exchange of commodities realised as the formal freedom and equality of every individual in bourgeois society, can the inadequacy of the standard be proved.

Jürgen Habermas in *Theorie und Praxis* in 1967 pointed out the close affinity between Marx's critique and the natural rights theory. As the legitimate heir to the natural law theory, political economy proved that the economic laws of society quarantee the realisation of the natural rights of man. In classical political economy the natural laws of society are supposed to fulfill the common interests of men. In proving that the free intercourse of the private property owners, in fact, excluded the mutual enjoyment of personal autonomy by all individuals, Marx also proved that the general laws of bourgeois society were devoid of the supposed economic righteousness:

> "Das Interesse der bürgerlichen kann dann mit dem aller Bürger nicht länger identifiziert werden;. . ." (Habermas 1967, 79).

All Marx had to do was to confront the liberal construction of the natural rights theory with the development of the same society in order to polemise with the bourgeois revolution. In producing philosophically a concept of itself, it could be criticised economically and taken at its face value. Consequently, Marx understood the bourgeois revolution as the emancipation of the bourgeoisie, and not as that of man. Men are recognised by law as free and equal persons but, at the same time, they are under the natural-born ("naturwüchsig") relations of an exchange society:

> "Sie (die politische Revolution − J.G.) verhält sich zur bürgerlichen Gesellschaft, zur Welt der Bedürfnisse, der Arbeit, der Privatinteressen, des Privatrechts, als zur Grundlage ihres Bestehens, als zur einer nicht weiter begründeten Voraussetzung, daher als zu ihrer Naturbasis." (MEW 1, 69; cf. Habermas 1967, 80).

By analogy, Lohmann's analysis of the immanent critique in Marx's *Capital* was based on the idea of the formal nature of the principles of freedom and equality which does not take into account the real basis of the constitution of the bourgeois society:

> "Es ist diese Herrschaft des vermittelnden Eigentums, das die integrierenden Freiheits-
> und Gleichheitsnormen spezifisch beschränkt. Diese sind ihrer Geltung nach formal und
> allgemein, in fact jedoch an die inhaltliche Bedingung des Privateigentums gebunden. Sie
> sind daher abstrakte Freiheits- und Gleichheitsnormen, die nur gelten, weil sie gleichgültig
> gegenüber der konkreten eigenen wie der anderen Individualität sind." (Lohmann 1980,
> 273–274).

Thus, freedom and equality are formal principles having validity only in the sphere of commodity circulation. The production process as the genetic constitutive process of society is based on the appropriation of the surplus value, which is in contradiction with the constituting principles of bourgeois society as postulated by natural law.

The structure of the first book of Marx's *Capital* can now be interpreted in the light of the distinction between the immanent and transcending critique; the immanent presentation ends with chapter 22, after which there are two more chapters (even though there are elements of transcending critique in earlier chapters, too). At the end of the immanent presentation the object is presented in its totality, as the process of reproduction of capital. On the one hand, capital is shown to be reproducing its own preconditions; the relation between capital and wage labour is continuously reproduced. Capital no longer needs any external historical conditions. On the other hand, the natural rights theory supposing that a right to property must be based exclusively on the appropriation of the products of one's own labour and the exchange of equals, is challenged to defend its legitimatory basis; the only possibility to legitimate capital would be to prove that capital is, at least originally or historically, the result of a capitalists's own labour. At this point capital, in order to legitimate itself, must refer to its historical origins and, consequently a historical presentation of the coming into being of capital is required. And historical analysis must enter Marx's critique of capital, too:

> "Von der Systematik seiner eigenen Legitimation wird das Kapital gezwungen, seine
> höchst eigenen Zirkel zu überschreiten: es muss seine historische Entstehung darstellen.
> An der Stelle, wo scheinbar alle Geschichte im Kapitalsystem erloschen ist, kommt sie auf
> das *ganze* System bezogen wieder hervor. (...) Die immanente Kritik hat quasi ihren
> Gegenstand jetzt da, wo sie ihnen haben will. Er muss sich selbst als einen geschichtlich
> gewordenen Gegenstand darstellen, – und dies unter Rechtfertigungsgesichtspunkten –,
> nachdem vorher schon seine normative Selbstwidersprüchlichkeit ihn als einen sich selbst
> aufhebenden Gegenstand *indizierte.*" (Lohmann 1980, 280–281).

Lohmann's conception of immanent and transcending critique was inspired by Karl Korsch's discussion of the different modes of critique in Marx's political economy (see Lohmann 1980, 289; note 6). Of the three different modes of critique ("transzendent, immanent und transzendentale Kritik") formulated by Korsch the "transzendent" mode of critique resembles Lohmann's concept of transcending critique:

> "Transzendent, die Grenzen der Ökonomie wirklich überschreitend, ist die Marxsche Kri-
> tik an jenen, zahlreichen, dem Umfang nach weniger stark hervortretenden, aber inhaltlich
> äusserst wichtigen Stellen, wo Marx, nachdem er die von der Politischen Ökonomie in
> ihrer klassischen Periode aufgestellten Sätze bis in ihre letzten theoretischen Konsequenzen
> verfolgt hat, am Ende auch noch den Rahmen der Ökonomischen Theorie selbst sprengt

und von der ökonomischen zu einer direkt geschichtlichen und gesellschaftlichen Darstellung der Entwicklung der bürgerlichen Produktionsweise und des hinter dem Gegensatz der beiden ökonomischen Kategorien 'Kapital' und 'Lohnarbeit' versteckten wirklichen Gegensatzen und Kampfes der gesellschaftlichen Klassen übergeht." (Korsch 1967, 220; cf. Korsch 1971a, 67—68).

In Korsch's conception there was, however, supposed to be a strong parallelism between the development of the Marxist theory and the proletarian class movement:

> "Die Entstehung der marxistischen Theorie ist, hegelisch-marxistisch gesprochen, nur die 'andere Seite' der Entstehung der realen proletarischen Klassenbewegung;..." (Korsch 1971b, 87).

Marxism is, as a phenomenon parallel to a social movement, not only a critical theory of bourgeois society, but at the same time a theory of the proletarian revolution, in a rather straightforward way (see Korsch 1967, 56; see also Schanz 1974, 39—42). Marx's critique of the bourgeois economy is based on the standpoint of the proletariat ("Standpunkt des Proletariats") as the only class that is not interested in the preservation and legitimation of the bourgeois conceptions (see Korsch 1971b, 138).

The transcending critique as explicated by Lohmann can be interpreted as being concerned with the consequences of development of the capitalist society for the participants or individuals concerned. The immanent critique shows how the natural laws of society do not, in fact, realise the freedom and the equality of the individuals as presented by classical political economics. The transcending critique has to do with the normative standards of the participants. It introduces into the discussion the fate of labouring men (or the lot of the working class); the standard of the transcending critique has something to do with the experiences and also the opposition and actual resistance of the participants. The elements of transcending critique can be found in the historiographic paragraphs in Marx's *Capital:*

> "In ihrer allgemeinen Gestalt zeigen die Passagen die historisch beschreibbaren Auswirkungen der Entwicklung des Kapitals auf das 'Geschick' der Menschen, vornemlich der Arbeiterklasse. Sie zeigen die Subsumierung vorkapitalistischer Arbeit- und Lebensweisen unter die Herrschaft des Kapitals, die Widerstandshandlungen und Kämpfe der Arbeiter um ein ihren Ansprüchen entsprechendes Leben, aber auch die Formierung ihrer Lebensprozesse und -umstände. Unmittelbarer Darstellunggegenstand sind, allgemein gekennzeichnet, die historischen Lebenszusammenhänge der Menschen in der kapitalistischen Gesellschaft." (Lohmann 1980, 259).

These passages characterise a horizon of universal history in the light of which the historical nature and limits of the capitalist mode of production become visible — and in them the object of immanent critique is transcended. The function of the transcending critique is, according to Lohmann, to justify the standard of immanent critique from a 'broader horizon' (see Lohmann 1980, 258—259):

> "Aufgabe des kritischen Aspekts der transzendierenden Kritik ist die Zurückschneidung der universalen Ansprüche des naturrechtlichen (Lockeschen) Selbstverständnisses der

> bürgerlichen Gesellschaft. Dazu bedarf die transzendierende Kritik eines Masstabes, dessen für mich stärkste Version in den historiographischen Passagen des Kapitalbuches impliziert ist." (Lohmann 1980, 254–255).

In the transcending critique the relation between presentation and critique ("Darstellung und Kritik") is different from that of immanent critique; the critical moment is the dominating one (see Lohmann 1980, 254).

A more important problem is, however, that transcending critique cannot be imbedded in the systematic, conceptual presentation in the same way as immanent critique necessarily is. It is, out of necessity, of a fragmentary and narrative character. In this sense it can be compared with the positive philosophy of Schelling:

> "Fassen wir nämlich dasjenige an der bürgerlich-kapitalistischen Wirklichkeit, was sich im Sinne der 'negativen Philosophie' Schellings begrifflich-systematisch aneignen lässt, allein als die Entwicklung der Kapitalformation, die in der immanenten Darstellung begrifflich erfasst und systematisch reproduziert ist, so bleibe in den historiographischen Passagen Darstellungsstoff 'übrig'. Es wäre durch die antizipierende Kraft der methodischen Anschauung aufgenommen, im Sinne der 'positiven Philosophie' Schellings wiedersugeben, d.h. nicht in der Form einer systematischen Begriffsentwicklung, sondern in einer erzählenden Darstellungsweise. Marx hätte also – bewusst oder nicht – deshalb auf eine systematische, begrifflich konsistente Darstellung des Gehaltes der historiographischen Passagen verzichtet und damit auf eine bergifflich konsistente Darstellung des normativen Masstabes der transzendierenden Kritik, weil dieser 'Stoff' seiner Natur nach im Denken begrifflich nicht adäquat reproduzierbar ist." (Lohmann 1980, 260; cf. also Theunissen 1976).

The comparison with Schelling should, however, be taken cautiously. Marx had explicitly criticised in his dissertation such a 'positive philosophy of reality'. The 'true immediacy' ("Wahre Unmittelbarkeit") had been used as a critical point by all the 'young' Hegelians; the reality beyond reason is set against the infinite power of reason. The analogy with Schelling should, therefore, be taken much more cautiously; the narrative form of Marx's transcending critique and its standards can be explicated, too:

> "Was mit der immanenten Bergifflichkeit des kapitalistisch-bürgerlichen Selbstverständnisses nicht theoretisch angeeignet, d.h. immanent systematisch dargestellt werden kann, wird einer erzählenden Darstellungsweise überantwortet, die aber gleichwohl noch einer vernünftigen Explikation zugänglich ist." (Lohmann 1980, 261).

Lohmann's explication of Marx's two forms of critique is convincing as such. There are, however, at least three problematic questions connected with Lohmann's interpretation of Marx's critique of political economy. Some problems arise from the fact that his interpretation was influenced by Habermas' dual conception of system and life world ("Lebenswelt"), even though Lohmann was at the same time explicitly criticising Habermas' conception of the normative standards valid in life world (cf. Habermas 1981).

First, Lohmann can be criticised for forgetting Marx's presentation of the capitalist society as a negative totality in another meaning. Fulda (1978, 194–195) emphasised that Marx's critique of political economy is a theory of a catastrophe in a specific sense. Capital is understood by Marx to be a self-contradictory principle; the reproduction of capital is continuously faced by the limits set by the very process of value increase. While increasing the productivity of labour and relative surplus value, capital is all the more getting rid of its own basis of value increase, living labour power. This conception gets its clearest expression in Marx's analysis of the development of crises in capitalism and his law of the falling rate of profit:

> "Das wichtige aber in ihrem (der Ökonomen – J.G.) Horror vor der fallenden Profitrate ist das Gefühl, dass die kapitalistische Produktionsweise an der Entwicklung der Produktiv-kräfte eine Schranke findet, die nichts mit der Produktion des Reichtums als solcher zu tun hat; und diese eigentümliche Schranke bezeugt die Beschränktheit und den nur historis-chen, vorübergehenden Character der kapitalistischen Produktionsweise; bezeugt, dass sie keine für die Produktion des Reichtums absolute Produktionsweise ist, vielmehr mit seiner Fortentwicklung auf gewisse Stufe in Konflikt tritt." (MEW 25, 252).

The element of crisis is a continuous and permanent structural moment in capitalism – and in the critique of political economy. It determines capital as 'negative' – as pointed out by Stapelfeldt. The possibility of crises or disharmony is already present in the duality of abstract and concrete labour, and the dual character of commodity as both value and use-value runs through the whole of Marx's presentation and defines the presentation as critique:

> "Nicht erst der Nachweis einer Mehrwertaneignung über den Äquivalententausch begrün-det die Theorie von Marx als Kritik, sondern die in alle Einzelbestimmungen eingehende Entzweiung von abstrakter und konkreter Arbeit. Die Lehre, dass das Geld nur aus dem Kontext der 'Verdopplung der Ware in Ware und Geld' verstanden werden kann, ist nicht nur als Resultat einer Ableitung jener Identifikation zu lesen, die Ricardo auf fun-damentaler Ebene seiner Theorie im Begriff des Wertmassstabes vollzogen hat und den Ausgangspunkt der durchgängigen Konstruktion eines Gleichgewichtzustandes bildet, son-dern zugleich als Nachweis einer misslungenen Identifikation, einer misslungenen Projek-tion des gesellschaftlichen Verhältnisses auf das Verhältnis des Menschen zur Natur. Die Harmonie, der Tausch von Waren zu ihren Werten, die Gleichsetzung von Gebrauchswer-ten als Werte, erweist sich als Disharmonie, Differenz der Wertformen: Möglichkeit von Krisen." (Stapelfeldt 1979, 244–245).

Secondly, the problem of the fetish character of the relations of commodity producers and the reification of social relations does not, in fact, fit very well into Lohmann's interpretation, even though he does discuss the problem of the reciprocal relations of indifference between private producers. The main problem of Lohmann's interpreta-tion, in this respect, is connected with the Habermasian concept of life world.

The mutual indifference characteristic of the relations between private producers ("Gleichgültigkeitsverhältnisse") is based, according to Lohmann, on abstract labour. This indifference between private producers culminates in the indifference in the self-understanding of the owners of labour power. The relation of indifference is an exam-ple of structural domination because its causes are not manifest but hidden. Marx was, however, – and this interpretation shows the close affinity of Lohmann's conception to

that of Habermas' — too harmless in his understanding of the indifference relations
because he understood human action exclusively in terms of goal-oriented productive or
instrumental action:

> "Die einseitige Fassung des fundamentalen Handlungsbegriffs, die Handlung nur als pro-
> duktiv-gegenständliche Tätigkeit verstehen kann, rächt sich in einer Unterbestimmung des
> Ausmasses von Indifferenz, die mit einer Reduktion auf abstrakte Arbeit gegeben ist."
> (Lohmann 1980, 271).

The problem of the relation of indifference between the actors was solved by Marx in
terms of reification and the fetish character of commodity: social relations take the form
of relations between things. Money is a clear indicator of this indifference. Lohmann
criticised the Marxian understanding of the fetish character because Marx was, at his
best, only able to criticise the world of work (formal and real subsumption of work) but
not the wider subsumption of the whole life world by capital. A system integration
based on indifference remains unstable as long as the ability to work has not taken the
commodity form of labour power and the relations of the whole life world take the
character of indifference:

> "Damit kommen weitere Indifferenzphänomene in den Focus der Analyse, die das Verhal-
> ten zu Anderen und das Sich-zu-sich-Verhalten des Arbeitenden betreffen. Diese, durch
> Gleichgültigkeit characterisierten Selbstverhältnisse des Arbeitskraftbesitzers, die eine
> Selbstversachlichung des eigenen und gemeinschaftlichen Lebens ausdrücken, bewirken
> weitere Indifferenzphänomene, die üder die Veränderung der 'Arbeitswelt' (...) in die
> historisch-soziale Lebenswelt des Menschen hineinwirken." (Lohmann 1980, 272).

According to Lohmann's critique Marx's conceptualisation of the life world remains
inadequate and undetermined:

> "Er kann nämlich jene Subsumierungsprozesse, für die er, vom System aus gesehen, die
> Begriffe der 'formellen und reellen Subsumption' für die Formierung der Arbeitswelt und
> der historisch-sozialen Lebenswelten entwickelt, vom Standpunkt des Subsumierten nur
> ungenügend begrifflich fassen (...) Die Formierung der Arbeitswelt ist dabei begrifflich
> noch am deutlichsten gefasst, weil eine aristotelisch- hegelsche Begrifflichkeit von Arbeit
> und Leben als kontrastierende Folie untergelegt ist." (Lohmann 1980, 277; cf. Lohmann
> 1984).

In Marx's analyses the life world does remain conceptually undetermined. It can, therefore, oppose the subsumption by capital neither conceptually nor in principle. This is
the main reason why Marx's conception of transcending critique presupposes a specific
form of presentation of its own. The presentation cannot, however, be theoretical and
conceptual but descriptive and argumentative. Its further explication would require a
conceptual presentation of the historical-social life world and would thus overstep the
limits of Marx's conceptualisation:

> "Die Explikation des Gehaltes der 'historischen Betrachtungen' als Darstellung historisch-
> sozialen Lebenswelten muss daher über Marxsens begrifflichen Rahmen hinausgehen."
> (Lohmann 1980, 278).

Lohmann did not, however, see Marx's concepts of the fetish character of commodity and reification of social relations as a critical answer to the problem of the autonomy of the individual and the creatability and producibility of history as formulated by the philosophy of history of the Enlightenment and classical political economy. Marx solved the problem of the 'invisible hand' (Smith) or 'nature's purpose' ("Naturabsicht"; Kant) by showing how social relations act as an independent and objectified alien power in relation to the acting individuals and are, at the same time, an objectification of their social labour or productive activity. Marx criticised the 'teleology of bourgeois society'. In his analysis the historical teleology is not in need of a metaphysical explanation — even though Marx used metaphorical expressions in characterising the turning upside down of social relations (see Kittsteiner 1980, 87—88).

The problem of the fetish character of social relations is important from the point of view of the interpretation of the Second International Marxism, too, because the subsumption of the life world was in a way taken into account by the famous thesis of immiseration, whereas the problem of the alien character of social relations can be seen to form a contrary interpretation of Marx's revolutionary perspective (see Mohl 1981; for a further discussion see the concluding chapter).

The third problem in Lohmann's interpretation is closely connected with the previous one. As has already been pointed out, Lohmann did not notice that even the mode of critique explicated by him as a transcending one is, in fact, an implicit critique of the basic presuppositions of John Locke's natural rights theory and Adam Smith's classical political economy, even though on a different level from the immanent critique. While emphasising the nature of transcending critique as introducing the perspective and critical standards of those living and struggling in capitalism, Lohmann did not notice that the discussion of the fate ("Geschick") of wage workers in *Capital* is a direct comment on a central legitimatory argument of classical political economy. Lohmann was right in emphasising that the transcending critique "entwickelt...die nur faktisch-historisch auffindbaren Gründe für ein Urteil über das Kapital" (Lohmann 1980, 283), but not necessarily right in emphasising that a further development of Marx's critical presentation — in the spirit of Marx — would require an explication of the critical standards present in the historical-social life world of the participants:

> "Eine theoretische Extrapolation des normativen Massstabes der transzendierenden Kritik muss auf diese historisch-moralische Selbstinterpretation der Beteiligten historisch-sozialer Lebenswelten zurückweisen." (Lohmann 1980, 282).

One of the main arguments of the present study is that the critical standards characterised by Lohmann as transcending, which were presented by Marx in the chapter on the general law of accumulation in *Capital*, can be understood as a critique of the basic postulate of classical political economy and its predecessor, natural rights theory concerning the increasing opulence and well-being of the greatest number of the members of the bourgeois society as a consequence of private property and accumulation of capital.

The previous discussion has emphasised the indebtedness of Marx's critique and analysis of capitalism to his predecessors, the modern natural rights theoreticians and classical political economists; the standards of both immanent and transcending critique are claimed to be essentially taken over from them.[2] Consequently, the following presentation will take up for closer study Marx's critique of the justification of appropriation and private property, of the normative principles of freedom and equality, and his discussion of the general law of accumulation and its consequences for the fate of the working class.

---

[2]   In analysing Marx's reception and critique of classical political economy and its predecessors it should be kept in mind that Marx was reconstructing a history of a theory, the labour theory of value and the theory of surplus value. He consequently read the works of classical political economy with a specific theoretical and systematic interest. Classical political economy was − in a specific sense − understood by Marx to be an adequate conceptual expression of the system of bourgeois society. The critique of the economic doctrine also provided a critique of the bourgeois society:

"Die Arbeit, um die es sich zunächst handelt, ist *Kritik der ökonomischen Kategorien*, oder, if you like, das System der bürgerlichen Ökonomie kritisch dargestellt. Es ist zugleich Darstellung des Systems und durch die Darstellung Kritik desselben." (MEW 29, 550)

2. JOHN LOCKE, ADAM SMITH AND KARL MARX'S CRITIQUE OF PRIVATE PROPERTY

There are two opposing interpretations of John Locke's *Two Treatises on Government* (1965 (1690)) relevant from the point of view of Marx's critical presentation. Macpherson (1972) interpreted Locke as having provided a justification of private property and the accumulation of capital. Tully's (1980) analysis of Locke's theory was an explicit critique of Macpherson's interpretation. In Locke's theory there is no place either for private property or for the accumulation of capital. On the contrary, in Tully's opinion Locke provided a justification for common property and the individuation of property not to be mixed with private property.

Locke's analysis of property begins with the statement that land and its products are originally given to mankind to be used in common:

> 'Whether we consider natural *Reason,* which tells us, that Men, being once born, have a right to their Preservation, and consequently to Meat and Drink, and such other things, as Nature affords for their Subsistence: Or *Revelation,* which gives us an account of those Grants God made of the world to *Adam,* and to *Noah,* and his Sons, 'tis very clear, that God, as King *David* says, Psalm CXV, xvi *has given the Earth to the Children of Men,* given it to Mankind in common.'' (Locke 1965 II, V, 25; 327).

If land and all the products of land are given by God to all mankind in common, how, then, can anyone have property in anything and even without the explicit consent of all the other members of the society? This is the problem Locke set out to solve in his *Treatise.* The ''deduction'', as Locke says, ''is as follows'':

> ''. . . every Man has a *Property* in his own *Person* (. . .) The *Labour* of his Body, and the *Work* of his Hands, we may say, are properly his.'' (Locke 1965 II, V, 27; 328−329).

The only way to appropriate things from nature legitimately is through one's own labour:

> ''Whatsoever then he removes out of the State that Nature hath provided, and left it in, he hath mixed his *Labour* with, and joyned to it something that is his own, and thereby makes it his *Property*.'' (Locke 1965 II, V, 27; 329).

Because labour adds to nature something which unquestionably belongs to the labourer, things are mixed, so to say, with his labour, and hence become his property.

The right to private property, the right to appropriate something from nature that was originally given to all men in common, is based on labour, and only labour.

There are, however, two important limitations regulating the appropriation of property. The first restriction explicitly states that every man has a right to the products of his labour only insofar as there is enough left for everybody else to take for the preservation of his life:

> "For this *Labour*, being the unquestionable Property of the Labourer, no Man but he can have a right to what that is once joyned to, at least where there is enough, and as good left in common to others." (Locke 1965 II, V, 27; 329).

The second limitation is the spoilage limitation: no one has a right to more than he − or his dependants − can personally make use of or consume before it spoils:

> "As much as any one can make use of to any advantage of life before it spoils; so much he may by his labour fix a Property in. Whatever is beyond this, is more than his share, and belongs to others. Nothing was made by God for Man to spoil or destroy." (Locke 1965 II, V, 31; 322).

Property in land is principally acquired in the same manner as in the products of land:

> "*As much Land* as a Man Tills, Plants, Improves, Cultivates, and can use the Product of, so much is his Property." (Locke 1965 II, V, 32; 332).

The same limitation applying to the products of land is also valid with regard to the appropriation of landed property: so long as there is enough land, of equal quality, left for others to cultivate, everyone has a right to the land he cultivates (see Locke 1965 II, V, 33; 333).

Because of the limitations imposed on property no man can appropriate more than he can add his labour to and no more than he can use for his own convenience:

> "The Measure of Property, Nature has well set, by the Extent of Men's *Labour, and the Conveniency of Life:* No Man's Labour could subdue, or appropriate all. (...) This *measure* did confine every Man's *Possession,* to a very moderate Proportion..." (Locke 1965 II, V, 36; 334).

The introduction of money, however, changes the original rules regulating the appropriation of property. By agreeing on the use of money, men make it possible to appropriate larger possessions which would, in fact, violate the original limitations regulating private possessions:

> "That the same *Rule of Propriety,* (. . .) that every Man should have as much as he could make use of, would hold still in the World, without straitning any body, since there is Land enough in the World to suffice double the Inhabitants had not the *Invention of Money,* and the tacit Agreement of Men to put a value on it, introduced (by Consent) larger Possessions, and a Right to them; which, how it has done, I shall, by and by, shew more at large." (Locke 1965 II, V, 36; 335).

The introduction of money is thus the first contract agreed upon by the inhabitants in the original state of nature, the second being the introduction of political power.

The introduction of money by the common consent of the members of society changes the original rule of property; the spoilage limitation can be overcome by introducing money which concretely — in the form of gold and silver — does not spoil or decay, thus making possible the hoarding of money and larger possessions without violating this restriction:

> "And thus *came in the use of Money*, some lasting thing that Men might keep without spoiling, and that by mutual consent Men would take in exchange for the truly useful, but perishable Supports of Life." (Locke 1965 II, V, 47; 343).

The tacit agreement to use money and put value on it also, out of necessity, entails agreement on unequal possessions:

> "But since Gold and Silver, being little useful to the Life of Man in proportion to Food, Rayment, and Carriadge, has its *value* only from the consent of Men, it is plain that Men have agreed to disproportionate and unequal Possession on the Earth, they having by a tacit and voluntary consent found out a way, how a man may fairly possess more land than he himself can use the product of, by receiving in exchange for the overplus, Gold and Silver, which may be hoarded up without injury to any one, these metals not spoiling or decaying in the hands of the possessor. This partage of things, in an inequality of private possessions, men have made practicable out of the bounds of Societie, and without compact, only by putting a value on gold and silver and tacitly agreeing in the use of Money." (Locke 1965, II, V, 50; 344).

The second limitation, the sufficiency rule is, however, more problematic. Locke was quite explicit that with the introduction of money men can have a right to larger possessions and thus they would not, in fact, leave enough for others to make use of.

According to Macpherson (1972) Locke was faced with the dilemma of at least two seemingly contradictory rules regulating the right to property, the right based on one's own labour under the limitations of the sufficiency rule, and the accumulation of money which obviously violates the sufficiency rule, even though overcoming the spoilage rule. Locke solved the contradiction caused by the introduction of money and legitimated the larger possessions by modifying his original sufficiency limitation; the private appropriation of landed property is shown to be in common benefit of mankind; the productivity of labour under private property yields a much more higher produce than land lying in waste:

> ". . .he who appropriates land to himself by his labour, does not lessen but increase the common stock of mankind. For the provisions serving to the support of humane life, produced by one acre of inclosed and cultivated land, are (to speak much within compasse) ten times more, than those, which are yielded by an acre of Land, of an equal richnesse, lyeing wast in common." (Locke 1965 II, V, 37; 336).

The accumulation of property is then legitimated by the fruits of labour used in larger possessions:

> "For 1 aske whether in the wild woods and uncultivated wast of America left to Nature, without any improvement, tillage or husbandry, a thousand acres will yeild the needy and wretched inhabitants as many conveniences of life as ten acres of equally fertile land in Devonshire where they are well cultivated?" (Locke 1965 II, V, 37; 336).

As Macpherson (1972, 211; note 4) has pointed out, this argument was added only in the third edition of Locke's *Treatise*. Macpherson summarised Locke's 'astonishing achievement' of solving the seemingly contradictory presumptions of his theory as follows:

> "The chapter on property, in which Locke shows how the natural right to property can, be derived from the natural right to one's life and labour, is usually read as if it were simply the supporting argument for the bare assertion offered at the beginning of the *Treatise* that every man had a natural right to property 'within the bounds of the Law of Nature'. But in fact the chapter on property does something much more important: it removes 'the bounds of the Law of Nature' from the natural property right of the individual. Locke's astonishing achievement was to base the property right on natural right and natural law, and then to remove all the natural law limits from the property right." (Macpherson 1972, 199).

Locke's main legitimatory argument is then that even "if there is not then enough and as good *land* left for the others, there is enough and as good (indeed a better) *living* left for others. And the right of all men to a living was the fundamental right from which Locke had in the first place deduced their right to appropriate land" (Macpherson 1972, 212).

To Locke, the purpose of money was not merely to facilitate the exchange of things produced for consumption,

> "that is, to enlarge, beyond the scale of barter, exchange between producers of goods intended for consumption.The characteristic purpose of money is to serve as capital. Land itself Locke sees as merely a form of capital." (Macpherson 1972, 206).

Further:

> "He identifies money and capital, and assimilates both to land". (Macpherson 1972, 206).

The purpose of agriculture, industry and commerce was the accumulation of capital, not to provide consumable income for its owner, but to beget further capital by profitable investment (see Macpherson 1972, 207). Machpherson's conclusion, then, is that Locke justified the specifically capitalistic appropriation of land and money. And the accumulation of capital is justified by Locke in the state of nature prior to the consent of civil society (see Macpherson 1972, 208–209).

Macpherson further argued that the fact that the accumulation of capital is read all the way back to the state of nature is further supported by Locke's assumption of a wage relationship existing in the state of nature.[1] The labour limitation supposed by

---

[1] Rainer Rotermundt (1976) further radicalised Macpherson's interpretation of Locke's theory: Locke read back into the state of nature both the use of money as capital and the wage labour relationship and the contrary assumption of private property which is based only on one's own labour. These contrary assumptions follow from the identification of relations to nature with social relations. The incentive to accumulate follows in Locke's analysis exclusively from the introduction of money, and money is identified with capital. Capital is thus identified with the natural properties of both money and land. (See Rotermundt 1976, 98–99). Thus, both the

Locke says that anyone is entitled to appropriate only as much as one has mixed one's labour with (see Macpherson 1972, 214). Only if one assumes that the wage relationship exists in the state of nature does it become possible to overcome the labour limitation; if the labour is the property of the labourer, it becomes fully alienable and exchangeable as a property in its bourgeois sense:

> "The labour thus sold becomes the property of the buyer, who is then entitled to appropriate the produce of that labour". (Macpherson 1972, 215).

In his study *A Discourse on Property* (1980) James Tully showed that there is no place for private property of for wage labour relationship in Locke's *Two Treatises* — Macpherson's interpreation is ungrounded. Locke did not justify private property — even less the accumulation of capital. In Locke's theory money is simply hoarded and it is the miser's desire to hoard money which Locke not only disapproved of but even regarded as unnatural. Tully's interpretation is especially interesting in this context while he explicitly criticised Macpherson's influential interpretation on which even Lohmann's analysis implicitly relied.

In Tully's opinion Macpherson's interpretation leads to a paradoxical conclusion. It was precisely Locke's opponents, Grotius, Pufendorf and Filmer, who proposed an exclusive rights theory and justified private property. Their theory employed natural law to protect exclusive rights by reducing it to the natural duty to abstain from another's property. According to Tully, Locke's theory was constructed in opposition to an unlimited rights theory; precisely the sort of theory that Marx took to be the typical justification of private property. (See Tully 1980, 131.) Macpherson was thus wrong in suggesting that Locke's theory

> ". . .'can be seen to be the product of the new relations of emergent capitalist society'. If this were true, then there would seem to be a tension in Macpherson's analysis of the seventeenth century at this point. The authors who adopt the private concept, Grotius, Filmer and Pufendorf, integrate it into their absolutist theories. The author who adheres to the common concept most emphatically is Locke." (Tully 1980, 79).

Locke, then, did not adopt a concept of private property but a concept of individual property (see Tully 1980, 111). Following Driver (1950, 91) Tully further argued that the identification of Locke's concept of property with private property is a relatively new phenomenon:

---

generalisation of commodity relations and the ownership of the means of production by the individual producers were assumed by Locke:

> "Die bürgerliche Gesellschaft wird dadurch sowohl ansatzweise historisch als auch naturhaft gegeben betrachtet, da sie zum einen in ihrer wesentlichen Bestimmung der gesellschaftlich verallgemeinerten Warenproduktion als menschliche Naturkonstante erscheint, zum anderen aber (. . .) entwickelt gedacht wird aus einem Zustand, in dem es die Trennung von Lohnarbeit und Kapital noch nicht gab." (Rotermundt 1976, 84–85).

"Early nineteenth century radicals fixed on Locke's theory of a natural property in the product of one's own labour and used it to legitimate revolt against the prevailing system of private property." (Tully 1980, 124).

Tully also suggested that Marx interpreted Locke in the spirit of this radical tradition.

According to Tully, Locke defined property as that which cannot be taken away without one's consent. But Locke's theory is not an unlimited rights theory because at the moment that cultivated fields and their products cease to be objects of use for a person they cease to be his property, and the inclusive rights of others apply (see Tully 1980, 124). Locke was, furthermore, by no means undermining the traditional obligations associated with property. On the contrary, he gave them a firm basis. Labour is not the sole means to entitle a person to the necessary means of support. In Locke's theory there are two additional natural titles to property: charity and inheritance (see Tully 1980, 131–132).

In addition to undermining the interpretation of Locke's theory as a justification of private property, Tully emphatically denied that Locke supposed wage labour relationship to have existed in the state of nature. In the 'turfs' passage to which Macpherson refers, Locke was only assuming a master-servant relationship:

"All that Locke assumes in the 'turfs' passage is a master-servant relation. It is not only not the wage relationship of capitalism, it is a fetter to the development of capitalism which was not supplanted until the late eighteenth century." (Tully 1980, 136).

In support of his interpretation Tully provided two arguments: First Locke assumed that a master-servant relation can only be established if a freeman has a choice not to become a servant. If for some reason there is no alternative available to him to support himself, then the relation cannot arise (see Tully 1980, 138). The second argument follows directly from Locke's own definition of labour:

"Since the labour of a person is defined as actions determined by the will of that person, it is logically impossible for an agent to alienate *his* labour. Therefore, what is sold by a freeman, and bought by another, is not his labour but, as Locke carefully writes, the 'Service he undertakes to do'." (Tully 1980, 138).

A person directed in his activity like a wage worker by a capitalist would not be a servant but a slave or a vassal, and would be part of a relation "to which Locke's servant is contrasted" (Tully 1980, 141).

Tully agreed with Macpherson that the introduction of money will, according to Locke's theory', lead to unequal possessions:

"As soon as money is introduced, some men begin to put more land under cultivation than is necessary for their uses and exchange the products they cannot use for money." (Tully 1980, 147).

But even in this respect Tully disagreed with Macpherson on one important question. Neither land nor money can possibly function as capital in Locke's theory:

"Land cannot be exchanged, only the products of it are alienable. There is no evidence in the *Two Treatises* that money functions as capital: it is simply hoarded." (Tully 1980, 149).

It is even more important to note that Locke thought that "the acceptance of money brings with it the fall of man" (Tully 1980, 150). Men begin to desire more than they need and as a consequence "some men's desires are no longer coincident with the law of nature but, rather, drive them to overstep it" (Tully 1980, 150). In Locke's opinion the introduction of money would lead to the violation of the law of nature if there were not some new rules to regulate the possession of land. Locke's solution to the problem of this new rule is civil law:

"The original proviso, that there is enough and as good (land − J.G.) left in common for others, no longer obtains and, therefore, natural appropriation without consent is invalid." (Tully 1980, 153).

Tully's conclusion of his discussion of Locke's theory of property, then, is that Locke justified neither private property nor unlimited appropriation, but proposed

". . .a system in which private and common ownership are not mutually exclusive but mutually related; private ownership is the means of individuating the community's common property and is limited by the claims of all other members". (Tully 1980, 170).

As already pointed out, Tully briefly referred to Marx as a representative of the radical interpretation of Locke's theory as justifying private property. In a manuscript written in 1861−63 Marx briefly mentioned Locke in a way that seems to support Tully's thesis. According to Marx, Locke represented two contrary conceptions. Locke presupposed both that the means of production are privately owned by every producer and that the capitalist relations of production prevail − in Marx's opinion these two contradictory presumptions were common to the whole succeeding political economy:

"Die allgemeine Vorstellung von Locke bis Ricardo daher die des *kleinbürgerlichen Eigentums*, während die von ihnen dargestellten Produktionsverhältnisse der kapitalistischen Produktionsweise angehören." (Marx 1969, 133).

If this were Marx's only comment on Locke, one could probably interpret Marx as sharing the early nineteenth century radicals' interpretation of Locke as defending capitalist private property − an interpretation which was followed by Macpherson. However, in *Theorien über den Mehrwert* which was written in the same period as the manuscript referred to earlier Marx discussed Locke's theory in more detail, and in this manuscript Marx's conclusions did not remarkably differ from those reached by Tully. In *Theorien* Marx wrote that Locke did not discuss any procedures of appropriation other than appropriation by labour; in Locke's theory the right to property is always based on one's own labour. But the property in question is not private property, it is individual property:

"Was Locke daher zu beweisen sucht, ist nicht der Gegensatz, dass (man) Eigentum noch durch andre procedures als Arbeit erwerben könne, sondern wie durch die individuelle Arbeit, trotz dem common property an der Natur, individuelles Eigentum geschaffen werden könne." (MEW 26.1., 342).

Marx further acknowledged that in Locke's case personal labour is the limit of property, and that one cannot own more than one can personally make use of. Through the introduction of money unequal possessions arise, but even then Marx acknowledged that in Locke's theory the just measure of personal labour prevails (see MEW 26.1., 342–343). Marx even notified that Locke's theory was opposed to the demands of landlords. In Locke's opinion the rent of land demanded by a landlord is not better than the interest received by any usurer.

Despite the fact that Marx thus clearly recognised that Locke's theory was not an affirmative theory of capitalist private property, he still emphasised the importance of Locke's conceptions to subsequent political economy. It shared with Locke the general idea that a title to property can only be created by personal labour. And the whole political economy succeeding Locke assumed that even in bourgeois society private property is based on personal labour:

> "Lockes Auffassung um so wichtiger, da sie der klassische Ausdruck der Rechtsvorstel-
> lungen der bürgerlichen Gesellschaft im Gegensatz zur feudalen und seine Philosophie
> überdies der ganzen späteren englischen Ökonomie zur Grundlage aller ihrer Vorstel-
> lungen diente." (MEW 26.1., 343).

The importance of Locke was further accentuated by the fact that Marx understood Locke to be the founder or predecessor of the labour theory of value: Locke comprehended value exclusively in terms of use value, but he also thought that labour makes up by far the greatest part of the value of any useful thing — the rest is added by nature (see MEW 26.1., 342).[2]

Even though Macpherson was obviously drawing too far-reaching consclusions from his reading of Locke's *Two Treatises*, he did pay attention to one important argument in Locke's theory which remains valid despite Tully's critique. Locke did not only assume that it is labour that transforms nature's products into useful things. Because labour creates the greatest part of the value of a product, the common stock of useful things is increased by cultivating land and adding more labour to nature's products. Even though the justification of private property and the accumulation of capital cannot — as shown by Tully — possibly be actualised in Locke's theory, he did assume that by cultivating land and by creating a right of property in it, man contributes to the support of human life by increasing the value of things useful to man. Thus labour and the property associated with it are beneficial to mankind in creating the conditions for a better human life.

The same social benefits associated with labour and property were explicitly thought by Adam Smith in *The Wealth of Nations* (1970 (1776)) to result from the increasing division of labour and from the increasing exchange of commodities — and from the

---

[2] Tully (1980, 144) formulated Locke's conception of value as follows: "Labour transforms nature into useful products, and so it is the source of value. . .". In Locke's theory labour is thus associated with use value, with the usefulness of its products to man.

establishment of private property closely connected with the division of labour. Once all unnatural barriers intervening with the free functioning of the economic laws of a commercial society have been removed,these laws will quarantee that the division of labour and exchange of commodities will lead to the general opulence of a nation, creating the possibilities of a human existence for the greatest number of its members. In Smith's opinion it was the continuously growing wealth of a nation that quaranteed a decent living even for the lower ranks of people.

According to Smith:

> ". . . in that original state of things, which precedes both the appropriation of land and the accumulation of stock, the whole produce of labour belongs to the labourer. He has neither landlord not master to share with him." (Smith 1970, 167).

In the natural law tradition Smith regarded the property in one's own labour as the fundamental property right on which all more developed property rights are based:

> "The property which every man has in his own labour, as it is the original foundation of all other property, so it is the most sacred and inviolable." (Smith 1970, 225).

Labour, also, is the ultimate measure of the value of commodities:

> "Labour alone, therefore, never varying in its own value, is alone the ultimate and real standard by which the value of commodities can at all times and places be estimated and compared. It is their real price; money is their nominal price." (Smith 1970, 136).

And further:

> "The real price of everything, what everything really costs to the man who wants to acquire it, is the toil and trouble of acquiring it. . . What is bought with money or with goods is purchased by labour as much as what we acquire by the toil of our body. (. . .) Labour was the first price, the original purchase-money that was paid for all things. It was not by gold or silver, but by labour, that all the wealth of the world was originally purchased; and its value, to those who possess it, and who want to exchange it for some new productions, is precisely equal to the quantity of labour which it can enable them to purchase or command." (Smith 1970, 133).

In the original "state of things, which preceeds both the appropriation of land and the accumulation of stock, the whole produce of labour belongs to the labourer" (Smith 1970, 167). The situation is, however, changed as soon as land becomes private property and stock is accumulated and the labourer becomes a wage labourer. Thereafter he has to share the produce of his labour with both the owners of stock and land. (See Smith 1970, 152 and 168.) Both the introduction of money and the accumulation of stock are originally based on the demands of the increasing division of labour:

> ". . . every prudent man in every period of society, after the first establishment of the division of labour, must naturally have endeavoured to manage his affairs in such a manner as to have at all times by him besides the peculiar produce of his own industry, a certain quantity of some one commodity or other, such as he imagined few people would be likely to refuse in exchange for the produce of their industry." (Smith 1970, 126—127).

In the original state of society, when every man produces for himself and there is seldom any exchange made, no stock need be accumulated. After the introduction of the division of labour only a small part of those commodities that he himself makes use of are produced by him. Money in the form of a commodity which is generally taken in exchange for the produce of other men's labour is a convenient means of solving the problem of accumulation of stock and exchange of commodities.

Smith claimed that after the accumulation of stock and the establishment of private property of land it is only natural that anyone interested in employing them is expected to get from the sale of their produce more than is sufficient to replace his stock. Otherwise "he could have no interest to employ a great stock rather than a small one, unless his profits were to bear some proportion to the extent of his stock" (Smith 1970, 151).[3]

The same is also true of the land which has become private property:

> "The landlord demands a share of almost all the produce which the labourer can either raise, or collect from it". (Smith 1970, 168).

The profits of stock and rent of land are, then, formed of a share of the produce of labour, which is the only thing that adds new value to things. On the other hand, the natural price of every commodity is, according to Smith, composed of three component parts forming its real price, wages, profits and rent, corresponding to the three sources of revenue, labour, stock and land:

> "In every society the price of every commodity finally resolves itself into some one or other, or all of those three parts; and in every improved society, all the three enter more or less, as component parts into the price of the far greater part of commodities." (Smith 1970, 153).

There is, however, yet a third conception of the determination of the value of commodities inherent in Smith's theory, the so-called labour command theory; the value of every commodity is determined by the amount of labour it can command or the value of the commodities it can be exchanged with, and not directly by the amount of labour that has been necessary to produce it:

> "The value of any commodity, therefore, to the person who possessed it, and who means not to use or consume it himself, but to exchange it for other commodities, is equal to the quantity of labour which it enables him to purchase or command." (Smith 1970, 133).

---

[3] Cf.:

> "In exchanging the complete manufacture either for money, for labour, or for other goods, over and above what may be sufficient to pay the price of the materials, and the wages of the workmen, something must be given for the profits of the undertaker of the work who hazards his stock in this adventure. The value which the workmen add to the materials, therefore, resolves itself in this case into two parts, of which the one pays their wages, the other the profits of their employer upon the whole stock of materials and wages, which he advanced." (Smith 1970, 151).

It is this labour command conception that leads to the problematic conclusion that it is possible to exchange a certain amout of labour for a greater amount of labour.

The increasing division of labour and private property was legitimated by Smith by the just distribution of necessities of life it occasions and by the advancement of the interests of society (see Musgrave 1976, 302–305). In *The Theory of Moral Sentiments* Smith argued that the economic laws of a society — the invisible hand — will even after the introduction of unequal possessions, quarantee the same distribution of the necessities of life prevailing under the conditions of equal possessions of land:

> "They (the landlords — J.G.) are led by an invisible hand to make nearly the same distribution of the necessaries of life, which would have been made, had the earth been divided into equal portions among all its inhabitants, and thus without intending it, without knowing it, advance the interest of the society, and afford means to the multiplication of the species. When Providence divided the earth among a few lordly masters, it neither forgot nor abandoned those who seemed to have been left out in the partition. These last too enjoy their share of all that it produces." (Smith 1979 (1759), 184–185).

In the *Wealth of the Nations* it is argued that the increasing division of labour will lead to increasing opulence of the nation, an opulence extending to the lowest ranks of people:

> "It is the great multification of the productions of all the different arts, in consequence of the division of labour, which occasions, in a well-governed society, that universal opulence which extends itself to the lowest ranks of people. Every workman has a great quantity of his own work to dispose of beyond what he himself has occasion for; and every other workman being exactly in the same situation, he is enabled to exchange a great quantity of his own goods for a great quantity of, or what comes to the same thing, for the price of a great quantity of theirs." (Smith 1970, 115).

The increasing division of labour is considered to cause an increasing national wealth and a consequent increase in the real wages of labour. According to Smith it is not the actual greatness of national wealth, but its continual increase which occasions a rise in the wages of labour (see Smith 1970, 172):

> "The liberal reward of labour, therefore, as it is the necessary effect, so it is the natural symptom of increasing national wealth." (Smith 1970, 176).

And this should be regarded as real advantage to a society:

> "Is this improvement in the circumstances of the lower ranks of the people to be regarded as an advantage or as an inconveniency to the society? The answer seems at first sight abundantly plain. Servants, labourers, and workmen of different kinds, make up the far greatest part of every great political society. But what improves the circumstances of the greater part can never be regarded as an inconveniency to the whole. No society can surely be flourishing and happy, of which the far greater part of the members are poor and miserable. It is but equity, besides, that they who food, clothe, and lodge the whole body of the people, should have such a share of the produce of their own labour as to be themselves tolerably well fed, clothed, and lodged." (Smith 1970, 181).

The increasing division of labour, being the original moving force behind the increasing opulence of nations "from which so many advantages are derived", is according to Smith,

"... not originally the effect of any human wisdom, which foresees and intends that general opulence to which it gives occasion. It is the necessary, though very slow and gradual consequence of a certain propensity in human nature which has in view no such extensive utility: the propensity to truck, barter, and exchange one thing for another." (Smith 1970, 117).

The natural progress of opulence of nations is a guarantee of the possibility of 'human existence' in society. A continuous economic progress guarantees even for the lower ranks of people a descent and human existence, an existence equally good or even far better than in any primitive society which, by contrast, are more equal, but miserably poor (see Hont & Ignatieff 1983, 1−2; see also Medick 1973, 281).[4]

As Istvan Hont and Michael Ignatieff have recently (1983, 1) shown the main question which Smith attempted to answer in his *Wealth of Nations* was exactly how a commercial society with its marked inequality of property still satisfied the basic needs of those who laboured for wages:

"Our argument is that the *Wealth of Nations* was centrally concerned with the issue of justice, with finding a market mechanism capable of reconciling inequality of property with adequate provision for the excluded." (Hont & Ignatieff 1983, 2).

According to Hont and Ignatieff (1983, 2) Smith's unique solution to the problem was included in his conception of the "productivity of modern forms of labour" (due to division of labour) and his natural price model.

In Marx's opinion the greatest merit of Adam Smith was that he was the first to become sensitive to the problem of the origins of surplus value. By reconstructing Smith's labour theory of value Marx showed that Smith was led to the conclusion that less labour can be exchanged for more labour, a conclusion contradicting his original law of value and the consequent postulate of equal exchange. From Marx's point of view the interesting and problematic result of Smith's analysis was that once the simple exchange of commodities is transformed into exchange between wage labour and capital, the law of value no longer holds but is reversed:

---

[4]   Hans Medick interpreted the natural progress of opulence to be the result of a civilisatoric dynamic caused by the artificial nature of needs of man (see Medick 1973, 251). He summarised Smith's conception of the natural state and the natural history of society as follows:

"Das Modell eines von der künstlichen Bedürfnisnatur des Menschen stimulierten, durch die institutionelle Garantie der Justices freigesetzten und regulierten historischen Prozess wirtschaftlichen Wachstums liefert Smith in Gestalt der Vorstellung eines 'Natural Progress of Opulence' nicht nur den Massstab einer normativen Naturgeschichte, mit Hilfe dessen er die empirische Geschichte des Menschen identifizieren, verstehen und kritisieren kann, es gibt ihm zugleich − als Telos des 'Natural Progress of Opulence' auch den Massstab eines 'Naturzustandes' an die Hand, mit Hilfe dessen er seine zeitgenössische Gesellschaft analysiert, um sie über sich selbst aufzuklären." (Medick 1973, 250).

"Es ist das grosse Verdienst A. Smiths, dass er gerade in den Kapiteln des ersten Buches
(. . .) wo er vom einfachen Warenaustausch und seinem Gesetz des Wertes übergeht zum
Austausch zwischen vergegenständlichter und lebendiger Arbeit, zum Austausch zwischen
Kapital und Lohnarbeit, zur betrachtung von Profit und Grundrente im allgemeinen, kurz
zum Ursprung des Mehrwerts, es fühlt, dass hier ein Riss eintritt, dass − . . . − das Gesetz
im Resultat faktisch aufgehoben wird, mehr Arbeit gegen weniger Arbeit (vom Standpunkt
des Arbeiters), weniger Arbeit gegen mehr Arbeit (vom Standpunkt des Kapitalisten)
ausgetauscht wird, und dass er hervorhebt und ihn förmlich irre macht, dass mit der
Akkumulation des Kapitals und dem *Grundeigentum* − also mit der Verselbständigung der
Arbeitsbedingungen gegenüber der Arbeit selbst − eine neue Wendung, scheinbar (und
faktisch das Resultat) ein Umschlag des Gesetzes des Werts in sein Gegenteil stattfindet."
(MEW 26.1., 58−59).

According to Marx Smith was right in emphasising that a change was taking place, but
he did not comprehend what really caused this change.[5] And what is equally important:
Smith did not understand that the exchange between wage labour and capital did not, in
fact, violate the original law of value and equal exchange, even though as a result of this
process of exchange the capitalist had indeed appropriated a surplus value. The ambivalence in Smith's theory of value resulted from his determination of the value of a
product both by the amount of alien labour it can command and by the amount of
labour that has been necessary to produce it. According to Marx, this led Smith to
confuse two clearly distinct problems in analysing the exchange of commodities.

Firstly, while emphasising the change caused by the introduction of the division of
labour, exchange of products, and production for a market Smith in fact problematised
the social character of labour:

". . . der Reichtum nicht mehr im Produkt der eignen Arbeit besteht, sondern in dem
Quantum fremder Arbeit, die dies Produkt kommandiert, der gesellschaftlichen Arbeit,
die es kaufen kann, welches Quantum durch das Quantum der in ihm selbst enthaltnen
Arbeit bestimmt ist. (. . .) Der Akzent liegt hier auf der mit der Teilung der Arbeit und
dem Tauschwert herbeigeführten Gleichsetzung *meiner* Arbeit und *fremder* Arbeit, in
andren Worten gesellschaftlicher Arbeit. . ." (MEW 26.1., 46−47).

Quantitatively the relation of exchange is determined by the amount of labour that has
been used in producing the commodities:

"Unter der Voraussetzung (dass der ganze Produkt der Arbeit gehört dem Arbeiter −
J.G.) ist der Arbeiter blosser Warenverkäufer, und der eine kommandiert die Arbeit des
anderen nur, sofern er mit seiner Ware die Ware der andren käuft. Er kommandiert also
mit seiner Ware nur soviel Arbeit des andren, als in seiner eignen Ware enthalten ist, da
beide nur Waren gegeneinander austauschen und der Tauschwert der Waren bestimmt ist
durch die in ihnen enthaltne Arbeitszeit oder Quantität Arbeit." (MEW 26.1., 49).

---

[5] Marx was clearly exaggerating his case in claiming that Smith clearly felt that a change
took place in his argumentation concerning the relations of exchange once capital had been
introduced. The contradictions of Smith's theory were reconstructed by Marx; Smith obviously
was not conscious of them.

Secondly, Smith's analysis of the exchange relations between the commodity producers included another emphasis — even though Smith did not adequately comprehend it — , the relation between living and materialised labour. This relation seems to violate the rule of the exchange of equal amounts of labour objectified in commodities:

> "Ein bestimmtes Quantum lebendiger Arbeit kommandiert nicht dassalbe Quantum vergegenständlichter Arbeit, oder ein bestimmtes Quantum in Ware vergegenständlichter Arbeit kommandiert ein grösses Quantum lebendiger Arbeit, als in der Ware selbst enthalten ist." (MEW 26.1., 43).

The problem of the relation of exchange between living and materialised labour can be solved when it is realised that in a society where the means of production belong totally to one or several classes, and where the ability to work ("Arbeitsvermögen") belongs to a different class, the class of workers, the product of labour in fact no longer belongs to the worker. If one demystifies Smith's conception of labour command and understands that it in fact refers to the relation between materialised and living labour, it can be interpreted to reveal the fact that the appropriation of surplus value begins at the moment when the means of labour belong to one class and the ability to work to another. In Marx's opinion this differentiation of the social functions of the classes or separation of the means of labour from the ability to work marks the beginning of capitalist society. (See MEW 26.1., 49.)

Smith did — according to Marx — have a notion that the profits are nothing but a reduction from the value that labour adds to the material of work (see MEW 26.1., 51). The profits originate in the part of labour which is not paid, even though it is bought by the owner of capital:

> "A. Smith hat damit selbst widerlegt, dass der Umstand, dass dem Arbeiter nicht mehr das ganze Produkt seiner Arbeit gehört, dass er es oder seinen Wert teilen muss mit dem Eigentümer des Kapitals, das Gesetz aufhebt, dass das Verhältnis, worin sich die Waren gegeneinander austauschen, oder ihr Tauschwert bestimmt ist durch das Quantum der in ihnen materialisierten Arbeitszeit." (MEW 26.1., 50).

The great merit of Smith was that he — without knowing it — emphasised the change that takes place in the relation of exchange after the introduction of capitalist production. Smith was, however, mistaken in believing that the relation between materialised and living labour violates the rule of equal exchange and occasions a change in the determination of the relative value of commodities. (See MEW 26.1., 52.)

Marx's solution to the contradiction of classical political economy as interpreted by him was the introduction of the concept of labour power. All the contradictions inherent in the political economy concerning the origins of profits and surplus value could be solved once the specific character of the commodity 'labour power' was developed: labour power has both a use value and an exchange value like any other commodity, the only difference being that its specific use value is its ability to create new value. Thus is was possible for Marx to show that the exchange between materialised labour and living labour follows the same rule of equal exchange as any exchange of commodities in a society of commodity production, i.e. in a society where private labour becomes social only through exchange, and where the products of labour only have use value to the buyers and exchange value to the sellers of commodities.

Marx's critique and analysis of the capitalis mode of appropriation and private property in *Capital* and in *Grundrisse* in particular was a direct comment on the anomalies he had identified in Smith's theory of value. According to Marx, in capitalism the right to property is transformed from one based on one's own labour into a right, first, to appropriate the products of alien labour and, second, to a duty to respect one's own labour and its products as belonging to another. Marx stated that in capitalism the exchange of equivalents — reflected in the legal rules governing private property — seems to be a mere appearance:

> "Der Austausch von Äquivalenten aber, der als die ursprüngliche Operation erschien, die das Eigentumsrecht juristisch ausdrückte, hat sich so gedreht, dass auf der einen Seite nur zum Schein ausgetauscht wird, indem der gegen lebendiges Arbeitsvermögen ausgetauschte Teil des Kapitals, erstens selbst *fremde Arbeit* ist, angeeignet ohne Äquivalent, und zweitens *mit einem Surplus von Arbeitsvermögen ersetzt werden muss*, also in fact nicht fortgegeben wird, sondern nur aus einer Form in die andre verwandelt wird. Das Verhältnis des Austauschs ist also gänzlich weggefallen, oder ist *blosser Schein.*" (Marx s.a., 362).

The relation between capital and labour only appears to be a relation of equivalents because, in fact, the result of exchange is the appropriation of surplus labour, and the capital which is exchanged against labour power is already a result of an earlier process of appropriation of alien labour or its product, and is consequently not based on one's own labour as presupposed by the original idea of the right to property. To speak of exchange as 'pure appearance' is, however, somewhat misleading. The relation between capital and labour power is namely one of exchange in reality. The relation is only one of appearance if one considers not a single act of exchange but the total relation of exchange between the class of capitalists and the class of wage workers (see Clarke 1982, 84). The relation is, then, only one of appearance — it could be interpreted — because the accumulated capital is already totally a result of the previous appropriation of surplus value. It does not in any way consist of the materialised labour of its owner. Further, the whole act of exchange belongs, according to Marx, to the sphere of circulation, which ignores the 'deeper' process of production as the consumption of use values and the creation of new value by labour power.

While discussing the transformation of surplus value into capital in *Capital* Marx also analysed the problems of the capitalist form of appropriation. The critique of the legal rules of capitalist appropriation and private property is, in a way, completed as soon as all the capital is shown to originate from the surplus value produced previously by the wage worker. The last legitimatory argument defending the right to private property as a right to the products of one's own labour loses its rationale:

> "Eigentum an vergangner unbezahlter Arbeit erscheint jetzt als die einzige Bedingung für gegenwärtige Aneignung lebendiger unbezahlter Arbeit in stets wachsender Umfang." (MEW 23, 609).

As soon as the production of commodities becomes generalised, labour power takes the
form of a commodity, too. And consequently the law of appropriation is reversed:

> ". . .sofern jede einzelne Transaktion fortwährend dem Gesetz des Warentausches ent-
> spricht, der Kapitalist stets die Arbeitskraft kauft, der Arbeiter sie stets verkauft, und wir
> wollen annehmen selbst zu ihrem wirklichen Wert, schlägt offenbar das auf Warenproduk-
> tion und Warenzirkulation beruhende Gesetz der Aneignung oder Gezetz des Privateigen-
> tums durch seine eigne, innere, unvermeidliche Dialektik in sein direktes Gegenteil um."
> (MEW 23, 609).

In *Grundrisse* Marx formulated the result of this transformation in similar terms as in
Capital: the exchange takes place only in appearance ("nur zum Schein ausgetauscht
wird"; Marx s.a., 362). The relation of exchange between the capitalist and the worker
is thus a mere appearance belonging to the process of circulation. It is a pure form,
alien to the contents of this process and mystifying them:

> "Der beständige Kauf und Verkauf der Arbeitskraft ist die Form. Der Inhalt ist, dass der
> Kapitalist einen Teil der bereits vergegenständlichten fremden Arbeit, die er sich unauf-
> hörlich ohne Äquivalent aneignet, stets wieder gegen grösseres Quantum lebendiger frem-
> der Arbeit umsetzt." (MEW 23, 609).

The right to property which was thought to be originally based on the products of one's
own labour is thus in reality reversed into the right to appropriate alien labour and its
products without a mutual equivalent:

> "Eigentum erscheint jetzt auf Seite des Kapitalisten als das Recht, fremde unbezahlte
> Arbeit oder ihr Produkt, auf Seite des Arbeiters als Unmöglichkeit, sich sein eignes Pro-
> dukt anzueignen. Die Scheidung zwischen Eigentum und Arbeit wird zur notwendigen
> Konsequenz eines Gesetzes, das scheinbar von ihrer Identität ausging." (MEW 23, 610).

The identity of property and labour, as postulated by the natural law theory and its
followers, classical political economists, is thus broken and reversed into a dissociation
of property and labour.

Marx, nevertheless, wanted to emphasise that this new capitalistic form of appropriation does not violate the original law of commodity exchange. Quite the contrary, it
results from the observance of this rule. The whole secret of the transformation of the
law of appropriation consists of the fact that even if the process of exchange of commodities is also conditioned by the difference in use values, it does not tell us anything
about the (productive) consumption of commodities, which only begins after the act of
exchange has been completed. (See MEW 23, 611).[6]

To Kautsky and other Marxists of the Second International capitalism was mainly to

---

[6] Cf.:

> "Im Ganzen der vorhandnen bürgerlichen Gesellschaft erscheint dieses Gesetz der Preise
> und ihre Zirkulation etc., als der oberflächliche Prozess, unter dem aber in der Tiefe ganz
> andere Prozesse vorgehn, in denen diese scheinbare Gleichheit und Freiheit der Individuen
> verschwindet." (Marx s.a., 159).

be blamed because it does not respect the right of the labourer to the products of his labour. Marx's critique of capitalist private property was more developed and complicated. First, Marx continuously emphasised that the capitalist form of appropriation does not violate the rule of commodity exhange. The mutual freedom and equality of commodity owners is respected even in the relation between capital and wage labour. Second, Marx analysis in fact implicitly included a critique of such a radical version of the natural rights theory which was later adopted by traditional Marxism. In Marx's opinion the title to property is never constituted by man's productive relation to nature.

Marx did not thus stop at the point of showing how appropriation is, in fact, transformed into its opposite form in capitalism. He also explained why classical political economy insisted on labour as remaining the basis for the right to property even in bourgeois society. The original appropriation of commodities, their production takes place outside the sphere of circulation. Within the process of circulation commodities can only be appropriated through exchange, i.e. the appropriation of the products of alien labour can only take place through the alienation of one's own labour. Consequently the only way to appropriate commodities seems to be exclusively through one's own labour:

"In den einfachen Austauschprozess, wie er sich in den verschiednen Momenten der Zirkulation auseinanderlegt, fällt zwar nicht die Produktion der Waren. Sie sind vielmehr als fertige Gebrauchswerte unterstellt. (. . .) *Der Entstehungsprozess der Waren, also auch ihr ursprünglicher Aneignungsprozess, liegt daher jenseits der Zirkulation."* (Marx s.a., 902).

Because the original appropriation of commodities does not belong to the sphere of circulation, the process in which the private property owners are born is postulated as being based on the original appropriation of nature's products through labour:

"Wie sie zu Privateigentümern geworden sind, *d.h. sich vergegenständlichte Arbeit angeeignet* haben, ist ein Umstand, der überhaupt nicht in die Betrachtung der einfachen Zirkulation zu fallen scheint." (Marx s.a., 903).

A commodity can be thought only to be a product of one's own labour, because the process through which the owners have become owners of commodities takes place, in a way, behind the backs of the exchangers:

"Indem *die Ware als Tauschwert nur vergegenständlichte Arbeit ist,* vom Standpunkt der Zirkulation aber, die selbst nur die Bewegung des Tauschwerts ist, fremde vergegenständlichte Arbeit nicht angeeignet werden kann ausser durch den Austausch eines Äquivalents, kann die *Ware in der Tat nichts sein als Vergegenständlichung der eignen Arbeit,* und wie die letztere in der Tat der faktische Aneignungsprozess von Naturprodukte ist, erscheint sie ebenso als der juristische Eigentumstitel." (Marx s.a., 903).

The process of circulation is a 'pure appearance' because it is based on conditions which are not set by it but which are given in relation to it:

"Die Zirkulation in sich selbst betrachtet ist *die Vermittlung vorausgesetzter Extreme.* Aber sie setzt diese Extreme nicht. Als Ganzes der Vermittlung, als totaler Prozess selbst muss sie daher vermittelt sein. *Ihr unmittelbares Sein ist daher reiner Schein.* Sie ist das *Phänomen eines hinter ihrem Rücken vorgehnden Prozesses."* (Marx s.a., 920).

According to Marx the right to private property is by all the modern economists since John Locke considered to be based on one's own labour; the title to property is thought to be a result of the objectification of one's own labour. The situation is, however, paradoxical, because the problem of the legitimation of property is actualised only in a society based on the division of labour and the production of commodities, in a society where labour becomes social only through exchange. The right to private property and the law of appropriation valid in simple commodity production are thought to be valid in a bourgeois society, too. They are transplanted into a capitalist society without recognising that their realisation is possible only in the 'golden period' of simple commodity production, in a state of society characterised by the ownership of the means of production by every individual producer. The right to private property in a bourgeois society is postulated into a historical period in which the conditions of this society were not at all present:

> "So dass sich das sonderbare Resultat ergäbe, dass die Wahrheit des Aneignungsgesetzes der bürgerlichen Gesellschaft in eine Zeit verlegt werden müsste, worin diese Gesellschaft selbst noch nicht existierte, – und das Grundgesetz des Eigentums in die Zeit der Eigentumslosigkeit." (Marx s.a., 904).

According to Marx analysis there is thus a paradox in the thinking of political economy: private property in a bourgeois society is legitimated by the appropriation of nature's products by labour, by the eternal relation of man to nature. This is a further consequence of the postulate that the right to property is read back into a hypothetical state of nature preceding the capitalist production of commodities and private property. The laws of bourgeois society are thus thought to be natural laws which are eternally valid. And consequently, the freedom and equality of every commodity owner and producer associated with private property and exchange of commodities are regarded to be the natural properties of man.

Marx argued that the ideas of freedom and equality of individuals as bourgeois ideas of justice in reality have their origin in the sphere of circulation, in the exchange of exchange values. As exchangers of commodities individuals are in fact free and equal:

> "Aus dem Akt des Austauschs selbst kehrt jedes der Subjekte als Endzweck des ganzen Prozesses in sich selbst zurück, als übergreifendes Subjekt. Damit ist also die vollständige Freiheit des Subjekts realisiert." (Marx s.a., 912).

Every subject is only an exchanger of commodities, and as such all are equal:

> "Als Subjekte des Austauschs ist ihre Beziehung daher die der *Gleichheit.*" (Marx s.a., 153).

Every individual recognises the other as an owner of a commodity, as an autonomous individual, and does not try to use force to seize the property of another. The act of exchange presupposes common consent even though both partners of exchange are only realising their egoistic interests:

> "Das allgemeine Interesse ist eben die Allgemeinheit der selbstsüchtigen Interessen." (Marx s.a., 156).

Marx summarized his ideas about equality and freedom by saying that the economic form, exchange, determines the subjects as equal while the contents of the process, the material needs which drive individuals to exchange with each other, determine their freedom. The exchange of exchange values is thus the 'productive basis of freedom and equality':

> "Gleichheit und Freiheit sind also nicht nur respektiert im Austausch, der auf Tauschwerten beruht, sondern der Austausch von Tauschwerten ist die produktive Basis aller *Gleichheit* und *Freiheit*. Als reine Ideen sind sie bloss idealisierte Ausdrücke desselben; als entwickelt in juristischen, politischen, sozialen Beziehungen sind sie nur diese Basis in einer andren Potenz. Dies hat sich denn auch historisch bestätigt." (Marx s.a., 156).

In order to express the economic relation, the relation between capital and wage labour as a legal relation, as a relation of property, all we have to do is — according to Marx — to analyse the process of value increase as a process of appropriation (see Marx s.a., 373).

The right to property is in capitalism, in fact, based on alien labour:

> "Zum Beispiel, dass die Surplusarbeit als Surpluswert des Kapitals gesetz wird, heisst, dass der Arbeiter sich nicht das Produkt seiner eignen Arbeit aneignet; dass es ihm als *fremdes Eigentum* erscheint; umgekehrt, dass die *fremde Arbeit* als Eigentum des Kapitals erscheint. Dieses zweite Gesetz des bürgerlichen Eigentums, worein das erste umschlägt (. . .) wird ebensowohl als Gesetz aufgestellt wie das erste. Das erste ist die Identität der Arbeit mit dem Eigentum; das zweite die Arbeit als negiertes Eigentum oder das Eigentum als Negation der Fremdheit der fremden Arbeit." (Marx s.a., 373).

Still, within the sphere of circulation the capitalist can only acquire the title to property, to an alien commodity by giving away his own commodity. And his own commodity can only be thought to have been produced by his own work. Both the capitalist and the wage worker are free and equal commodity exchangers who own their own commodities, money capital and labour power, respectively, and can only acquire the other's property by exchange and mutual consent.[7]

As has already been pointed out private property and the ideas of freedom and equality are paradoxically thought by classical political economy to have their full validity in the golden period, in the postulated state of nature preceding bourgeois society. This idea is based on the contradictory assumptions of both the identity of producer and appropriator ('simple commodity production') and the generalisation of

---

[7] Cf.:

> "Um diese Dinge als Waren aufeinander zu beziehen, müssen die Warenhüter sich zueinander als Personen verhalten, deren Willen in jenen Dingen haust, so dass der eine nur mit dem Willen des anderen, also jeder nur vermittelst eines, beiden gemeinsamen Willensakts sich die fremde Ware aneignet, indem er die eigne veräussert. Sie müssen sich daher wechselseitig als Privateigentümer anerkennen. Dies Rechtsverhältnis, dessen Form der Vertrag ist, ob nun legal entwickelt oder nicht, ist ein Willensverhältnis, worin sich das ökonomische Verhältnis wiederspiegelt." (MEW 23, 99)

commodity relations, relations of the exchange of exchange values.[8] The whole ambiguity follows — as seen from Marx's critical perspective — from the identification of abstract with concrete labour, which leads to the identification of social relations with the relations of nature. In the classical thinking labour constitutes both the intersubjective relations of exchange and man's relation to nature, the original appropriation of nature's products. By mixing nature with labour man appropriates nature's products and achieves a title to property. By objectifying his labour man creates a common denominator for his and others' products, thus constituting the exchange relations. As products of his very labour commodities are alienable and can be exchanged with each other. Men enter into social relations as private property owners.

According to Marx's own self-understanding the discovery of the dual character of labour, the distinction between abstract and concrete labour, was the 'great discovery' which made it possible for him to criticise and solve the anomalies of classical political economy (see Marx 1867, 7; cf. MEW 23, 56). It still is labour, but now abstract labour, a special social form of labour, that constitutes the social relations of commodity exchangers. Labour as concrete labour produces use values and constitutes man's relation to nature, his exchange of substance with nature. More concretely, the analyses of the dual character of labour and the production process of capital made it possible to show how surplus value is created 'both outside and inside circulation'; the specific use value of labour power is to create new value which is materialised in the production process, whereas the exchange between capital and wage labour still follows the rule of equal exchange. The value of labour power (and the wages of wage labourer in the ideal case) is determined by the costs of its reproduction. Even though fully compensating the wage worker, the capitalist is still able to appropriate surplus value. Marx's discovery also made it possible for him to understand how capitalist private property — which seems to be based exclusively on the labour of its owner — in reality, is based on the appropriation of the products of alien labour. The unity of property and labour is destroyed. The pronounced inequality of possessions cannot be justified by the general well-being of the whole nation as Smith and Locke were inclined to think. As Marx understood it, in a bourgeois society accumulation of misery takes place alongside the accumulation of richness (see chapter II.4.).

---

[8]   The mistake of the utopian socialists (especially Proudhon) resulted from similar contradictory assumptions. According to Marx, they wanted to preserve the relations of commodity exchange and private property but get rid of their consequences, capital and money:

"Andrerseit zeigt sich ebensosehr die Albernheit der Sozialisten (. . .), die demonstrieren, dass der Austausch, der Tauschwert etc. *ursprünglich* (in der Zeit) oder ihrem *Begriff* nach (in ihrer adäquanten Form) ein System der Freiheit und Gelichheit aller sind, aber verfälscht worden sind durch das Geld, Kapital etc. . . . Es ist ein ebenso frommer wie dummer Wunsch, dass der Tauschwert sich nicht zum Kapital entwickle, oder die den Tauschwert produzierende Arbeit zur Lohnarbeit." (Marx s.a., 160).

3. THE PRINCIPLE OF LABOUR

There seems to be an ambivalence in Marx's presentation of commodity circulation in the beginning of *Capital*. On the one hand, circulation as presented in *Capital* is an 'outer surface' (''Oberfläche'') under which the production of commodities and of surplus value is hidden. It is, however, the necessary starting point of the analysis from which the more developed determinations are derived (see Hochberger 1974, 166–174). The exchange of equivalents is the starting point of the transformation of money into capital:

> ''Die Verwandlung des Geldes in Kapital ist auf Grundlage dem Warentausch immanenter Gesetze zu entwickeln, so dass der Austausch von Äquivalenten als Ausgangspunkt gilt. (. . .) Seine Schmetterlingsentfaltung muss in der Zirkulationssphäre vorgehn.'' (MEW 23, 180–181).

On the other hand, Marx, on several occasions discussed the transformation of money into capital (and the development of commodity into money) as if he were describing a process of transformation from a historically preceding, more simple exchange and circulation of commodities into a later, more developed one:

> ''Warenproduktion und Warenzirkulation können stattfinden, obgleich die weit überwiegende Produktenmasse, unmittelbar auf den Selbstbedarf gerichtet, sich nicht in Ware verwandelt, der gesellschaftliche Produktionsprozess also noch lange nicht in seiner ganzen Breite und Tiefe vom Tauschwert beherrscht ist. Die Darstellung des Produkts als Ware bedingt eine so weit entwickelte Teilung der Arbeit innerhalb der Gesellschaft, dass die Scheidung zwischen Gebrauchswert und Tauschwert, die im unmittelbaren Tauschhandel erst beginnt, bereits vollzogen ist. Eine solche Entwicklungsstufe ist aber den geschichtlich verschiedensten ökonomischen Gesellschaftsformationen gemein. (...) Dennoch genügt erfahrungsmässig eine relativ schwach entwickelte Warenzirkulation zur Bildung aller dieser Formen. Anders mit dem Kapital.'' (MEW 23, 184).

In *Capital* and *Grundrisse* Marx's critical intention was to prove that the appropriation of surplus value and the accumulation of capital is completely possible following the rules of commodity circulation; the development of capitalist production follows from simple circulation of commodities according to its own immanent laws. The law of appropriation of simple commodity production is transformed into the law of capitalist appropriation, but the very rules of exchange of commodities remain the same in capitalism, too:

"Sagen dass die Dazwischenkunft der Lohnarbeit die Warenproduktion fälscht, heisst sagen, dass die Warenproduktion, will sie unverfälscht bleiben, sich nicht entwickeln darf. Im selben Mass, wie sie nach ihren eignen immanenten Gesetzen sich zur kapitalistischen Produktion fortbildet, in demselben Mass schlagen die Eigentumsgesetze der Warenproduktion um in Gesetze der kapitalistischen Aneignung." (MEW 23, 613).

By analogy, while discussing the transformation of the values of commodities into product prices Marx similarly referred to a historically preceding less developed exchange of commodities which takes place directly according to values. Value is, then, both theoretically and historically the 'prius', the primary determinator, of the capitalist mode of production. In Marx's *Capital* the capitalist commodity production was thus understood to have developed from a simple production of commodities characterised by the individual ownership of the means of production by every producer. In simple commodity production appropriation of products was really based on one's own labour and only labour could create a right to private property:

"Der Austausch von Waren zu ihren Werten oder annähernd zu ihren Werten erfordert also eine viel niedrigre Stufe als der Austausch zu Produktionspreisen, wozu eine bestimmte Höhe kapitalistischer Entwicklung nötig ist. (. . .) Abgesehn von der Beherrschung der Preise und der Preisbewegung durch das Wertgesetz, ist es also durchaus sachgemäss, die Werte der Waren nicht nur theoretisch, sondern historisch als das prius der Produktionspreise zu betrachten. Es gilt dies für Umstände, wo dem Arbeiter die Produktionsmittel gehören, und dieser Zustand findet sich, in der alten wie in der modernen Welt, beim selbstarbeitenden grundbesitzenden Bauer und beim Handwerker." (MEW 25, 186).

On the other hand, Marx was quite explicit in his statement that only after the introduction of the wage relation and, consequently, the accumulation of capital does the production of commodities become the general and dominating form of production:

"Erst da wo die Lohnarbeit ihre Basis, zwingt die Warenproduktion sich der gesamten Gesellschaft auf; aber auch erst da entfaltet sie alle ihre verborgnen Potenzen." (MEW 23, 613).

It was Friedrich Engels who in his interpretation of Marx's *Capital* canonised the conception of a 'simple commodity production'. In *Anti-Dühring* the simple commodity production is understood to be a specific mode of production preceding capitalism (see MEW 20, 250). This conception was preceded by the interpretation of the historical nature of Marx's presentation already in Engels' review (1859) of Marx's *Zur Kritik der politischen Ökonomie*. Marx's method was, according to Engels, basically historical:

"Wir gehen bei dieser Methode aus dem ersten und einfachsten Verhältnis, das uns historisch, faktisch vorliegt, hier also von dem ersten ökonomischen Verhältnis, dass wir vonfinden." (MEW 13, 475).

The simple and historically first relation is that of two commodities in exchange. Political economy consequently, takes the concept of a commodity as its starting point. The logical presentation and development of categories in Marx's work generally follows their actual historical development:

"Womit diese Geschichte anfängt, damit muss der Gedankengang ebenfals anfangen, und sein weiterer Fortgang wird nichts sein als das Spiegelbild, in abstrakter und theoretisch konsequenter Form, des historischen Verlaufs; ein korrigiertes Spiegelbild, aber korrigiert nach Gesetzen, die der wirkliche geschichtliche Verlauf selbst an die Hand gibt, indem jedes Moment auf dem Entwicklungspunkt seiner vollen Reife, seiner Klassizität betrachtet werden kann." (MEW 13, 475).

The history of political economy ("die literarischen Abspiegelungen") generally speaking follows the development from the more simple to the more complex relations corresponding to the actual development of these relations. It must, however, be freed and abstracted from many accidental turns in their development. In the logical presentation or analysis these contingencies have been eliminated and, consequently, the historical development is presented in its pure form. (See MEW 13, 475.)

In his recension Engels did not, anyhow, yet postulate the existence of simple commodity production as a historical stage of production preceding capitalism. He even stated that the analyses in the beginning of the treatise started from the commodity of a fully developed commodity exchange:

"Betrachten wir nun die Ware nach ihren verschiedenen Seiten hin, und zwar die Ware, wie sie sich vollständig entwickelt hat, nicht wie sie sich im naturwüchsigen Tauschhandel zweier ursprünglicher Gemeinwesen erst mühsam entwickelt, so stellt sie sich uns dar unter den beiden Gesichtspunkten von Gebrauchswert und Tauschwert,. . ." (MEW 13, 476).

Even though it is unclear whether Engels thought that a fully developed exchange of commodities was only possible after the wage relation had been introduced, his statement nevertheless problematised the historical interpretation (see also Backhaus 1981, 119).

Engels' interpretation of the logical presentation as corresponding to the actual historical one was further and more strongly developed in his preface to the third volume of *Capital* dated 1894 and in his afterword and supplement to the edition of 1895 (see Backhaus 1981, 120–121). Now Engels directly stated as a historical fact that there had existed a long period of commodity production in which exchange had taken place directly according to values and in which the means of production had belonged to the individual producers themselves.[1] And Engels further claimed that Marx's theory of value was valid for the whole period of simple commodity production:

"Mit einem Wort: das Marxsche Wertgesetz gilt allgemein, soweit überhaupt ökonomische Gesetze gelten, für die ganze Periode der einfachen Warenproduktion, also bis zur Zeit, wo diese durch den Eintritt der kapitalistischen Produktionsform eine Modifikation er-

---

[1] "Danach wird es wohl klar sein, warum Marx am Anfang des ersten Buches, wo er von der einfachen Warenproduktion als seiner historischen Voraussetzung ausgeht, um dann weiterhin von dieser Basis aus zum Kapital zu kommen — warum er da eben von der einfachen Ware ausgeht und nicht von einer begrifflich und geschichtlich sekundären Form, von der schon kapitalistisch modifizierten Ware,..." (MEW 25, 20).

> fährt. (. . .) Das Marxsche Wertgesetz hat also ökonomisch-allgemeine Gültigkeit für eine Zeitdauer, die vom Anfang des die Produkte in Waren verwandelnden Austausches bis ins fünfzehnte Jahrhundert unserer Zeitrechnung dauert." (MEW 25, 909).

The law of value is approximated as having governed the exchange of commodities for a period of about five to seven thousand years.

Engels' interpretation was made even more problematic by the fact that he seemed to think that the law of value resulted from conscious action on the part of the producers:

> '... wie also können sie (die Produzenten im Mitteialter − J.G.) diese ihre Produkte mit denen anderer arbeitenden Produzenten austauschen anders als im Verhältnis der daruf verwandten Arbeit? (. . .) Für die ganze Periode der bäuerlichen Naturalwirtschaft ist kein andrer Austausch möglich als derjenige, wo die ausgetauschten Warenquanta die Tendenz haben, sich mehr und mehr nach den in ihnen verkörperten Arbeitsmengen abzumessen." (MEW 25, 907).

And further:

> "Die Leute im Mittelalter waren so imstande, jeder dem andern die Produktionskosten an Rohstoff, Hilfsstoff, Arbeitszeit mit ziemlicher Genauigkeit nachzurechnen − wenigstens, was Artikel täglichen Gebrauchs betraf." (MEW 25, 907−908).

The law of value would thus in Engels' interpretation be not a law which, even though executed by the acts of exchange of individuals, still functioned blindly behind the backs of these individual actors. It would simply be a method of counting the expenses of production.[2]

Marx's own self-understanding of his method and Engels' interpretation of it has been problematised in recent contributions by Hans-Georg Backhaus (1978; 1981; see also Backhaus 1974; 1975). Backhaus pointed out that Marx's method of presentation cannot be historical because a concept of a premonetary market economy cannot be constructed in a non-contradictory manner:

> "Der Begriff einer premonetären Ware sollte als ein *denkunmöglicher* erkannt werden." (Backhaus 1978, 38).

Marx's analysis of the form of value should be understood essentially as a contribution to the theory of money. In his analysis of the form of value Marx criticised both Ricardo and Bailey. (See Backhaus 1981, 127.) Ricardo, in studying only the quantitative determination of value, did not understand the relation of his labour theory of

---

[2] Backhaus ironically formulated what Engels seemed to think happened in the ancient society of fishermen and hunters. Fishermen and hunters could not supposedly exchange their products because the incommensurability of their use values excluded the possibility of exchange. One fine day they were nevertheless lucky enough to get the idea of abstracting from the use value of their commodities and the concrete character of their labour. They found out that the property of being products of labour in general is the necessary common property which makes it possible to exchange their commodities with each other − which had not succeeded earlier. (See Backhaus 1981, 124.)

value to money. He did not pose the question why the contents must appear in a specific form (or why labour presents itself as value; see MEW 23, 95). On the contrary, Bailey argued that money and value simply result from the actual relations of exchange, value is a contingent quantitative relation of two commodities — whereas Marx emphasised that, in reality, exchange is first constituted by value; the value of commodities is a necessary precondition for exchange (see MEW 26.3, 137). Backhaus' idea was that Marx's critique of Bailey in the third volume of *Theorien* proved that Marx's presentation in the first chapters of *Capital* should be understood as a metacritique of Bailey's critique of Ricardo (see Backhaus 1981, 130).[3]

Bailey's merit in relation to Ricardo was, according to Marx, that he abandoned the problem of the constant measure of value so essential to Ricardo's labour theory of value (see MEW 26.3, 130—131). Bailey was right in claiming that it is not necessary to suppose that the value of the commodity in which all other commodities are measured is a constant entity. Bailey did, however, deny that in order to be able to be exchanged, two commodities must have a common quality which is different from their existence as useful objects, things:

> "Statt dessen geht er alle Kategorien der Ökonomie durch, um stets die einformige Litanei zu wiederholen, dass der Wert das Austauschverhältnis von Waren ist und daher nichts von diesem Verhältnis Unterschiednes." (MEW 26.3, 137).

Bailey justified his argument by the observation that because the quantitative relations of commodities in exchange and consequently their money prices are not constant and vary from one act of exchange to another, the actual relation of two commodities in exchange determines their respective values. To Bailey, the concept of value was only a fictional and metaphysical entity wrongly deduced from the existence of money:

> "Der *Wertbegriff* wird nur gebildet — daher der Wert aus bloss quantitativem Verhältnis, worin Waren gegeneinander ausgetauscht werden, in etwas von diesem Verhältnis Unabhängiges verwandelt (. . .) — *weil* ausser den Waren *Geld* existiert, und wir so gewohnt sind, die Werte von *Waren* nicht in ihrem Verhältnis zueinander, sondern als Verhältnis zu einem *Dritten*, als ein von dem *unmittelbaren* Verhältnis unterschiednes drittes Verhältnis (zu betrachten). Bei B(ailey) ist es nicht die Bestimmung des Produkts als Wert, das zur Geldbildung treibt und im *Geld* sich ausdrückt, sondern es ist das Dasein des Geldes, das zur Fiktion des Wertbegriffs treibt. (. . .) Indem Herr B(ailey) nun nachweist, dass Geld als äussres Mass der Werte — und Darstellung des Werts — seinen Zweck erfüllt, obgleich es einen *veränderlichen* Wert hat, glaubt er die Frage nach dem Begriff des Werts — der von der Veränderlichkeit der Wertgrösse der Waren nicht affiziert wird — beseitigt zu haben, und in der Tat nicht mehr nötig zu haben, (sich) überhaupt etwas unter Wert zu denken." (MEW 26.3, 143).

---

[3] Rubin (1973, 65—71) — whose work Backhaus did not refer to — had already earlier presented a similar interpretation of Marx's critique of Bailey. Rubin, however, did not in this context discuss Ricardo's faulty understanding of the money form, even though he otherwise seemed to come practically to the same conclusion concerning the role of money in Marx's reasoning (see Rubin 1973, 89). Neither did Rubin relate his discussion to the problem of the historical and logical character of Marx's presentation. (For a further discussion of Rubin's interpretation see pp. 211—212.)

The problem of the determination of an objective value was shown by Bailey to be an unnecessary problem because the presentation of the value of a commodity in money does not exclude the possible change in the value of this commodity (money) (see MEW 26.3, 143).

The result of Marx's critique of Bailey was, however, not only that in order to be exchanged two commodities must have something in common, they must be qualitatively similar and be able to be measured on the same dimension. Marx also stated that Bailey was right in emphasising that the value of a commodity can only be expressed in its relation to another commodity — or more correctly it must present its value in that of another commodity, or more generally, they must both express their value in that of a third commodity, money. This problem was totally neglected by Ricardo who, consequently, could not understand the relation of his theory of value to money. On the other hand, Ricardo was right as opposed to Bailey in understanding labour to be the immanent substance of value.[4] Bailey did not pose the problem correctly because he did not analyse money as a qualitative 'transformation' of commodities, only as a quantitative one (see MEW 26.3, 135).

According to Marx, Ricardo emphasised that labour is the common inner substance of value. Ricardo, however, neglected to study the specific form in which labour first becomes this substance of value:

> "Die Waren können alle aufgelöst werden in labour als ihre Einheit. Was R(icardo) nicht untersucht, ist die *spezifische* Form, worin labour als Einheit der Waren sich darstellt. Daher begreift er das Geld nicht." (MEW 26.3, 136).

According to Marx, in order to be able to present themselves in money, in a third commodity, commodities must have a common qualitative property; their quantitative relation presupposes a common denominator:

> "Eine *Einheit*, die sie zu denselben — zu Werten macht — als Wert qualitativ gleichmacht, ist schon unterstellt, damit ihre Werte und Wertunterschiede sich in dieser Weise darstellen. Drücken alle Waren ihre Werte in Gold z.B. aus, so ist dieser ihr Goldausdruck, ihr Goldpreis, ihre Gleichung mit dem Gold, eine Gleichung, aus der ihr Wertverhältnis zueinander erhellt, berechnet werden kann, denn sie sind nun ausgedrückt als *verschiedne Quanta Gold*, und in dieser Art sind die Waren in ihren *Preisen* als gleichnahmige und vergleichbare Grössen dargestellt." (MEW 26.3, 131—132).

In order to be able to present their value in money, commodities must be identical in some respect:

> "Sonst wäre das Problem, den Wert jeder Ware in Gold auszudrücken, unmöglich zu lösen, wenn nicht Ware und Gold oder jede zwei beliebige Waren als Werte, Darstellungen derselben Einheit, ineinander ausdrückbar wären." (MEW 26.3, 132).

---

4 Cf. Marx:
"Unsere Analyse bewies, dass die Wertform oder der Wertausdruck der Ware aus der Natur des Warenwerts entspringt, nicht umgekehrt Wert und Wertgrösse aus ihrer Ausdrucksweise als Tauschwert." (MEW 23, 75).

The quantitative relations of commodities are determined by the quantity of simple or medium labour that has been used in producing them. But the labour forming the substance of value is not primarily simple or medium labour. Commodities are essentially products of private labour. As value the commodity must, on the contrary, be a product of social or general labour. The whole problem can be formulated as the question of how private labour can present itself as its direct opposite, as social or general labour:

> "... diese verwandelte Arbeit ist als ihr unmittelbares Gegenteil *abstrakt allgemeine Arbeit,* die sich daher auch in einem allgemeinen Äquivalent darstelle. Nur durch ihre Veräusserung stellt sich die individuelle Arbeit wirklich als ihr Gegenteil dar. Aber die Ware muss diesen allgemeinen Ausdruck besitzen, bevor sie veräussert ist. Diese Notwendigkeit der Darstellung der individuellen Arbeit als allgemeiner ist die Notwendigkeit der Darstellung einer Ware als Geld. (. . .) Erst durch ihre wirkliche Verwandlung in Geld, den Verkauf, gewinnt sie diesen ihren adäquaten Ausdruck als Tauschwert. Die erste Verwandlung ist bloss theoretischer, die zweite wirklicher Prozess." (MEW 26.3, 133).

Commodities are produced by private labour, which becomes social only through exchange, and their value must consequently be presented in a socially general form. And because private labour must be transformed into general, social labour, commodities must present their value in a specific commodity, money:

> "Weil das Produkt nicht als unmittelbarer Gegenstand der Konsumption für die Produzenten produziert wird, sondern nur als *Träger des Werts,* sozusagen als Anweisung auf bestimmtes Quantum aller Darstellungen der gesellschaftlichen Arbeit, sind alle Produkte gezwungen, als *Werte* sich eine von ihrem Dasein als Gebrauchswerte unterschiedne Daseinsform zu geben. Und es ist diese Entwicklung der in ihnen enthaltnen Arbeit als gesellschaftlicher, es ist die Entwicklung ihres *Werts,* das die Geldbildung bedingt, die Notwendigkeit der Waren, sich als *Geld* füreinander darzustellen — was bloss heisst: (als) selbständige Daseinsformen des Tauschwerts —, und sie können dies nur, indem sie eine Ware aus dem lot ausschliessen, alle ihre Werte in dem Gebrauchswert dieser ausgeschlossnen Ware messen, die in dieser ausschlieslichen Ware enthaltne Arbeit daher unmittelbar in *allgemeine, gesellschaftliche* Arbeit verwandeln." (MEW 26.3, 142—143).

Backhaus' central conclusion was that the circulation of commodities as analysed by Marx in *Capital* is principally different from the simple exchange of commodities. The concept of a premonetary commodity is a *contradictio in adjecto,* and, consequently, it is impossible to think of an exchange process for premonetary commodities (see Backhaus 1981, 155). Marx's theory of value should be understood as a critique of a premonetary theory of value (see Backhaus 1981, 141). Marx was interested in developing an inner and necessary relation between value and money (the genesis of money form; see MEW 23, 62). When Marx asked the question: why does this content appear in this form, he also seemed to think that value cannot be thought of without its form of appearance (see Backhaus 1981, 128). Value cannot be analysed correctly without its form of appearance, money, and money can only be understood as a form of appearance of an 'absolute' or objective value. Value does not exist without price and money.

Backhaus' interpretation is especially interesting because he discussed the possible reasons for Marx's attempt to justify his theoretical procedure in *Capital* as an ideal reflection of the real historical process of the development of money and capital. According to Backhaus, Marx — and even less Engels — did not seem to understand what he really was doing; Marx obviously felt unable to justify his categorial analysis and was therefore forced to take refuge in a pseudo-dialectical reasoning concerning the historical nature of his presentation (see Backhaus 1981, 156—158).

In *Grundrisse* Marx explicitly stated that

> "Dieser dialektische Entstehungsprozess ist nur der ideale Ausdruck der wirklichen Bewegung, worin das Kapital wird. Die späteren Beziehungen sind als Entwicklung aus diesem Keim heraus zu betrachten." (Marx s.a., 217).[5]

It was Engels who suggested to Marx that results obtained dialectically should be justified historically in more detail. The evidence supporting Marx's theory should be taken from history. According to Engels, Marx already had enough material at his disposal to prove the necessity of the historical development of money (see MEW 31,303).

Backhaus argued that the material at Marx's disposal was, in fact, totally insufficient to prove any such hypothesis. Instead of being able to correct his 'idealistic manner' of reasoning materialistically, Marx adopted Aristotle's argument, which had also been adopted by Adam Smith. According to Smith money was invented in order to surpass the problems of exchange brought by an increasing division of labour. Money was invented to overcome the difficulties encountered in the exchange of commodities (see Backhaus 1981, 157—158). Marx thought he had discovered a materialistic correction to his logical and seemingly idealistic development or deduction of categories — a task he had set out to solve in *Grundrisse:*

> "Es wird später nötig sein, eh von dieser Frage abgebrochen wird, die idealistische Manier der Darstellung zu korrigieren, die den Schein hervorbringt, als handle es sich nur um Begriffsbestimmungen und die Dialektik dieser Begriffe. Also vor allem die Phrase: das Produkt (oder Tätigkeit) wird Ware; die Ware Tauschwert; der Tauschwert Geld." (Marx s.a., 69).

It was thus Marx's intended materialism which — according to Backhaus — was the main reason for his historical fables about simple commodity production and the historical development of money.

Marx, in fact, referred on several occasions to the necessity of introducing money because of the increasing division of labour and the increasing exchange of products, as if

---

[5]   In his introduction to *Grundrisse,* in which Marx explicitly reflected on his method of presentation, he clearly formulated an opposite thesis:

> "Es wäre als untubar und falsch, die ökonomischen Kategorien in der Folge aufeinanderfolgen zu lassen, in der sie historisch die bestimmenden waren. Vielmehr ist ihre Reihenfolge bestimmt durch die Beziehung, die sie in der modernen bürgerlichen Gesellschaft aufeinander haben, und die genau das umgekehrte von dem ist, was als ihre naturgemässe erscheint oder der Reihe der historischen Entwicklung entspricht." (Marx s.a., 28).

money had been invented in order to overcome the difficulties encountered in actual exchange of products in a period of history in which premonetary exchange of commodities had prevailed:

> "Je weiter sich die Teilung der Arbeit entwickelt, um so mehr hört das Produkt auf, ein Tauschmittel zu sein. Es tritt die Notwendigkeit eines allgemeinen Tauschmittels ein, unabhängig von der spezifischen Produktion eines jeden."(Marx s.a., 113).

And further:

> "Die Schwierigkeiten, die im Tauschhandel liegen, kann das Geld nur aufheben, indem es sie verallgemeinert, universell macht." (Marx s.a., 68).

In *Capital* the formulation of the same problem was more problematic. The existence of a general equivalent was seen to be necessary to any exchange between several commodities, but the introduction of money was still understood as a solution to the difficulties due to the increasing division of labour:

> "Die Notwendigkeit dieser Form (einer allgemeinen Wertform – J.G.) entwickelt sich mit der wachsenden Anzahl und Mannigfaltigkeit der in den Austauschprozess eintretenden Waren. Die Aufgabe entspringt gleichzeitig mit den Mitteln ihrer Lösung. Ein Verkehr, worin Warenbesitzer ihre eignen Artikel mit verschiednen andren Artikeln austauschen und vergleichen, findet niemals statt, ohne dass verschiedne Waren von verschiednen Warenbesitzern innerhalb ihres Verkehrs mit einer und derselben dritten Warenart ausgetauscht und als Werte verglichen werden." (MEW 23, 103).

Backhaus saw the reason for Marx's insistence on the categorial presentation corresponding to actual historical development of the different forms of value as a desire to proceed materialistically and to correct his seemingly idealistic manner of presentation. On could, however, claim that there were other reasons for Marx's procedure, reasons that are closely connected with another essential interpretative argument of Backhaus'. For Backhaus, Marx's 'labour theory of value' was a necessary consequence of his conception of an objective value: the idea of the necessary form of the appearance of value (money) could only be developed on the basis of an objective theory of value and, consequently, labour theory of value. An objective or 'absolute' value can only be based on labour:

> 'It is evident that such an 'absolute' value only can be understood in the meaning of labour theory of value." (Backhaus 1981, 141).

It is not, however, at all clear why such an absolute value should be exclusively understood in this meaning. On the contrary, it could be claimed that such a position is highly problematic; and Marx's introduction of the concepts of abstract and concrete labour as producing use value and value, respectively, was rather straightforward, without any specific grounds. Stapelfeldt (1979, 111) interestingly pointed out that Marx's introduction of abstract labour in his reasoning as the identical property of the commodities making possible their exchange is highly problematic. The definition was justified only through negation; according to Marx's reasoning the common quality on which the identity of labour's products is based cannot be any substantial or natural quality of theirs, or their use value, because as use values commodities evidently are qualitatively different. The only possible identical quality of commodities after the abstraction or negation of their natural qualities or use values is their property as products of labour in general: "Sieth man nun vom Gebrauchswert der Warenkörper ab so bleibt ihnen nur noch eine Eigenschaft, die von Arbeitsprodukten" (MEW 23, 52). Marx did not, however, give any further arguments in favour of the identification of the common quality found in the products of labour with labour in general.[6]

As Stapelfeldt pointed out, the difficulty in Marx's operation of abstraction culminates in its result. Marx abstracted from the determination of products as products of labour and once more got as the result − abstract human − labour:

> "Denn Marx abstrahiert ja von Arbeitsprodukten stellt als Resultat aber nur noch − abstrakt menschliche − Arbeit vor." (Stapelfeldt 1979, 115).

One further problem in Marx's procedure of abstraction is the definition of use value as a product of useful or concrete labour. In the beginning of his discussion of the dual character of a commodity, Marx defined use values simply as useful things which satisfy human needs. In discussing the dual nature of labour Marx said that as such they are the product of useful activity:

> "Man hat also gesehn: in dem Gebrauchswert jeder Ware steckt eine bestimmte zweckmässig produktive Tätigkeit oder nützliche Arbeit." (MEW 23, 57).

According to Stapelfeldt, Marx needed a more determined definition of use value, or a definition of the identical quality of use values for his further argument (see Stapelfeldt 1979, 115). Use values are not simply useful things. Use values are also products of labour, of a specific productive or useful activity:

> "Als Bildnerin von Gebrauchswerten, als nützliche Arbeit, ist die Arbeit daher eine von allen Gesellschaftsformen unabhängige Existenzbedingung des Menschen, ewige Naturnotwendigkeit, um den Stoffwechsel zwischen Mensch und Natur, also das menschliche Leben zu vermitteln." (MEW 23, 57).

In Stapelfeldt's opinion, Marx's procedure of abstraction was only legitimate because of the presupposed truth imbedded in classical political economy. Marx's analysis of a

---

[6] Marx's argument was consequently not convincing as such. It is easy to think of other common identical qualities of products in use. The price of commodities can be understood as being determined by their potential demand and supply, as was pointed out by Böhm-Bawerk in his classical critique of Marx's labour theory of value (see Böhm-Bawerk 1973 (1896)), which amounts to their determination by the marginal utilities. To take another extreme example, as was shown by Simmel (1900), one could also postulate a specific metaphysical sphere of values; or one could interpret value as a specific socially determined quality of commodities due to the social form of organisation of labour, as was the case in Rubin's theory of abstract labour and value (see Rubin 1973 (1924)).

commodity is only understandable when it is understood that it takes place within this tradition of thought, which becomes evident during the problematised argumentation of abstract labour as determining the common quality of commodities. Marx's dual reference to labour makes his close relation to natural rights theory and classical political economy evident (see Stapelfeldt 1979, 117). Marx did not, however, only adopt the concept of labour from classical political economy. He also criticised it for its ambivalence. In Marx's opinion classical political economy lacked the understanding of the dual nature of labour. In classical political economy the concept of labour referred both to man's relation to nature and to the intersubjectivity of social relations, and remains thus indifferentiated. After the introduction of the dual concept of labour, the different use values and concrete products of labour can, on the one hand, be regarded as equal because abstract labour has been objectified in them. Their comparability is based on abstract labour. On the other hand, the concrete labour producing use values is closely tied to nature's substance and is in every case as different as its products. They cannot thus be considered as identical to one another. In order to emphasise the contrast, Marx named the equal substance of commodities as 'abstract human labour', and understood it to be a result of abstraction. But abstract labour can, on the other hand, only be the common quality of commodities because labour is, in fact, materialised in use values; they are in some strong sense products of labour. The classical political economy never understood this difference in its concept of labour and was criticised by Marx accordingly (see Stapelfeldt 1979, 121—122).

It is essential, however, that the concept of value shares with that of 'concrete labour' the idea that labour has in reality been objectified and materialised in its products (see Stapelfeldt 1979, 133—134). The reproduction of social relations thus takes place within the production of use values — the value has concrete labour as its necessary precondition — which in Stapelfeldt's opinion determines Marx's doctrine as both materialistic and dialectical:

> "Materialistisch ist die Kritik der Politischen Ökonomie, weil sie zeigt, dass der Wert die Abstraktion vom Verhältnis des Menschen zur Natur ist, darum in konkreter Arbeit die Bedingung seiner Möglichkeit hat und Arbeitsprodukte identifizierend zu seiner Erscheinungsform herabsetzt. Dialektisch ist dieser Materialismus, weil er die Erfahrung einer Entzweiung von gesellschaftlichem Verhältnis und Verhältnis des Menschen zur Natur, von abstrakter und konkreter Arbeit formuliert. (. . .) Die Lehre vom 'Doppelcharakter der in den Waren dargestellten Arbeit' bestimmt die Kritik der Politischen Ökonomi als dialektische Theorie." (Stapelfeldt 1979, 224).

As Stapelfeldt has pointed out Marx's critique of the concept of labour was only convincing because of its close conceptual relation to classical political economy. It adopted its standards of critique from the latter:

> "Die Kritik der Politischen Ökonomie vermag sich nur zu konstituieren, indem sie am Falschen, den Aporien der klassischen Politischen Ökonomie ansetzt, diese durch den Nachweis einer in alle Einzelbestimmungen eingehenden Entzweiung von abstrakter und konkreter Arbeit auflöst und damit sowohl die Erfahrungsbasis des Kritisierten nennt als auch den eigenen Maßstab der Kritik gewinnt." (Stapelfeldt 1979, 251—252).

'The critique was directed against both the capitalist mode of production and its scientific expression. It aimed at destroying the claim of reason of the bourgeois society, the concept of reasonal society which projects the social relations into natural relations, into man's relations to nature (see Stapelfeldt 1979, 64–65).

Marx did not, however, only redefine the concept of labour by introducing his conception of the dual character of labour. He redefined the concept of labour in another sense, too – and in so doing radicalised the critical potency of his analysis. It was essential to Marx that through labour the very goal-oriented activity of man is materialised in its products and objectified in the social relations, too. According to Lange (1980, 55) this conceptual redefinition of labour already took place in the *Ökonomisch–philosophische Manuskripte* of 1844, in which Marx discovered labour to be the real principle of national economy:

> "Der Gegenstand, den die Arbeit produziert, ihr Produkt, tritt ihr als ein *fremdes Wesen*, als eine von dem Produzenten *unabhängige Macht* gegenüber. Das Produkt der Arbeit ist die Arbeit, die sich in einem Gegenstand fixiert, sachlich gemacht hat, es ist die *Vergegenständlichung* der Arbeit. Die Verwirklichung der Arbeit ist ihre Vergegenständlichung." (MEW Erg.Bd. 1., 511–512).

In Marx's manuscript objectification ("Vergegenständlichung") became synonymous with becoming a material object. Labour is, then, materialised very concretely in the products of labour (see Lange 1980, 56). Marx's conceptual operation made it possible for him to radicalise the concept of labour into a model of objectification or alienation and use it as a critical model:

> "Sie erlaubt es ihm zu sagen, 'dass das Kapital nichts als aufgehäufte Arbeit ist'. Erst so wird die Arbeit zu dem, zu dem sie gemacht zu haben Marx Adam Smith als sein grösstes theoriegeschichtliches Verdienst zugerechnet hat, zum 'Prinzip' und zwar 'zum einzigen Prinzip der Nationalökonomie'." (Lange 1980, 68–69).

The concept of objectification of labour made it possible for Marx to understand and to criticise the national economic state of affairs ("nationalökonomischer Zustand") or bourgeois society, and the process of private property. Private property and the relations of bourgeois society are reduced to the worker's alienated self-relation to himself and to his alienated relation to the products of his own labour (the product of his labour, his very labour process, and the essence of human species ("Gattungswesen") all become alienated). The very opposition of classes in a bourgeois society is based on the missing self- and object relation of the worker (see Lange 1980, 81–82).

The same idea of materialisation and objectification of labour was strongly present in *Capital*, too.

> "Ein Gebrauchsgegenstrand oder Gut hat also nur einen Wert, weil abstrakt menschliche Arbeit in ihm vergegenständlicht ist." (MEW 23, 53).

By analogy, the use value of a commodity represents materialised labour. The main difference of Marx's later critique of political economy in relation to the manuscript of

1844 was that labour was no longer understood to be the real principle of the bourgeois society. According to Marx it was now wrong to say that capital is just the result of accumulated labour. In *Grundrisse* Marx for instance claimed that the characterisation of capital as accumulated labour in no way described the capital in specific, but in fact any instrument of production (see Marx s.a., 7; see also Lange 1980, 146).

Lange, however, claimed that while beginning the presentation of *Capital* with commodity and money, Marx was, in fact, still indirectly beginning it with the category of labour. Labour did not then become the very principle of national economy but its contradictory principle:

> "Dass die Arbeit im nationalökonomischen Zustand der spezifisch ökonomischen bestimmungen der Lohnarbeit unterliegt, setzt nach Marx voraus, dass die Arbeitskraft der ökonomischen Bestimmung der Ware unterworfen ist. Deshalb kann die kritische Darstellung des nationalökonomischen oder kapitalistischen Gesellschaftszustands nicht mit der Arbeit beginnen, wie sie gemäss dem Entäusserungsmodell des Handelns (in sich einiges) Prinzip wäre ... nur als zerrissenes, widersprüchliches Prinzip ist die Arbeit im nationalökonomischen Zustand Prinzip. Als solches ist sie selber ein aufzudeckender Widerspruch, ja *der fundamentale* Widerspruch, auf dem noch der Widerspruch von Arbeit und Kapital, der Klassenantagonismus beruht. Daher kann die Arbeit nicht Ausgangspunkt der scheinhafte Einheiten destruirenden und immer fundamentalere Widersprüche aufdeckenden Darstellung sein, obwohl sie selbst als entfremdet 'an sich' oder 'für uns' – die theoretischen Beobachter – Prinzip ist." (Lange 1980, 150).

In *Capital* Marx did not begin his analysis with the concept of labour, or with alienated labour, but with the concept of commodity. Labour, then, is conceptually redefined; labour producing commodities has a dual character. Labour is no longer – as it was in *Ökonomisch-philosophische Manuskripte* – the fundamental principle of the national economy, from which all further consequences ensue, but a principle of a contradictory nature. Despite this self-critique and conceptual redefinition Marx was, however, strongly indebted to classical political economy and its predecessor, the natural law theory. It was the concept of labour and the labour theory of value which Marx interpreted to be the rational core of classical political economy. And certain important elements of it can already be found in natural rights thinking. Classical thinking does, however, result in anomalies as reconstructed by Marx, because of its misunderstanding of the dual character of labour and the specific historical and social form of labour in a society ruled by commodity exchange. But still one can agree with Schanz (1981, 260) – and Lange – in interpreting labour as the most important concept in Marx's *Capital*, too.

As has already been pointed out Marx's argument included another important conceptual redefinition of the concept of labour which was not present in classical political economy or natural rights theory. Marx understood labour to be materialised and objectified in its products, in commodities. It was essential for instance for Marx to emphasise that abstract labour could only be objectified in the material products of labour. In discussing his value form analysis Marx stated that human labour power is always objectified in a specific form, in the product of specific concrete labour:

> "Verwirklichen, vergegenständlichen kann sie sich nur, sobald die menschliche Arbeits-
> kraft in *bestimmter Form* verausgabt wird, als *bestimmte* Arbeit, denn nur der *bestimmten*
> Arbeit steht ein Naturstoff gegenüber, ein äusseres Material, worin sie sich vergegenständ-
> licht." (Marx 1867, 18).

Marx was ridiculing Hegelian concepts, which can objectify themselves without any external substance:

> "Bloss der Hegelsche 'Begriff' bringt es fertig, sich ohne äussern Stoff zu objektifieren."
> (Marx 1867, 18).

From his conception of objectification it also follows that the value of a commodity can only appear in the use value of another commodity; in Marx's opinion value must appear and it can only come into appearance in the relation of two commodities. As stated by Marx, one peculiarity of the value form is that use value becomes the form of appearance of its direct opposite, value, or to put it in another way, concrete labour becomes the form of appearance of its opposite, abstract labour. (See MEW 23, 71 and 73.)

In another context Marx wrote that it is wrong to say that labour is the sole source of richness. Nature is equally a source of use value, the universal substantial form of richness:

> "Die Arbeit *ist nicht Quelle* alles Reichtums. Die *Natur* ist ebensosehr die Quelle der
> Gebrauchswerte (und aus solchen besteht wohl das sachliche Reichtum!) als die Arbeit, die
> selbst nur die Äusserung einer Naturkraft ist, der menschlichen Arbeitskraft." (MEW 19,
> 15).[7]

Marx furthermore added that only insofar as man relates himself to nature as its owner and treats it as belonging to him, does his labour become the source of use values and consequently of richness. It is only because man cannot objectify his labour without the necessary means and objects of production originally created by nature that private property and capital, too, are possible at all. Otherwise any man possessing his own labour power exclusively could work and support himself without the consent of the person owning and controlling the instruments of labour and the necessary resources of nature (see MEW 19, 15).

Taking into account Marx's redefinition of labour and discussion of the concept of labour, it becomes possible to explicate his critique of private property and the form of capitalist appropriation. Marx's critique was twofold: It is not man's relation to nature via labour that constitutes private property. Private property is not based on man's right to appropriate the products of his own labour. Private property furthermore has the exchange of commodities as its necessary precondition. It is first established in a society where private labour is transformed into social through exchange of commodities. But it

---

[7] In *Capital* Marx approvingly paraphrased William Petty:
> "Die Arbeit ist sein Vater (des stofflichen Reichtums − J.G.),. . . und die Erde seine
> Mutter." (MEW 23, 58).

was equally important for Marx to understand that commodities are appropriated from nature by materialising labour in them, and the materialisation of labour is not possible without the corresponding potentialities of nature. Marx then not only criticised what, in his understanding, was the fundamental legal conception of private property in classical political economy. He also adopted and − by redefining the concept of labour − radicalised its central insight. In capitalism private property is not based on labour; in fact, the products of alien labour are approriated by capitalists without an equivalent. And in general, it never is labour − the productive relation of man to nature − that constitutes private property. Legal and political ideas are only reflexions or expressions of more fundamental social relations of production. Still even for Marx − and even in capitalism − products are originally appropriated from nature by labour. It is the labour power, the productive activity of the worker, that is materialised in commodities, and in the material elements of richness in general.

As has already been pointed out, Backhaus claimed that it was Marx's intended materialism that made him attempt to justify his value form analysis as corresponding to an actual historical development from less developed forms of value into more developed ones. Considering the previous discussion of Marx's concept of labour one can, however, go even further and claim that it was Marx's labour theory of value − recognised by Backhaus as the only alternative to determine an objective value − that is to be blamed. The same problem can also be formulated as follows: because of his labour theory of value Marx, in fact, did analyse the production of commodities before circulation and exchange of commodities. At the beginning of *Capital* Marx does not only analyse the simple circulation of commodities but the simple production of commodities, too.

Rubin (1973, 110) recognised that there is a seeming ambivalence in Marx's reasoning at this point: on the one hand, value and abstract labour were already presupposed before the exchange of commodities could take place, and on the other hand, value was first constituted in the very process of exchange.[8] The same duality of reasoning can also be formulated in Rubin's own words as follows:

---

[8]   Sohn-Rethel's critical interpretation of Marx's analysis of the forms of value pointed out the same ambivalence as Rubin's. Sohn-Rethel went even further and suggested that Marx's analysis at the beginning of *Capital* is inconsistent because Marx does not clearly distinguish between the problems of the magnitude and the form of value (see Sohn-Rethel 1978, 21; see also Sohn-Rethel 1972, 235).

Inspired by Sohn-Rethel's interpretation Pietilä (1984) has in a recent article proposed an original solution to the problem of the relation between the 'historical and logical' in Marx's analysis of the form of value corresponding to the quantitative and qualitative aspects pointed out by Sohn-Rethel. The first level consists of "a 'logical' theory aiming to show that money is nothing but 'the necessary form of expression of the immanent value measure of commodities, viz. the labour time' " (Pietilä 1984, 63). "The second level, in turn, would indicate the *historical development* of the structure of exchange relations and the necessities of this structure − *precisely in the premonetary era*" (Pietilä 1984, 64). Pietilä's interpretation is problematic because there hardly is any analysis of the development of the structure of exchange relations in *Capital* except of the

"Indem Marx zeigte, dass es ohne Wertform keinen Wert gibt, legte er zugleich präzise dar, dass diese gesellschafliche Form ohne die Arbeitssubstanz, die sie erfüll, leer bleibt." (Rubin 1973, 81).

Rubin solved the problem by assuming that in production oriented towards a market, the very production process already has a specific social form, it is labelled by exchange from the very beginning (see Rubin 1973, 112). Production and circulation of commodities thus are mutually conditioned. But Rubin's argument did not really solve the problem; it only reformulated it. The same ambivalence is also present in Marx's two-fold critique of both Ricardo and Bailey, a critique discussed both by Backhaus (see pp. 200–201) in the context of the logical and historical presentation in Marx's *Capital* and in the present context by Rubin himself (see 1973, 72). As was already pointed out in Marx's reconstruction of the history of political economy Bailey and Ricardo were made to criticise one another. Ricardo's fault, then, was that he neglected to analyse the specific form of labour, the value form which first constitutes value. Ricardo, in Marx's opinion, however, correctly identified the substance of value with labour. The other debater, Bailey, did not admit that exchange presupposes that commodities have an objective value, a common quality making their exchange possible, and consequently he dismissed the whole concept of value as a metaphysical entity not needeed by political economy. But Bailey's theory, too, had its own merits. He correctly recognised that the value of a commodity can only appear in its relation to another commodity. Thus, both Bailey and Ricardo provided certain invaluable insights adopted by Marx in his analysis of value and value form.

The importance of Marx's critique of Ricardo received special emphasis in Backhaus' analysis. For the present argument, Marx's critique of Bailey is more important. In rejecting value as an unnecessary entity for the analysis of the exchange of commodities, Bailey failed to understand that in order to be exchanged, two commodities must already possess a common qualitative property making their exchange possible. And like Ricardo, Marx identified this common quality with value, and the substance of value with labour. Without being an independent item in Marx analysis – value admittedly was always thought to be connected with its value form, as pointed out by Rubin (see Rubin 1973, 81–82) – the elements of a labour theory of value were indispensable to Marx's theory. They can be said to form the Ricardian – and Smithian – heritage in Marx's thinking. They can also be said to constitute Marx's Marxism.

It can now be claimed that by identifying value with a specific social form of labour, and by identifying the substance of value with labour, Marx opened up his argumenta-

---

exchange of commodities. The form of value analysed by Marx always is the form of value of a commodity, the use value of a commodity becomes the form of appearance of the value of another commodity. And consequently, the quantitative and form aspects are closely intertwined in Marx's argumentation. Therefore Marx's presentation can hardly be read as both an analysis of primitive (premonetary) exchange of products and an analysis of a developed exchange of commodities, respectively. As will be shown in the present study, it is exactly – to use Sohn-Rethel's expression – the 'quantitative' aspect of value in Marx's reasoning that explains his historicising intention.

tion to a historical interpretation of the development of value forms. It was thus Marx's labour theory of value that led him to present those 'pseudodialectical fables' referred to by Backhaus.[9] Because of the labour theory of value it becomes reasonable to assume that any commodity exchanged for another already has a value, a common quality making the exchange possible, and that any two products in exchange inevitably are exchanged according to their value, since labour already has been objectified in them. On the other hand, Marx evidently thought that products of labour have a commodity form only insofar as they are produced in order to be exchanged, only insofar as they are produced for a commodity market; i.e. only insofar as the commodity form has become the general form of the products of labour.[10] But if it is admitted that the value of a commodity also preceeds its exchange, if commodities have a value only insofar as labour has in fact been objectified in them, then it is resonable for Marx to think that the less developed value forms really are independent forms historically preceding the forms of money and capital. Consequently, even a less developed exchange of commodities inevitably follows the rule of equal exchange.

The element of a labour theory of value in Marx's reasoning similarly explains why he, on several occasions, while discussing the transformation of the forms of appropriation, seemed to think that there had, in fact, existed before and alongside capitalism a form of commodity production characterised by the private ownership of the means of production by every individual producer. Even though he explicitly criticised classical political economy for its postulate of a natural society (identified with bourgeois society) − a natural state in which labour's products belonged to the very man who had produced them by his own labour and in which private property was constituted by appropriating nature's products by labour − one could still claim that he came very close to postulating such a society himself.

One could, like Lange (1980, 175−176), rescue Marx by saying that he assumed the existence of simple commodity production only counterfactually. But Marx did not proceed counterfactually. He did not simply say that even if we were to suppose − following classical political economy and John Locke − that there once existed a natural society in which nature's products were exclusively appropriated and a legitimate title to property created either by one's own labour or by exchanging the products of one's own labour with the products of other men's equal amount of labour, and even

---

[9] This does not mean that Backhaus' suggestion of Marx's intended materialism as the reason leading to his 'pseudodialectical fables' should be totally rejected either. Marx obviously thought that the categories developed by him were 'real' abstractions in the sense that they corresponded to a state of affairs that had existed in its pure form in history; in capitalism value appears only in different modified forms, hence it must have appeared in its pure form at some previous historical stage.

[10] Cf. Marx's compact formulation in *Capital:*

"Indem sie ihre vershiedenartigen Produkte einander im Austausch als Werte gleichsetzen, setzen sie ihre verschiednen Arbeiten einander als menschliche Arbeit gleich. Sei wissen das nicht, aber sie tun es." (MEW 23, 88).

if we were, in addition, to suppose that the law of value is preserved intact even in capitalism, the truth about capitalism still is that alien labour and its products are in fact appropriated and that one has to respect one's labour and its products as belonging to another. Marx's postulate was a stronger one as he explicitly stated that if commodities are produced by individual producers owning their own means of production, then their exchange takes place directly according to their value and one can achieve a title to property only by one's own labour. And he furthermore claimed that such a simple commodity production had existed at various times and in various places in history.

One could also summarise the result of the above analysis as follows: the analysis of the simple circulation of commodities in *Capital* does not only consist of an abstraction of certain aspects of capitalist circulation of commodities. It is not an abstraction which must be taken as the starting point for the development of the theoretical presentation because it determines the specific social and historical character of the capitalist society as interpreted by Rubin (1973, 43—49). Via the labour theory of value and the specific radicalisation of the concept of labour, the production of commodities is introduced into the analysis from the very beginning. Labour has, in fact, been materialised and objectified in a commodity, otherwise it would not possess the dual character of use value and value. In discussing the opposite laws of appropriation in simple commodity production and in capitalism respectively, or the equality and freedom of the commodity owners and exchangers, Marx only added one more condition or characteristic to his determination of simple circulation. Simple commodity production then is a specific form of production having its own social conditions; it is equal to simple circulation of commodities plus the private ownership of the means of production by every individual producer.

In his *Critique of the Gotha Programme,* one of his last writings, Marx formulated in a condensed form his critical standpoint, which clearly showed that he had not departed so far from the theoretical standpoint of classical political economy by turning its standards of natural society into critical standards of bourgeois society. According to Marx, in any imaginable society labour always is the real source of richness, and anyone not working himself can only be living at the cost of the labour of others:

> "Da die Arbeit die Quelle alles Reichtums ist, kann auch in der Gesellschaft sich niemand Reichtum aneigen, ausser als Produkt der Arbeit. Wenn er also nicht selber arbeitet, lebt er von fremder Arbeit und eignet sich auch seine Kultur auf Kosten fremder Arbeit an." (MEW 19, 16).

From this formulation it is but a short step to understanding the central contradiction of capitalism in terms of the violation of the original rule of appropriation valid in simple commodity production.[11] Thus it is not surprising that Marx obviously approved of and

---

[11]   There is, however, one important difference between Marx's and Engels' ideas. Marx obviously did not think that simple commodity production equaled to a specific mode of production of its own as Engels and later Marxists, Kautsky among them, were inclined to do. Marx simply

even contributed to Engels' interpretation of the fundamental critical result of his theory of capitalism as presented in *Anti-Dühring* (see MEW 20, VII). The way Engels — and Kautsky — put it there is a basic contradiction in capitalism between the private mode of appropriation inherited from the stage of simple commodity production and the increasing socialisation of production. Marx in fact never formulated his own standpoint in quite the similar terms, but if one understands Engels' contradiction as a shorthand formulation of the thesis that even in capitalism it is the labour power or, more specifically, the combined power of wage workers united in the production process by capital, that, in the last instance, is the source of value and richness, Marx would probably recognise it as his own.

---

thought that simple commodity production had taken place at different times and in different places alongside with different modes of production, and that simple commodity production can take place alongside capitalism, too. The relation between simple commodity production and capitalism was not understood by Marx as a process of historical transformation leading from one mode of production into another followed by the increasing socialisation of production. All that Marx suggested was that simple commodity production is an independent form of production — and that the different value forms are historically independent forms of value, too — having a reality of their own.

4. THE THEORY OF INCREASING MISERY AND THE CRITIQUE OF CAPITALISM

One of Lohmann's main ideas discussed already earlier, was that there are, inherent in Marx's presentation, elements of critique which can be called transcending. These elements can be localised in the discussions of the fate of the working class and of the forces and struggles of opposition in capitalism. The normative standards of the partici- pants present another form of critique of capitalism different from that of immanent critique. In *Die Revolution in der Theorie von Karl Marx* Sieferle (1979) interpreted Marx's discussion of the general law of accumulation in a rather similar sense. To him, there is inherent, and partly hidden, in Marx's presentation a phenomenological level, a description of the experience of the wage workers of the exploitation and repression of capitalism which justities Marx's expectations of the increasing revolutionary conscious- ness of the working class.

Sieferle's starting point was a problem connected with the revolutionary perspective in Marx's *Capital.* According to Sieferle, Marx was − at his best −able to determine the foundations of the objective reified thought forms produced by the capitalist mode of production and to show how the consciousness of the owners of different revenue sources (capital, land, labour) is system affirmative. On the other hand, Marx was forced to argue the necessity of the development of the revolutionary consciousness of the working class because of his historico−philosophical preconceptions. His expecta- tions of the development of revolutionary consciousness were based on the analysis of capital accumulation. The theories of collapse and immiseration, as formulated at the end of the first volume of *Capital,* can be understood to determine both the objective and subjective limits of capitalism. The subjective experience of the growing misery of the wage workers is the basis of experience ("Erfahrungsbasis") necessary for the development of a non-affirmative consciousness. This made it reasonable and justifiable for Marx to cherish his revolutionary hopes and expectations despite the seemingly iron-cage character of capitalism.

Sieferle's interpretation is interesting because it problematised some of the central themes of the 'Zusammenbruch' theory. According to Sieferle, in *Capital* Marx was only developing the inner contradictions of capitalism. The presentation did not seem to include any phenomenological level on which the analysis of the development of a revolutionary consciousness could be based. The secret or mystery of surplus production and exploitation can be revealed only through scientific analysis of the essence of capitalism; they always remain hidden from the everyday consciousness.[1] The everyday experience of a wage worker does not include any such experience that could directly reveal the exploitative nature of capitalism to him. The problem could be formulated even more generally: is the exploitative nature of capitalism something that is revealed only to a scientist who is able and willing to follow the categorical exposition of the critique of political economy?[2] What, then, is the revolutionary perspective in *Capital?*

Marx's *Capital* did, however, according to Sieferle, include such a phenomenological level after all. It did analyse the fate of the working class under capital accumulation. Marx was, indeed, describing the purpose of his further presentation at the beginning of the chapter on the general law of capital accumulation as follows:

> "Wir behandeln in diesem Kapitel den Einfluss, den das Wachstum des Kapitals auf das Geschick der Arbeiterklasse ausübt. Der wichtigste Faktor bei dieser Untersuchung ist die Zusammensetzung des Kapitals und die Veränderungen, die sie im Verlauf des Akkumulationsprozesses durchmacht." (MEW 23, 640).

In Sieferle's opinion such considerations were unnecessary in Marx's earlier studies because the proletarian situation was characterised as one of total negativity:

> "The negativity of the proletarian situation as determined in the early concept of the materialistic theory of bourgeois society (in *Deutsche Ideologie* — J.G.) excluded the possibility of the continuous survival of a fully developed capitalistic society (. . .) This society

---

[1] Cf. Marx's formulation in *Capital:*

"Übrigens gilt von der Erscheinungsform, 'Wert und Preis der Arbeit' oder 'Arbeitslohn', im Unterschied zum wesentlichen Verhältnis, welches erscheint, dem Wert und Preis der Arbeitskraft, dasselbe, was von allen Erscheinungsformen und ihrem verborgnen Hintergrund. Die ersteren reproduzieren sich unmittelbar spontan, als gang und gäbe Denkformen, die andre muss durch die Wissenschaft erst entdeckt werden. Die klassische politische Ökonomie stösst annähernd auf den wahren Sachverhalt, ohne ihn jedoch bewusst zu formulieren. Sie kann das nicht, solange sie in ihrer bürgerlichen Haut steckt." (MEW 23, 564).

[2] Lange formulated the same problem in another context:

" 'An sich' oder 'für uns' als theoretische Beobachter ist das Kapital seiner Gebrauchswertseite nach betrachtet nichts als vergegenständlichte Arbeit und seiner Wertseite nach betrachtet nichts als vergegenständlichte Arbeits*zeit*. Und im Produktionsprozess werden die scheinhaften Trennungen, die durch die Eigentumsregeln der Zirkulation in den Selbstvermittlungszusammenhang der Arbeit getragen werden und ihr, als sozialer Klasse, einen Gegensatz im Kapital entstehen lassen, auch tatsächlich aufgehoben. Aber solange diese Aufhebung nur 'an sich' oder 'für uns' ist und nicht auch 'für es (bzw. sie)', nämlich die beteiligte und betroffene Arbeit — und d.h.: solange aus den sachlichen Produktionsverhältnissen nichts folgt im Hinblick auf Ansprüche der Arbeit(er) auf ihr Produkt und die Kontrolle des Produktionsprozesses, die der Kapitalist ausübt — bleibt der fundamentale Widerspruch auch latent." (Lange 1980, 214).

must have been destroyed at the very moment the proletariat had developed into a socially relevant class." (Sieferle 1979, 171).[3]

The analysis in *Capital* comes to a different conclusion: the surface of bourgeois society forms an effective legitimation instance and all experiences are reflected through the mystified forms of its surface. If the ideas of freedom and equality of the commodity owners are preserved intact in capitalism as Marx thought, one would have expected him to have paid more explicit attention to the problems of the possible destruction of the reified consciousness. One would, indeed, have expected Marx to have included in his presentation in *Capital* a phenomenology of class consciousness that would have shown how the mystification of the thought forms could be destroyed and the universal consciousness of the historical nature of capital could be enfolded. (See Sieferle 1979, 172; cf. Scharrer 1976, 20—21.)

Sieferle looked for the reasons for the neglect of an explicit discussion of the problem in *Capital* in the historical situation of the workers' movement in Marx's day. The practical evidence of the socialist movement was so obvious that it would have been uninteresting for Marx to try to justify theoretically the practical possibility of a revolutionary labour movement. According to Sieferle, it was the expanding and continuing reproduction of capital as experienced in England which, however, should have made Marx to problematise the question of system conforming behavior and consciousness of the working class. In Sieferle's opinion, from today's perspective it is quite clear that Marx had strong illusions about the revolutionary substance of this movement. And it has become almost commonplace to assert that Marx was taking the birth pains of capitalism to be its death agony. (See Sieferle 1979, 172—173.)

The nearest Marx ever came to the presentation of the problem of revolution in *Capital* was his analysis of the situation of wage workers under the law of capital accumulation. The tendential law of the falling rate of profit shows the objective limits of capital reproduction: in its everlasting hunger for surplus value by increasing the productivity of labour and, consequently, by increasing the share of relative surplus value, capital increasingly dismisses its own living basis, labour power.[4] If this tendency

---

[3]   As Marx and Engels wrote in *German Ideology:*
"Nur die von aller Selbstbetätigung vollständig ausgeschlossenen Proletarier der Gegenwart sind imstande, ihre vollständige, nicht mehr borniert Selbstbetätigung, die in der Aneignung einer Totalität von Produktivkräften und der damit gesetzten Entwicklung einer Totalität der Fähigkeiten besteht, durchsetzen." (MEW 3, 68).

[4]   "Über einen gewissen Punkt hinaus wird die Entwicklung der Produktivkräfte eine Schranke für das Kapital; also das Kapitalverhältnis eine Schranke für die Entwicklung der Produktivkräfte der Arbeit. (. . .) Die letzte Knechtschaft, die die menschliche Tätigkeit annimmt, die der Lohnarbeit auf der einen, des Kapitals auf der andren Seite, wird damit abgehäutet, und diese Abhäutung selbst ist das Resultat der dem Kapital entsprechenden Produktionsweise; die materiellen und geistigen Bedingungen der Negation der Lohnarbeit und des Kapitals, die selbst schon die Negation frührer Formen der unfreien gesellschaftlichen Produktion sind, sind selbst Resultate seines Produktionsprozesses. In schneidenden

towards falling rate of profit shows the objective limits of capitalism, the law parallel to it, the capitalist law of relative overpopulation, shows the subjective limits of capitalism.

After abandoning the Ricardian position of the determination of wages through the physical existence minimum and the iron law of wages in the 1850's (see Vygodskij 1970, 20−21; see also Schanz 1981, 289), Marx no longer adhered to a straightforward theory of the continuously growing misery of the wage workers. The wage worker does not necessarily represent absolute poverty any more, as he did in Marx's earlier writings. The increasing productivity of labour makes it possible for the real wages (and consumption) of the workers to rise even as the value and price of his labour power decrease and the rate of surplus value increases. Consequently, the worker does not in this respect necessarily have any subjective experience of the contradictory character of the capital relation and of any direct immiseration of his economic or social position:

> "In dem Moment, wo die Verelendung nur noch in Relation zur Entwicklung des Kapitals gesehen wird, der Lebensstandard aber steigt, kann die Verelendungstheorie nicht mehr beanspruchen, für die Erklärung der Entstehung von revolutionärem Bewusstseins etwas herzugeben. Eine Verelendung, die nicht als solche sinnlich erfahren wird, kann nicht als 'Not' Ausdruck der 'Notwendigkeit' sein." (Sieferle 1979, 198; cf. Wagner 1976, 15−16).

The immiseration theory was, however, preserved intact in another way by Marx. Due to the increasing organic composition of capital (the relation of constant to variable capital) total capital accumulated faster than its variable part; as Marx understood it, the amount of employed workers does not increase in tact with the accumulated capital:

> "Einerseits attrahiert also das im Fortgang der Akkumulation gebildete Zuschusskapital, verhältnismässig zu seiner Grösse, weniger und weniger Arbeiter. Andrerseits repelliert das periodisch in neuer Zusammensetzung reproduzierte alte Kapital mehr und mehr früher von ihm beschäftigte Arbeiter." (MEW 23, 657).

There is a continuously increasing reserve army of unemployed workers in capitalism:

> "Mit der durch sie selbst produzierten Akkumulation des Kapitals produziert die Arbeiterbevölkerung also in wachsendem Umfang die Mittel ihrer eignen relativen Überzähligmachung. Es ist dies ein der kapitalistischen Produktionsweise eigentümliches Populationsgesetz . . ." (MEW 23, 660).

The rationale of the increasing industrial reserve army from the point of view of capital is its influence on the demand and supply of labour power and, consequently, on the wage level. Wages are automatically kept in control. The price of labour power tends

---

Widersprüchen, Krisen, Krämpfen drückt sich die wachsende Unangemessenheit der produktiven Entwicklung der Gesellschaft zu ihren bisherigen Produktionsverhältnissen aus. Gewaltsame Vernichtung von Kapital, nicht durch ihm äussre Verhältnisse, sondern als Bedingung seiner Selbsterhaltung, ist die schlagendste Form, worin ihm advice gegeben wird to be gone and to give room to a higher state of social production." (Marx s.a., 635−636).

towards the existential minimum under circumstances of decreasing demand and increasing supply of labour power. The following formulation shows clearly, according to
Sieferle (see 1979, 201–202), that Marx was, even in *Capital,* introducing the concept
of growing misery, once again:

> "Die Akkumulation von Reichtum auf dem einen Pol ist also zugleich Akkumulation von
> Elend, Arbeitsqual, Sklaverei, Unwissenheit, Brutalisierung und moralischer Degradation
> auf dem Gegenpol, d.h. auf Seite der Klasse, die ihr eignes Produkt als Kapital pro-
> duziert." (MEW 23, 675).

The possibility of the experience of the 'universal negativity' of the position of the
working class, which in Sieferle's opinion is a precondition of the destruction of capitalism, is after all a subjectively experienced phenomenon in Marx's later thinking, too,
because of the growing army of unemployed and the consequent misery and suffering of
the wage workers under capitalism. Thus Marx was not in need of presenting any more
specific problematisation of the development of the consciousness of the working class
on a phenomenological level that would have shown how the mystification of the
surface can be penetrated and overcome. (See Sieferle 1979, 202.)

Sieferle criticised Marx's presentation of the capitalist law of population or the law of
relative overpopulation because it is based on the idea of the increasing organic composition of capital. The same critique which can be directed at the 'falling rate of profit
doctrine' can be directed at the population law. A priori, one cannot forecast any
necessity for a continuously growing reserve army. Sieferle's critique of this law was
almost a standard one: only *if* the value composition of capital were necessarily to rise
and only *if* the rate of surplus value were not to rise fast enough, would the expected
conclusion follow (see Sieferle 1979, 162–163).

One could, however, easily add some more doubts about the validity of the law.
Marx was drawing from it conclusions that quite obviously could be drawn only at a
later stage of his presentation. The general law of accumulation was an absolute and
abstract law, as pointed out by Wagner (1976, 79–81). The expected conclusions could
possibly follow only after the introduction of the problems of realisation and competition, etc. The accumulation of capital was in the first volume of *Capital* analysed in its
'pure form' and, consequently, it can only be shown that – in relation to its own growth
– capital continuously strives to get rid of its own basis of value increase, living labour,
by increasing both absolute and relative surplus value and the productivity of labour.
From this one cannot draw any conclusions concerning the historical fate of the working
class, even less concerning the necessity for any continuously increasing misery. All that
Marx could at this stage of his presentation say was that there is a tendency towards the
existence of a *relative* overpopulation, i.e. relative to the accumulated capital; capital
accumulates faster than employment increases. But at the same time employment can
be increasing as well, even though at a slower rate. Even though one were to accept the
doctrine of the increasing organic composition of capital, it would not be correct to
deduce from it any empirical forecasts about increasing overpopulation and unemploy-

ment, even less about any necessary decrease in the real wages of labour power or about the increasing misery of the proletariat. And it is in principle as impossible to have any experience of the relative — relative to the reproduction of capital — over-population and relative pauperisation of the proletariat as it is to experience the growing relative exploitation (or 'relative immiseration').

Whatever one thinks about the doubts about the nature of the general law of accumulation, Sieferle's interpretation is in any case interesting because he claimed that Marx's *Capital* included a phenomenological level of presentation relevant to the development of class consciousness. In analysing the consequences of capital accumulation Marx was explicitly discussing the historical fate of the proletariat under capitalism. More specifically, Marx was trying to show that the inner contradictions and limitations of the production of surplus value come into appearance on the surface of society in an empirically apprehensible way, as the misery and poverty of the workers. Thus the universal negativity inherent in the social category of wage labour can be experienced by the majority of the population; the wage workers come to realise that the capital relation must be overthrown to allow the free development of the individual. The wage worker as an 'absolute pauper' representing 'absolute negativity' is not only something that scientific analysis of the essence of capitalism can reveal. It is also something that every worker can and must feel in his own body and soul.

One could claim that the role of the theory of immiseration in Second International Marxism and in Kautsky's thinking in specific, is very similar to that explicated by Sieferle in discussing Marx's *Capital*. Just as crisis development, centralisation of capital, and the generalisation of wage labour were thought to reveal the objective limits of capitalism, so the increasing misery was thought to express its subjective limits. The revolutionary consciousness is born out of the insight that capitalism has nothing to offer the working masses. While making the capitalists richer wage workers are doomed to ever increasing misery. As already pointed out, the central role of the law of the increasing misery of the working class was accepted to be a crucial element of Marxism by both the orthodox Marxists and the 'revisionists' of the Second International. They only disagreed on the empirical validity of the law.

It may, however, be doubted whether Marx's discussion of the capitalist law of population could in any way be understood either as a phenomenological level of the analysis of consciousness (Sieferle) or as a discussion of the normative standards of the participants forming part of Marx's transcending critique (Lohmann). The discussion is namely closely connected with the postulates and conclusions of classical theories of bourgeois society. It is here suggested that Marx's discussion of the general law of accumulation and the fate of the working class in *Capital* should be considered strictly in the context of his critique of political economy. Marx was, first of all, criticising the respective laws of Ricardo (1971 (1817)) and Malthus (1970 (1798)) and trying to prove that the tendency towards increasing overpopulation and the falling rate of profit are not eternal natural laws but, on the contrary, historical laws which are specific to capitalism. For Ricardo the falling rate of profit resulted from the diminishing productivity of land taken into use cumulatively (see Ricardo 1971, 71–72; cf. Marx s.a., 499–450). In *Capital* Marx was directly commenting on Malthus:

> "Mit der durch sie selbst produzierten Akkumulation des Kapitals produziert die Arbeiter-bevölkerung also in wachsendem Umfang die Mittel ihrer eignen relativen Überzählig-machung. Es ist dies ein der kapitalistischen Produktionsweise eigentümliches Populations-gesetz, wie in der Tat jede besondere historische Produktionsweise ihre besonderen, histo-risch gültigen Populationsgesetze hat. Ein abstraktes Populationsgesetz existiert nur für Pflanze und Tier, soweit der Mensch nicht geschichtlich eingreift." (MEW 23, 660).

There is, however, yet another context which is even more relevant to the interpreta-tion of Marx's law of accumulation and overpopulation. In *Capital* Marx stated:

> "Die Bewegung des Getsetzes der Nachfrage und Zufuhr von Arbeit auf dieser Basis vollendet die Despotie des Kapitals. Sobald daher die Arbeiter hinter das Geheimnis kommen, wie es angeht, dass im selben Mass, wie sie mehr arbeiten, mehr fremden Reichtum produzieren und die Produktivkraft ihrer Arbeit wächst, sogar ihre Funktion als Verwertungsmittel des Kapitals immer prekärer für sie wird; sobald sie entdecken, dass der Intensitätsgrad der Konkurrenz unter ihnen selbst ganz und gar von dem Druck der re-lativen Übervölkerung abhängt;. . ." (MEW 23, 669).

The law of supply and demand of labour power in a sense completes the analysis of the despotism of capital in Marx's critique of political economy: as soon as wage workers come to recognise that they, in fact, produce richness alien to themselves in the form of capital while becoming poorer themselves capitalism has come to an end. By reproducing capital on an enlarging scale they reproduce their own situation as wage workers, a situation characterised by both insecurity and brutality.

In the *Ökonomisch–philosophische Manuskripte* of 1844 the same idea was already formulated in abstract terms:

> "Der Arbeiter wird um so ärmer, je mehr Reichtum er produziert, je mehr seine Produk-tion an Macht und Umfang zunimmt." (MEW Erg.Bd. 1., 511).

And in *Grundrisse* the conclusion can be found in a more developed form already resembling Marx's analysis in *Capital:*

> "Es (das Arbeitsvermögen – J.G.) hat nicht nur den fremden Reichtum und die eigne Armut produziert, sondern auch das Verhältnis dieses Reichtums als sich auf sich selbst beziehenden Reichtums zu ihm als der Armut, durch deren Konsum es neue Lebensgeister in sich zieht und sich von neuem verwertet." (Marx s.a., 357).

And further:

> "Es zeigt sich hier, wie progressiv die objektive Welt des Reichtums durch die Arbeit selbst als ihr fremde Macht sich ihr gegenüber ausweitet und immer breitere und vollere Existenz gewinnt, so dass relativ, im Verhältnis zu den geschaffnen Werten oder den realen Bedingungen der Wertschöpfung die bedürftige Subjektivität des lebendigen Arbeitsver-mögens einen immer grelleren Kontrast bildet." (Marx s.a., 359).

The discussion of the general law of accumulation and the fate of the working class in *Capital* can then be interpreted to be a more developed formulation of the above ideas.[5] By showing the mechanism through which the reproduction and accumulation of capital makes the capitalist richer and the worker poorer, Marx is concluding his critique of the natural rights thinking and classical political economy. The analysis of the reproduction of capital proved how the value increase of capital takes place at the cost of living labour and how wage labour continuously reproduces the social force that dominates the life activity of the worker. The production of a relative overpopulation, the other side of the accumulation of capital, shows furthermore that while continuously reproducing the conditions of further accumulation of capital, wage labour simultaneously reproduces its own relative superfluousness. The wage worker thus continuously reproduces the relation of domination of capital over himself, or the domination of dead over living labour, a domination which most concretely comes into appearance as the relative overpopulation of workers:

> "Die kapitalistische Akkumulation produziert vielmehr, und zwar im Verhältnis zu ihrer Energie und ihrem Umfang, beständig eine relative, d.h. für die mittleren Verwertungsbedürfnisse des Kapitals überschüssige, daher überflüssige oder Zuschuss-Arbeiterbevölkerung." (MEW 23, 658).

The other side of the accumulation of capital is the accumulation of misery as explicitly stated by Marx:

> "Es bedingt eine der Akkumulation von Kapital entsprechende Akkumulation von Elend." (MEW 23, 675).

In Marx's critique of capitalism the original identity of labour, property and use value as postulated by John Locke and Adam Smith was definitely broken. Rather than increasing the conveniences of human life by adding more labour to nature's products as promised by Locke, those who work are deprived of even the mere necessities of life and of the very means of their living. Neither does the increasing wealth of a nation — followed by inequality of property — guarantee that a human existence will extend even to the lowest ranks of people, as promised by Smith. The general well-being of the greatest number does not follow from the growing wealth of a nation. The accumulation of capital results more in the most inhuman existence of the greatest number of people, the working class. In Marx analysis the accumulation of capital completes the despotism of capital (cf. Nielsen 1980), and proves the dependence of the wage worker on the

---

[5] In *Critique of the Gotha Programme* Marx referred approvingly to a formulation according to which the misery of the working class is continuously increasing while the capitalists are becoming all the richer:

> "Im Mass, wie die Arbeit sich gesellschaftlich entwickelt und dadurch Quelle von Reichtum und Kultur wird, entwickeln sich Armut und Verwahrlosung auf seiten des Arbeiters, Reichtum und Kultur auf seiten des Nichtarbeiters." (MEW 19, 17).

conditions of the reproduction of capital leading to the utmost brutality and insecurity of the whole life situation of the wage workers.[6]

At the end of the first volume of *Capital* Marx thus implicitly claimed that bourgeois society does not keep its promise of reason as formulated by classical thinking, and the legitimation of private property, money and capital through their social consequences, the human existence of mankind, cannot be justified. Marx, was, however, clearly exaggerating his case, while emphasising the almost continuous and inevitable immiseration of the working class.[7]

But it clearly was not sufficient for Marx only to prove that wage labour produces richness in a form alien to itself and that, whether or not better paid, wage labour continuously reproduces the capital relation — and the conditons of its own further existence — on a larger scale. Marx did not only stop at the point of proving that wage labour both reproduces on the one side more capitalists and on the other side more wage workers and the continuous dominance of capital over itself, as stated at the beginning of the chapter on the general law of accumulation:

> "Umstände, worin sich die Lohnarbeiter erhalten und vermehren, ändern jedoch nichts am Grundcharakter der kapitalistischen Produktion. Wie die einfache Reproduktion fortwährend das Kapitalverhältnis selbst reproduziert, Kapitalisten auf der einen Seite, Lohnarbeiter auf der andren, so reproduziert die Reproduktion auf erweiterter Stufenleiter oder die Akkumulation das Kapitalverhältnis auf erweiterter Stufenleiter, mehr Kapitalisten oder grössere Kapitalisten auf diesem Pol, mehr Lohnarbeiter auf jenem. (. . .) Akkumulation des Kapitals ist also Vermehrung des Proletariats." (MEW 23, 641−642).

[6]   The list of the 'vices' of capital quoted by Marx is impressive:

". . . innerhalb des kapitalistischen Systems vollziehn sich alle Methoden zur Steigerung der gesellschaftlichen Produktivkraft der Arbeit auf Kosten des individuellen Arbeiters; alle Mittel zur Entwicklung der Produktion schlagen um in Beherrschungs − und Exploitationsmittel des Produzenten, verstümmeln den Arbeiter in einen Teilmenschen, entwürdigen ihn zum Anhängsel der Maschinen, vernichten mit der Qual seiner Arbeit ihren Inhalt, entfremden ihm die geistigen Potenzen des Arbeitsprozesses im selben Masse, worin letzterem die Wissenschaft als selbständige Potenz einverleibt wird; sie verunstalten die Bedingungen, innerhalb deren er arbeitet, unterwerfen ihn während des Arbeitsprozesses der kleinlichst gehässigen Despotie, verwandeln seine Lebenszeit in Arbeitszeit, schleudern sein Weib und Kinder unter das Juggernaut-Rad des Kapitals." (MEW 23, 674).

[7]   As shown by Carlsen et al. (1980; see also Schanz 1981) there is an important dimension in Marx's thinking concerning the civilisatoric dynamism of capitalism especially pronounced in *Grundrisse*. According to Marx, the development of a free and rich individuality with universal needs and capacities results from the civilisatoric influence of capital. Marx never explicitly reflected on the relation between his conception of the civilisatoric influence of capital in *Grundrisse* and the results of his analysis of the fate of the working class in *Capital*. At first sight, there would seem to be in Marx's thinking a duality similar to that presented by Kautsky concerning the position of the working class in capitalism. According to Kautsky there are both elevating and repressive tendencies operating in capitalism. Whereas the elevating tendencies in Kautskýs argumentation always are connected with the struggle of the working class against capitalism, in Marx's thinking they are, however, inherent in the very civilisatoric dynamism of capital.

Evidently Marx wanted to prove more — more than could actually be proved on the basis of his premises. He wanted to prove that the existence of the proletariat, the greatest number of the people in capitalism, is inclined to become more brutal and inhuman in a very concrete sense. Thus Marx opened up his case for a direct empirical interpretation — and falsification — of his theory and a historical critique of it. At least certain parts of his analysis can legitimately be understood to form a historical prognosis of the ever-worsening economic and social condition of the working class in capitalism. And it was the Second International Marxism that adopted this interpretation and prophecy as its own and absolutised it into the very cornerstone of its scientific socialism.

CONCLUSION

The main purpose of the present study has been to analyse and reconstruct the theory of capitalism formulated and developed by Karl Kautsky at the turn of the present century. The specific importance of Karl Kautsky's contribution to the development of Marxism lies in the fact that in interpreting and commenting on what he understood to be the essential ideas of Karl Marx's economic thought, he explicitly and more or less systematically formulated a doctrine that can be claimed to constitute the common core of the social theory of traditional Marxism. Despite the obvious and important differences in the conceptions of the leading Marxists of the time − especially in their strategic and political conclusions − in their understanding of the nature of capitalism they share important common ideas. These ideas have far-reaching consequences for their analysis of imperialism, for the evaluation of the conditions of the future revolution and for the understanding of the coming socialist society.

Kautsky's Marxism springs from certain crucial misunderstandings in his interpretation of Marx's theory of capitalism: his interpretation of Marx's *Capital* fails to pay attention to the specific character of Marx's theory as a critique of political economy. Still, a critical reconstruction of the social theory of traditional Marxism is not only useful in pointing out differences in Marx's and Marxism's analysis and critique of bourgeois society. It also leads to the problematisation and re-evaluation of certain crucial conceptions in Marx's own reasoning. Marxism does not only represent what could be called a deformation of Marx's critique of political economy, there is a Marxism of Marx, too.

Kautsky's most original contribution to the development of Marxism lies in his formulation of the laws of capitalist development. In Kautsky's own understanding these laws were already presented by Marx in his *Capital*. Consequently, Kautsky understood it as his task both to defend Marx's theory against attempts at empirical falsification and to apply it in analysing the development of the present capitalism and the conditions for a socialist revolution. His understanding of the law of capital accumulation as a historical and empirical law predicting the continuous concentration and centralisation of capital did, however, already include a specific interpretation of Marx's theory of capitalism.

In Kautsky's opinion, the main importance of Marx's *Capital* lay in the fact that it proved that, due to the centralisation of capital, a capitalist society is polarised into essentially two classes where − to quote an apt characterisation by Arato (1973−74, 6)

— "an insignificant non-working minority owns everything and a working majority owns next to nothing (except their labour power)". The inevitable polarisation of bourgeois society also included the proletarisation of the vast majority of its population. While destroying the economic basis for the existence of the old middle classes (various producers owning their own means of production), the concentration of property in a few hands concretely showed that there is no return to a previous historical stage in society. The future socialist society is the only alternative open to the working class for improving its lot in society.

Continuous immiseration of the working class is the other side of the concentration thesis. In Kautsky's opinion the social and economic position of the proletariat, the great majority of the population in advanced capitalist countries, was doomed to deteriorate. The development of capitalism as predicted by Marx's theory thus created both the objective and the subjective conditions for a socialist revolution. The objective conditions were ripening due to the continuous concentration of capital, and the increasing misery of the working class was equally inevitably leading to the formation of a revolutionary working class, the subject of the coming socialist revolution.

In Kautsky's understanding these developmental laws of capitalism were empirical historical laws describing the general tendency of capitalism towards greater concentration and polarisation. They furthermore predicted the inevitability of the future dissolution of capitalism. The whole socialist doctrine rested on the validity of these laws. If they were refuted, then socialism would lose its scientific status and the labour movement would be deprived of the consciousness of the inevitability of its goal of socialism. In this respect Kautsky's defence of Marxism against Bernstein's critique was revealing. On the one hand Kautsky claimed that Bernstein's critique was totally misdirected. Marxism was not a theory of the collapse of capitalism. On the other hand Kautsky was ready to agree that if Bernstein's critique were justified — if Bernstein had succeeded in proving the empirical invalidity of the concentration thesis — then the whole idea of the coming socialist revolution would have to be abandoned.

There was in Kautsky's conception of capitalism another component which was directly adopted from Engels' *Anti-Dühring* and which was of equal theoretical importance. In *Anti-Dühring* Engels had formulated the basic contradiction of capitalism in terms of the increasing socialisation of production and the still prevailing private mode of appropriation. According to Engels, in the simple commodity production historically preceding capitalism every property owner appropriates the products of his own labour, whereas in capitalism the products are no longer products of individual labourers even though they still are appropriated by private property owners. In simple commodity production the right to private property was genuinely based only on one's own labour, in capitalism products of alien labour are appropriated even though they are no longer products of private labour even but are produced collectively by wage workers. In a socialist society, in which the means of production have been socialised, the mode of appropriation would once again correspond to the true nature of production, in fact, already socialised in capitalism.

In Engels' reasoning this contradiction really was the basic contradiction of capitalism from which all the other contradictions — including industrial crises — followed. In Kautsky's conception the role of this contradiction was — if possible — even more accentuated. He interpreted Marx as having presented in his *Capital* the historical development of capitalism from an earlier mode of production, that of simple commodity production. This interpretation was already suggested by Engels, but one can claim that it has even more important consequences for Kautsky's reasoning. Kautsky claimed that there was a curious shortcoming in Marx's presentation of *Capital*. Marx did not provide the necessary historical facts in describing the transformation of simple commodity production into capitalism. And Kautsky even suggested that the analysis should be complemented by these facts first giving support and making understandable Marx's historical theory.

The most important consequence of Kautsky's discussion of the transformation of the mode of appropriation is that his critique of capitalism comes close to a radical version of natural rights theory. Kautsky — and for that matter Engels, too — in fact postulated a hypothetical stage of simple commodity production during which the right to private property was based on one's own labour. It was the right to appropriate nature's products by one's own labour that formed a title to property. It is only labour that creates a legitimate right to property. Private property and private mode of appropration prevail in capitalism, but the original right to appropriate the products of one's own labour is violated. Capitalism is, consequently, criticised because it does not respect this original rule.

Neither Engels nor Kautsky demanded a return to an original or natural state of society, to simple commodity production, as some early nineteenth century radicals did. In the opinion of Marxists these radicals were utopian socialists who did not understand that the development of capitalism had made such a return impossible. The specific Marxist contribution to a critique of capitalism which directed the natural rights theory against capitalist private property consisted of the idea of the socialisation of production. In capitalism products are not appropriated from nature privately; they are the products of the collective labour of wage workers socialised in the production process by capital. Consequently there cannot be any return to simple commodity production and legitimate private property. The original right to appropriate the products of one's own labour must be substituted by the right of the working class, the collective worker, to appropriate the products of its collective labour.

The historical laws of the development of capitalism and the basic contradiction of capitalism formed the two poles of Kautsky's historical interpretation of Marx's *Capital*. This interpretation had important consequences for Kautsky's understanding of modern capitalism, too. These consequences were manifested most clearly in his analysis of imperialism. The different proposals and attempts to analyse and discuss the new emerging features of capitalism generally gathered under the concept of imperialism were certainly inspired by the immediate political problems facing different Social Democratic Parties both before and during the First World War. The weight given to different factors — protective tariffs, colonial policy, export and import of capital and raw materials, overproduction, militarism, and the threat of war — in different theories of imperialism could certainly partly be explained by differences in the political and economic situation in different European countries.

The partly competing and partly converging proposals for analysing imperialism were, however, not only aimed at clarifying the immediate political tasks and conditions of action of the socialist parties. By characterising present capitalism either as imperialism or monopoly capitalism something theoretically more ambitious was assumed. The theories of imperialism indicated that capitalism was developing or had already developed into a new phase or stage which had transformed the functioning of its political and economic mechanisms demanding a new political orientation of the Social Democratic Parties. Although there obviously are important differences of opinion regarding imperialism and monopoly capitalism in the theories of Hilferding, Kautsky, Lenin and Luxemburg — the main representatives of the theory of imperialism analysed in this study — all the respective conceptions share a common understanding of what is the essential nature of capitalism: capitalism is essentially a society characterised by the expropriation of the products of labour of the majority of the population, the working class, by a handful of property owners, the owners of the means of production. Capitalism is a society of exploitation, and the exploitative nature of capitalism was understood to become both more severe and more evident insofar as capitalism was developing according to its own economic laws.

The specific relevance of the conceptions of imperialism to the analysis of Marxism is that, in a sense, imperialism first reveals the truth about capitalism. In imperialism the exploitative nature of capitalism was manifested in a most conspicuous manner. During the age of imperialism the majority of the population is exploited by cartels and finance capitalists not only in the capacity of producers but in the capacity of consumers as well. Cartels and finance capital do not only exploit the working class; other groups in society are exploited as well: the middle classes, peasants, and other smallholders, even industrial capitalists are exploited by finance capital. Exploitation is not restricted to the people of the imperialist countries. The exploitation of colonies in various forms is of growing importance.

It was Hilferding's theory of finance capital that formulated these consequences most explicitly. In Hilferding's opinion capitalism was due to develop towards the formation of a single general cartel which would consciously regulate the distribution of the whole national product among a general cartel and the rest of the people, respectively. Hilferding's conception was based on the extrapolation of the tendencies inherent in capitalism as understood by the majority of the Marxists of the time. The logical outcome of these tendencies would be the formation of a general cartel. The antagonistic nature of capitalism would be developed to its extremes and in capitalism governed and regulated by a general cartel the remaining antagonism would be an antagonism of distribution exclusively.

In Kautsky's opinion imperialism was essentially a political method adopted by the capitalist state to guarantee the profits of cartels and finance capital. Colonial policy (annexation of colonies) and high import tariffs were the basic methods of imperialist states. They were furthermore political measures which were in the interests of the finance capital exclusively. Kautsky's famous idea of ultra-imperialism was a further direct extrapolation of Hilferding's conception of a general cartel. In ultra-imperialism international cartels would regulate the quantity of production, prices of commodities and the distribution of profits among themselves. The formation of ultra-imperialism was a logical consequence of the tendencies towards centralisation of capital inherent in capitalism as understood by Kautsky. Ultra-imperialism would be a consciously re-gulated society based on the exploitation of the rest of the people by a few international cartels.

Even though principally denying the possibility of the development of capitalism towards the formation of a general cartel and the establishment of ultra-imperialism, and even though emphasising imperialism as a necessary stage of capitalism determined by its economic development — and not only as a political method of the state through which the power of cartels was exercised — Lenin, too, understood imperialism as being essentially a forceful method of finance capital and monopolies to appropriate high profits resulting either from international transfers of capital, regulations of competition or finance operations.

As has already been pointed out, there is a feature common to all these explanations. In all of them the profits of finance capital, cartels, or monopolies do not specifically result from the relation between capital and wage labour. It is not the different methods of surplus value production that are analysed. In imperialism capitalists are furthermore able to appropriate high profits by methods that directly and clearly violate the rule of equal exchange of commodities which in Marx's understanding was respected even in the relation between wage labour and capital. The profits of cartels are increased by artificially regulating competition, either by selling at a high price or buying at a low price; exported capital can raise a high profit or interest; and dividends on stock are increased in value by finance operations. The importance of finance capital and export of capital in the theories of imperialism is especially revealing: in imperialism capital is no longer directly related to the process of production, but profits are redistributed among different capital owners. In the hands of finance capital and cartels private property becomes a right of the more powerful to appropriate and distribute profits in their interests. In this sense, then, imperialism reveals the truth about capitalism. In imperialism capitalists are exploiting the people without even an illusion of equality in their relations. Private property is furthermore clearly separated from the production process, from the appropriation of nature's products by labour which alone can create a rightful title to property. In claiming that imperialism and the reign of finance capital marked the end of technical development, the development of the productive forces, Kautsky and Lenin were presenting more than a doubtful empirical generalisation; private property was deprived of its transhistorical legitimation. Capital no longer had a progressive function in organising the labour process. In characterising imperialism as parasitic capitalism, Lenin thus summerised his analysis more aptly than he perhaps realised.

The previous discussion has emphasised the common features in the different theories of imperialism. In Kautsky's conception there were, however, interesting features that were not shared by others. As was already pointed out, Kautsky understood imperialism as being basically a political method of capitalist states. Imperialism was only one of the possible answers to the problem of overproduction which he understood to be a chronic problem in capitalism. According to Kautsky the continuous threat of overproduction resulted from the different expansive capacities of industrial and agrarian production. Whereas industrial production could in principle be expanded without limits, there were natural limits to the growth of agrarian production. By opening up new markets for industrial products and new raw material resources colonies — at least temporarily — relieved the imperialist countries of the problem of overproduction. Protective tariffs had a similar function by restricting foreign competition. In Kautsky's opinion imperialism was only in the interests of finance capital. It had forced the state to adopt an imperialist policy. In this context of discussion Kautsky formulated his famous thesis about the possible alternatives to imperialism which were suggested by him in different articles: ultra-imperialism and a democratic union of states. In ultra-imperialism world-wide cartels would regulate both production quantities, market prices and the distribution of profits. A democratic union of states would, on the contrary, restore the principle of free trade within its borders. These alternatives would both be more favourable to the working class than imperialism. The democratic alternative of free trade would in particular be more favourable both to the development of productive forces — a criterion constantly applied by Kautsky in evaluating different political measures — and to the wage workers as well. Still, both ultra-imperialism and the democratic union of states must finally be replaced by the socialist alternative, the final goal of the proletariat and socialist movement.

Even though resembling Luxemburg's idea of the necessity of non-capitalist markets for the continuous accumulation of capital, which was closely related to the conception that there are absolute, final limits to the expansion of capitalism, Kautsky's emphasis on overproduction as a central cause of imperialism can be said to constitute his original contribution to the theories of imperialism. But even in this respect there are certain important similarities in Kautsky's, Lenin's and Luxemburg's reasoning.

In Kautsky's analysis the natural restrictions of agrarian production give rise to imperialist politics. Hilferding found out that cartels agreed on restrictions on competition in order to prevent the devaluation of capital fixed in such means of production which could not easily be transferred to other fields of production. In Lenin's analysis, the increasing size of the production units necessitated by technical development was one of the reasons for free competition to be substituted by monopolistic restrictions on competition. One feature common to all these explanations is that monopoly capitalism or imperialism is explained by some peculiur technical or natural properties of the labour process. On the one hand imperialism was thus understood as a system in which profits were appropriated and distributed in the interests of powerful groups of capitalists, on the other hand the production process was analysed in terms of the technical labour process.

Kautsky, Luxemburg and Lenin all emphasised the violent and reactionary nature of imperialism. It was partly explained by the political forces active in imperialism. The bourgeoisie was understood as having given up its former democratic aspirations and as having taken refuge in violent methods of repression both in its relation to the 'domestic' working class and in international relations. There were, however, other more deeply rooted reasons explaining this strategic evaluation of imperialism. It could namely be claimed that it was not only imperialism that was understood as reactionary; capitalism in general was reactionary. To both Kautsky and Lenin democracy and equality were simply tactical weapons used by the rising bourgeoisie in its struggle against feudalism and absolutism. They were political ideals that in principle had nothing to do with the social relations of a bourgeois society. It was Kautsky's conception of democracy and dictatorship that is especially revealing in this respect, too.

The role of democracy in Kautsky's thinking is rather peculiar; it determines his specific position in the political spectrum of the Second International Marxists. To Kautsky, democracy was not only — as it was to many a Marxist — the most effective political institution to be used in organising and schooling a socialist and revolutionary working class. Parliamentary democracy also offered the best possible measuring stock for evaluating the actual strength of the proletarian organisations. To Kautsky democracy was not, however, only a tactical question. He was obviously a principal democrat by conviction. In Kautsky's opinion socialism without democracy was only a caricature of socialism. He demanded that the democratic rights of the minority should be respected during the socialist revolution and proclaimed that parliamentary democracy would be the ideal form of a socialist rule. Kautsky was, however, equally convinced that the socialist transformation of bourgeois society would not be a process of gradual transition. It would be a revolutionary process, preceded by a political revolution. And — at least until the Russian Revolution — Kautsky also thought that this revolutionary transformation of society would take place under a dictatorship of the proletariat.

It was the way he combined parliamentary democracy and the dictatorship of the proletariat in his thinking that was peculiar to Kautsky's political position. There was not, however, any contradiction in his thinking. According to his definition the dictatorship of the proletariat would be equal to Social Democratic majority rule in parliament. As soon as the Social Democratic Party occupied the majority of the seats in parliament, it would declare a socialist revolution under the auspices of the dictatorship of the proletriat. But a dictatorship of the proletariat would respect democratic principles, it would realise the will of the majority while also respecting the rights of the minority.

The main reason for Lenin's well-known accusation of Kautsky as a renegade of Marxism was Kautsky's disapproval and critique of the Russian Revolution and the Bolshevik model of the dictatorship of the proletariat. Lenin accused Kautsky of adopting only a formal concept of democracy which did not pay attention to the real class character of the bourgeois state. To Lenin, the real class character of the state was the decisive criterion according to which a Marxist should judge it. The ruling class of a society always establishes its class rule in a state irrespective of its possible democratic constitution. But even Lenin recognised that in Russia the socialist revolution must be preceded by a democratic one, and he also shared Kautsky's opinion of the importance of democratic institutions as a training ground for the proletarian organisations. But otherwise the question of democracy was rather irrelevant to Lenin. It was always the class character of the state that was the decisive factor.

Despite their radically different stands on questions of democracy and dictatorship Kautsky's and Lenin's positions were similar in that in their view democracy and equality obviously did not have anything to do with the social relations of a bourgeois society. Democracy was either an alien principle in capitalism, its only adherent being the working class, or it was relevant only from the tactical point of view as just another form of bourgeois class rule. It can be claimed that this understanding of democracy in capitalism and its role in the socialist revolution is closely connected with the conception of capitalism as essentially a society in which a small minority of property owners directly exploits the great majority of the population, a society in which the fruits of the labour of the working class are appropriated by the capitalists. In such a society there is no place for any freedom and equality of its members; it is a reactionary society in which even the most elementary needs of the greatest number are repressed. Continuous misery is all the working class can expect. If the capitalism of free competition preceding imperialism was still understood as fulfilling its historical mission of developing the productive forces, imperialism was deprived even of this justification. Thus the reactionary nature of capitalism was manifest in it in a most conspicuous manner.

Marx's critique of the capitalist mode of appropriation differs remarkably from Marxism's critique of private property, and consequently his critique of capitalism is also more subtle. In *Capital* and *Grundrisse* Marx did not formulate any basic contradiction of capitalism in terms of the still prevailing private mode of appropriation and the increasing socialisation of production. At first sight his critique had a similar target. It was directed at the basic assumption of classical political economy, the legitimation of private property as being based on one's own labour. Marx's discussion of the transformation of the mode of appropriation seems to resemble the thesis presented in *Anti-Dühring*. According to Marx, in capitalism the mode of appropriation has been transformed into its opposite. While being originally based on one's own labour in simple commodity production, in capitalism the result of the transaction between capital and wage labour is that the products of alien labour have been appropriated. In fact, however, Marx's critique of political economy could be directed at Engels' formulation of the basic contradiction of capitalism, too. In classical political economy the right to private property was postulated as being based on the right to appropriate nature's products by labour. It is labour that creates a legitimate right to private property. In Marx's opinion this postulate leads to a naturalisation of the social relations of bourgeois society as private property is not constituted by man's relation to nature; it is a legal expression of the more fundamental social relations of production and has different contents in different social formations. Marx did not, however, only disqualify the conception of private property and appropriation postulated in classical political economy by stating that in capitalism private property is not based on one's own labour. His critique also included an explanation of the reasons which led classical political economy to make such a postulate. In Marx's opinion, the legitimation of private property by labour is, in a sense, a valid form of thought in the bourgeois society.

In Marx's understanding political economy postulated an original appropriation of the products of one's own labour and a property right based on it, because if only the process of circulation of commodities is analysed, then the products of alien labour could only be thought to have been appropriated by exchanging them with the products of one's own labour. Thus the commodities exchanged must originally have been produced by the respective commodity owners. If the rule of equal exchange has furthermore been respected (as assumed by political economy), then the commodities produced by alien labour can only be appropriated by exchanging them with the products of one's own labour of equal value.

There is, however, another side to Marx's critique of political economy which was equally neglected by traditional Marxism. In making a distinction between the form and the contents of the process of appropriation, Marx recognised that there is an essential truth imbedded in classical political economy. The form of capitalist appropriation respects the rule of equal exchange as the relation between capital and labour power is one of exchange of commodities. In the process of commodity circulation the mutual freedom and equlity of the commodity exchangers (including the owner of the labour power) are respected. In Marx's own words, the process of circulation is the productive basis for the legal ideas of freedom and equality in a bourgeois society. Freedom and equality are, however, by nature formal, because the result of the capitalist commodity circulation is that surplus value has been appropriated. Capital has increased in value, but the owner of the commodity labour power leaves the process in the same capacity as he entered it, the value of his commodity has − in the ideal case − been preserved. In entering the production process the wage worker is furthermore subordinated under the 'despotism of the factory'. Freedom and equality are by nature formal, because the wage worker is not in command of the material means of the objectification of his own labour power. The very productive activity of the worker is subjected under an alien will. The result of the process is that surplus value has been appropriated, even though the process of exchange respects the rule of equal exchange, and the commodity exchangers are in the sense of classical thinking free and autonomous individuals.

While adopting only one element of Marx's critique of capitalist appropriation and private property, traditional Marxism understood capitalism as just another exploitative society in which the products of the labouring class are forcibly exploited by property owners. Thus Marxism totally ignored Marx's conception of capital as a rather specific relation of exploitation. And due to this neglect, the result of which was most drastically expressed in the theories of imperialism, Marxism came close to a radical version of the natural rights theory. Capitalism was to be blamed because it did not respect the original right of the worker to his own products.

Even though one could perhaps interpret Marxism as implicitly presenting an immanent critique of capitalism (capital as a violation of an original property rule), it still fell short of understanding the specific character of Marx's *Capital* as a critique of political economy. Marx's critique of political economy included both a critique of the postulated naturalness of the social relations of bourgeois society and a critique of bourgeois society with its own normative standards of freedom and equality. To claim that Marxism did not understand the specific character of Marx's theory of capitalism as a critical theory amounts to the same as to claim that Marxism did not understand the importance of Marx's determination of the dual nature of labour, in Marx's own view his most original theoretical invention. The postulate of the naturalness of social relations, of social relations which were based on man's relation to nature, was a consequence of the failure to comprehend the specific social form of labour in bourgeois society. The secret of the origins of surplus value could also be revealed once the determination of the dual nature of the labour power had been invented. Marx's critique of both capital and private property had as its prerequisite the critique of the concept of labour.

In discussing the transformation of the mode of appropriation in capitalism even Marx seemed to refer to an earlier mode of appropriation from which the capitalist mode had been developed. In the simple commodity production preceding capitalism the appropriation of commodities and private property, too were, in fact, based exclusively on one's labour. But in contrast to Kautsky's and Engels' Marxism, Marx was careful to stress that private property is not constituted by man's relation to nature. It is only in a society in which private labour is transformed into social labour by exchange that private property is constituted. It is thus wrong to naturalise the social relations of a society of commodity production. But in sense even Marx adopted what he understood to be the rational kernel of classical political economy through a critical reconstruction of its theories of surplus value. His dual redefinition of the concept of labour preserved and even radicalised the central idea of classical political economy (which was preceded by natural rights thinking) that labour is the original price that has been paid for commodities. Through the productive activity of man his labour is materialised in its products. It is labour — even if not labour alone — that creates richness in society, a multiplicity of use values, which in capitalism (temporarily) appear in the form of commodities. Even in capitalism it is then the labour of the wage worker that creates richness by materialising in the products of labour. It is labour that forms the substance of value, and it is labour time that determines the quantity of value. Even though emphasing that value is a specific social form of commodities, a social function ascribed to them in exchange, Marx definitely identified the substance of value with abstract labour.

Thus it is understandable that Marx obviously approved of and even contributed to Engels' formulation of the basic contradiction of capitalism in terms of the socialisation of production and private mode of appropriation. Marx would undoubtedly recognise it as a shorthand formulation of his own critical thesis that even in capitalism, as in any society, it is labour that creates richness; any man not working himself lives at the cost of others. Even though drastically overlooking Marx's critique of political economy, Marxism thus still preserves intact a central component of Marx's critique of capitalism, condensed in the labour theory of value which Marx adopted from Ricardo and which he even found *in statu nascendi* in the whole history of classical political economy. It is this labour theory of value that can be said to constitute Marx's Marxism.

In another context Alexa Mohl identified in Marx's thinking an element that has equally been preserved in Marxism. In her study *Verelendung und Revolution* (1981; see also Mohl 1979; 1983) Mohl identified two distinct conceptions about the socialist revolution and the determination of the revolutionary subject. These conceptions are mutually exclusive and their relationship was never explicitly reflected on by Marx, even though elements of both of them can be found even in Marx's mature works, in his critique of political economy. Mohl calls the first conception objectivistic, the second the model of practical emancipation. According to the objectivistic version, the coming socialist revolution is an inevitable outcome of the economic development of capitalism revealed by its scientific analysis. Its central thesis is that it is the increasing misery of the working class that qualifies it as the genuine executor of revolution.

The concept of practical emancipation, on the other hand, emphasises Marx's theory of capitalism as a critical theory. The development of the revolutionary subject is not thought to be predetermined by the development of capitalism. The very goals and aspirations of different actual emancipatory movements assume special importance in this conception. Even though Mohl was not discussing explicitly the role of different standards of critique in Marx's theory, in this respect her interpretation resembles Lohmann's idea of a transcending critique. Mohl is interested in the relation between the critical theory and emancipatory movements. In her opinion the role of the critical theory is to clarify the self-understanding of practical movements about their goals and conditions of action, but it does not dictate any such goals of action. Theory, then, is not the dominating partner of the revolutionary movement. And what is even more important, the model of practical emancipation did not identify the revolutionary subject exclusively with the proletariat. (See Mohl 1981, 126–127.)

Mohl's interpretation is especially interesting because she identified elements of an objectivistic theory of revolution not only in certain stages of the development of Marx's thought, but practically in all Marx's main writings. The thesis of immiseration and the presumption of the proletariat as representing absolute poverty can be found both in the *Ökonomisch–philosophische Manuskripte* of 1844 and in *Die heilige Familie* (MEW 2, 38; see also Mohl 1981, 25–28). The idea is then elaborated further in Marx's writings at the end of the 1840's, *Elend der Philosophie* (MEW 4 (1847/48)) and *Lohnarbeit und Kapital* (MEW 6 (1849)), written in the period in which Marx adopted most uncritically Ricardos's theory of value and the determination of wages by the existential minimum of the wage worker (see MEW 6, 406; see also Tuchscheerer 1968,

287–290; 314–315). The conception of immiseration and the idea that it is the steadily deteriorating social position of the working class that forces it to accomplish the socialist revolution can be found in Marx's *Capital,* too, particularly in the chapter dealing with the accumulation of capital.

Even though it cannot be denied that there are formulations in Marx's *Capital* and in his earlier works that would suggest that Marx did in fact present an objectivistic theory of revolution as interpreted by Mohl, it is more reasonable to interpret the discussion of the fate of the working class in *Capital* as an essential element of Marx's critical theory. Mohl's characterisation of the objectivistic theory of revolution would, on the other hand, be an apt description of Marxism's conception of revolution analysed in this study.

According to Kautsky the belief in the inevitability of the coming revolution was not based on any expectation of the automatic collapse of capitalism. In a sense, socialism will not be an automatic end–result of the development of capitalism, because the coming revolution can only be accomplished by a proletariat impregnated by socialist consciousness representing not only misery and moral degradation but also higher learning and even higher moral standards developed in its organisations during the struggle against capitalism. In Kautsky's opinion the party of the working class was in the possession of the most scientific knowledge about society and its development. Scientific socialism was indipensable to the labour movement. It united the proletariat in its struggle, and it coud fulfil this function most effectively by proving the necessity of the abolition of capitalism and the inevitability of the socialist goal. According to Kautsky, science cannot, however, dictate any goals of action to a socialist movement. It would be wrong in principle to deduce any such goals or ideals from the scientific analysis of society. Despite his strong emphasis on the will and conscious activity of the proletariat, as indispensable preconditions for the coming revolution, Kautsky's conclusions were deterministic: the very same development of capitalism that was expected to lead to an increasing polarisation of bourgeois society was just as automatically and inevitably expected to create the executor of the revolution, a revolutionary, socialist working class.

There is a seeming paradox in Kautsky's discussion of the relation between scientific socialism and the working class. First, the formation of a revolutionary working class is thought to be an automatic and unproblematic result of the development of capitalism. Second, Kautsky, followed by Lenin, definitely presumed that within the working class there could not develop a socialist revolutionary consciousness all by itself. The proletariat could only become conscious of its immediate economic interests (its spontaneous consciousness was, Lenin claimed, mostly trade-unionistic) and these particular interests might even be opposed to the general genuine interest of the proletariat, the establishment of a socialist society. It was then the task of the Social Democrats in possession of scientific socialism to assist the proletariat, to school and to organise it, and to make it conscious of its genuine interests and historical mission. Scientific socialism then both becomes redundant in its relation to the proletarian movement, because there cannot be any doubt about the future development of a revolutionary socialist working class, and it is presumed to be the necessary constituent of the revolutionary movement, because first socialist intellectuals (Kautsky) or professional revolutionaries (Lenin) bring an insight of the inevitability of the socialist goal into the labour movement.

As has already been pointed out, Mohl's identification of an objectivistic theory of revolution in Marx's *Capital* is problematic. Even if one can recognise an immiseration thesis in Marx's discussion of the fate of the working class under capital accumulation, it has been suggested in this study that this discussion should be interpreted in another context. It is in general highly problematic to interpret Marx's *Capital* as including any theory of revolution, at all, as there is no analysis of the conditions determining the development of socialist consciousness of the wage workers.

Marx's analysis did not simply introduce other standards into his critique of bourgeois society, normative standards of actual emancipatory movements, as suggested by Lohmann's interpretation. Marx's discussion of the fate of the working class under capital accumulation is rather directed at the claim of a reasonable society as presented by classical political economy and its predecessor, natural rights theory. Bourgeois society does not keep its promise of a natural and reasonable society guaranteeing the general well-being of the greatest number and the human existence of its members. By showing that while developing according to its immanent laws capitalism continuously creates a relative overpopulation and threatens to deprive the wage workers of their very means of existence, Marx in a sense concluded his critique of political economy, a critique in which the normative standards of the very bourgeois society are directed against this society. Thus in interpreting Marx as having predicted the continuous immiseration of the working class in capitalism and as having made it a cornerstone of his theory of revolution, Marxism certainly miscomprehended Marx's critical intention, but still it cannot be denied that even to Marx the brutality and the degradation of the life situation of wage workers showed in a most drastic way that capitalism must give way to a higher social formation.

Even though one were to admit that Mohl's characterisation of the role and function of Marx's critical theory as a kind of enlightened discussion partner of practical emancipatory movement obviously grasps an essential feature of Marx's critique of political economy, one can still claim that there are important theoretical reasons for Marx to identify the subject of revolution with the proletariat. In Mohl's interpretation Marx's critical theory is identical to Marx's critique of reification. It does not identify the subject of the revolution with the proletariat because the reification of social relations can in principle be experienced by all the members of a bourgeois society. (See Mohl 1981, 117—120.) It can, on the contrary, be claimed that it is the critique of reification that definitely identifies the general human emancipation with the emancipation of the proletariat in Marx's thinking. Marx's discussion of the fate of the working class, and his determination of the wage worker as representing absolute poverty, are an integral part of his critique of reification, too.

Marx's analysis of the dual nature of a commodity and of labour power resulted in the recognition of the turning upside down of all social relations of which money and capital are further expressions. According to Marx in a society of commodity production private labour is only transformed into social labour through exchange. Because a necessary precondition of this transformation is that the use value of a specific commodity (money) becomes the manifestation of the value of all other commodities, all the social relations between the producers take the form of relations between things:

> "Das geheimnisvolle der Warenform besteht also einfach darin, dass sie den Menschen die gesellschaftlichen Charaktere ihrer eignen Arbeit als gegenständliche Charaktere der Arbeitsprodukte selbst, als gesellschaftliche Natureigenschaften dieser Dinge zurückspiegelt, daher auch das gesellschaftliche Verhältnis der Produzenten zur Gesamtarbeit als ein ausser ihnen existierendes gesellschaftliches Verhältnis von Gegenständen. Durch dies Quidproquo werden die Arbeitsprodukte Waren, sinnlich übersinnliche oder gesellschaftliche Dinge." (MEW 23, 86).

Due to the analysis of the value form of a commodity, the experience of reification described in *Ökonomisch—philosophische Manuskripte* as the alienation of labour or the self-alienation of the human species is finally explained in *Capital*. The analysis of the 'national economic state of affairs' (bourgeois society) cannot start with the concept of labour and the alienation of labour, because in bourgeois society labour takes a specific value form and, consequently, neither richness nor social relations appear as they are in reality. The analysis of the dual nature of labour makes it possible to comprehend why the products of labour take a thing-like character in relation to the very producers; the social totality is not constituted by the conscious actions of its members. The fable of simple commodity production in which the producers calculate their labour time used to produce commodities and in which they thus consciously constitute their mutual social relations is seriously wrong:

> "Die Menschen beziehen also ihre Arbeitsprodukte nicht aufeinander als Werte, weil diese Sachen ihnen als bloss sachliche Hüllen gleichartig menschlicher Arbeit gelten. Umgekehrt. Indem sie ihre verschiedenartigen Produkte einander im Austausch als Werte gleichsetzen, setzen sie ihre verschiednen Arbeiten einander als menschliche Arbeit gleich. Sie wissen das nicht, aber sie tun es. Es steht daher dem Werte nicht auf der Stirn geschrieben, was er ist. Der Wert verwandelt vielmehr jedes Arbeitsprodukt in eine gesellschaftliche Hieroglyphe." (MEW 23, 88).

In Marx's manuscript of 1861—63, a prework of *Capital*, the concept of capital as a 'value increasing its value' is still in some sense undeveloped. Partly for this reason the manuscript is especially interesting. In the manuscript Marx was still discussing both the different form of surplus value production and the reproduction of capital simultaneously. In analysing the reproduction of capital Marx was constantly emphasising that the material means of the existence of the worker, the means of the objectification of his labour power, are in alien hands, subordinated under an alien will. In this sense the wage worker is a representative of absolute poverty:

> "Er (der Arbeiter − J.G.) ist als solcher, seinem Begriff nach, Pauper, als die Personification und der Träger dieses für sich, von seiner Gegenständlichkeit isolirten Vermögens." (MEGA II 3.1, 35).

And further:

> "Damit er gezwungen ist, sein Arbeitsvermögen statt einer Waare, worin sich seine Arbeit vergegenständlicht, zu verkaufen (. . .) dazu ist vorausgesetzt, dass die gegenständlichen Bestimmungen zur Verwirklichung seines Arbeitsvermögens, die Bedingungen zur Vergegenständlichung seiner Arbeit fehlen, abhanden gekommen sind, und vielmehr als Welt des Reichtums, des gegenständlichen Reichtums einer fremden Willen unterthan, ihm als Eigenthum der Waarenbesitzer in der Circulation fremd gegenüberstehn, als fremdes Eigenthum." (MEGA II 3.1, 32).

Because the conditions of the objectifiction of his labour power are in alien hands, the worker is bound to get poorer:

> "Er muss sich vielmehr verarmen, indem die schöpferische Kraft seiner Arbeit als Kraft des Capitals, als *fremde Macht* sich ihm gegenüber etablirt. Er entäussert sich der Arbeit als Productivkraft des Reichtums; das *Capital* eignet sie sich als solche an. (. . .) Dem Arbeiter gegenüber *wird* also die Productivität seiner Arbeit *fremde Macht*, überhaupt seine Arbeit, soweit sie nicht *Vermögen* sondern Bewegung, *wirkliche* Arbeit ist; das Capital umgekehrt verwerthet sich selbst durch *Aneignung fremder Arbeit."* (MEGA II 3.1, 143).

In this manuscript Marx emphasised that there is a fundamental difference between the material means of production and their capital form: capital ist not just equal to the means and instruments of production. Even though the conditions of the objectification of labour power seem to be opposed to the worker in their transhistorical capacity of material means of production, they do in fact subordinate the living labour power only insofar as they take the specific social form of capital:

> "Der Werth, die vergegenständlichte Arbeit bekommt diess Verhältnis zur lebendigen Arbeit nur so weit ihm das Arbeits*vermögen* als solches gegenübersteht, d.h. also andererseits wieder, so weit die *gegenständlichen Bedingungen* der Arbeit − . . . − ihm selbst in getrennter Selbständigkeit, unter der Controlle eines fremden Willens, gegenüberstehen. Obgleich daher Arbeitsmittel und Material als solche nicht Capital sind, erscheinen sie selbst als *Capital*, weil ihre Selbständigkeit, ihre selbstische Existenz gegenüber dem Arbeiter und daher die Arbeit selbst ihrem Dasein eingewachsen ist." (MEGA II 3.1, 86).

In analysing the value increase process Marx stated that the commodity labour power has a specific and peculiar use value: it produces a new value. As a consequence, in selling his labour power the wage worker gives away to the buyer the right to consume his commodity in a way similar as the seller of any commodity. Labour power is, however, a specific kind of commodity as it cannot be separated from the personality of the worker. The worker has to enter the process of its consumption together with the commodity he has exchanged:

"Da aber die Arbeit zugleich Lebensäusserung des Arbeiters selbst, Bethätigung seiner eignen persönlichen Fertigkeit und Fähigkeit ist — eine Bethätigung, die von seinem Willen abhängt, zugleich Willensäusserung desselben ist — überwacht der Capitalist den Arbeiter, controllirt die Bethätigung des Arbeitsvermögens als eine ihm gehörige Action." (MEGA II 3.1, 83).

An important conclusion follows from the above argument:

". . . zeigt ein Phänomen, das in seinem Resultat und in seiner Bedingungen gänzlich fremd ist, nicht nur den Gesetzen der einfachen Circulation, sondern ihr auch zu widersprechen scheint. Erstens ändert sich die sociale Position von Verkäufer und Käufer in dem Productionsprocess selbst. Der Käufer wird der Commandant des Verkäufers, soweit dieser mit seiner Person als Arbeiter in den Consumptionsprocess des Käufers selbst eingeht. Es wird ausser dem einfachen Austauschprocess ein Herrschafts— und Dienverhältnis, dass sich aber von allen anderen historischen Verhältnissen dieser Art dadurch unterscheidet, dass es nur aus der spezifischen Natur der Waare folgt, die der Verkäufer verkauft,. . ." (MEGA II 3.1, 93—94).

In this study it has been argued that Marx's discussion of the fate of the working class under capital accumulation should be understood as an essential conclusion of his critique of political economy. Now the same conclusion could be formulated as follows: Marx's thesis about the insecurity and the degradation of the life situation of the wage worker is an integral part of his critique of reification, too. The very starting point for his analysis of capital is that the wage worker represents absolute poverty while he is deprived of the material means of objectification of his labour power. In the form of capital these means are opposed to living labour as an alien power, as a power commanding his own productive activity. To Marx the cyclical increase in a relative overpopulation, the growing rate of unemployment, shows in a drastic manner the real character of capital as an alien power; the material conditions of the objectification of living labour, the very means of the existence of the wage worker, are in the form of capital conditions of which he is not a master.

Now, Marx was careful to stress that it is only in the form of capital that the means and substance of the objectification of labour power become that kind of an alien power. Otherwise the process would be irreversible. But it is of equal importance that in the means and substance of the productive activity of the labour power, labour has, in fact, been materialised; they represent former objectified — dead — labour. The historical mission to end the prehistory of mankind belongs to the proletariat — even if it does not recognise this itself — because in a way the reification of the social relations is its own produce. It is the labour of the wage worker that has been materialised in the use value of commodities and objectified in the value of commodities. It is the relation of the labour of the individual worker to the total social labour that takes an objectified, independent form of relations between things. And the productive powers of capital are in fact nothing but the productive powers of living labour only temporarily alienated from it. And as such they can in principle be returned to what they in reality are, the capacities and abilities of living labour.

Because of his redefinition of the concept of labour Marx's critique of capitalism implicitly proposes a non-metaphysical solution to the question of the producibility of history. As pointed out by Kittsteiner (1980) Marx demystified an idea common to the philosophy of Enlightenment which claimed that in acting according to their own interests or purposes − often against each other − men unintentionally and unconsciously realise a hidden plan or a reasonable goal in history. This idea was expressed, for instance, in Kant's metaphor of 'nature's purpose' or in Smith's 'invisible hand.' By introducing his dual conception of labour Marx both preserved the idea that men make their own history and that history is by nature alien, realising a goal which is not intended by the individual actors. The use values of commodities are a product of a specific purposive activity of man which, in Marx's understanding, is by nature transhistorical. But because labour power takes the form of a commodity, a value form, its products have a specific thing-like character and the relations of the commodity producers have become reified. Men are subordinated under the independent, alien character of the products of their own labour. Thus they are not the real subjects of their history.

In Marx's communism − beyond reification − this prehistory of mankind would come to an end. As Marx said, in the sphere of material production there would always remain an element of nature's compulsion and the productive activity of man can never become the arena of man's self-realisation; the real empire of freedom would only begin beyond the empire of necessity, beyond need and labour. But even within the empire of necessity men would consciously, and with human dignity, regulate their exchange of substance with nature; in the realm of freedom man's activity would be genuinely free. It would only have a goal in itself or − in other words − the goal of the activity would be included in the very process of action. (See MEW 25, 828.)

Kautsky's Marxism has no place for a critique of reification. In Kautsky's communism the anarchy of production has been overcome; man has learned to master the laws of his own social development, in the same sense as he has already learned to master the laws of nature. The development of society can be controlled just as natural forces are controlled:

> "An Stelle der anarchischen Waarenproduktion tritt die planmässig bewusste Organisation der gesellschaftlichen Produktion; die Herrschaft des Produkts über den Produzenten hat ein Ende. Der Mensch, der immer steigendem Masse Herr der Naturkräfte geworden, wird damit auch Herr der gesellschaftlichen Entwicklung." (Kautsky 1906c, 268).

Kautsky continued his characterisation of the principles of future society by quoting Engels' famous dictum:

> "Erst von da an werden die Menschen ihre Geschichte mit vollem Bewusstsein selbst machen, . . . erst von da werden die von ihnen in Bewegung gesetzten, gesellschaftlichen Ursachen vorwiegend in stets steigendem Masse auch die von ihnen gewollten Wirkungen haben. *Es ist der Sprung der Menscheit aus dem Reich der Nothwendigkeit in das Reich der Freiheit.*" (Kautsky 1906c, 268; cf. also MEW 20, 264).

To Kautsky and Engels, then, communism would not mark the end of the prehistory of mankind, the end of reification, but the consciously regulated utilisation of the natural-like laws governing the development of human society. In Engels' words "die Gesetze ihres eignen gesellschaftlichen Tuns, . . . werden dann von den Menschen mit voller Sachkenntnis angewandt und damit beherrscht" (MEW 20, 264). In a planned socialist society social causes would finally have the intended causes once the societal laws were recognised and mastered, but still the social activity of man would be regulated by laws similar to those of nature. According to Engels' famous slogan, freedom is equal to the recognition of necessity (see MEW 20, 106).

Kautsky's and Engels' Marxism is closer to classical political economy than to Marx's critique of it. But the critical potency of Marx's theory of capitalism is no less dependent (and by no means less questionable) on the classical formulation of the essential social issue of modern society expressed in the Philosophy of Enlightenment. Marx's critique of reification would maintain its critical potency if it would still be reasonable to claim that there is a hidden plan in history realising the human existence of man. Marx's idea of a free association of producers would only be convincing if history were a result of the objectification of the principle of labour, of the perfectification of the purposive, productive activity of socialised man or the human species.

BIBLIOGRAPHY

Alter, I. (1930): *Demokratija protiv revolucia. Učenie Kautskogo o revolucii.* Moskva: Izd. Kommunističeskoi Akademii.

Arato, Andrew (1973—74): The Second International. A Reexamination. *Telos 18*, pp. 2—52.

Backhaus, Hans-Georg (1974): Materialen zur Rekonstruktion der Marxschen Werttheorie. In *Gesellschaft. Beiträge zur Marxschen Theorie 1.* Frankfurt am Main: Suhrkamp Verlag.

Backhaus, Hans-Georg (1975): Materialen zur Rekonstruktion der Marxschen Werttheorie 2. In *Gesellschaft. Beiträge zur Marxschen Theorie 3.* Frankfurt am Main: Suhrkamp Verlag.

Backhaus, Hans-Georg (1978): Materialen zur Rekonstruktion der Marxschen Werttheorie 3. In *Gesellschaft. Beiträge zur Marxschen Theorie 11.* Frankfurt am Main: Suhrkamp Verlag.

Backhaus, Hans-Georg (1981): Om forholdet mellem det "logiske" og det "historiske" i Marx' kritik af den politiske økonomi. *Kurasje 27/28*, pp. 119—165.

B(ebel), A(ugust) (1891—92): Zum Erfurter Parteitag. *Die Neue Zeit*, 1. Bd., pp. 33—36.

Bernstein, Eduard (1896—97a): Allgemeines über Utopismus und Eklektizismus. *Die Neue Zeit*, 1. Bd., pp. 164—171.

Bernstein, Eduard (1896—97b): Eine Theorie der Gebiete und Grenzen des Kollektivismus. *Die Neue Zeit*, 1. Bd., pp. 204—213.

Bernstein, Eduard (1896—97c): Der Gegenwärtige Stand der industriellen Entwicklung in Deutschland. *Die Neue Zeit*, 1. Bd., pp. 303—311.

Bernstein, Eduard (1896—97d): Die neue Entwicklung der Agrarverhältnisse in England. *Die Neue Zeit*, 1. Bd., pp. 772—783.

Bernstein, Eduard (1896—97e): Die sozialpolitische Bedeutung von Raum und Zahl. *Die Neue Zeit*, 2. Bd., pp. 100—107.

Bernstein, Eduard (1897—98a): Der Sozialismus und die gewerbliche Arbeit der Jugend. *Die Neue Zeit*, 1. Bd., pp. 37—44.

Bernstein, Eduard (1897—98b): Der Kampf der Sozialdemokratie und die Revolution der Gesellschaft. 1. Polemisches, 2. Die Zusammenbruchstheorie und die Kolonialpolitik. *Die Neue Zeit*, 1. Bd., pp. 484—497, 548—557.

Bernstein, Eduard (1897—98c): Das realistische und das ideologische Moment im Sozialismus. *Die Neue Zeit*, 2. Bd., pp. 225—232, 388—395.

Bernstein, Eduard (1904): *Die Voraussetzungen des Sozialismus und die Aufgaben der Sozialdemokratie.* Stuttgart: J.H.W. Dietz Nachf.

Blumenberg, Werner (1960): *Karl Kautskys literarisches Werk. Eine bibliographische Übersicht.* 's-Gravenhage: Mouton.

Braionovič, S.M. (1979): Karl Kautsky. In I.S. Narskij, B.V. Bogdanov and M.T. Iovčuk (eds.): *Marksistkaja filosofija v XIX veke. Razvitie marksistkoi filosofii vo vtoroi polovine XIX veka. Kniga vtoraja.* Moskva: Nauka.

Braionovič, S.M. (1982): *Karl Kautsky — evolucija ego vozzrenii.* Moskva: Nauka.

Böhm-Bawerk, Eugen von (1973): Zum Abschluss des Marxschen Systems. In F. Eberle, (ed.): *Aspekte der Marxschen Theorie 1. Zur metodischen Bedeutung des 3. Bandes des "Kapital".* Frankfurt am Main: Suhrkamp Verlag.

Carlsen, J., H.-J. Schantz, L.-H. Schmidt and H.-J. Thomsen (1980): *Kapitalisme, behov og civilisation 1—2.* Aarhus: Modtryk.

Clarke, Simon (1982): *Marx, Marginalism and Modern Society. From Adam Smith to Max Weber.* London and Basingstoke: Macmillan Press.

Colletti, Lucio (1971): *Bernstein und der Marxismus der Zweiten Internationale.* Frankfurt am Main: Europeische Verlagsanstalt.

Donner, Ingrid (1978): "Das Kapital" von Karl Marx in der theoretischen Arbeit Kautskys während der zweiten Hälfte der achtziger Jahre. In... *unser Partei einen Sieg erringen. Studien zur Entstehungs- und Wirkungsgeschichte des "Kapitals" von Karl Marx.* Berlin: Die Wirtschaft.

Driver, C.H. (1950): John Locke. In F.J.C. Hearnshaw (ed.): *The Social and Political Ideas of Some English Thinkers of the Augustan Age A.D. 1650—1750.* New York: Barnes & Noble.

Ebbighausen, Rolf (ed.) (1974): *Monopol und Staat. Zur Marx-Rezeption in der Theorie des staatsmonopolistischen Kapitalismus.* Frankfurt am Main: Suhrkamp Verlag.

Engels, Friedrich (1971, MEW 13): Karl Marx. "Zur Kritik der Politischen Ökonomie" (Rezension). Pp. 468—477 in Karl Marx and Friedrich Engels: *Werke,* 13. Bd. Berlin: Dietz.

Engels, Friedrich (1969, MEW 19): Die Entwicklung des Sozialismus von der Utopie zur Wissenschaft. Pp. 189—228 in Karl Marx and Friedrich Engels: *Werke,* 19. Bd. Berlin: Dietz.

Engels, Friedrich (1971, MEW 20): Herrn Eugen Dürhings Umwälzung der Wissenschaft ("Anti-Dühring"). Pp. 5—303 in Karl Marx and Friedrich Engels: *Werke,* 20. Bd. Berlin: Dietz.

Engels, Friedrich (1970, MEW 22): Zur Kritik des sozialdemokratischen Programmentwurfs 1891. Pp. 225—240 in Karl Marx and Friedrich Engels: *Werke,* 22. Bd. Berlin: Dietz.

Engels, Friedrich (1970, MEW 22): Einleitung zu Karl Marx` "Klassenkämpfe in Frankreich 1848 bis 1850". Pp. 509—527 in Karl Marx and Friedrich Engels: *Werke,* 22. Bd. Berlin: Dietz.

Engels, Friedrich (1969, MEW 25): Vorwort zum Dritten Band des Kapitals. Pp. 7—30 in Karl Marx and Friedrich Engels: *Werke,* 25. Bd. Berlin: Dietz.

Engels, Friedrich (1969, MEW 25): Ergänzung und Nachtrag zum III. Buche des "Kapitals". Pp. 895—919 in Karl Marx and Friedrich Engels: *Werke,* 25. Bd. Berlin: Dietz.

Engels, Friedrich (1969, MEW 31): Ein Brief an Karl Marx 16.6.1867. Pp. 303—304 in Karl Marx and Friedrich Engels: *Werke,* 31. Bd. Berlin: Dietz.

Engels, Friedrich (1967, MEW 35): Ein Brief an Karl Kautsky 12.9.1882. Pp. 356—358 in Karl Marx and Friedrich Engels: *Werke,* 35. Bd. Berlin: Dietz.

Engels, Friedrich (1968, MEW 39): Ein Brief an Werner Sombart 11.3.1895. Pp. 427—429 in Karl Marx and Friedrich Engels: *Werke,* 39. Bd. Berlin: Dietz.

Fulda, Hans Friedrich (1978): Dialektik als Darstellungsmethode im "Kapital" von Marx. *Ajatus.* Yearbook of the Philosophical Society of Finland, vol. 37, pp. 180—216.

Furtschik, M. (1929): Kautskys "Marxismus". *Die Internationale,* Jg. 12, pp. 658—660, 678—685, 705—709, 774—781.

Gottschalch, Wilfried (1962): *Strukturveränderungen der Gesellschaft und politisches Handeln in der Lehre von Rudolf Hilferding.* Soziologische Abhandlungen, Heft 3. Berlin: Duncker & Humblot.

Groh, Dieter (1973): *Neqative Integration und revolutionärer Attentismus. Die deutsche Sozialdemokratie am Vorabend des Ersten Weltkrieges.* Frankfurt am Main, Berlin and Wien: Ullstein.

Gronow, Jukka (1975): Monopolin käsitteestä (On the concept of monopoly). *Tasa-arvon ja demokratian tutkimus TANDEM.* Tutkimusraportti, no. 6. Helsinki.

Gronow, Jukka (1978): Om tillkomsten av Lenins verk om imperialismen. *Nordisk Forum 17,* pp. 88—100.

Gustafsson, Bo (1969): *Marxism och revisionism. Eduard Bernsteins kritik av marxismen och dess idéhistoriska förutsättningar.* Ekonomisk-historiska studier 4. Uppsala: Svenska bokförlaget.

Habermas, Jürgen (1967): *Theorie und Praxis.* Sozialphilosophische Studien. Neuwied am Rhein and Berlin: Luchterhand.

Habermas, Jürgen (1981): *Theorie des kommunikativen Handelns. Handlungsrationalität und gesellschaftliche Rationalisierung.* 1−2 Bd. Frankfurt am Main: Suhrkamp Verlag.

Haug, W.F. (1974): *Vorlesungen zur Einführung ins "Kapital".* Köln: Pahl-Rugenstein.

Hilferding, Rudolf (1902−03): Der Funktionswechsel des Schutzzolles. Tendenz der modernen Handelspolitik. *Die Neue Zeit,* 2. Bd., pp. 274−281.

Hilferding, Rudolf (1968): *Das Finanzkapital.* I−II Bd. Frankfurt am Main: Europeische Verlagsanstalt.

Hilferding, Rudolf (1973a): *Organisierter Kapitalismus. Referat und Diskussion.* Sozialökonomische Studientexte 10. Rotdruck.

Hilferding, Rudolf (1973b): Böhm-Bawerks Marx-Kritik. In F. Eberle (ed.): *Aspekte der Marxschen Theorie* 1. *Zur metodischen Bedeutung des 3. Bandes des "Kapital".* Frankfurt am Main: Suhrkamp Verlag.

Himmelmann, Gerhard (1978): Die Rolle der Werttheorie in Bernsteins Konzept der politischen Ökonomie. In H. Hiemann and T. Meyer (ed.): *Bernstein und der demokratische Sozialismus.* Berlin and Bonn: J.H.W. Dietz Nachf.

Hobson, John (1948): *Imperialism. A Study.* London: Georg Allen & Unwin.

Hochberger, Hunno (1974): Probleme einer materialistischen Bestimmung des Staates. In *Gesellschaft. Beiträge zur Marxschen Theorie 2.* Frankfurt am Main: Suhrkamp Verlag.

Hont, Istvan and Michael Ignatieff (1983): Needs and Justice in the Wealth of Nations: An Introductory Essay. In I. Hont and M. Ignatieff (eds.): *Wealth and Virtue. The Shaping of Political Economy in the Scottish Enlightenment.* Cambridge: Cambridge University Press.

Horowitz, David (1970): *Imperialismus und Revolution. Neue Fakten zur gegenwärtigen Geschichte.* Berlin.

Hühnlich, Reinhold (1981): *Karl Kautsky und der Marxismus der II. Internationale.* Schriftenreihe für Sozialgeschichte und Arbeiterbewegung, 22. Bd. Marburg: Verlag Arbeiterbewegung und Gesellschaftswissenschaft.

Il'enkov, E.V. (1980): *Leninskaja dialektika i metafizika pozitivizma.* Moskva: Politizdat.

Jordan, Dirk (1974a): Der Monopolbegriff im System der Kritik der politischen Ökonomi. In R. Ebbighausen (ed.): *Monopol und Staat. Zur Marx-Rezeption in der Theorie des staatsmonopolistischen Kapitalismus.* Frankfurt am Main: Suhrkamp Verlag.

Jordan, Dirk (1974b): Der Imperialismus als monopolistischer Kapitalismus. Zur Imperialismus − Analyse Lenins als Basis der Theorie des staatsmonopolistischen Kapitalismus. In R. Ebbighausen (ed.): *Monopol und Staat. Zur Marx-Rezeption in der Theorie des staatsmonopolistischen Kapitalismus.* Frankfurt am Main: Suhrkamp Verlag.

Kautsky, Benedikt (ed.) (1955): *Friedrich Engels' Briefwechsel mit Karl Kautsky.* Wien: Danitsia.

Kautsky, John H. (1961): J.A. Schumpeter and Karl Kautsky. Parallel Theories of Imperialism. *Midwest Journal of Political Science 5,* pp. 101−128.

Kautsky, Karl (1893−94): Ein sozialdemokratischer Katechismus. *Die Neue Zeit,* pp. 361−369, 402−410.

Kautsky, Karl (1894−95a): Die Intelligenz und die Sozialdemokratie. *Die Neue Zeit,* 2 Bd., pp. 10−16, 43−49, 74−80.

Kautsky, Karl (1894−95b): Unser neuestes Agrarprogramm. *Die Neue Zeit,* 2. Bd., pp. 557−565, 586−594, 620−624.

Kautsky, Karl (1897−98): Ältere und neuere Kolonialpolitik. *Die Neue Zeit,* 1. Bd., pp. 769−781, 801−816.

Kautsky, Karl (1899a): *Bernstein und das sozialdemokratische Programm. Eine Antikritik.* Stuttgart: J.H.W. Dietz Nachf.

Kautsky, Karl (1899b): Bernstein's Streitschrift. I–III. *Vorwärts,* Nr. 64, 65, 66; 16., 17., 18.3.1899.

Kautsky, Karl (1899c): *Die Agrarfrage. Eine Uebersicht über die Tendenzen der modernen Landwirtschaft und die Agrarpolitik der Sozialdemokratie.* Stuttgart: J.H.W. Dietz Nachf.

Kautsky, Karl (1899d): Nochmals Bernsteins Streitschrift. 1–3. *Vorwärts,* Nr. 82, 84, 85; 8., 11., 12.4.1899.

Kautsky, Karl (1900): Deutschland, England und Weltpolitik. I–II. *Vorwärts,* Nr. 105, 107; 8., 10.5.1900.

Kautsky, Karl (1900–01): Problematischer gegen wissenschaftlichen Sozialismus. *Die Neue Zeit,* 2. Bd., pp. 355–361.

Kautsky, Karl (1902–03a): Die Drei Krisen des Marxismus. *Die Neue Zeit,* 1. Bd., pp. 723–731.

Kautsky, Karl (1902–03b): Klassenintresse – Sonderintresse – Gemeinintresse. *Die Neue Zeit,* 2. Bd., pp. 240–245, 261–274.

Kautsky, Karl (1902–03c): Was nun? *Die Neue Zeit,* 2. Bd., pp. 389–398.

Kautsky, Karl (1902–03d): Der Dresdener Parteitag. *Die Neue Zeit,* 2. Bd., pp. 809–815.

Kautsky, Karl (1903): Die Handelsverträge und der Zolltariff. *Vorwärts,* Nr. 130; 7.6.1903.

Kautsky, Karl (1904): Vorrede. In K. Marx: *Theorien über den Mehrwert.* Aus dem nachgelassenen Manuskript "Zur Kritik der politischen Ökonomie". Ed. by Karl Kautsky. Erster Band. *Die anfänge der Theorie vom Mehrwert bis Adam Smith.* Stuttgart: J.H.W. Dietz Nachf.

Kautsky, Karl (1904–05): Patriotismus, Krieg und Sozialdemokratie. 1. Der Patriotismus, 2. Der Krieg. *Die Neue Zeit,* 2. Bd., pp. 343–348, 364–371.

Kautsky, Karl (1905–06): Mein Verrat an der russischen Revolution. *Die Neue Zeit,* 2. Bd., pp. 854–860.

Kautsky, Karl (1905): Vorrede. In K. Marx: *Theorien über den Mehrwert.* Aus dem nachgelassenen Manuskript "Zur Kritik der politischen Ökonomie". Ed. by Karl Kautsky. Zweiter Band. *David Richardo.* Stuttgart: J.H.W. Dietz Nachf.

Kautsky, Karl (1906a): *Das Erfurter Programm in seinem grundsätzlichen Theil erläutert.* Stuttgart: J.H.W. Dietz Nachf.

Kautsky, Karl (1906b): *Ethik und materialistische Gesichtsauffassung.* Stuttgart: J.H.W. Dietz Nachf.

Kautsky, Karl (1906c): *Karl Marx' Oekonomische Lehren.* Stuttgart: J.H.W. Dietz Nachf.

Kautsky, Karl (1907a): Die Nutzen der Kolonien für die Arbeiter. I–III. Vorwärts, Nr. 11, 13, 17; 13., 16., 20.1.1907.

Kautsky, Karl (1907b): *Sozialismus und Kolonialpolitik. Eine Auseinandersetzung.* Berlin: Buchhandlung Vorwärts.

Kautsky, Karl (1907–08a): Zum 1. Mai. *Die Neue Zeit,* 2. Bd., pp. 113–115.

Kautsky, Karl (1907–08b): Verelendung und Zusammenbruch. *Die Neue Zeit,* 2. Bd., pp. 540–551, 607–612.

Kautsky, Karl (1908–09): Sozialistische Kolonialpolitik. *Die Neue Zeit,* 2. Bd., pp. 33–43.

Kautsky, Karl (1909a): Ein Brief über Marx and Mach. *Der Kampf. Sozialdemokratische Monatschrift,* 2. Bd. Wien: Georg Emmerig, pp. 451–452.

Kautsky, Karl (1909b): *Der Weg zur Macht. Politische Betrachtungen über das Hineinwachsen in die Revolution.* Berlin: Buchhandlung Vorwärts.

Kautsky, Karl (1910): Vorrede. In K. Marx: *Theorien über den Mehrwert.* Aus dem nachgelassenen Manuskript "Zur Kritik der politischen Ökonomie". Ed. by Karl Kautsky. Dritter Band. *Von Ricardo zur Vulgärökonomie.* Stuttgart: J.H.W. Dietz Nachf.

Kautsky, Karl (1910–11): Finanzkapital und Krisen. *Die Neue Zeit,* 1. Bd., pp. 764–772, 797–804, 838–846, 874–883.

Kautsky, Karl (1911a): *Parlamentarismus und Demokratie.* Stuttgart: J.H.W. Dietz Nachf.

Kautsky, Karl (1911b): *Handelspolitik und Sozialdemokratie. Populäre Darstellung der handelspolitischen Streitfragen.* Berlin: Buchhandlung Vorwärts, Paul Singer.

Kautsky, Karl (1911c): Demokratische Probleme. I Massen und Führer. II Staat und Partei. *Vorwärts,* Nr. 56, 57; 7., 8.3.1911.

Kautsky, Karl (1912–13): Der jungste Radikalismus. *Die Neue Zeit,* 1. Bd., pp. 436–446.

Kautsky, Karl (1913–14): Der Imperialismus. *Die Neue Zeit,* 2. Bd., pp. 908–922.

Kautsky, Karl (1914): *Der politische Massenstreik. Ein Beitrag zur Geschichte der Massenstreikdiskussionen innerhalb der deutschen Sozialdemokratie.* Berlin: Buchhandlung Vorvärts, Paul Singer.

Kautsky, Karl (1915a): *Nationalstaat, imperialistischer Staat und Staatenbund.* Nürnberg: Verlag der Fränkischen Verlagsanstalt.

Kautsky, Karl (1915b): *Die Internationalität und der Krieg.* Berlin: Buchhandlung Vorwärts, Paul Singer.

Kautsky, Karl (1916–17a): Der imperialistische Krieg. *Die Neue Zeit,* 1. Bd., pp. 449–454, 473–487.

Kautsky, Karl (1916–17b): Imperialismus und reaktionäre Masse. *Die Neue Zeit,* 2. Bd., pp. 102–109.

Kautsky, Karl (1916–17c): Die Aussichten der russischen Revolution. *Die Neue Zeit,* 2. Bd., pp. 9–20.

Kautsky, Karl (1917): Die Erhebung der Bolschewiki. *Leipziger Volkszeitung,* 15.11.1917.

Kautsky, Karl (1918): *Die Diktatur des Proletariats.* Wien: Volksbuchhandlung, I. Brand.

Kautsky, Karl (1919a): *Die historische Leistung von Karl Marx. Zum 25. Todestag des Meisters.* Berlin: Buchhandlung Vorwärts, Paul Singer.

Kautsky, Karl (1919b): *Die Sozialisierung und die Arbeiterräte. Bericht, erstattet dem 2. Kongress der Arbeiter-, Soldaten- und Bauernräte Deutschlands am 14. April 1919.* Wien: Volksbuchhandlung, I. Brand.

Kautsky, Karl (1919c): *Terrorismus und Kommunismus. Ein Beitrag zur Naturgeschichte der Revolution.* Berlin: Verlag Neues Vaterland.

Kautsky, Karl (1920): Eduard Bernstein. *Die Weltbühne, Wochenschrift für Politik – Kunst – Wirtschaft.* XVI Jg., 2. Berlin: Verlag der Weltbühne. pp. 43–49.

Kautsky, Karl (1924): Karl Kautsky. In F. Meiner (ed.): *Die Volkswirtschaftslehre in Selbstdarstellung.* Leipzig: Felix Meiner.

Kautsky, Karl (1927): *Die materialistische Geschichtsauffassung.* 1–2. Bd. Berlin: J.H.W. Dietz Nachf.

Kautsky, Karl (1960): *Erinnerungen und Erörterungen. Materialen für eine Autobiographie.* Ed. by B. Kautsky. Gravenhage: Mouton.

Kautsky, Karl (1968a): Das Görlitzer Programm. In A. Langer (ed.): *Karl Kautsky. Texte zu den Programmen der deutschen Sozialdemokratie 1891–1925.* Köln: Verlag Jacob Hegner.

Kautsky, Karl (1968b): Grundsätze und Forderungen der Sozialdemokratie. Erläuterungen zum Erfurter Programm. In A. Langer (ed.): *Karl Kautsky. Texte zu den Programmen der deutschen Sozialdemokratie 1891–1925.* Köln: Verlag Jacob Hegner.

Kautsky, Karl (Nachlass A 48): Einleitung zu "Handelspolitik und Sozialdemokratie" (the Russian Edition 1906). Manuscript. *Kautsky Nachlass A 48.*

Kittsteiner, Heinz-Dieter (1980): *Naturabsicht und unsichtbare Hand. Zur Kritik des geschichtsphilosophischen Denkens.* Frankfurt am Main, Berlin and Wien: Ullstein.

Korsch, Karl (1967): *Karl Marx.* Frankfurt am Main and Wien: Europeische Verlagsanstalt and Europa Verlag.

Korsch, Karl (1971a): Die materialistische Geschichtsauffassung. In K. Korsch: *Die materialistische Geschichtsauffassung und andere Schriften*. Ed. by E. Gerlach. Frankfurt am Main: Europeische Verlagsanstalt.

Korsch, Karl (1971b): *Marxismus und Philosophie*. Ed. by E. Gerlach. Frankfurt am Main and Wien: Europeische Verlagsanstalt and Europa Verlag.

Kraus, Rainer (1978): *Die Imperialismusdebatte zwischen Wladimir I. Lenin und Karl Kautsky. Eine Vergleichende Analyse ihrer Theorien*. Frankfurt am Main, Bern and Las Vegas: Peter Lang.

Lange, Ernst Michael (1980): *Das Prinzip Arbeit*. Frankfurt am Main, Berlin and Wien: Ullstein.

Leineweber, Bernd (1977): *Intellektuelle Arbeit und kritische Theorie*. Frankfurt am Main: Verlag Neue Kritik.

Lenin, V.I. (1967, SW 1): What is to be done? Pp. 97–256 in V.I. Lenin: *Selected Works*, vol. 1. Moscow: Progress Publishers.

Lenin, V.I. (1967, SW 1): Two Tactics of Social-Democracy in the Democratic Revolution. Pp. 455–566 in V.I. Lenin: *Selected Works*, vol. 1. Moscow: Progress Publishers.

Lenin, V.I. (1967, SW 1): The War and Russian Social-Democracy. Pp. 655–663 in V.I. Lenin: *Selected Works*, vol. 1. Moscow: Progress Publishers.

Lenin, V.I. (1967, SW 1): Imperialism, the Highest Stage of Capitalism. Pp. 673–777 in V.I. Lenin: *Selected Works*, vol. 1. Moscow: Progress Publishers.

Lenin, V.I. (1967, SW 2): The Tasks of the Proletariat in Our Revolution. Pp. 21–53 in V.I. Lenin: *Selected Works*, vol. 2. Moscow: Progress Publishers.

Lenin, V.I. (1967, SW 2): The State and Revolution. Pp. 263–360 in V.I. Lenin: *Selected Works*, vol. 2. Moscow: Progress Publishers.

Lenin, V.I. (1967, SW 3): The Proletarian Revolution and the Renegade Kautsky. Pp. 39–127 in V.I. Lenin: *Selected Works*, vol. 3. Moscow: Progress Publishers.

Lenin, V.I. (1967, SW 3): "Left-wing" Communism – an Infantile Disorder. Pp. 333–420 in V.I. Lenin: *Selected Works*, vol. 3. Moscow: Progress Publishers.

Lenin, V.I. (1963, CW 3): The Development of Capitalism in Russia. In V.I. Lenin: *Collected Works*, vol. 3. Moscow: Progress Publishers.

Lenin, V.I. (1964, CW 21): Socialism and War. The Attitude of the R.S.L.P. Towards the War. Pp. 295–338 in V.I. Lenin: *Collected Works*, vol. 21. Moscow: Progress Publishers.

Lenin, V.I. (1974, CW 22): Preface to N. Bukharin's Pamphlet, Imperialism and the World Economy. Pp. 103–107 in V.I. Lenin: *Collected Works*, vol. 22. Moscow: Progress Publishers.

Lenin, V.I. (1974, CW 39): Notebooks on Imperialism. In V.I. Lenin,: *Collected Works*, vol. 39. Moscow: Progress Publishers.

Lenin, V.I. (1967): *Materialism and Empirio-criticism. Critical Comments on a Reactionary Philosophy*. Moscow: Progress Publishers.

Leontev, L.A. (1969): *Leninskaja teorija imperializma*. Moskva: Nauka.

Lichtheim, Georg (1964): *Marxism. A Historical and Critical Study*. London: Routledge and Kegan Paul.

Linder, Marc (1973): *Reification and the Consciousness of the Critics of Political Economy. Studies in the Development of Marx' Theory of Value*. Copenhagen: Rhodos.

Locke, John (1965): *Two Treatises on Government*. A Critical edition with an Introduction and apparatus criticus by Peter Laglett. New York, Scanborough and London: Mentorbook.

Lohmann, Georg (1980): Gesellschaftskritik und normativer Maßstab. Überlegungen zu Marx. In A. Honneth and U. Jaeggi (eds.): *Arbeit, Handlung, Normativität. Theorien des historischen Materialismus 2*. Frankfurt am Main: Suhrkamp Verlag.

Lohmann, Georg (1984): "Wealth" as an Aspect of the Critique of Capital. In Rethinking Marx. *Argument – Sonderband AS 109*, pp. 86–90.

Luxemburg, Rosa (1963): *The Accumulation of Capital*. London: Routledge and Kegan Paul.
Luxemburg, Rosa (1970a): Sozialreform oder Revolution? In Rosa Luxemburg:*Politische Schriften*. Leipzig: Verlag Philipp Reclam.
Luxemburg, Rosa (1970b): Massenstreik, Partei, Gewerkschaften. In Rosa Luxemburg:*Politische Schriften*. Leipzig: Verlag Philipp Reclam.
Macpherson, C.B. (1972): *The Political Theory of Possessive Individualism*. London, Oxford and New York: Oxford University Press.
Malthus, Thomas Robert (1970): *An Essay on the Principles of Population and A Summary View of the Principle of Population*. Harmondsworth: Penguin Books.
Mannheim, Karl (1960): *Ideology and Utopia. An Introduction to the Sociology of Knowledge*. London: Routledge & Kegan Paul.
Marx, Karl (1867): *Das Kapital. Kritik der politischen Ökonomie*. Erster Band. Hamburg: Verlag von Otto Meisner.
Marx, Karl (1969): *Resultate des unmittelbaren Produktionsprozesses. Das Kapital*. I Buch. Der Produktionsprozess des Kapitals. VI Kapitel. Frankfurt am Main: Verlag Neue Kritik.
Marx, Karl (s.a.): *Grundrisse der Kritik der politischen Ökonomie*. Frankfurt am Main and Wien: Europeische Verlagsanstalt and Europa Verlag.
Marx, Karl (1968, MEW Erg. Bd. 1): Ökonomisch—philosophische Manuskripte aus dem Jahre 1844. Pp. 463–588 in Karl Marx and Friedrich Engels: *Werke*. Ergänzungsband. Erster Teil. Berlin: Dietz.
Marx, Karl (1970, MEW 1): Ein Brief an Ruge. September 1843. Pp. 343–346 in Karl Marx and Friedrich Engels: *Werke*, 1. Bd. Berlin: Dietz.
Marx, Karl (1970, MEW 1): Zur Judenfrage. Pp. 347–377 in Karl Marx and Friedrich Engels: *Werke*, 1. Bd. Berlin: Dietz.
Marx, Karl (1971, MEW 4): Das Elend der Philosophie. Pp. 63–182 in Karl Marx and Friedrich Engels: *Werke*, 4. Bd. Berlin: Dietz.
Marx, Karl (1970, MEW 6): Lohnarbeit und Kapital. Pp. 397–423 in Karl Marx and Friedrich Engels: *Werke*, 6. Bd. Berlin: Dietz.
Marx, Karl (1969, MEW 19): Kritik des Gothaer Programms. Pp. 11–32 in Karl Marx and Friedrich Engels: *Werke*, 19. Bd. Berlin: Dietz.
Marx, Karl (1969, MEW 19): Randglossen zu Adolph Wagners "Lehrbuch der politischen Ökonomie". Pp. 355–383 in Karl Marx and Friedrich Engels: *Werke*, 19. Bd. Berlin: Dietz.
Marx, Karl (1969, MEW 23): Das Kapital. Kritik der politischen Ökonomie. Erster Band. In Karl Marx and Friedrich Engels: *Werke*, 19. Bd. Berlin: Dietz.
Marx, Karl (1969, MEW 25): Das Kapital. Kritik der politischen Ökonomie. Dritter Band. In Karl Marx and Friedrich Engels: *Werke*, 25. Bd. Berlin: Dietz.
Marx, Karl (1973, MEW 26.1): Theorien über den Mehrwert. Erster Teil. In Karl Marx and Friedrich Engels: *Werke*, 26.1. Bd. Berlin: Dietz.
Marx, Karl (1974, MEW 26.3): Theorien über den Mehrwert. Dritter Teil. In Karl Marx and Friedrich Engels: *Werke*, 26.3. Bd. Berlin: Dietz.
Marx, Karl (1970, MEW 27): Ein Brief an Ludwig Feuerbach 11.8.1844. Pp. 425–428 in Karl Marx and Friedrich Engels: *Werke*, 27. Bd. Berlin: Dietz.
Marx, Karl (1970, MEW 29): Ein Brief an Ferdinand Lassalle 22.2.1858. Pp. 549–552 in Karl Marx and Friedrich Engels: *Werke*, 29. Bd. Berlin: Dietz.
Marx, Karl (1976, MEGA II, 3.1.): Zur Kritik der politischen Ökonomie (Manuskript 1861–63). In Karl Marx and Friedrich Engels: *Gesamtausgabe*. Zweite Abteilung, 3. Bd., 1.T. Berlin: Dietz.
Marx, Karl and Friedrich Engels (1969, MEW 2): Die heilige Familie oder Kritik der kritischen Kritik. Gegen Bruno Bauer und Konsorten. In Karl Marx and Friedrich Engels: *Werke*, 2. Bd. Berlin: Dietz.

Marx, Karl and Friedrich Engels (1969, MEW 3): Die Deutsche Ideologie. In Karl Marx and Friedrich Engels: *Werke*, 3. Bd. Berlin: Dietz.

Marx, Karl and Friedrich Engels (1971, MEW 4): Manifest der kommunistischen Partei. Pp. 459—493 in Karl Marx and Friedrich Engels: *Werke*, 4. Bd. Berlin: Dietz.

Mathias, Erich (1957): Kautsky und der Kautskyanismus. Die Funktion der Ideologie in der deutschen Sozialdemokratie vor den ersten Weltkrieg. In I. Fetscher (ed.): *Marx-Studien*. Zweite Folge. Tübingen: J.C.B. Mohr (Paul Siebeck).

Medick, Hans (1973): *Naturzustand und Naturgeschichte der bürgerlichen Gesellschaft*. Göttingen: Vandenhoeck und Ruprecht.

Mohl, Alexa (1979): ''Wissenschaftlicher Sozialismus'', was ist das? *Prokla 36*, pp. 77—109.

Mohl, Alexa (1981): *Verelendung und Revolution oder das Elend des Objektivismus*. Frankfurt am Main and New York: Campus Verlag.

Mohl, Alexa (1983): Karl Marx und die Selbstverständigung unserer Zeit über ihre Kämpfe und Wunsche. *Prokla 50*, pp. 59—77.

Musgrave, Г.A. (1976): Adam Smith on Public Finance and Distribution. In T. Wilson and A.S. Skinner (eds.): *The Market and the State. Essays in Honor of Adam Smith*. Oxford: Oxford University Press.

Negt, Oskar (1974): Marxismus als Legitimationswissenschaft. Zur Genese der stalinistischen Philosophie. In N. Bucharin and A. Deborin (eds.): *Kontroversen über dialektischen und mechanistischen Materialismus*. Frankfurt am Main: Suhrkamp Verlag.

Neusüss, Christel (1972): *Imperialismus und Weltmarktbewegung des Kapitals*. Erlangen: Politladen.

Nielsen, Kurt Aagaard (1980): Åndsarbejde og videnskabskritik. *Kurasje 23/24*, pp. 185—215.

Pannekoek, Anton (1911—12): Massenaktion und Revolution. *Die Neue Zeit*, 2. Bd., pp. 541—550, 589—593, 609—616.

Pannekoek, Anton (1912—13): Marxistische Theorie und revolutionäre Taktik. I—II. *Die Neue Zeit*, 1. Bd., pp. 272—281, 365—373.

Parvus (Alexander Helphand) (1895—96): Der Weltmarkt und die Agrarkrisis. *Die Neue Zeit*, 1. Bd., pp. 197—202, 276—283, 335—342, 514—526, 554—560, 621—631, 654—663, 747—758, 781—788, 818—827.

Parvus (Alexander Helphand) (1897): *Die Gewerkschaften und die Sozialdemokratie*. Dresden.

Parvus (Alexander Helphand) (1900—01a): Die Handelspolitik und die Doktrin. *Die Neue Zeit*, 1. Bd., pp. 580—589.

Parvus (Alexander Helphand) (1900—01b): Industriezölle und der Weltmarkt, *Die Neue Zeit*, 1. Bd., pp. 708—716, 772—784.

Parvus (Alexander Helphand) (1901): *Die Handelskrisis und die Gewerkshaften*. München.

Paul, Hans-Holger (1978): *Marx, Engels und die Imperialismus-Theorie der II. Internationale*. Hamburg: VSA-Verlag.

Pietilä, Veikko (1984): The Logical, the Historical and the Forms of Value — Once Again. *Argument — Sonderband AS 109*, pp. 62—67.

Plechanow, G. (1897—98): Bernstein und der Materialismus. *Die Neue Zeit*, 1. Bd., pp. 545—555.

Postone, Moishe (1978): Necessity, Labour, and Time: A Reinterpretation of the Marxian Critique of Capitalism. *Social Research 45*, pp. 739—788.

Postone, Moishe and Barbara Brick (1982): Critical Pessimism and the Limits of Traditional Marxism. *Theory and Society 11*, pp. 617—658.

Projekt Klassenanalyse (1972): Leninismus — neue Stufe des wissenschaftlichen Sozialismus? Zum Verhältnis von Marxscher Theorie, Klassenanalyse und revolutionärer Taktik bei W.I. Lenin. *Reihe Studien zur Klassenanalyse 2/1—2/2*. Westberlin: VSA.

Projekt Klassenanalyse (1976): *Kautsky. Marxistische Vergangenheit der SDP?* Westberlin: VSA.

Przeworski, Adam (1977): Proletariat into a Class: The Process of Class Formation from Karl Kautsky's The Class Struggle to Recent Controversies. *Politics & Society 7*, pp. 343–401.

Radek, Karl (1911–12): Zum unseren Kampf gegen den Imperialismus. I–II. *Die Neue Zeit, 2.* Bd., pp. 194–199, 233–241.

Reichelt, Helmut (1971): *Zur logischen Struktur des Kapitalbegriffs bei Karl Marx.* Frankfurt am Main and Wien: Europeische Verlagsanstalt and Europa Verlag.

Ricardo, David (1971): *On the Principles of Political Economy and Taxation.* Harmondsworth: Penguin Books.

Rosdolsky, Roman (1968): *Zur Entstehungsgeschichte des Marxschen "Kapital". Der Rohentwurf des Kapital 1857–1858.* 1–2. Bd. Frankfurt am Main: Europeische Verlagsanstalt.

Rosenberg, A. (1962): *Demokratie und Sozialismus. Zur politischen Geschichte der letzten 100 Jahre.* Frankfurt am Main: Europeische Verlagsanstalt.

Rotermundt, Rainer (1976): *Das Denken John Lockes. Zur Logik bürgerlichen Bewusstseins.* Frankfurt am Main: Campus Verlag.

Rozental, M.M. (1973): *Die dialektische Methode der politischen Ökonomie von Karl Marx.* Westberlin: Verlag das europeische Buch.

Rubin, I.I. (1973): *Studien zur Marxschen Werttheorie.* Frankfurt am Main: Europeische Verlagsanstalt.

Salvadori, Massimo (1979) *Karl Kautsky and the Socialist Revolution 1880–1938.* London: New Left Books.

Schanz, Hans-Jørgen (1974): *Til rekonstruktionen af kritikken af den politiske økonomis omfangslogiske status.* Aarhus: Modtryk.

Schanz, Hans-Jørgen (1981): *Traeck af behovsproblematikkens idehistorie med saerligt henblik på Marx og Engels.* Aarhus: Modtryk.

Scharrer, Manfred (1976): *Arbeiterbewegung im Obrigkeitsstaat. SDP und Gewerkschaft nach dem Sozialistengesetz.* Berlin: Rotbuch Verlag.

Schimkowsky, Reinhard (1974a): Exkurs über Hilferding: Vom Generalkartell zur Konzeption des organisierten Kapitalismus. In R. Ebbighausen (ed.): *Monopol und Staat. Zur Marx-Rezeption in der Theorie des staatsmonopolistischen Kapitalismus.* Frankfurt am Main: Suhrkamp Verlag.

Schimkowsky, Reinhard (1974b): Zur Marx-Rezeption bei Hilferding. Die Bestimmungen von Konkurrenz und Monopol im "Finanzkapital". In R. Ebbighausen (ed.): *Monopol und Staat. Zur Marx-Rezeption in der Theorie des staatsmonopolistischen Kapitalismus.* Frankfurt am Main: Suhrkamp Verlag.

Schubert, Joachim (1973): Die Theorie des staatsmonopolistischen Kapitalismus – Kritik der zentralen Aussagen. *Mehrwert 4*, pp. 1–102.

Schwarz, Winfried (1974): Das "Kapital im allgemeinen" und die "Konkurrenz" im ökonomischen Werk von Karl Marx. Zu Rosdolskys Fehlinterpretation der Gliederung des "Kapital". In *Gesellschaft. Beiträge zur Marxschen Theorie 1.* Frankfurt am Main: Suhrkamp Verlag.

Schwarz, Winfried (1980): *Von "Rohentwurf" zum "Kapital". Die Strukturgeschichte des Marxschen Hauptwerks.* Westberlin: Verlag das europeische Buch.

Sieferle, Rolf Peter (1979): *Die Revolution in der Theorie von Karl Marx.* Frankfurt am Main, Berlin and Wien: Ullstein.

Simmel, Georg (1900): *Die Philosophie des Geldes.* Leipzig: Duncker & Humblot.

Smith, Adam (1970): *The Wealth of Nations.* Books I–III. With an Introduction by Andrew Skinner. Harmondsworth: Penguin Books.

Smith, Adam (1979): *The Theory of Moral Sentiments.* The Glasgow Edition of the Works and Correspondence of Adam Smith. Ed. by D.D. Raphael and A.L. Macfie. Oxford: Clarendon Press.

Sohn-Rethel, Alfred (1972): *Geistige und körperliche Arbeit. Zur Theorie der gesellschaftlichen Synthesis*. Frankfurt am Main: Suhrkamp Verlag.

Sohn-Rethel, Alfred (1978): Gespräch über "die Genese der Ideen von Warenform und Denkform". In H.D. Dombrowski et al. (eds.): *Symposium Warenform − Denkform*. Frankfurt am Main: Suhrkamp Verlag.

Stapelfeldt, Gerhard (1979): *Das Problem des Anfangs in der Kritik der Politischen Ökonomie*. Frankfurt am Main and New York: Campus Verlag.

Steenson, Gary P. (1978): *Karl Kautsky 1854−1938. Marxism in the Classical Years*. Pittsburgh: University of Pittsburgh Press.

Steinberg, H-J. (1973): *Sozialismus und deutsche Sozialdemokratie. Zur Ideologie der Partei vor dem I. Weltkrieg*. Bonn and Bad Godesberg: Verlag für Litteratur und Zeitgeschehen.

Steinberg, H-J. (1978): Die Herausbildung des Revisionismus von Eduard Bernstein im Lichte des Briefwechsels Bernstein − Kautsky. In H. Heimann and T. Meyer (eds.): *Bernstein und der demokratische Sozialismus. Bericht über den wissenschaftlichen Kongress "Die historische Leistung und die aktuelle Bedeutung Eduard Bernsteins"*. Berlin and Bonn: J.H.W. Dietz Nachf.

Stephan, Cora (1974): Geld- und Staatstheorie in Hilferdings "Finanzkapital". Zum Verhältnis von ökonomischer Theorie und politischer Strategie. In *Gesellschaft. Beiträge zur Marxschen Theorie 2*. Frankfurt am Main: Suhrkamp Verlag.

Theunissen, Michael (1976): Die Aufhebung des Idealismus in der Spätphilosophie Schellings. *Philosophisches Jahrbuch im Auftrag der Görres − Gesellschaft*. 1. Halbband, 83. Jg., pp. 1−29.

Theunissen, Michael (1978): *Sein und Schein. Die kritische Funktion der Hegelschen Logik*. Frankfurt am Main: Suhrkamp Verlag.

Trotsky, L. (1921): *Terrorismi ja kommunismi* (Terrorism and communism). Kuopio: Savon kansan kirjapaino.

Tuchscheerer, W. (1968): *Bevor "Das Kapital" entstand*. Berlin: Akademie Verlag.

Tully, James (1980): *A Discourse on Property. John Locke and his Adversaries*. Cambridge: Cambridge University Press.

Wagner, Wolf (1976): *Die Verelendungstheorie − eine hilflose Kapitalismuskritik*. Frankfurt am Main: Fischer Taschenbuch Verlag.

Vasilevskij, E.G. (1969): *Razvitie vzgljadov V.I. Lenina na imperializm*. Moskva: Izd. Moskovskogo universiteta.

Videnskab og kapital. Bidrag til udviklingen af en socialistisk politik for de videregående udannelser (1974). Århus and København: Modtryk and Kurasje.

Vorländer, Karl (1911): *Kant und Marx*. Tübingen: J.C.W. Mohr (Paul Siebeck).

Vorländer, Karl (1924): Kautsky als Philosoph. In R. Hilferding (ed.): Karl Kautsky. Dem Wahrer und Mehrer der Marxschen Lehre zum 70ten Geburtstage. *Die Gesellschaft*. Berlin: Dietz, pp. 19−24.

Vygodskij, V.S. (1970): *K istorii sozdania 'Kapitala'*. Moskva: Mysl.

Zeleny, Jindřich (1968): *Die Wissenschaftslogik bei Marx und "Das Kapital"*. Berlin: Akademie Verlag.

Communicated 16 December 1985 by Erik Allardt
Printed August 1986

Ekenäs Tryckeri Aktiebolag
Tammisaari − Ekenäs